Every Drop *of* Blood

Also by Edward Achorn

The Summer of Beer and Whiskey:
How Brewers, Barkeeps, Rowdies, Immigrants, and a Wild
Pennant Fight Made Baseball America's Game

Fifty-Nine in '84:
Old Hoss Radbourn, Barehanded Baseball, and the
Greatest Season a Pitcher Ever Had

Every Drop *of* Blood

THE MOMENTOUS SECOND INAUGURATION OF ABRAHAM LINCOLN

EDWARD ACHORN

Atlantic Monthly Press
New York

FIRST EDITION

Published simultaneously in Canada
Printed in the United States of America

First Grove Atlantic hardcover edition: March 2020

This book was set in 11 pt. Janson by Alpha Design & Composition of Pittsfield, NH.

Library of Congress Cataloging-in-Publication data is available for this title.

ISBN 978-0-8021-4874-2
eISBN 978-0-8021-4876-6

Atlantic Monthly Press
an imprint of Grove Atlantic
154 West 14th Street
New York, NY 10011

Distributed by Publishers Group West

groveatlantic.com

20 21 22 23   10 9 8 7 6 5 4 3 2

To my mother

"...until every drop of blood drawn with the lash, shall be paid by another drawn with the sword..."

—ABRAHAM LINCOLN, Second Inaugural Address

CONTENTS

IMAGE CREDITS

Image credits for the insert section are as follows:

Image 1.1: Library of Congress, Prints & Photographs Division, DAG no. 1224 (Cabinet A).

Image 1.2: Library of Congress, Prints & Photographs Division, LC-DIG-ppmsca-19219.

Image 2.1: Library of Congress, Prints & Photographs Division, LC-B813- 1764 A-1 [P&P] LOT 4192.

Image 2.2: National Portrait Gallery, Smithsonian Institution, object number NPG.2002.87.

Image 2.3: Brady-Handy photograph collection, Library of Congress, Prints & Photographs Division, LC-BH82- 2460 B [P&P].

Image 3.1: Timothy H. O'Sullivan (American, about 1840 - 1882). *A Harvest of Death*, Gettysburg, Pennsylvania, July 4, 1863, Albumen silver print. 17.8 × 22.1 cm (7 × 8 11/16 in.), 84.XO.1232.1.36. The J. Paul Getty Museum, Los Angeles.

Image 3.2: Civil War photographs, 1861-1865, Library of Congress, Prints and Photographs Division, LC-B817- 7929 [P&P].

Image 4.1: Library of Congress, Prints & Photographs Division, LOT 6286, p. 15 [P&P].

Image 4.2: Library of Congress, Prints & Photographs Division, LC-B813- 1747 B [P&P].

Image 4.3: Library of Congress, Prints & Photographs Division, LC-BH82- 5341 B [P&P].

Image 5.1: Library of Congress, Prints & Photographs Division, LC-F81- 2009 [P&P].

Image 5.2: Library of Congress, Prints & Photographs Division, DRWG/US - Meyer, no. 2 (B size) [P&P].

Image 6.1: Library of Congress, Prints & Photographs Division, LC-DIG-ppmsca-19671.

Image 6.2: Library of Congress, Prints & Photographs Division, LOT 14043-2, no. 697 [P&P].

Image 6.3: Library of Congress, Prints & Photographs Division, LC-DIG-ppmsca-19421.

Image 7.1: National Archives and Records Administration, item number 530494.

Image 7.2: Library of Congress, Prints & Photographs Division, LC-USZ62-122395.

Image 7.3: Brady-Handy photograph collection, Library of Congress, Prints and Photographs Division, LC-BH82- 5077 C [P&P].

Image 8.1: Library of Congress, Prints & Photographs Division, LC-B813- 6532 A [P&P].

Image 8.2: Library of Congress, Prints & Photographs Division, LC-DIG-ppmsca-53391.

Image 8.3: Library of Congress, Prints & Photographs Division, LC-BH82- 2417 [P&P].

Image 8.4: Library of Congress, Prints & Photographs Division, LC-BH831- 565 [P&P].

Image 9.1: Sisters of Mercy of the Americas, Mercy Heritage Center, Belmont, North Carolina.

Image 9.2: Metropolitan Museum of Art, Harris Brisbane Dick Fund, 1933, accession number 33.65.306.

Image 10.1: Photograph courtesy of Hillsdale College. Frederick Douglass. Edwin Burke Ives (1832-1906) and Reuben L. Andrews, January 21, 1863, Howell Street, Hillsdale, MI, Carte-de-visite (2 1/2 x 4 in), Hillsdale College.

Image 10.2: Library of Congress, Prints & Photographs Division, PGA - Ritchie (A.H.)—First reading . . . (D size) [P&P].

Image 11.1: Alderman Library, University of Virginia, via the Walt Whitman Archive, ID number 013.

Image 11.2: Library of Congress, Prints & Photographs Division, LC-USZ62-79930.

Image 12.1: Library of Congress, Prints & Photographs Division, LC-DIG-ppmsca-19233.

Image 12.2: Library of Congress, Prints & Photographs Division, LC-BH826- 476 [P&P].

Image 12.3: Carol M. Highsmith's America, Library of Congress, Prints and Photographs Division, LC-DIG-highsm-04748.

Image 13.1: Gilman Collection, Metropolitan Museum of Art, accession number 2005.100.1118.

Image 13.2: Brady-Handy photograph collection, Library of Congress, Prints and Photographs Division, LC-BH835- 26 [P&P].

Image 14.1: Library of Congress, Prints & Photographs Division, LC-BH826-1516 [P&P].

Image 14.2: Library of Congress, Prints & Photographs Division, LC-USZ62-2578 (b&w film copy neg.).

Image 14.3: Library of Congress, Prints & Photographs Division, LC-USZ62-279 (b&w film copy neg.).

Image 15.1: Library of Congress, Prints & Photographs Division, LC-USA7-16837.

Image 15.2: Library of Congress, Prints & Photographs Division, LC-DIG-ppmsc-02927.

Image 16.1: Courtesy of Heritage Auctions, HA.com.

Image 16.2: National Portrait Gallery, Smithsonian Institution, object number NPG.83.241.

PROLOGUE
THE NATION'S WOUNDS

Saturday, February 25, 1865

The wound refused to heal. Nearly ten months after a Confederate bullet shattered his thighbone at the Battle of the Wilderness, Selden Connor was still trapped in a hospital bed on a cold morning in Washington, D.C., hounded by pain. Doctors had hoped the two sides of the broken femur, the splinters sawed off, might fuse back together, making Connor whole again. But the bad leg, four and a half inches shorter than the good one, was too weak to stand on without snapping. It kept becoming infected and needed to be drained periodically of putrid pus.

Connor was a strikingly tall twenty-six-year-old, keenly intelligent, with a commanding presence, a cascading beard, and dark, calm eyes. As a Phi Beta Kappa graduate of Tufts College bent on a career in law, he had once had an extraordinarily bright future. Now, a week before Abraham Lincoln's inauguration to another term, Connor was one more shattered casualty of an extraordinarily cruel and murderous war.

A less resolute man than Lincoln might have backed away from this catastrophic struggle with a united South bent on its independence. Breaking the might of the largest slave society in the world—probably the largest slave society in human history—was always going to be an enormous challenge.

The erudite and experienced man who had preceded Lincoln in the White House, Pennsylvania Democrat James Buchanan, did not have the slightest intention of going to war after Southern states seceded in the wake of Lincoln's election in 1860. Given that the United States of America was supposed to be a voluntary partnership, his attorney general, James Sullivan Black, had advised Buchanan, the *New York Times* reported, that "military force would not only be useless, but pernicious, as a means of holding the States together." President Buchanan accordingly informed the members of Congress in December 1860 that, under the Constitution, they might rescue the nation "by conciliation, but the sword was not placed in their hand to preserve it by force." Opponents of war could also reflect on the sobering example of the American Revolution eight decades earlier, of resistance so fierce and widespread that even Britain, possessing the world's strongest military, could not subdue it.

But Lincoln, an Illinois lawyer raised in poverty and regarded by the Washington establishment as a vacillating rube, soon proved to be of much sterner stuff than his predecessor. In the face of one disastrous battle after another that left Americans fearfully scanning long lists of the dead and wounded for the name of a husband or son, he refused to bend from his course of crushing the rebellion and forcing the shattered pieces of the nation back together, though the prospect often seemed as doubtful as trying to fuse Connor's broken femur. The only executive experience Lincoln had before stepping into the White House was running a two-man law office, yet he brilliantly coordinated the powers of the federal government and its massive war effort to support his mission. By 1865, four years of Lincoln's brutal, unremitting pressure was at last breaking the Confederacy. But the price had been horrendous. Nearly 750,000 young men had died so far, many rolled into unmarked graves far from home and loved ones. Countless thousands of survivors had been left, like Connor, debilitated or horribly disfigured.

When the war started, virtually no one had expected savagery on this scale, an appalling blot on a country conceived in liberty and dedicated to the Enlightenment values of self-government and the peaceful resolution of political differences. Lincoln himself, a frequent visitor at Union hospitals, was horrified. As the president's friend Ward Hill Lamon recalled, "it was the havoc of the war, the sacrifice of patriotic

Prologue xvii

lives, the flow of human blood, the mangling of precious limbs in the great Union host that shocked him most,—indeed, on some occasions, shocked him almost beyond his capacity to control either his judgment or his feeling." Lincoln had dedicated his life to the rule of law and the peaceful settlement of differences. He argued that each man, white or black, carried the spark of divinity and merited freedom. And then he presided over the wholesale slaughter of America's young men.

"The dead, the dead, the dead—*our* dead, or South or North, ours all . . . our young men once so handsome and so joyous, taken from us—the son from the mother, the husband from the wife, the dear friend from the dear friend," Brooklyn poet Walt Whitman lamented. "And everywhere among these countless graves . . . we see, and ages yet may see, on monuments and gravestones, singly or in masses, to thousands or tens of thousands, the significant word *Unknown*." As Lincoln's first term approached its end in the winter of 1865, bodyguard William H. Crook recalled, "death was on every hand, the black badge of mourning was seen on every side; and those connected with the White House, where centered the entire nervous system of the nation, felt the strain of conflict, the grief and sorrow, so poignantly and so constantly that it is no wonder gayety and lightness of spirit were absent for the most part." Beyond the carnage, the war was virtually bankrupting the nation, costing a staggering $4 million a day, an unimaginable $1.4 billion a year—about $22 billion today, though in the much poorer and less populous America of 31 million people in 1865, the impact of such spending was immensely greater. Before the war, in 1860, the entire federal budget was a comparatively paltry $63.1 million.

In fighting the war relentlessly, assuming vastly greater power than any president had before him, Lincoln had used every weapon he could get his hands on—massive borrowing; the nation's first federal income tax; the jailing of journalists; the imposition of martial law across the nation, with the use of military tribunals to imprison tens of thousands of civilians who were suspected of making trouble; the draft; and, most notably, the emancipation of as many African Americans as possible and their subsequent enlistment in the destruction of the Confederacy. Through these actions, he had earned the loathing of countless Americans, North and South.

Confederate captain Elijah P. Petty of Texas, later killed in battle, expressed the emotions of millions of Southerners when he begged his wife to inculcate in their children "a bitter and unrelenting hatred to the Yankee race. . . . They have invaded our country and devastated it and are continuing to do so. They have murdered our best citizens & continue to do so and all because we insist upon the unalienable right of self government." Southerners did not usually call the conflict the Civil War. They called it Lincoln's War or the War of Northern Aggression. In their view, the Yankees and their immigrant hordes had come to destroy the hearths and homes of a graceful South where whites and blacks had managed to live peacefully for generations. A Southern officer, in writing a letter, paused to address any Union soldier who might intercept it:

> You god damned bloody, Negro-stealing, cowardly son of a bitch! . . . I hope your damned brain more than it is now may become the abode of the vile, pestiferous vermin. That your skulking eyes may gangrene and wither in their sockets—that your damned lying tongue may feaster and cleave to the roof of your shameless mouth—that your damned canting throat may become tremors from nothing but loathsome pus—that your Yankee intestines may putrify—may your damned paunch fill with boils and cancers and abcesses, and I send an eternal carcass-odor to your damned codfish-plied nostrils. In fact that you yourself, you dirty villain, may land in the seventh hell and blister forever.

In the North, as well, Americans despised Lincoln for his ruthless conduct of the war. In 1861, Union soldiers arrested Baltimore newspaper editor Frank Key Howard, the grandson of Francis Scott Key, author of "The Star-Spangled Banner," for writing an editorial critical of Lincoln's suspension of habeas corpus, basic civil liberties, in Maryland. Oblivious to irony, they clapped Howard in Fort McHenry, the very site of the gallantly waving banner in the passionately patriotic poem that had become the lyric of the national anthem. "The flag which he had then so proudly hailed, I found waving over the same place, over the victims of as vulgar and brutal a despotism as modern times have witnessed," Key's grandson wrote bitterly. Many found it especially troubling that, as young Americans fell by the thousands, this backwoods politician incessantly told funny and often earthy stories to political cronies and White House visitors. The London-based *Standard* branded him "a foul-tongued and ribald punster" who was the "most despicable tyrant of modern days."

Some critics considered Lincoln worse than a vulgar and brutal despot; he was a decidedly second-rate leader, his incompetence responsible for the war's insane butchery. In the spring of 1863, *The Dubuque* (Iowa) *Herald*, citing Lincoln's haggard appearance, observed: "No wonder the President looks wretched; no wonder he looks as if the ghosts of half a million of his slaughtered countrymen were pointing to their ghastly wounds, and accusing him of being their murderer!" The Reverend Sabin Hough, a longtime critic of Lincoln's use of violence to break the South, wrote in 1864: "There is death at the heart of this glory & greatness. This war is murder & nothing else. . . . My heart is sick of this horrible carnage." The *La Crosse Democrat* of Wisconsin opined that July that Lincoln had lost the country: "Patriotism is played out . . . [and] all are tired of this damnable tragedy." On the left, abolitionist and women's rights activist Elizabeth Cady Stanton called the president "Dishonest Abe" and blasted "the incapacity and rottenness" of his administration. If he was reelected, she vowed to her friend Susan B. Anthony, "I shall immediately leave the country for the Fijee Islands."

Lincoln's chances of being reelected in November 1864 seemed so small, and the public's hatred of him and his damnable war so intense, that the president on August 23 wrote down a grim promise, asking his Cabinet members to endorse the back of it without reading it: "This morning, as for some days past, it seems exceedingly probable that this Administration will not be re-elected. Then it will be my duty to so co-operate with the President elect, as to save the Union between the election and the inauguration; as he will have secured his election on such ground that he can not possibly save it afterwards. A. LINCOLN."

Better war news—notably, General William Tecumseh Sherman's capture of the vital Southern industrial and railroad center of Atlanta—combined with strenuous efforts by the administration to get out the pro-Lincoln soldiers' vote, changed the momentum. With eleven Confederate states not participating—Alabama, Arkansas, Florida, Georgia, Louisiana, Mississippi, North Carolina, South Carolina, Tennessee, Texas, and Virginia—Lincoln defeated the former commander of his Union forces, Democrat George B. McClellan, amassing 2.1 million votes to the general's 1.8 million, and 212 electoral college votes to his opponent's 21. In a country riven in two, America's men—women did not yet vote—gave Lincoln their support to subdue the South and end the war. Still, the shift of a few thousand votes in several key states could have led to the president's defeat in the electoral college.

In Richmond, the capital of the Confederacy, the *Daily Dispatch* found it appalling that the people of the North had reelected "a vulgar tyrant . . . whose career has been one of unlimited and unmitigated disaster; whose personal qualities are those of a low buffoon, and whose most noteworthy conversation is a medley of profane jests and obscene anecdotes—a creature who has squandered the lives of millions without remorse and without even the decency of pretending to feel for their misfortunes; who still cries for blood and for money in the pursuit of his atrocious designs." Such an outcome, the paper argued, underscored that the Yankees were unfit for the sacred freedom that had been bequeathed them by the Founders. The *Daily Richmond Examiner* warned that the election had placed the Union's immense military, economic, and industrial power firmly "in the hands of those who have vowed to destroy us, to seize our lands and houses, to beggar our children, and brand our names forever as the names of felons and traitors." There was no middle course left: "We must be victors, or we must be annihilated." Many Northerners, in truth, prayed that the

Confederate ringleaders who had brought this misery on the nation—from President Jefferson Davis on down—would soon be captured and hanged for treason.

For nearly four years, Southerners had fought with incredible bravery for their independence, and their spirit was not yet extinguished. Peace negotiations in early February 1865 had raised hopes in the South of separation. But after Lincoln insisted that the South must drop its independence and kill the institution of slavery as the conditions for ending the war, "a new and irrepressible fire of indignation and resistance . . . warmed every heart" fighting for the Confederacy, a pro-Southern correspondent to the *Times* of London asserted on February 16. "I think I can promise Mr. Lincoln that he has in General Lee's army a nut to crack which will severely try the jaws not only of General Grant, but also of General Sherman." At a mass meeting in Richmond on February 6, Davis vowed he would yet "teach the insolent enemy" a lesson, especially Lincoln, who had "plumed himself with arrogance" in demanding the South's surrender. The Confederate president reassured the crowd that he "could have no common country with the Yankees," and "if any man supposed that under any circumstances he could be an agent of the reconstruction of the Union he mistook every element of his nature. With the confederacy he would live or die." Davis thanked God that he "represented a people" of the same mind—brave Southerners "too proud to eat the leek, or bow the neck to mortal man." Thousands in his audience, though suffering terribly as the Union choked off the capital's access to food, medicine, and clothing, roared their approval.

Yet millions of Americans still shared Lincoln's unshakable belief that this exceptional nation had to be stitched back together, as the best hope for freedom's survival in a world governed by brute power. Selden Connor was one. Like many of his fellow soldiers, he had grown up in a close-knit family in a small town rooted in patriotism—in his case, Fairfield, Maine, population 2,753 in 1860. In early 1861, he was studying law, writing elegant poetry in his spare time, when South Carolina and its Confederate allies bombarded Fort Sumter in Charleston Harbor and brought down the American flag. When President Lincoln called for seventy-five thousand volunteers to suppress "combinations too powerful" to be stopped by law enforcement, Connor responded. "The motive that impelled me to enlist was common to most soldiers of the Union Army—the desire to avenge the insult to the flag and to maintain the integrity of the Union," he recalled.

Over the next three years, Connor had stared down death and agony in some of the most terrifying encounters of the war—the corpse-strewn battlefields of the Virginia Peninsula, Antietam, Fredericksburg, Chancellorsville, Gettysburg, and others, where swarms of bullets making a *whit-whit* sound and terrifying screaming shells haphazardly tore into or sliced off arms, legs, genitals, intestines, and jaws, knocked out teeth and eyes, and smashed or removed heads. The odds finally caught up to him in the chaos of the Battle of the Wilderness, on May 6, 1864. A colonel, he was leading the Nineteenth Maine Voluntary Infantry Regiment, trying to hold off a Confederate flank attack along a path through the dense woods called the plank road, acting on his own initiative to save the lives of countless fellow soldiers, when "something like a sledgehammer struck my left thigh and felled me to the ground." Nothing would ever be the same for him again. A surgeon at a filthy field hospital went to work. Rather than amputate the leg, the doctor removed several inches of the shattered bone. "The ends of the bone were trimmed out . . . and sawed off smooth," Connor coolly informed his sister in a letter. Though his prognosis was poor, Connor insisted he was not downcast, for he had given his all to save the nation and, he assured his sister, "if my life is lost for the cause, it will be without a regret."

Alerted by a heart-stopping telegram, Connor's father, William, a well-to-do lumber baron and former Maine state legislator who had aided in the rise of Vice President Hannibal Hamlin, rushed to Virginia. From there, the father warned the family to prepare for the worst. Doctors kept the leg on a steeply inclined plane, but Connor suffered intensely, and the wound became infested with wriggling maggots. Still, the strong-willed young colonel survived the first days, then weeks, and endured the jarring misery of a move by cart and boat to Washington's

Sixth Street Wharf, where rows of horse-drawn ambulances lined up to transport many such broken men. From there, he was hauled to Douglas Hospital, near the corner of New Jersey Avenue and I Street. Journalist Noah Brooks described the scene in late May 1864, at the very time Connor was transported: "Boatloads of unfortunate and maimed men are continually arriving at the wharves and are transported to the various hospitals in and around Washington in ambulances or upon stretchers, some of the more severely wounded being unable to bear the jolting of the ambulances. There are twenty-one hospitals in this city and vicinity and every one of them is full of the wounded and the dying." Congressman Isaac N. Arnold long remembered Lincoln's anguish at the sight. "Look yonder at those poor fellows," he said. "I cannot bear it. This suffering, this loss of life is dreadful."

One month after Connor's fall, President Lincoln promoted the young man to brigadier general, while Connor was still alive to appreciate the honor. After the wound disastrously hemorrhaged and doctors concluded he was too weak to survive amputation, the Bangor *Daily Whig & Courier* broke the news to Maine readers that Connor had perished. "The day before his death, his appointment as Brigadier General was approved by the Senate," it noted, "a tardy but honorable recognition of gallant and meritorious service." In truth, Connor had somehow survived the crisis. His father returned to Maine, and the family, recognizing that the patient needed more attention than the hospital staff could provide, sent Selden's bright and lively seventeen-year-old brother, Virgil, to Washington to watch over him. Virgil moved into his brother's hospital room, number six, where Lieutenant Benjamin Emigh of Pittston, Pennsylvania, soon joined them. While storming Lee's defenses outside Petersburg, Virginia, on June 17, the former store clerk had been shot by a musket ball that tore off one of his testicles and lodged in his left hip. Doctors sawed off Emigh's leg below the knee—and later, when the wound would not heal, at mid-thigh.

Both patients suffered miserably. When Harriet Eaton, a nurse from Portland, Maine, visited Douglas Hospital in October, she was moved by the sight of Connor lying flat on his back with his leg hanging in a frame. "Noble-looking man, I was more indignant than ever at the work of rebel bullets," she wrote in her diary. "He seems very cheerful and hoping against hope, for they tell him it is very doubtful whether the bones will connect as they form. He showed me the pieces that had come out, some of which were the new formation." Through it all, Connor somehow maintained his spirits. In recent days, he had entertained fellow patients by reading aloud long stretches of Charles Dickens's sprawling novel *Nicholas Nickleby*, when his kid brother thought he should be resting. "I tried to get him to stop just now, but he couldn't 'see it,'" Virgil wrote home. On the anniversary of his wounding, Selden would write to his mother: "One year ago today I tumbled over in the Wilderness, and I am still on my back, helpless and immoveable. I have suffered much in that twelve-month, but the consciousness that I fell while doing my duty, and the kindness I have experienced at the hands of so many friends, kindness so much beyond my deserts, have made the memory of this year almost a pleasant one." Such was the caliber of some of the men Lincoln was feeding into the meat grinder of war.

When young Virgil wasn't tending to his brother, he was busy making the social rounds of wartime Washington, visiting the Capitol, dancing with the city's belles, paying New Year's Day calls. He attended a party at the home of Speaker of the House Schuyler Colfax, where he enjoyed "a view of the elite of the city," gazed at the many "very handsome" young ladies who were "distressingly draped" in dresses that concealed their charms, and ate so much ice cream that he was left with "an unpleasant feeling under the second button of my vest, resembling an ache." He marked his eighteenth birthday on January 10. On Wednesday, February 22, he marveled at the spectacular illumination of the city's great public buildings in honor of George Washington's birthday and recent Union victories. In a matter of days, Virgil and Selden's father was expected to join the crowds pouring into the city for Lincoln's inauguration, a celebration the teenager keenly anticipated.

Less grateful for the kindness of others than his brother, Virgil was annoyed on this Saturday by the incessant chatter of a visitor named Mrs. Sampson—no doubt Sarah Sampson, of Bath, Maine, a strong-willed but good-hearted woman who faithfully tended to sick and wounded men from her state in Washington hospitals. While visiting room six on that dreary day, "she kept her tongue a flying all the time she was here," Virgil complained. "Her's is hung in the middle if any woman's ever was."

That afternoon, a mile and a half away, a man who depended on his own tongue—as a diplomat and accomplished flatterer, though he was nervous about his English skills—approached the White House.

Adolphe Pineton, the Marquis de Chambrun, a thirty-three-year-old Paris lawyer, had just arrived in Washington to study Lincoln and the war's progress, though his cover story claimed that he was helping the French legation grapple with tariff questions. He brought with him an abiding interest in the United States. He had married into the family of the Marquis de Lafayette, the French aristocrat famous for helping General Washington win the Revolutionary War, and he enjoyed a close friendship with Alexis de Tocqueville, the author of *Democracy in America*, a celebrated book written in the 1830s to inform the decaying Old World about the vibrant young country.

Earlier that Saturday, Chambrun had paid a visit to Joseph C. G. Kennedy, the director of the U.S. Census Bureau, in his office at the Interior Department. A brilliant statistician who was friendly with the president, Kennedy informed the diplomat that Mary Todd Lincoln was holding a reception that afternoon; the two of them could go together, if the marquis would like. Though Chambrun fretted that he had not yet been formally presented to the president, Kennedy assured him there would be no breach of diplomatic protocol, since Lincoln, harried by duty, did not attend his wife's levees.

The diplomat and the bureaucrat arrived at the White House in a cold rain at about three o'clock, stepping under the portico onto the worn paving stones that had been trod on by many presidents. "The reception was almost over. Many guests had already left," the marquis recounted in a letter to his wife. "In we went." When he was ushered through the tall lobby into the Blue Room, with its floor-to-ceiling windows, deep blue walls, and gold hangings, humming with chatter and women's laughter, the marquis felt a wave of panic rush through him. "I at once perceived a tall man standing near the door, surrounded by an atmosphere of great respect. No mistake was possible; it was Mr. Lincoln himself!" The president had turned up at his wife's event, after all. "What an anxious moment! Here I was alone, without anyone to help, obliged to say a polite word in English to each of them. No possibility of retreat, though."

While waiting in line to shake the president's hand, the French aristocrat sized up the famous rail-splitter, a figure whose exaggerated features and country mannerisms had been lampooned throughout the Western world. Many who had met this peculiar president were, in truth, stunned by his rude appearance. "To say that he is ugly, is nothing; to add that his figure is grotesque is to convey no adequate impression," British journalist Edward Dicey informed his readers in 1862.

> Fancy a man six-foot[-four] high, and thin *out of* proportion, with long bony arms and legs, which, somehow, seem to be always in the way; with great rugged furrowed hands, which grasp you like a vise when shaking yours; with a long scraggy neck, and a chest too narrow for the great arms hanging by its side. Add to this figure a head, cocoa-nut-shaped and somewhat too small for such a stature, covered with rough, uncombed and uncombable hair, that stands out in every direction at once; a face furrowed, wrinkled, and indented, as though it had been scarred by vitriol; a high narrow forehead, and, sunk deep beneath bushy eyebrows, two bright, somewhat dreamy eyes, that seem to gaze through you without looking at you; a few irregular blotches of black bristly hair, in the place where beard and whiskers ought to grow; a close-set, thin-lipped, stern mouth, with two rows of large white teeth, and a nose and ears, which have been taken by mistake from a head of twice the size. Clothe this figure, then, in a long, tight, badly fitting suit of

black, creased, soiled, and puckered up at every salient point of
the figure (and every point of this figure *is* salient); put on large
ill-fitting boots, gloves too long for the bony fingers . . . and then
add to all this an air of strength, physical as well as moral, and a
strange look of dignity coupled with all this grotesqueness; and
you will have the impression left upon me by Abraham Lincoln.

Richard Henry Dana Jr., the snobbish author of the memoir *Two Years
before the Mast*, felt only disgust for the sprawling man he met at the
White House. "Such a shapeless mass of writhing ugliness as slouched
about in the President's chair you never saw or imagined," he wrote.

Yet the president did not strike Chambrun as a grotesque figure.
Rather, the famous Lincoln seemed a stooping, sad-looking man who
obviously possessed both deep resolve and great intelligence. "He is
exceedingly thin, not so very tall. His face denotes an immense force of
resistance and extreme melancholy. It is plain that this man has suffered
deeply." While Lincoln still bore the marks of his country upbringing,
the marquis found nothing there to diminish his stature as a leader.
"The elevation of his mind is too evident; the heroic sentiments are
so apparent that one thinks of nothing else. Nobody could be less of
a parvenu. As President of a mighty nation, he remains just the same
as he must have appeared while felling trees in Illinois. But I must add
that he dominates everyone present and maintains his exalted position
without the slightest effort."

After a fifteen-minute wait, Kennedy introduced the marquis to
President Lincoln. "His eyes are superb," Chambrun wrote, "large and
with a very profound expression when he fixes them on you." Through
his accented English, Chambrun managed to inform the president
that "my whole heart was engaged on the side of his political ideals;
that I participated enthusiastically in his present success and that of
his armies, feeling, as I did, that Union victory was the victory of all
mankind." Lincoln seemed very pleased with this analysis. He "took
both of my hands in his and said how glad he was to find his policies
so well understood."

Lincoln had long reflected on the meaning of the nation's struggle. Fifteen months earlier, in a short speech at the dedication of a national cemetery at the Gettysburg battlefield, he had described the Civil War as a test of whether a system of self-government could long endure in this world. Though America had been ripped apart by forces of partisan division that were all too characteristic of republics, Lincoln believed that all humanity had a stake in the survival of this remarkable country. But in the months since that address, the president had been pondering the nation's wounds and finding a deeper lesson in the terrible war.

The marquis moved on to Mary Lincoln, who was standing a few steps away at the center of another circle of people. Mrs. Lincoln, famous for her low-cut dresses, wore a single bracelet, no necklace, and "must have been pretty when young," Chambrun unchivalrously informed his wife. Now she was tired and middle-aged, a rather plump, short woman in "an ample silk gown." A prisoner of strong emotions, the First Lady had suffered greatly during the war, losing her husband's attention to an unending crisis that had aged him terribly, enduring the slander of political tongues and the vicious snobbery of Washington society, battling severe headaches, seeking relief in shopping, and getting into fearful financial troubles that she hid from Mr. Lincoln. All that was nothing to the agony of watching their beloved eleven-year-old son, Willie, suffer and die from a mysterious illness. The journalist Murat Halstead dismissed Mrs. Lincoln as "a fool—the laughing stock of the town, her vulgarity only the more conspicuous in consequence of her fine carriage and horses and servants in livery and fine dresses, and her damnable airs." The Boston abolitionist Lydia Maria Child called her a "vulgar doll" decked out in "foreign frippery." Mary Lincoln's hometown Democratic newspaper, the *Illinois State Register*, cruelly painted her as a "sallow, fleshy, uninteresting woman in white laces, & wearing a band of white flowers about her forehead, like some overgrown Ophelia." In a scornful letter to his wife after one of Mary's receptions, Senator James W. Nesmith, a Democrat from Oregon, remarked that the First Lady "had her bosom on exhibition" and "a flower pot on her head." Mrs. Lincoln, who used to "cook Old Abe's dinner and milk the cows," he continued, now seemed eager "to exhibit her milking apparatus to public gaze." In the face of such contempt by many Washington insiders, Mary carried on in her ceremonial role. In introducing the marquis to her, Kennedy mentioned his family link to Lafayette. Given that connection, the marquis told her, she "would easily understand how greatly I rejoiced in the success of Mr. Lincoln and the United States of which, at heart at least, I felt myself a citizen." The First Lady seemed to comprehend his English, "and looked pleased at what I tried to express."

Kennedy and the marquis proceeded through the East Room, where a regimental band was playing patriotic airs. Soon they were back out the front door and onto Pennsylvania Avenue. But the day was not over.

Kennedy took his new friend along to his house at 380 H Street to fetch one of his two daughters for a far more impressive reception than Mary Lincoln's humdrum affair. They were going to a much-anticipated "matinee" at the mansion of three dazzling Washington celebrities: Supreme Court chief justice Salmon Portland Chase, his lovely daughter, Kate, age twenty-four, and her thirty-four-year-old husband, Senator William Sprague of Rhode Island, one of the richest men in the United States.

While waiting for Miss Kennedy to appear, Kennedy and Chambrun smoked cigars and chatted. When she finally emerged, the young woman was wearing, to the marquis's astonishment, a sumptuous gown. "I asked her what kind of reception this would be." It turned out that the matinee was in fact a dress ball, starting oddly in the afternoon, with the shutters drawn to darken the house as if it were already night—a concession to religious convention, since there could be no dancing on the Lord's Day, which would commence at midnight. "Fortunately, I had a white tie," the marquis wrote. Off they went to a three-story, red brick townhouse at the corner of Sixth and E, both streets lined with expensive carriages disgorging the city's well-dressed elites. "This mansion is the finest in Washington, and Mrs. Sprague has a reputation for wit and beauty which the Washington ladies are rather impatient of, as I myself was able to observe," the marquis tartly reported. Even amidst the terrible war, jealousies and social climbing were rampant in the capital city.

This was the glittering event the city's sophisticates and powerbrokers flocked to attend, not a dull reception at the run-down White House with those vulgar Lincolns. Washington's most fashionable people admired the handsome fifty-seven-year-old chief justice for his calm and imperial manner and his unflinchingly liberal politics. For many years, society gossips had been disseminating the details of the great man's private life, tragic even by the measure of his time. One beloved wife after another—three all told—had perished from illness, as had three of his daughters. Unwilling to suffer more, Chase had remained a widower for the previous thirteen years, courageously throwing himself into antislavery work and relying on Kate, his effervescent surviving daughter from his second marriage, for love and support. She regarded him—a gutsy man in the liberal vanguard of the Republican Party, a former Ohio governor and U.S. senator, then a brilliant treasury secretary before becoming chief justice—as infinitely superior to the absurdly gauche, joke-cracking lawyer who had finagled his way into the White House. For its part, Washington society, especially its men, found her fascinating. The *Washington Chronicle* praised her "rare virtues of heart and mind" and said that, when she attended to guests in her home, "these graces sparkle and radiate like gems of dazzling splendor." Another admirer found her "tall and slender and exceedingly well formed. . . . Her little nose, somewhat audaciously tipped up . . . fitted pleasingly into her face with its large, languid, but at the same time vivacious hazel eyes, shaded by long dark lashes and arched over by proud eyebrows. The fine forehead was framed in waving, gold-brown hair. She had something imperial in the pose of the head, and all her movements possessed an exquisite natural charm." Kate emerged as the leading hostess of Washington, far surpassing the dumpy, hot-tempered First Lady, just as this evening's showy festivities would surpass Mrs. Lincoln's plain afternoon reception.

Hurt by Kate's pretentions and ill-concealed disdain, Mary Lincoln hated her with a fury—and was still furious at the president's loyal secretaries, John Nicolay and John Hay, for having invited Chase and his daughter to a state dinner in 1864 against her expressed will. Behind her back, the two aides called the First Lady "the Hell Cat" and "Her Satanic Majesty." While detesting Mary, twenty-six-year-old Hay adored Kate and seemed to have formed a rather intimate friendship with her. Three weeks before her wedding, he took her to Ford's Theatre to see *The Pearl of Savoy*, and was amused to see the "statuesque Kate cry like a baby" over the maudlin play. Hay, no doubt jealous, disdained her filthy-rich husband, dismissing him as "a small insignificant youth who bought his place" as Rhode Island governor and then U.S. senator with the money generated by his family's lucrative cotton mills. The *Brooklyn Daily Eagle* held a similar view. "Personally, Mr. Sprague is not attractive; pecuniarly, he is—seven millions." Raised to focus on calico production, he seemed a weedy, weird young man devoid of social graces and education. In the Senate, the *Eagle* predicted, Sprague "will make no speeches, for he neither writes nor talks; he will not contribute to the dignity of the Senate, for he is small, thin, and unprepossessing in appearance; he will vote regularly and just as Papa Chase tells him; and he will always regret that he forsook his congenial factory, where he made a mark and could hold his own with the best of them, for the marble halls of the legislators, whom he can neither influence nor comprehend."

Miss Chase's 1863 wedding to the Rhode Island senator, in this very house, had been the most brilliant social event in the city since wealthy Southerners, regarded as the gracious aristocrats of Washington, had departed in late 1860, in advance of the war. The newspapers provided extensive coverage of the grand display of elegance and riches, with *Harper's Weekly* magazine offering readers a view of Kate's stunning tiara of matched pearls and diamonds, a wedding gift from Sprague. The slender bride had looked strikingly beautiful in her white velvet gown and point-lace veil, holding orange blossoms, as she stood at the top of the stairs, while Chase waited at the foot, ready to lead his daughter

to the Episcopal bishop of Rhode Island, stationed in the center of the
room. As part of the entertainment that night, the U.S. Marine Band
struck up "The Kate Chase March," specially composed for the occasion. The haggard president had attended alone, without the resent-
ful First Lady. Paying homage to an important Cabinet member one
week before delivering his address at Gettysburg, Lincoln stayed for
a good while to "'take the cuss off' the meagerness of the Presidential
party," one reporter noted. By the end of the event, "Kate looked tired
out and languid," Hay observed, "especially at the close of the evening
when I went to the bridal chamber to say goodnight." Many believed
she married Sprague for his money, sacrificing her happiness to fund
her father's political ambitions.

Certainly, she had used her husband's wealth to purchase and then
tastefully renovate her father's mansion, with an eye toward bringing
Washington's elites to her door. And on this damp February evening in
1865, "the whole of Washington society was there," the marquis boasted,
"[and] I was presented to all those whom it might be interesting for me
to know." The Washington *Evening Star* gushed, in its account, "The
Chief Justice of the Supreme Court of the United States—father of
Mrs. Sprague—Members of both Houses of Congress, Governors, Ex-
Governors, Cabinet Ministers, Foreign Ministers, and other dignitaries
with their wives and daughters, were among the delighted throng . . . the
good, the distinguished, the accomplished and the beauty and fashion
of the Metropolis, and of very many of the States of this Union." The
Washington correspondent for the *New York Express* reported: "Magnificent salons welcomed them, and lighted tapers, and Chinese lanterns,
and a Government band of music." As for Kate, the "lady host was in
all the grace of youth and beauty, and the splendor of toilette."

Even in the depths of winter, the hosts seemed untroubled by the
wartime shortages and skyrocketing prices that afflicted lesser mortals.
"The elegant mansion of the Senator was decorated as became his great
wealth, and as became the accomplishments and graces of his beautiful
wife. The air throughout the different apartments of the edifice was
redolent with the perfumes of a thousand flowers, and music lent its

enchantment to the whole," the *Evening Star* reported. The hosts had gone to the extraordinary expense of building a temporary fifty-by-one-hundred-foot dancing hall for the occasion on the lawn behind the house. It was "draped, gauzed, festooned, flagged, flounced, and all ravishing to the eye, with incense and beauty." It "resembled more the abode of fairies . . . than a place for common mortals to dance." And they danced. "Beautifully trained," they "wound themselves up in their gauze, and lost and re-lost themselves in the mazes of their misty dance, to the astonishment of all rural beholders. No Ballet corps on the Academy floor could beat the spectacle."

Some found the frenetic partygoing of that winter, while the nation's young men still died in agony, disgraceful. The wives of capitalists made rich by the war—"shoddy upstarts," as one critic called them—shamelessly exhibited their wealth and beauty. "Point lace, diamonds, &c., &c., are paraded with a lavishness of display ill-suited to the times. It is remarked by everyone conversant with society here in former hours, that the extravagance of this season, in the way of dressing, &c., is unprecedented," wrote one Washington columnist. Some of the women attending these society events had suspiciously rough hands, indicating that they had risen from a class of manual laborers. The *New York Express* correspondent mused, "Is not Washington gay? Is there any war? Is not war a blessing?"

Guests chatted excitedly about the man of the hour, General William Tecumseh Sherman. His western army of tough, wiry young men had captured Atlanta and marched through Georgia, breaking free from its supply chain and living off the land. The army was now finishing the work of mauling South Carolina, the first state to secede, harshly punishing its civilians for instigating civil war. Sherman had made his intentions clear in a letter to his superiors on Christmas Eve, after seizing the important port of Savannah. "We are not only fighting hostile armies, but a hostile people, and must make old and young, rich and poor, feel the hard hand of war, as well as their organized armies," he wrote. With grim satisfaction, the general was leaving a trail of terror and hunger in his wake, sending a message of Union dominance that the Southern people could not ignore. "Thousands who had been deceived by their lying newspapers to believe that we were being whipped all this time now realize the truth, and have no appetite for a repetition of the same experience," Sherman wrote. Lincoln had approved this cruel strategy as a means of bringing the war to its swiftest possible conclusion, but the hatred and resentment the North was stirring up could only be imagined. One of the South's "lying newspapers," the *Richmond Whig*, sputtered that the stories of burned and pillaged plantations were exaggerated, and Confederate forces would give Sherman his comeuppance yet. Still, the writer was sure that Northerners, heartless by nature, delighted in the reports. "One would imagine the whole Yankee nation to be afflicted with Sherman on the brain," the *Whig* argued the day before the Chase party, adding with sarcasm: "How charming the spectacle, how grateful to the Yankee mind, which . . . can satiate its cravings by imaginings of inextinguishable conflagration and unresisted destruction."

Among the crowd of partygoers, the marquis found Lincoln's war secretary, Edwin Stanton, a shrewd, ornery, short, thickset man, with a long, fleecy salt-and-pepper beard, tiny wire-rimmed glasses, and a tendency to bounce on his heels. The war secretary made a point of informing the French diplomat that victory was finally on the horizon, assuring him that Sherman "must, at this very moment, be marching on Richmond, that he would not linger in North Carolina but would merely go through the State." North Carolina governor Zebulon Baird Vance was urging his people to resist Lincoln's army, citing the example of the Confederacy's General Robert E. Lee, a model of courage and dignity whom no one could imagine "bowing at the footstool of a low, blackguard Illinois cross-roads lawyer, to beg for his life for the sake of his wife and children." It seemed doubtful, though, that such appeals could rally significant opposition anymore. If all went as planned, Sherman would brush aside any opposition, march his troops north rapidly to join Grant outside the Confederate capital, and close the trap on Lee's Army of Northern Virginia.

Another noted guest that evening was a twenty-two-year-old naval officer named William B. Cushing, who had shown incredible

audacity on the night of October 27, 1864, in rowing a small skiff to
the side of the ram *Albemarle* in the Roanoke River, affixing a torpedo,
and blowing up the last important ironclad in the Confederates' deci-
mated navy. Trying to escape the misery of war at the Chase mansion
in the glow of a young woman's beauty, the officer "danced fanatically
and . . . never left the side of a pretty girl in a rose-colored dress with
whom he seemed on the best of terms," the marquis recounted. Having read the newspaper accounts of Cushing's stirring heroism, "I felt
I must tell him that his bravery was equaled only by the fidelity of his
devotion. But he was so entranced by the rose-colored damsel that he
scarcely answered."

The only thing the marquis disliked about the lavish matinee was
the buffet supper. "The dining room was so small that it was difficult
to get near the sideboard, and quite impossible for ladies to do so."
Men had to bring them food, with everything "on the same plate after
the custom of the country," to the Frenchman's disgust. The marquis
supplied two women with plates, but he chose not to eat, finding his
appetite dulled by this crude American practice. "Except for this detail,
I must say that it would be impossible to find more elegant and correct
society, where so many distinguished officers and handsome men of
excellent manners were gathered."

"And everybody was there," the *New York Express* account noted.
But not everybody. Such distinguished, handsome, and elegant men as
Selden Connor could no longer attend society dances. And the most
notable man of all in Washington was not at the Chase party either,
and as little missed. Abraham Lincoln had writing to do. For many
months, while consumed with the endless details of his difficult work,
he had been thinking of deeper matters, pondering the meaning of
this monstrous war. During the stressful dark nights when the clicking
telegraph at the War Department had brought news of yet another
Union defeat—of dead and shattered young men by the thousands
splayed across once-peaceful fields and orchards, leaving behind homes
of loving mothers, forever broken, embittered fathers, and wives and
children robbed of love and sustenance—Lincoln had struggled to make

sense of the nation's ordeal, trying to comprehend how a just God could inflict such suffering on good people and searching his mind for some way to ease the hatreds that threatened to divide the United States for generations. He well understood that ending the war was only the start. The president planned to express his understanding during the inaugural ceremonies the following Saturday, in a taut address that, he hoped, would be much more than a political speech. Indeed, it would prove to be so. Lincoln would not live to experience its impact, but the brief discourse by the Illinois crossroads lawyer would come to be regarded as a profound statement about the American experience, and its elegance and excellence would far outshine all the best people at the Chase mansion on that Saturday evening in February.

CHAPTER 1

BLOODY GASHES ON THE FACE OF HEAVEN

Friday night, March 3, 1865

On the eve of Lincoln's inauguration to a second term, the bedridden Selden Connor and his eighteen-year-old brother Virgil waited for their father to arrive from Maine. To the brothers' surprise, a family friend named Cal showed up first, on one of the trains packed so full that even women had to stand. For days, the railroads had been disgorging thousands of strangers from all parts of the Union, out for amusement in the nation's capital in defiance of the miserable weather and what the *New York Herald* called "the liquefied condition of the streets and avenues." After a winter so bleak and so cold that the Potomac had frozen over, March had begun drearily. Rain had been falling since Thursday morning, and visitors confronted wind-whipped mists as they lugged their carpetbags and plodded alongside muddy streets under halos of flickering gaslights while looking for lodging. Four years earlier, in the days leading up to Lincoln's first inauguration, Washington's *Evening Star* recalled, "the weather was dry, and tornadoes of dust swept through the streets," leading officials to send out work crews to sweep up the avenue. This time, stubborn rain had made sweeping up impossible, and "the streets were covered with a thick coating of mud, carrying out the saying that Washington alternates from dust to mud or *vice versa*."

Women tried to lift their flowing, ankle-length skirts to keep them out of the mire—no easy task. But there was music and laughter, eating and drinking everywhere. Itching to escape the stale and fetid confines of Douglas Hospital for the fun erupting outside, Cal and Virgil decided to set off on their own. The elder Connor was surely among the thousands who, fearing there would be no place to stay in Washington, had postponed their arrival until Saturday morning, remaining in Philadelphia, Baltimore, or Wilmington until the last minute. But others were eager to join the throng early, including known thugs and pickpockets who, smelling an opportunity, had come from as far away as Boston. Police detectives and soldiers had been assigned to watch out for them.

Like many in Washington, Navy Secretary Gideon Welles had a house full of guests in town for the inauguration. A conservative lawyer-politician and Connecticut newspaper editor with a long white beard—Lincoln humorously called him "Father Neptune"—Welles had to focus on serious matters this night. He had just received an alarming request from Henry Halleck, the chief of staff of the Union military effort, to lock down Washington's navy yard in advance of the inauguration. "The city full of people. General Halleck has apprehensions that there may be mischief. Thinks precautions should be taken," Welles scrawled in his diary. Halleck, known for his nervous habit of scratching both elbows at the same time, tended to be excessively anxious. "I do not participate in these fears," Welles wrote, "and yet I will not say it is not prudent to guard against contingencies." Ominous rumors swept Washington that "something was going on," the *Evening Star* reported, "indicating that trouble was anticipated from some undeveloped quarter."

Halleck doubled the military guard and ordered the bridges and roads into Washington watched closely. The *Star* learned that the Eighth Illinois Cavalry had pushed out from its encampment at the Fairfax, Virginia, courthouse, on orders to look for suspicious characters on the country roads. Ornery-looking men "in grizzled costume were to be seen upon the streets" of Washington, suggesting "something portending." The fears were not unreasonable, given that an untold number of Southern spies were embedded in the nation's capital and Confederate agents had tried to set New York City itself ablaze just three months earlier. Soldiers wearing the blue uniform of the U.S. Army patrolled the streets, keeping watch, many of them African American, a sight few people could have imagined four years earlier. The soldiers competed for space on the soaked wooden sidewalks with wide-eyed tourists, drunken revelers, and brass bands blasting patriotic tunes into the soggy air.

Ulysses S. Grant, commander of all the Union forces, thought it best not to attend the inauguration while tens of thousands of still-lethal Confederate soldiers were entrenched in front of him and liable to attempt a breakout at any moment. But Grant sent a slew of high-ranking officers from his headquarters at City Point, Virginia, outside Petersburg. They boarded a special steamer that chugged through the slanting rain down the James River, into Chesapeake Bay and up the Potomac River to the Sixth Street Wharf in Washington. One of the gold-spangled military honchos stepping down the plank was a conscientious and fearless major general, Alexander Webb, who had been present at the Battle of the Wilderness when Selden Connor was shot down. "Are you hit, Colonel?" he cried. "I've got it this time, General," Connor responded in agony. Six days after his colonel fell, Webb was atop his horse leading the brigade at Spotsylvania when a minié ball pierced the corner of his right eye, passed along the skull, and exited behind his ear. He was hauled to the Gordon House in Fredericksburg, Virginia, the same hospital where Connor was fighting for his life before being transported to Washington. When Webb, who miraculously escaped brain damage, discovered that his colonel was in the house, he sent him a gallant message expressing regret for not lending Connor his horse to transport him after his wounding. Connor responded with commensurate chivalry. "I sent back the reply that I could not have made any use of the horse and therefore he need not have any regrets for not offering it." Webb healed more readily than Connor. After being sidelined for six months, he had returned to work as the chief of staff to General George Meade, the commander of the Army of the Potomac. Deeply respected by his peers, Webb was accorded the honor of helping to represent the army at Lincoln's inauguration.

Many tired travelers discovered that the hotels in Washington were hopelessly full. Such fashionable houses as Willard's Hotel—the famous nest of politicians and lobbyists that, as novelist Nathaniel Hawthorne observed, "may be more justly called the centre of Washington and the Union than . . . the Capitol, the White House, or the State Department"—tried to accommodate the overflow by filling their hallways with cots and mattresses. The Lincoln and Johnson Club, the big local Republican organization, managed to provide beds for one thousand people, while Washington fire companies put up fellow firefighters who came to march in the parade. But accommodating everyone was impossible. The city's population had nearly doubled during the war. Even before the inauguration crowds arrived, the capital was bursting with outsiders conducting the business of an unexpectedly huge and protracted struggle.

This teeming, slapdash city was not to everyone's taste. "Of all the detestable places Washington is first," Manhattan lawyer George Templeton Strong complained. "Crowd[s], heat, bad quarters, bad fair [fare], bad smells, mosquitos, and a plague of flies transcending everything within my experience. . . . Beelzebub surely reigns here, and Willard's Hotel is his temple." Foul-smelling animal pens dotted the city. The streets were full of rooting hogs, dirt, decaying horse manure, and rotting animal carcasses that waited to be picked up by the city carrion cart. Dilapidated and unfinished structures teetered alongside handsome new ones. "Its buildings, like its population, present a most incongruous medley, from the sublime to the ridiculous. Beauty and deformity are grouped together—with a great preponderance of the latter," journalist Lois Bryan Adams wrote. Washington was "a cesspool into which drained all the iniquity and filth of the nation," wrote a *New York Times* reporter who arrived in 1862. "It was filled with runaway Negroes, contractors, adventurers, office-seekers, gamblers, confidence men, courtesans, uniformed officers shirking their duties, and the riff-raff, the outscourings of all creation." A Michigan soldier visiting the capital in November 1861 found it dominated by three large groups of people. The first was soldiers. The other two, he wrote in his diary, were "politicians & prostitutes, both very numerous & abt equal in numbers, honesty & morality."

The worst of Washington's physical features was surely the reeking City Canal, which ran from Seventeenth Street south of the White House, passed along the north end of the Mall, and veered south at the foot of Capitol Hill in two branches that fed into the Anacostia River. Built at great expense to accommodate fat barges and encourage trade with the West, it was a majestic eighty feet wide at points. But it never drew much traffic, and by the 1850s, whatever use it once had as a canal was over. Now it was nothing but a stinking open cesspool, attracting swarms of flies and mosquitoes for much of the year and emitting a stench of human waste that, on the worst days, reached the White House. Benjamin Brown French, the commissioner of public buildings—and the man in charge of Saturday's inaugural festivities—had urged Congress nearly three years earlier to do something about the crumbling waterway: "It is the grand receptacle of nearly all the filth of this city. The waste from all the public buildings, the hotels, and very many private residences is drained into it," he wrote in a March 11, 1862, report. "Unless something be done to clear away this immense mass of fetid and corrupt matter, the good citizens of Washington must during some hot seasons, find themselves visited by a pestilence!" Nothing had been done.

None of this deterred the throngs of people out that evening to celebrate Lincoln's second term. After years of fear and mourning, Americans were ready to lose themselves in a celebration.

One of the liveliest parties was at the North Capitol Street home of John W. Forney, the secretary of the Senate and the publisher of the *Washington Chronicle*, a paper so slavishly loyal to the administration—and so amply rewarded for it with government printing contracts—that critics branded Forney "Lincoln's dog." The politician-publisher rented the old Mills House, built in George Washington's day, and turned it into a salon for the city's elites. His famous soirees, noted for their free-flowing liquor, attracted such celebrities as the photographer Mathew Brady, the Shakespearean actor Edwin Forrest, and the portrait painter Charles Loring Elliott. "My guests were always numerous enough to fill every room in the house, including the basement," Forney recalled. "They were men of all ideas, professions, and callings. We had no test but devotion to our country. We met like a band of brothers—the lawyer, the clergyman, the editor, the reporter, the poet, the painter, the inventor, the politician, the stranger, the old citizen, the Southerner and the Northerner, the soldier and the statesman, the clerk and the Cabinet Minister, and last, not least, President Lincoln himself." On this eve of the inauguration, Forney was holding a stag party in honor of Andrew Johnson of Tennessee, the vice-president-elect.

Forney, a former Democrat, had urged the Republicans to choose Johnson as Lincoln's running mate on the strength of his fierce and courageous leadership as military governor of Tennessee. Heading into an 1864 campaign that many party leaders expected to lose, the Republican Party had rebranded itself the National Union Party in a desperate bid to lure pro-war voters of other persuasions. Accordingly, the delegates to the party's 1864 nominating convention were open to the idea of balancing the ticket, and they jettisoned Lincoln's loyal and gentlemanly vice president, Republican Hannibal Hamlin, in favor of the pugnacious former Democratic senator and slaveholder.

Johnson was a self-made man, a humble tailor born in a log cabin in North Carolina and reared by illiterate parents. Determined to make a name for himself, he ventured into politics, working his way up from alderman to congressman to governor to U.S. senator to military governor to vice-president-elect with a message of anti-elitism that resonated with struggling white men. Forney considered the five-foot-eight populist his "beau-ideal of a representative and radical Democrat." Others found his hot temper and fiery denunciations repulsive. Gideon Welles, for one, rated Johnson "a coarse, vulgar creature." When Lincoln asked Thaddeus Stevens, a radical Republican from Pennsylvania, what he thought of the man, the congressman reportedly replied:

"Mr. President, Andrew Johnson is a rank demagogue, and I suspect at heart a damned scoundrel."

Johnson certainly presented a startling contrast to Lincoln. While the president kept his emotions in check, eased stress with jokes, and believed that grudges and personal attacks rarely paid off in politics, his 1864 running mate was humorless, quick to form resentments, and ready to smear opponents as base men acting from the worst of motives. In a stump speech in Louisville, Kentucky, in October, Johnson fiercely denounced the "pseudo Democratic party" as "the rebel party of the United States, composed in part of the lurking rebels and traitors in our midst, who are as much engaged in the attempted overthrow of our Government as the traitors under Jeff Davis"—even though the party's standard-bearer was George B. McClellan, formerly the Union's chief general. While Lincoln feared a spirit of vengeance would hamper the nation's reunification, Johnson believed the rich elites of the slaveholding aristocracy should pay a dear price for fomenting a rebellion against their country. His backers hoped this tough new vice president would stiffen Lincoln's spine. "I found fault with Abraham, because I thought him too tardy, and that he treated Treason too tenderly," New York lawyer Thomas Shankland wrote to Johnson after the election, "but God hath been good to Abraham, and perhaps you may strengthen him, for he needs a little starch."

Lincoln found common cause with Johnson, though, in their stubborn faithfulness to the Union. Johnson had refused to leave the U.S. Senate even after his adopted Tennessee formally joined the Confederacy, earning death threats and bitter enemies back home. In March 1862, after large portions of Tennessee fell under the control of Union forces, Lincoln appointed Johnson military governor—an exceedingly dangerous job in a state riven by violent hatreds and roving guerilla bands. Johnson provided tough, fearless, and deeply unpopular leadership. After arriving in Nashville, he arrested the city council for sedition and jailed seven ministers for refusing to take a loyalty oath. "Treason must be made odious," he proclaimed. Many despised him for his harsh and tactless leadership. Southern sympathizers regarded him a mere tool of the arrogant North. "No man in Tennessee . . . has done more than Andrew Johnson to create, to perpetuate and embitter in the minds of the Southern people, that feeling of jealousy and hostility against the free States, which has at length culminated in rebellion and civil war," wrote the *Nashville Press*, branding him "bigoted and intolerant." The paper presciently claimed that he had "but one aim, the Vice Presidency of the United States." Johnson was "the very lick spittle" of the Northern "school of negrophilists," the newspaper asserted on another occasion, adding that he was "aiming at his own selfish aggrandizement, by fanning the flames of sectional discord."

In early 1865, organized Confederate forces had been driven away from Tennessee. At Johnson's urging, white Unionists—the only Tennesseans permitted to participate—voted on February 22 to abolish slavery in the state, acting by the suspiciously lopsided margin of 25,293 votes to 48. Profoundly grateful that their chains were forever broken, black citizens of Nashville pooled their meager resources to present Johnson with a gold watch, in recognition of his "untiring energy in the cause of Freedom." Unbeknownst to them or to the editors who accused him of "Negrophilia," however, Johnson was by then concerned about the increasingly vociferous demands by Republicans in Congress for black civil rights. Ending slavery to win the war was one thing, but compelling white Southerners to accept the social and political equality of people he privately referred to as "niggers"—and whom Johnson saw as inherently lazier, more violent, and less educable than whites—was another. Most Southerners would fiercely resist such pressure by Washington. The former tailor, steeped in the values of white working people, believed the only way to sew the country back together was to avoid revolutionary social change.

For a time, Johnson seemed reluctant to go to Washington at all. Recovering from a bout of typhoid fever, he explored with Forney the idea of remaining in Tennessee and working on stabilizing the state until well after Inauguration Day. Though the Senate secretary dutifully researched the matter, informing Johnson that six vice presidents had been away from the nation's capital when their terms began, Forney begged Johnson not to delay. The pro-war Democrats who had linked up with Lincoln would get cut out of the action in the new administration, he feared, if Johnson were not on the scene, and radical Republicans, with their plans for crippling Southern whites, might hold too much sway with Lincoln. "The personal partizans of Mr. Lincoln will be on the ground, and I think you should be here, if only for a few days to see the people who look to you to assist in shaping a generous, magnanimous and national policy," Forney advised him.

Lincoln put a stop to the dithering by peremptorily ordering Johnson to get to Washington. The Cabinet had concluded unanimously that "it is unsafe for you not to be here on the 4th of March," Lincoln wrote to Johnson, in a brief and pointed letter. He did not explain the Cabinet's fears, though it was obviously essential that power be transferred smoothly should Confederate sympathizers make good on their threats to assassinate the president. Altogether, Lincoln found the vice president's reticence to share in the celebration odd. "This Johnson is a queer man," he told an Illinois crony.

Johnson headed to Washington alone, feeling weak and ill. He took with him a new black frock coat, silk vest, and doeskin pants for his inauguration, but not his wife, Eliza, whose help he could have used. By Monday, February 27, Johnson had made it to the Burnet House in Cincinnati. There he met up with his friend and fellow politician, Stanley Matthews, and shared his concerns with him. "You and I were old Democrats. . . . I will tell you what it is, if the country is ever to be saved it is to be done through the old Democratic Party" rather than the radical Republicans. They may have opened a bottle at some point. When a crowd of Lincoln supporters gathered outside to serenade the vice-president-elect with the help of Menter's Cornet Band, Johnson appeared dutifully on the balcony in the keen air to make a few hoarse remarks. But something was obviously wrong. While Johnson was still "the same plain citizen of former years," a *Cincinnati Daily Gazette* reporter observed, he seemed "somewhat the worse for the wear and tear of the past year or two." He did not speak with "as clear a voice or, it seemed to us, as clear a head as we have heard him on previous occasions." Perhaps he was drunk. The man from the *Cincinnati Enquirer*, taking dictation, found his notes useless. In his brief speech, Johnson blurted out "three or four 'fellow citizens' in every line" and otherwise made little sense. He "appeared to be suffering from a severe physical weakness."

In this woozy condition, Johnson moved on to Washington, where on this Friday he formally resigned his post as military governor of Tennessee and then headed over to Forney's house. Still feeling weak, he welcomed the opportunity for fortification from his friend's well-stocked bar.

Heavy drinking was underway all over the city. Many men eager for a good time headed for a thirteen-block neighborhood south of Pennsylvania Avenue and north of Ohio Avenue that had been nicknamed Hooker's Division—both for the army of prostitutes working its streets, "hooking" eager customers, and for the hordes of soldiers who had served under General Joseph Hooker and availed themselves of its shabby gambling dens, crowded saloons, and busy bordellos. The number of brothels in Washington had exploded during the war. "There are at present, more houses of this character, by ten times, in the city than have ever existed here before, and loose characters can now be counted by the thousands," the Washington *Evening Star* complained in 1863. The *Star* estimated that five thousand prostitutes were working in Washington and another twenty-five hundred in Georgetown and Alexandria. Young soldiers aching for release provided steady business for the city's colorfully named houses: Fort Sumter; the Ironclad; Headquarters, U.S.A.; the Wolf's Den (kept by Mrs. Wolf); the Haystack (kept by Mrs. Hay); Madam Russel's Bake Oven. Filth leaking from the City Canal oozed into the neighborhood's unpaved streets, "and the feet of the people passing churned the soft ground into black and odorous mud," the *Washington Post* wrote. "Thieves and unprincipled men and women, as ready to cut a throat as pick a pocket, flourished," preying on gullible visitors "without fear of law or justice."

Those with slightly elevated tastes and thicker purses might venture to Mary Hall's handsome three-story brick brothel at 459 Maryland Avenue, closer to the Capitol. With eighteen "inmates" in Miss Hall's employ, the bordello may have been the biggest and poshest in the city, serving its guests bottle after bottle of expensive French champagne. The Provost Marshal's Department of Washington, Twenty-Second Army Corps, which kept a close watch on underground activities, rated it a "Class 1" establishment. Such "parlor" or "upper-ten" houses were known for their expensive Brussels carpets, suites of red-plush furniture, and beautiful and often cultured women, some of them Southern belles. Mary Hall's sparkling young ladies were not always perfectly genteel, to be sure. Three found themselves arrested after a drunken carriage ride through the Union capital in 1863, during which they boisterously cheered for Jefferson Davis and belted out a favorite Confederate anthem, "The Bonnie Blue Flag." On the eve of the inauguration, the women of such houses were doing brisk business.

The railroad stations were alive with steam engines, arriving with a squeal of brakes and chuffing away for more passengers. A 7:30 p.m. train disgorged hundreds of healthy young males representing three volunteer fire companies from Philadelphia, here for the next day's inauguration parade—the celebrated Good Will, Franklin, and Perseverance hose companies, which brought along their engines, colorful uniforms, and marching bands. Their local comrades in firefighting, members of the Washington City Fire Department and the United States Steam Fire Brigade, cheered the Philadelphians' arrival, and a band on the platform struck up George F. Root's "The Battle Cry of Freedom," the stirring 1862 tune that had served the previous fall as Abraham Lincoln's unofficial campaign song.

In most cities, volunteer companies were fraternal and often partisan organizations, Democratic or Republican, stocked with young men eager to display their manly virtues and advance themselves professionally. They were crucial in halting the fearsome blazes that could easily consume America's great wooden metropolises—as Chicago would discover six years later when an inferno devoured much of the city. At the depot's crowded main saloon, Washington mayor Richard Wallach formally greeted these important political allies. A balding man with a protruding belly, sagging eye pockets, and immense sideburns, the mayor wished the visitors a pleasant stay. "There may be circumstances which would render it a little disagreeable—as, for instance, wet and mud; but to these firemen were always familiar," he joked. The firemen roared three cheers for the politician.

They enjoyed dinner at the Russell House, then formed in a procession and marched through the mist, the mud, and the crowds to the White House, American music blaring, their torches lighting up "the fog of the avenue with a curious sort of silvery haze," a reporter for the *Evening Star* noticed. They expected Lincoln to come out and make a little speech, like the mayor, but it turned out the president was not at the Executive Mansion, after all; he had gone up to the Capitol. No matter; the firemen marched over to the Union Engine House, at Nineteenth and H Streets, where the city's prized fire engine, Hibernia, was stored and kept polished to a gleam. A technological marvel built by the great Reaney and Neafie works in Philadelphia, Hibernia had defended Fort Monroe, at the mouth of the James River in Virginia, when the Union worried that the fearsome Confederate ironclad *Merrimack* might set the place ablaze. After the *Merrimack* was scuttled, the engine was sent to protect Washington. Named in honor of the Irish immigrants prevalent in firefighting, the Hibernia inspired awe in neighborhood boys, including the president's eleven-year-old son, Tad. That Monday, Lincoln had scrawled a message to William Dickson, head of the military-operated fire department, to "please pump the water out of a certain well, which Tad will show," using Hibernia. The rambunctious boy, who suffered from a speech impediment and hated schooling, liked to insert himself into the middle of White House activities, and Lincoln was an indulgent father.

As crowds celebrated on the eve of Lincoln's inauguration, a *New York Herald* reporter telegraphed his impressions to his newsroom: "The streets resound with the music of bands," marching in front of the "military, civic and political associations" that were "arriving almost hourly to proceed in the grand pageant."

A twenty-two-year-old clerk in Edwin Stanton's War Department could hear the hubbub outside his boardinghouse near the corner of Sixth and H Streets. "Numbers of bands of music were on the streets discoursing patriotic airs, and thousands of officers and soldiers in gay uniforms enlivened the scene," Louis J. Weichmann recalled. "It was too exciting an occasion for me to remain indoors." After supper, Louis asked his roommate, John Surratt, age twenty, to take a walk.

The two young men had been friends for years, having met while studying for the Roman Catholic priesthood at Saint Charles College in Catonsville, Maryland. While Weichmann tended to be thoughtful, nervous, and timid, his younger friend was a brash and active lad. Weichmann found Surratt striking, describing him as "tall, erect, slender, and boyish, with a very prominent forehead and receding eyes. His nose was sharp, thin, and aquiline; his face bore an unusually keen and shrewd expression." Neither Weichmann nor Surratt had much of an aptitude for the priesthood, it turned out, and when Surratt's father died unexpectedly in 1862, John readily returned to his farming village of Surrattsville in southern Maryland, a hotbed of anti-Union sentiment. Thomas Nelson Conrad, a leading Confederate spy who regularly stopped at the Surratts' tavern, thirteen miles south of Washington, described the father as "an impetuous southerner, full of intense prejudice and hate toward the Yankees—as was almost everyone in Southern Maryland—outspoken in his convictions and proud of every Southern victory." Weichmann, meanwhile, frustrated over being refused entry to Saint Mary's seminary in Baltimore, moved on to Washington, where he worked for a time as the principal of a Catholic boys' school before landing a plum job that paid more than twice as much—as a clerk in the War Department's Office of the Commissary General of Prisoners. The young friends stayed in touch, and Weichmann decided to move in with Surratt in his widowed mother's Washington townhouse, which she had turned into a boardinghouse for income.

By then, young John was living an extraordinary double life. Steeped in his late father's fierce devotion to the Southern cause, he had linked up with the Confederate Secret Service, making use of his skills as a horseman to carry dispatches about Union activities to boats that were waiting at night, hiding in shadowy inlets on the Potomac River. "We had a regular established line from Washington to the Potomac, and I being the only unmarried man on the route, I had most of the hard riding to do," Surratt recalled some years later. If discovered, the boy might have been summarily shot or hanged as a traitor and a spy. No doubt the information he gathered, gleaned from allies working in government positions, aided Confederate planning and contributed to the death of Union soldiers. But the young man craved excitement, and he was not worried. "I devised various ways to carry the dispatches—sometimes in the heel of my boots, sometimes between the planks of the buggy," he explained. "I confess that never in my life did I come across a more stupid set of detectives than those generally employed by the U.S. Government." When his mother moved to her townhouse, John shifted his base of operations to Washington, conducting espionage under the cover of working for the Adams Express Company, which distributed the packages pouring into the city for the boys in blue at the front. "It was a fascinating life to me. It seemed as if I could not do too much or run too great a risk," he asserted.

Weichmann joined the family in November 1864, at a rent of thirty-five dollars a month, finding the boardinghouse "just as orderly, decent, and respectable as any home in Washington." He took a liking to John's mother, Mary Surratt. "Her steel gray eye was quick and penetrating," but her "manner was genial and social and she had the rare faculty of making a stranger feel at home at once in her company," he recalled. Like her son and her late husband, Mrs. Surratt was devoted "body and soul" to the cause of Southern independence. "I never met one in all my experience who so earnestly, and I might add so conscientiously, defended and justified the Southern cause as she," Weichmann recounted in a manuscript he penned years later, published decades after his death as *A True History of the Assassination of Abraham Lincoln and of the Conspiracy of 1865*. "Next to her church and family, her love for the South was her meat and drink." Such sentiments did not seem to bother the Union war clerk. He regularly escorted Mary Surratt to Sunday Mass at Saint Patrick's Church at Tenth and F Streets, half a block from Ford's Theatre.

Around the breakfast table at the boardinghouse the previous Tuesday, February 28, she had shown great interest in a passage in that morning's newspaper, reprinted from the *Louisville Daily Journal*: "We have reason to say that the rebels are expecting very soon to startle the whole country, and astonish the world. No matter what our reason may be, it is a good one." Mary asserted confidently that "something was going to happen to Old Abe which would prevent him from taking his seat; that General Lee was going to execute a movement that would startle the *whole world*." Though Weichmann insisted Mrs. Surratt never shared with him what she meant, he had a pretty good idea of one plan of attack, according to the man who occupied the desk next to his at the commissary general's office.

Brevet Major Daniel H. L. Gleason, a discharged Massachusetts cavalry officer, was one of the unimaginably brave men this war had thrust into action. During a raid in 1864, he had been clubbed in the head and slashed with a saber that cut into his skull, yet he had kept on fighting. His wounds were still not fully healed in January 1865, when he went to work alongside Weichmann. Gleason had mixed feelings about his colleague. "Physically and intellectually he was a giant," he said of Weichmann, "but in bravery I should call him a dwarf." Like many young men in the North, Weichmann was terrified of the draft, his fear culminating in the thought of being fed into Grant's lethal front lines, "and I was chaffing him in regard to that," Gleason recalled.

But it was not just conscription that scared Weichmann. During this week leading up to Lincoln's inauguration, he pulled Gleason into a small supply room and unburdened himself. "His face wore a look of misery and fear, and perspiration ran down his cheeks. I thought he had gone crazy," Gleason recounted. Weichmann confessed "he had been carrying a terrible secret, which so weighed on him that he must confide it to me." He revealed to Gleason that there was a plot underway to kidnap Abraham Lincoln: "The time set was Inauguration Day, March 4, as there would be so many strangers in the city that people's attention would be diverted, and this would give [the culprits] a better chance to operate." Plans had been made to have men and horses ready and waiting across the Potomac River, with the goal of getting the president to Richmond as quickly as possible. "He said," Gleason continued, "all arrangements, every detail, had been made, and they only waited for March 4th; there was not the slightest chance of failure, and now the time was drawing near to act." Gleason strongly advised Weichmann to go to the provost marshal's office immediately and "lay open the plot." Fearful, perhaps, of being arrested as an accomplice, Weichmann ignored Gleason's advice and kept mum as Lincoln's inauguration approached.

Now, on the eve of the big event, with bands playing and crowds thronging the wet streets, Weichmann and Surratt strolled down Sixth Street. They sauntered past the stately brick mansion that Salmon P. Chase and his daughter Kate had opened to the city's elites six days earlier. When they reached the National Hotel, as overloaded as Willard's, they saw to their left the illuminated dome of the U.S. Capitol looming in the distance. They turned right, toward the White House, walking along the storefronts of Pennsylvania Avenue, wending through the mobs of visitors and avoiding the mud thrown by passing vehicles.

For all the excitement around them, Surratt seemed preoccupied. At Eighth Street, he made an excuse and peeled off, leaving Weichmann on his own. Louis wandered along the sidewalks for a while, drinking in the music and the excited talk around him before heading back home around at around seven p.m. Climbing the front steps, he opened the front door, stepped into the hall, and glanced over to the parlor on his left. There, to his surprise, he saw Surratt seated and already engaged in an animated conversation with a slender, stunningly handsome twenty-six-year-old with large hazel eyes, a dark mustache, perfect white teeth, and dark curly hair.

The visitor was someone Weichmann recognized, a famous man—the actor John Wilkes Booth.

Weichmann had been boasting to his coworker Gleason about his proximity to the star. "I rather considered it a fine thing to be acquainted with Booth, for he was a leading actor of the day, a good fellow, and a descendent from a most famous family," Weichmann recalled. His father was the legendary actor Junius Brutus Booth; his brother Edwin was an acclaimed Shakespearean performer. Indeed, the starstruck Weichmann found it odd that this urbane celebrity had grown so close to his unsophisticated friend, often engaging in intense discussions with him just out of earshot. "Surratt was a young man hardly out of his teens with no experience at all in the active pursuits of life, having spent the greater portion of his brief existence on a small farm," Weichmann observed. Booth, by contrast, "was not only an accomplished actor, but a man who could be called a finished scholar in the ways of the world. . . . He was familiar with the tinsel and glitter of theatrical life, and was always a boon and welcome companion among his fellow actors. He was a worldly man given to wine, women, and conviviality."

Booth was also an ardent supporter of the Southern cause. A Maryland man who had grown up in a family that hired slaves as well as whites to work its farm, Booth had mourned the death of the United States he knew, radically transformed by Lincoln.

In that, he was not unlike millions of his fellow Democrats. In a November 5 editorial, three days before the 1864 election, the *Cleveland Plain Dealer* had expressed their widely held sentiments:

> *Do you want four more years of war?*
> *Vote for Lincoln.*
> *Do you want the Constitution utterly destroyed?*
> *Vote for Lincoln.*

. . . .

Do you want the degraded Negroes made your social and political equals?
Vote for Lincoln.
Do you want the Union of your fathers forever destroyed?
Vote for Lincoln.
Do you want to be arrested and confined in loathsome dungeons without
     process of law and without hope of release?
Vote for Lincoln.

The North had indeed voted for Lincoln. Many Democrats sullenly returned to their lives, but Booth refused to accept the verdict. Every day, he stewed in his hatred for the president. Planning a response so startling that he felt he must explain himself to the world, the actor wrote a passionate declaration of his views and left it with his sister Asia in Philadelphia in February, locking it in her basement safe until it would be needed. In his manifesto, Booth poured out his grief and rage over what Lincoln had done, in tearing down the institution of slavery, undermining the Constitution, making the central government a tyrannical power over the states, disrupting the social order, and creating conditions for racial strife that would lead, the actor feared, to the "total annihilation" of African Americans.

"This country was formed for the *white* not for the black man," he wrote. "Yet, heaven knows *no one* would be willing to do, *more* for the negro race than I. Could I but see a way to still better their condition." Like many Americans, in the North as well as South, Booth still believed that slavery, for all its abuses, had provided work, food, shelter, medical care, welfare in old age, and some of the graces of Christian civilization to what he considered a sadly inferior race of people who would have endured harsher and briefer lives in an Africa torn by tribal warfare. Later in March—ironically, in Booth's own hearing—Lincoln would offer a pithy rejoinder to that point of view: "Whenever I hear any one arguing for slavery I feel a strong impulse to see it tried on him personally." But Booth could only have dismissed such a quip as nonsense, because in his view the races were starkly unequal. In the ruthless competition of a free society, the actor believed, most African American men would quickly be reduced to violence and crime. A race war would end in their extermination.

Booth had watched in horror as Lincoln sent his armies of invasion against Southern people who wanted only to live apart from the North in peace, with their institution of slavery protected and nurtured. He saw a despotic president prosecuting the conflict with increasing brutality, unleashing the hellish terror of Sherman's forces on helpless women, children, and the aged in Georgia and South Carolina, waging an inhuman war of attrition in Virginia, jailing thousands of citizens without trial, attacking free speech, and bringing contempt on America and its sacred emblem—the red, white and blue. "How I have loved the *old flag*, can never now be known," Booth wrote in his declaration. "O How I have longed to see her break from the mist of blood and death that circles round her folds, spoiling her beauty and tarnishing her honor. But no, day by day has she been dragged deeper and deeper into cruelty and oppression, till now (in my eyes) her once bright red stripes look like *bloody gashes* on the face of Heaven."

The man who had wrought these disasters was to be sworn in on March 4—to what Booth was certain would be another four years of despoiling the flag, destroying American ideals, and trying to make blacks the equals of whites. Lincoln had to be stopped. To that end, Booth had all but abandoned his lucrative acting career to answer a different calling. America's founders, he was certain, would have risked everything to oppose Lincoln. "To hate tyranny to love liberty and justice, to strike at wrong and oppression, was the teaching of our fathers. The study of our early history will not let *me* forget it, And may it never," Booth wrote in his manifesto.

The morning before the inauguration, a southern Maryland man whom Booth had cultivated, a doctor named Samuel Mudd, paid a visit to the Surratt Boarding House looking for the actor. Then he evidently headed to the National Hotel, where Booth lived. Sometime later, Marcus P. Norton, a patent lawyer from Troy, New York, was bent over his desk in room 77 of the National, working on a motion for a case, when a stranger burst in uninvited, a man with a balding head and a shaggy goatee, wearing a black suit, clutching his hat in his hand. "He appeared somewhat excited, made an apology, and said he had made a mistake; that he wanted to see Mr. Booth," Norton recalled. Later, the lawyer identified the agitated visitor as Dr. Mudd "or a man exactly like him." For some reason, Booth's associates seemed anxious to talk to him on the day before the inauguration. One was Surratt, who had strolled by Booth's hotel that evening with Weichmann, and now was conversing intently with the actor back at the boardinghouse.

Weichmann interrupted Booth and Surratt to make a proposal. The Capitol was lit up that night. As the bright white light glowing atop its great new dome signaled, Congress was in session, rushing to pass legislation before its session expired at noon the next day. President Lincoln was in the building, signing bills into law as they were brought to him. The First Lady, along with throngs of tourists, was there to watch the famous politicians in action. Outside, on the east front, a dripping wooden platform awaited the festivities the next day, the swearing-in and the delivery of the inaugural address. Weichmann suggested the three of them pay a visit.

Booth agreed. They set off.

CHAPTER 2

ONE AND A HALF TIMES BIGGER

Friday night, March 3, 1865

Sometime before Louis Weichmann and John Surratt strolled past the house that evening, a striking figure ascended the twelve front steps of the towering brick mansion of Salmon P. Chase, at Sixth and E Streets. Dressed in a fine suit, the visitor was a six-foot-tall man in his late forties, with ramrod posture, an exceedingly stern demeanor, flashing brown eyes, a sharp black beard, and an exploding mane of dark hair streaked with gray. Though African American, he was here not as a tradesman or a servant to be routed to the back door, as might have been expected. To the contrary, he was an honored guest.

The son of a black woman and a white man, Frederick Douglass had been born in about 1818 into slavery in Talbot County, Maryland. After escaping his enslavement in 1838, he made extraordinary use of his freedom, employing his fierce willpower and surpassing eloquence to become one of America's leading abolitionist editors and orators, as well as its most prominent African American man. With enormous courage, he held a mirror up to his country, going so far as to question its deep pride in its exceptionalism, born of its magnificent revolution. In a searing Independence Day speech in 1852, Douglass asked:

> What, to the American slave, is your 4th of July? I answer; a day that reveals to him, more than all other days in the year, the gross injustice and cruelty to which he is the constant victim.

To him, your celebration is a sham; your boasted liberty, an
unholy license; your national greatness, swelling vanity; your
sounds of rejoicing are empty and heartless; your denuncia-
tion of tyrants, brass fronted impudence; your shouts of liberty
and equality, hollow mockery; your prayers and hymns, your
sermons and thanksgivings, with all your religious parade and
solemnity, are, to him, mere bombast, fraud, deception, impiety,
and hypocrisy—a thin veil to cover up crimes which would
disgrace a nation of savages. There is not a nation on the earth
guilty of practices more shocking and bloody than are the people
of the United States, at this very hour.

Such comments gnawed at Illinois lawyer Abraham Lincoln, a fervent
believer in the stupendous moral achievement of the nation's founding. While running for the Senate two years after Douglass's oration,
Lincoln in a speech cited such bitter criticism of the United States as
one of the reasons he detested slavery. "I hate it," he said, "because it
deprives our republican example of its just influence in the world—
enables the enemies of free institutions, with plausibility, to taunt us as
hypocrites—causes the real friends of freedom to doubt our sincerity."

Even so, the deeply pragmatic Lincoln had long advocated moderate policies designed to weaken slavery. Before becoming president,
he defied those who favored outright abolition, preferring a strategy
of blocking the institution's spread to the territories being settled, in
hope that it would eventually die off where it was. As president, he
was cautious about proclaiming the emancipation of slaves and full
civil rights for those freed. While Lincoln was too conservative for his
taste, Douglass found a kindred soul in Salmon P. Chase, an early, brave,
and dynamic opponent of slavery. As a rising lawyer in Ohio, Chase
had faced down a mob besieging an abolitionist newspaper and fought
for black people's rights in the teeth of death threats. He had given
Douglass moral and financial support by subscribing to his newspaper,
the *North Star*. While Lincoln clung tenaciously to the disintegrating
Whig Party until the mid-1850s, Chase boldly left the Whigs in 1841

to join the antislavery Liberty Party. As a U.S. senator, he had worked with such men as John Parker Hale of New Hampshire and Charles Sumner of Massachusetts, fighting slavery in the face of their colleagues' ostracism and hatred. Douglass greatly admired the three because they stubbornly "refused to be inoculated with the pro-slavery virus of the times." As governor of Ohio from 1856 to 1860, Chase had championed other liberal causes as well, including prison reform, public education, and women's rights.

Now, as the sixth chief justice of the United States Supreme Court, Chase had invited Douglass to join him and his beloved daughter, Kate, on this eve of the inauguration to take tea—a dramatic statement of support for racial equality at a time when white leaders rarely mixed socially with black people. He "welcomed me to his home and his table when to do so was a strange thing in Washington, and the fact was by no means an insignificant one," Douglass recalled. Perhaps Chase showed Douglass something he proudly displayed on his dining room sideboard—a silver pitcher given to him in 1845 by Cincinnati's African American community, in gratitude for his courageous service to its people.

Douglass was not easily impressed with anyone, but he found Chase's qualities striking. "There was a dignity and grandeur about the Chief Justice which marked him as one born great," he observed. Others agreed. William Howard Russell of the *Times* of London thought Chase the most intelligent and distinguished member of Lincoln's Cabinet when he served as treasury secretary, from March 1861 to July 1864, keeping America afloat financially while it burned through billions of dollars trying to break the Southern rebellion. Russell described Chase as "tall, of good presence, with a well formed head, fine forehead, and a face indicating energy and power." Chase had piercing eyes and an utter confidence that he was uniquely equipped to lead the nation. Lincoln himself deeply respected his abilities, saying, "Chase is about one and a half times bigger than any other man that I ever knew."

Chase certainly believed he was a much bigger man than Lincoln. As treasury secretary, he had started playing a double game, serving his president while maneuvering to replace him as the party's nominee in 1864. His aims were not unrealistic, given his popularity with the party's liberal base. Horace Greeley of the *New York Tribune*, perhaps the nation's most influential newspaper editor, informed Chase in September 1863, "If in 1864 I could *make* a President (not merely a candidate) you would be my first choice." The editor sent *Tribune* stockholder Benjamin Camp to Washington to meet with Chase, who noted gleefully in his diary that Camp "proposed plan for collecting public sentiment in my favor as candidate for Presy." In the view of many, Lincoln had proved to be too sluggish, too indecisive, and in some ways, too unpresidential to be an effective leader against the greatest threat the country had ever faced. When Lincoln went to Gettysburg to deliver his noted address in November 1863, Secretary of State William H. Seward loyally traveled with him, but Chase declined, preferring to distance himself from a president who seemed headed for political oblivion. "Let the dead bury the dead," Congressman Thaddeus Stevens, a radical Republican from Pennsylvania, sardonically advised Chase.

Using his superb oratorical skills to set himself apart from the president, Chase had ventured out on his own that October, stumping in Ohio and Indiana before adoring crowds while ostensibly going home to vote in state elections in Columbus. Lincoln, who knew he needed Democratic as well as Republican support to win the war, had insisted, over and over, that his sole purpose in fighting was the conservative one of restoring the Union. But Chase, in stem-winding speeches that got national attention, argued that the war's meaning was far more profound and uplifting than that. On a flag-festooned platform outside the statehouse in Indianapolis, where he was greeted by a huge cheering throng, Chase argued that there was a hidden reason this war had gone on and on. "Even after the rebellion had become flagrant, you remember how forbearing the President was, how forbearing everybody was. I used to get impatient sometimes, and wanted this military thing done, and that military thing done, and the rebellion crushed out at once. Why was it not crushed out at once? Why was it that everything moved so slowly?" At the time of the 1860 election, Lincoln, Chase, and the Republican Party had sought merely to limit the spread of slavery, in hope that the institution might someday fade away. But the war had swept everyone far beyond that.

Could it have been, Chase asked, because God had a different plan for America? "Nothing seems clearer to me than that those of us who never desired to touch the institution of slavery in the slave States, but only to prevent its extension beyond State limits, were not moving in the path of God's providence, and that this war came upon us in order that the nation might be born again into a new life, ennobled and made glorious by justice and freedom." Chase admitted it was "presumptuous" to try to interpret God's will, yet "I cannot help thinking that this country has a great work before it, which it cannot fulfill while it remains a slaveholding country." George Washington, Chase explained to the crowd, believed that "God was in the American Revolution bringing a mighty nation to birth. Am I wrong in the reverent belief that God is in this second revolution, bringing this same mighty nation to a second birth?" Strikingly, at Gettysburg a month later, Lincoln would speak similarly, though more eloquently, of the nation's "new birth of freedom." Lincoln had worked out very similar ideas, as well, about the role of divine justice in this war.

Chase's themes resonated powerfully with many radicals, including Douglass. The great black leader was among those who hoped Lincoln would be denied the nomination in 1864, specifically for his refusal to commit to the outright eradication of slavery and for his general indifference to the plight of African Americans. "Abraham Lincoln is no more fit for the place he holds than was James Buchanan," Douglass declared in July 1862, "and the latter was no more the miserable tool of traitors than the former is allowing himself to be." Lincoln had "steadily refused to proclaim, as he had the constitutional and moral right to proclaim, complete emancipation to all the slaves of rebels. . . . The country is destined to become sick of . . . Lincoln, and the sooner the better." It seemed clear to Douglass that Lincoln cared only about restoring the Union, even if that meant leaving many black people enslaved.

The president himself could not have articulated that view any more nakedly than in his August 22, 1862, letter to editor Greeley, which was quickly reprinted in papers throughout the country. "If there be those who would not save the Union, unless they could at the same time *save* slavery, I do not agree with them. If there be those who would not save the Union unless they could at the same time *destroy* slavery, I do not agree with them. My paramount object in this struggle *is* to save the Union, and is *not* either to save or to destroy slavery," Lincoln wrote. "If I could save the Union without freeing *any* slave I would do it, and if I could save it by freeing *all* the slaves I would do it; and if I could save it by freeing some and leaving others alone I would also do that. What I do about slavery, and the colored race, I do because I believe it helps to save the Union; and what I forbear, I forbear because I do *not* believe it would help to save the Union." All this led Douglass to conclude that Lincoln was "pre-eminently the white man's President, entirely devoted to the welfare of white men," treating black people as "at best only his step-children." Given that, Douglass sought an alternative. "When there was any shadow of a hope that a man of a more decided anti-slavery conviction and policy could be elected, I was not for Mr. Lincoln."

In January 1864, while there was still a chance the Republicans would ditch the unpopular president, Douglass laid out his concerns in an address at Cooper Union in New York. This war, he observed, had "planted agony at a million hearthstones, thronged our streets with the weeds of mourning, filled our land with mere stumps of men, ridged our soil with 200,000 rudely-formed graves, and mantled it all over with the shadow of death." It had thwarted commerce and "piled up a debt, heavier than a mountain of gold to weigh down the necks of our children's children." And what was the cause of it all? "We all know it is Slavery. Less than half a million of Southern slaveholders—holding in bondage four million slaves—finding themselves outvoted in the effort to get possession of the United States Government, in order to serve the interests of Slavery, have madly resorted to the sword—have undertaken to accomplish by bullets what they failed to accomplish by ballots. That is the answer." But all that misery, Douglass argued, was a worthy sacrifice. The world had never "seen a nobler or grander war than that which the loyal people of this country are now waging against the slave-holding Rebels. The blow we strike is not merely to free a country or continent—but the whole world from Slavery—for when Slavery fails here—it will fall everywhere. We have no business to mourn over our mission. We are writing the statutes of eternal justice and liberty in the blood of the worst tyrants as a warning to all after-comers." Jefferson Davis was right that the North's goal was no longer restoring the United States, as Lincoln had claimed, but remaking it, by crushing constitutional protections for slavery and ending the nation's way of life. That was exactly what America needed, Douglass said. "No war but an Abolition war; no peace but an Abolition peace," he insisted. An abolition peace meant more than the end of slavery; it meant equal rights for black Americans at last, in the North as well as the South: "While a respectable colored man or woman can be kicked out of the commonest street car in New York where any white ruffian may ride unquestioned—we are in danger of a compromise with Slavery."

The nation's sacrifices would be squandered if its leaders stopped short. And the ever-hedging Lincoln, Douglass warned his audience, did not seem to be up to the challenge of leading America to its true destiny of freedom and racial equality. "Until we see the election of November next, and that it has resulted in the election of a sound Anti-Slavery man as President, we shall be in danger of a slaveholding compromise," he cautioned. Douglass bitterly criticized Lincoln for "the absence of all moral feeling" in his statements about slavery and the "heartless sentiments" he had expressed in his letter to Greeley. If Lincoln had "a warm heart and high moral feeling," instead of the numbed soul of a calculating politician, "he would welcome, with joy unspeakable and full of glory, the opportunity provided by the Rebellion to free the country from the matchless crime and infamy" of slavery. "But policy, policy, everlasting policy, has robbed our statesmanship of all soul-moving utterances."

Chase had the high moral feeling required to liberate the black people of America, Douglass believed. Chase fully agreed that he was

Lincoln's better, finding the man's crass behavior and endless politicking ill-befitting a president in a time of crisis. "Mr. Chase honestly felt his superiority to Mr. Lincoln in some respects, and could not be reconciled to his undignified manners and strange ways," Maunsell Bradhurst Field, assistant secretary of the treasury from 1863 to 1865, recalled. Journalist Noah Brooks noted that Chase was "reserved, unappreciative as to jokes, and has a low opinion of Presidential humor and fun generally." The leading contenders for the Republican nomination could hardly have been less alike—Lincoln with his disheveled clothes and slouching posture, his leg thrown over a chair arm, his endless telling of off-color jokes, and his cackling at the works of lowbrow humorists, which he read aloud before Cabinet meetings; Chase with his stuffy decorum, upright posture, expensive, well-tailored suits, and his decision to fit up his private offices, as Brooks observed, "with Axminster carpets, gilded ceilings, velvet furniture, and other luxurious surroundings which go to hedge about a Cabinet Minister with a dignity quite appalling to the unaccustomed outsider." His pomposity, in truth, could be hard to take. Ohio senator Benjamin Wade observed, "Chase is a good man but his theology is unsound. He thinks there is a fourth person in the Trinity."

For all his dignity and moral probity, Chase was susceptible to flattery and gifts. As treasury secretary, he had fallen under the spell of an ingenious Philadelphia investor named Jay Cooke, the brother of an editor Chase had known back in Ohio. "I see Chase is in the Treasury —and now what is to be done? . . . Can't you inaugurate something whereby we can all safely make some cash?" Jay Cooke had asked his brother at the start of the administration. In the months and years to come, the investor managed to cultivate Chase's friendship by extending him loans and steering him to lucrative investments. Cooke, in return, made millions as Chase's special agent selling government bonds, while using insider information to reap huge returns on the stock market. And Chase's son-in-law, William Sprague, flirted with treason by secretly opening cotton trade with the Confederacy.

To help finance the war, Chase introduced paper money—bills nicknamed "greenbacks" for the color of ink used on them—America's first national currency. Printed in amounts that outstripped gold reserves, the paper bills fueled inflation, robbing many Americans of the value of their savings, but the printing kept money flowing to the essentially bankrupt government. Chase planned to engrave a powerful slogan, "In God We Trust," on the nation's two-cent coin, and proposed using it on paper money, which supposedly prompted Lincoln, with his intimate knowledge of the Bible, to joke: "If you are going to put a legend on the greenback, I would suggest that of Peter and Paul, 'Silver and gold I have none, but such as I have I give to thee.'" The money's value soon tracked the fortunes of the Union. By July 1864, as faith in Lincoln and his war evaporated, the value of greenbacks had plummeted to the point that $258 in paper bills were required to equal $100 in gold.

In a remarkable display of his outsize ego, Chase put not George Washington's face on the initial one-dollar bill but his own. He placed Lincoln's face on the ten-dollar bill, one of "the higher priced notes, and my own, as was becoming, on the smaller ones," he explained, failing to add that there were vastly more of the "smaller ones" in circulation. Of course, those dollars were an extraordinary free political advertisement for Chase. Journalist Brooks scoffed: "Mr. Chase is large, fine looking, and his well flattered picture may be found on the left hand end of any one dollar greenback, looking ten years handsomer than the light [gray] haired Secretary." The currency had an effect. Cries of "Hurrah for old Greenbacks!" greeted Chase in the Midwest in 1863.

Though a friend to Lincoln, Brooks had to admit Chase was a formidable candidate who might well end up taking the oath of office in March 1865. "An ambition for the chair of State is honorable, as much so in Chase as in Lincoln," he conceded. The two leading Republicans held similar views, though Lincoln carefully calibrated his positions to public opinion, since he considered public support vital to the effective prosecution of the war. "Chase's views and sentiments are not manufactured for the occasion," Brooks explained to his readers. "His lifelong record, his splendid public services, his uncompromising hostility to every form of oppression and slavery, his purity of character—all these are too well known to need recapitulation, and these, added to his statesmanlike abilities, make him an eminently fit candidate for what is known as the radical wing of the loyal party of the North. If our people are ready now to go into an election upon Chase's avowed platform of 'Freedom for all,' he will be the next President." Brooks summed up the two men's approaches this way: "Chase keeps ahead of public sentiment; Lincoln prefers to be led by it."

By 1864, Lincoln's friends were warning him that Chase "was at work night and day laying pipe" for the presidency, using his control over fifteen thousand Treasury jobs to advance his candidacy. Chase believed a feckless Lincoln could not outlast one term, since no president had been elected to a second term since Andrew Jackson in 1832. In a private conversation with Navy Secretary Gideon Welles, Chase lamented that "the want of energy and force of the President" had "paralyzed everything," adding that Lincoln's "weakness was crushing us." Supreme Court justice David Davis, Lincoln's Illinois friend who had brilliantly managed his dark-horse victory at the 1860 Republican convention, compared Chase's conduct to "eating a man's bread and stabbing him at the same time."

Lincoln shrugged off reports of Chase's underhanded candidacy. "I have determined to shut my eyes, as far as possible, to everything of the sort," he said. "Mr. Chase makes a good Secretary and I shall keep him where he is. If he becomes President, all right, I hope we may never have a worse man." Lincoln even joked that the presidential bug might drive Chase to new heights of performance. He recalled a farmer back in Illinois whose horse was plagued by a stinging fly while pulling a plow. When asked why he did not brush off the pest, the farmer noted that the horse, in trying to escape from it, had raced up and down the field, completing its work much faster. "Why, *that's all that made him go!*" the farmer said. "Now, if Mr. [Chase] has a presidential *chin fly* biting him, I'm not going to knock him off, if it will only make his department *go*," Lincoln laughed. In a conversation with his aide John Hay, Lincoln seemed "much amused at Chase's mad hunt after the Presidency. He says it might win. He hopes the country will never do worse." But in the same discussion, Lincoln revealed some bitterness about Chase's determined pursuit, observing, "I suppose he will, like the blue-bottle fly, lay his eggs in every rotten spot he can find."

In truth, Lincoln was deeply troubled about securing the nomination. Knowing well that military heroes made powerful candidates, he especially feared the enormously popular Ulysses S. Grant and felt compelled to send out feelers to decipher the mighty general's intentions. When J. Russell Jones, a U.S. marshal and friend of the general, came by the White House one night about eight, bringing back a letter from Grant stating emphatically that "nothing could induce me to think of" running for president, Lincoln was vastly relieved, both for himself and the country. He had already dealt with the political machinations of one general, George B. McClellan, who refused to fight the war as aggressively as Lincoln wished and would be the Democrats' presidential nominee in 1864. Jones recalled that Lincoln put both of his hands on his shoulders, and said, "My son, I can't tell how deeply gratified I am. You don't know how deep the Presidential maggot can gnaw into a man's brain."

In Chase's case, he chose to keep quiet, fearing an acrimonious fight might alienate the radical wing of the party, which he needed to secure the nomination. Mary Lincoln, who was already livid about the arrogance of Kate Chase in attempting to lead Washington society, smoldered about the maneuvering of Kate's father to replace her husband. She found it galling that Lincoln kept this viper in his Cabinet. New York political boss Thurlow Weed, a close ally of Lincoln, regarded Chase as a dangerous adversary. Weed lamented to a friend in December 1863 that Chase's end-of-the-year "Treasury report is very able, and his huge banking machine will make him strong. But how pitiable it is to know his eye is single—single—not to the welfare of the country in an unselfish cause, but to the presidency. Mr. Lincoln says that he is 'trying to keep the maggot out of his brain.'"

In January 1864, in an effort funded largely by Chase's son-in-law, Sprague, powerful Washington insiders formed a group called the Republican National Executive Committee to advance Chase's candidacy. It included Senator John Sherman, brother of the famous

general, Congressman (and future president) James Garfield, and Senator Samuel C. Pomeroy, a friend and ally of Douglass. The next month,
an anonymous "circular" began quietly making the rounds among party
leaders. Brutally direct, it warned that Lincoln's reelection was impossible, given the "union of influences which will oppose him." Lincoln,
in any event, was incapable of fully advancing "the cause of human
liberty, and the dignity of the nation," and under his demonstrably
weak leadership, the war would "continue to languish." Fortunately,
there was an alternative. "We find united in the Hon. Salmon P. Chase
more of the qualities needed in a President . . . than are combined in
any other candidate." Chase was a "statesman of rare ability and an
administrator of the highest order," with a popularity in the party ranks
that amazed "even his warmest admirers." Lincoln's allies immediately
sent the sitting president this alarming document. "The treasury rats
are busy night and day and becoming more and more unscrupulous,"
White House aide John Nicolay fumed in a February 17 letter to his
colleague John Hay after being shown the "scurrilous anonymous pamphlet to injure the Prest."

Inevitably, the letter made it into print, where it exploded like a
bombshell, dramatically exposing the fissure in the Republican Party.
Welles shrewdly predicted "it would be more dangerous in its recoil
than its projectile," harming those who fired the salvo more than their
target. Sure enough, it badly wounded Chase. The great treasury secretary was revealed as a treacherous opportunist. Lincoln's supporters,
including many he had meticulously placed in patronage jobs, rushed to
the president's defense, while Chase's allies, smelling political danger,
hastily abandoned any further efforts to shove Lincoln aside before
the party's convention in June. Senator Sherman huffily denied a *New
York Times* report that he had distributed the letter to his constituents,
insisting, "I do not believe in secret circulars." While Sherman admitted
that he preferred Chase's nomination, "as I believe Gov. Chase has more
ability than Mr. Lincoln," he stressed he would bend to the party's will.
"If Mr. Lincoln should be nominated he will receive my hearty support."
The backlash grew so intense that Republican legislators from Chase's

own state of Ohio hastened to meet and pass a resolution supporting Lincoln. A similar vote in Rhode Island, which Chase's son-in-law had failed to nail down, signaled the end of his candidacy. Stunned by the hostile reaction, the heartbroken Chase had little choice but to "ask that no further consideration be given to my name." Yet some doubted Salmon P. Chase had given up entirely. As the *New York Herald* punned, "the salmon is a queer fish; very shy and very wary, often appearing to avoid the bait just before gulping it down."

Chase also wrote to the president, protesting that he knew nothing about the circular and offering to resign. Lincoln replied that he had known for weeks of the secret plot against him, adding with ice-cold disdain that he would not force Chase's departure: "Whether you shall remain at the head of the Treasury Department is a question which I will not allow myself to consider from any stand-point other than my judgment of public service; and, in that view, I do not perceive occasion for a change." Though Chase stayed on, the two men had reached a breaking point and could barely speak to each other. Lincoln made sure Chase's supporters paid a dear price for their machinations, weakening them by denying them patronage, while a conservative ally, Congressman Frank Blair, brother of the president's first postmaster general, twisted the knife, vilifying Chase on the House floor and calling for a formal investigation of corruption in his department, with Chase the obvious target.

In June, when Lincoln moved to replace a loyal Chase ally at the U.S. Custom House in New York, a patronage haven controlled by the Treasury Department, the aggrieved secretary proffered his resignation. The previous three times Chase had threatened to leave, Lincoln had beseeched him to stay on rather than upset the financial markets and the Republican base. This time, with the party's nomination firmly in hand, Lincoln coldly accepted Chase's request, to the secretary's astonishment and chagrin. "Of all I have said in commendation of your ability and fidelity I have nothing to unsay," Lincoln wrote, "and yet you and I have reached a point of mutual embarrassment in our official relations which it seems cannot be overcome or longer sustained consistently with the public service." One Treasury official begged Lincoln to reconsider, warning that the resignation could set off a panic on Wall Street. "Mr. President, this is worse than another Bull Run defeat," he fretted, recalling the first great Union battlefield disaster that had shaken the nation. But Lincoln had made up his mind to be rid of Chase, and he had the standing to do it.

Remarkably, that was not the end of their relationship. After the death of Chief Justice Roger B. Taney that October, Iowa congressman and radical Republican Josiah B. Grinnell pleaded with Lincoln to appoint Chase to the seat. "Are you sure the seat of a chief justice will not heighten rather than banish political ambition?" Lincoln asked him, adding: "It ought to banish it; so high and honorable a place should satisfy and engross any American." Grinnell insisted that it would. "Well, you are of good hope on the outside," Lincoln said, "but I must do the right thing in this critical hour."

    In the five months since his resignation from the Cabinet, Chase had indeed been playing politics, consulting with Senate Republicans on a reconstruction plan that former postmaster general Montgomery Blair feared would deprive white Southerners of their right to run their states after the war. Chase's scheme, Blair warned Lincoln in a lengthy memo, would "put the blacks and whites on equality in the political control of a government created by the white race for themselves." Indeed, former slaves, who were largely illiterate and ill-equipped by their stunted experience to rule, "may become themselves the masters of the Government created by another race" if former Confederates were denied the right to vote. White Southerners would react furiously to such a social and racial reversal, threatening the nation's reunification. Blair harbored hopes of being appointed to the Supreme Court himself and believed Lincoln, as a Kentucky-born pragmatist rather than a Northern ideologue, would share his concerns about Chase.

    Lincoln indeed wanted to make it easy for white Southerners to return to the fold. He preferred that the states work out for themselves the thorny details of civil rights for newly freed black people. In

December 1863, the president issued an executive order permitting Louisiana to reintegrate into the Union on easy terms: when a mere 10 percent of the number of people who had voted in 1860 took an oath of allegiance and pledged to abide by the Emancipation Proclamation, issued on January 1, 1863, which permanently freed its slaves.

This was anathema to radicals, who wanted to remake America, not permit white Southerners to return to power as if nothing had happened. In April 1864, two prominent free black men from New Orleans, Jean Baptiste Roudanez and Arnold Bertonneau, traveled to the North seeking support for black enfranchisement under the state's reconstructed government. At a dinner in their honor at Boston's Parker House, Douglass pleaded with attendees, including radical senator Charles Sumner, to use their political power to ensure "the complete, absolute, unqualified enfranchisement of the colored people of the South, so that they shall not only be permitted to vote, but to be voted for, eligible to any office." Anything less would expose blacks to the tender mercies of their former oppressors. Douglass's disgust with Lincoln's sluggish pragmatism had grown to the point that he considered the president to be positively malevolent. In a private letter to a British abolitionist in June, Douglass bitterly noted, "The President has virtually laid down this as the rule of his statesmen: Do evil by choice, right from necessity." Far from desiring to extend the vote to African Americans in the South, Lincoln seemed to be working against it. "This is extremely dishonorable," Douglass wrote. "No rebuke of it can be too strong from your side of the water."

Were Chase raised to chief justice, Blair warned in his memo, such potentially explosive questions of policy might be wrenched from Lincoln's hands, since Chase could well rule that his fellow radicals in Congress, and not the president, held the constitutional authority to control postwar reconstruction. "Mr. Chase and his followers," after all, had long tried to "counteract most of the leading measures to which you committed your own destiny, and that of the nation."

But Lincoln had already made up his mind. He would appoint Chase. Lincoln admired his work ethic and intellect. He knew the choice would play well with the Senate's powerful liberals, who controlled Supreme Court confirmations. More important, as chief justice, Chase could be expected to sustain two of Lincoln's key policies—the emancipation of slaves and the radical financial measures adopted to fund the war—since he had served on the Cabinet and "would only be sustaining himself." American and European investors in the government's securities would feel reassured. Lincoln did not discuss another obvious benefit: the appointment would surely shelve Chase politically, since he would be consumed by the heavy burdens of the job. When Lincoln's allies pleaded with him to finish off this exasperating adversary by denying him power, Lincoln answered, "Mr. Chase is a very able man. He is a very ambitious man, and I think on the subject of the presidency, a little insane. He has not always behaved very well lately, and people say to me, Now is the time to crush him out. Well, I'm not in favor of crushing anybody out. If there is anything that a man can do and do it well, I say, let him do it. Give him a chance." His aide Nicolay was flabbergasted: "Probably no other man than Lincoln would have had, in this age of the world, the degree of magnanimity to thus forgive and exalt a rival who had so deeply and so unjustifiably intrigued against him." But Lincoln explained, "I should despise myself if I allowed personal differences to affect my judgment of his fitness for the office of Chief Justice."

The delighted Senate confirmed the nomination within hours of receiving it, on December 6, 1864. But if the newly reelected Lincoln thought he had blunted Chase's appetite for politics, he was badly mistaken. Chase continued to work with powerful senators bent on shaping a postwar landscape of full black and white equality, come what may. After Christmas, William Sprague, visiting New York City, clipped an article from the *New York Herald* headlined "Chief Justice and the Presidency" and sent it to Kate, noting that it was "upon the subject of our own conversation." The paper opined: "Those politicians who counted upon Mr. Chase retiring from the political arena on assuming the position and duties of Chief Justice of the highest tribunal are destined to soon be relieved of that delusion. Mr. Chase has no idea of being permanently shelved. His influence will soon be seen in political circles in more ways than one." Gideon Welles believed the same, writing in his diary on February 22, "There is no man with more fierce aspirations than Chase, and the bench will be used to promote his personal ends."

Sure enough, as Sherman ravaged the South in late 1864, Chase freely vented his concerns to an ally: "I fear our good President is so anxious for the restoration of the Union, that he will not care sufficiently about the basis of representation. In my judgment, there is none sound except absolute justice for all, and ample security for justice in law and suffrage." Chase even lobbied Lincoln to give freed blacks the vote. "I most respectfully but most earnestly commend these matters to your attention," he wrote to the president, lecturing: "God gives you a great place and a great opportunity. May He guide you in the use of them." Chase still believed that Lincoln, heading into a second term, was not up to the immense moral challenges of his high position in these historic times.

On the day after his celebrated "matinee" party, which the *Evening Star* had found so impressive, the chief justice raised the contentious political issue in his address to the National Freedmen's Relief Association in the U.S. House of Representatives. "Shall the loyal blacks of rebel States be permitted to protect themselves, and protect white loyalists also by their votes, from new oppressions by amnestied but still vindictive rebels?" he asked. Chase said he knew how the American people would answer. "They will say, 'Let ballots go with bullets; let freedom be defended by suffrage.'" After the speeches, the black choir of the Fifteenth Street Presbyterian Church rose to sing national hymns that took on new and poignant meaning in the wake of slavery's defeat. "My country 'tis of thee, sweet land of liberty," they sang. "And, stranger still, the evening was closed by the same lips" singing "The Battle Hymn of the Republic," wrote journalist Lois Bryan Adams, "the immense audience rising to their feet and joining in the chorus with an enthusiasm which made those frescoed walls and gilded ceilings ring as they never rung before. Is not the world, too, 'Marching on'?"

Now, on the windy, misty eve of Lincoln's inauguration five days later, Chase was in his stately Washington house, trying out a new black judicial robe that had just been tailored for him. With heavy symbolism, the escaped slave Frederick Douglass assisted Chase's beloved daughter, Kate, in placing the ceremonial robe over her father's broad shoulders. He would wear it while administering the presidential oath of office the next day to Abraham Lincoln, a man whom all three in that room considered inferior to the grand and dignified chief justice.

After Douglass departed, Chase called for his carriage. Like John Wilkes Booth, he felt drawn this night to the center of the political action. Bringing Kate with him, beautifully adorned in a silk dress certain to charm Washington society, Chase headed to the Capitol to pay a call on the president and to see what the chief justice's friends in Congress were up to.

CHAPTER 3

A MESSAGE FROM GRANT

Friday night, March 3, 1865

A reporter for the Washington *Evening Star* noticed that the Capitol gave off a curious silvery glow in the misty night air, much like the effect of the torches of the firemen marching to the White House, though on a far grander scale. Massive lights on the roofs over the House and Senate, signifying they were in session, were "illuminating the heavens with a brilliant halo seen for miles away into the country." A huge American flag flying over the Capitol shone brilliantly in the night, its red, white, and blue "thus emblazoned, every fold in the glorious ensign being brought out in radiant relief."

During Lincoln's first inauguration four years earlier, the Capitol's new iron dome had been only half-finished, a truncated vision of national glory, its naked ribs reaching to the sky. Some had argued that the building effort should be halted during the war, given the enormous cost and the loss of workmen to the Union Army. But Lincoln recognized that completing the task would say something important. "If people see the Capitol going on, it is a sign we intend the Union shall go on," he said. The finished dome on display confirmed the president's confidence. On Wednesday, March 1, the poet Walt Whitman had savored the results. "Tonight I have been wandering awhile in the capitol, which is all lit up. The illuminated rotunda looks fine. I like to stand aside and look a long, long while, up at the dome; it comforts me somehow."

Now, two nights later, thousands more Americans were drawn to it. All over the city, strangers hauling carpetbags and finding no lodging "were bolting in every direction in a dazed hap-hazard sort of way, and a good many of them found their way to the brilliantly lighted and comfortably warmed Capitol as if with an eye to quartering there for the night," the *Evening Star* reported. As a bonus, they could watch famous politicians rise to speak in the House and Senate chambers. For some visitors, the real thing came as a shock, particularly the grubbier House members. "They behave disgracefully, putting their legs on the desks, their hands in their pockets, roaming about, spitting &c.," wrote Ellen Low Mills, the daughter of a wealthy New York shipping magnate. "One was smoking and one combing his hair." Journalist Lois Bryan Adams found it a shame that Americans in town to see "the august assemblies of the nation's lawgivers" for the first time "too often witness scenes fitter to be enacted in the bar-room of a country tavern than in these national halls of legislation." She noted that some members were so drunk that, when rising to make a speech, they were "obliged to hold themselves balancing between two desks, one hand grasping each, in order to keep up the pretense of standing." The *New York Times*, on the other hand, was happy to observe that the evening was "not disgraced by personal quarrels, nor were there any prominent or noisy manifestations of drunkenness as heretofore." Former Massachusetts governor John H. Clifford, invited to the inauguration, found the proceedings interesting, "though they were not calculated to elevate one's idea of the dignity of the American Congress." He spent that night chatting with the incoming treasury secretary, Hugh McCulloch, who, unlike his predecessor, Salmon P. Chase, was "a pleasant amiable man but evidently not a great one." And he met Admiral David Farragut, famous for his "Damn the torpedoes, full speed ahead" attack on Mobile Bay, whom Clifford found to be "a simplehearted jolly 'old boy.'"

It was the last night of the Thirty-Eighth Congress. The frenzied scene at the Capitol, every gaslight flaring, was a biennial ritual, a tribute to the procrastination that was endemic to the institution.

Until a hard deadline confronted them, the nation's representatives and senators could not stomach the panicked horse trading and painful concessions required to get their work done. In the days leading up to the end, members worked long hours, and in an all-night marathon session on March 3, they raced to pass the remaining bills before their power vaporized at noon on March 4, as a new Congress took over.

Newspaper reporters, trying to keep pace with their machinations, crowded the press gallery and worked the halls for tidbits, among them Noah Brooks, thirty-four, the bearded and balding Washington correspondent of the *Sacramento Daily Union*. A Maine man, he signed his pieces "Castine," in honor of his lovely birthplace on Penobscot Bay, about seventy miles east of Selden Connor's Fairfield. In his painful and circuitous route to the journalistic citadel of Washington, Brooks had failed as a merchant and journalist in Illinois and a farmer in Kansas before seeking his fortune in gold-rush California. But there, as editor of the *Daily Appeal* in Marysville, north of Sacramento, Brooks had suffered the anguish of seeing both his wife, Caroline, and their daughter die during childbirth. In 1862, on his own now, he started over again, coming east alone to cover Washington. Soon enough, papers up and down the West Coast began to reprint Brooks's richly detailed and highly opinionated dispatches. But like many ambitious correspondents who were barely scraping by, Brooks kept his eyes open for other opportunities in the capital.

Back in Illinois in the 1850s, while reporting on campaign speeches, Brooks had met a remarkable figure, a tall, tousled one-term congressman who combined country mannerisms with unexpected eloquence and a capacity for brilliant political insight. Brooks was struck by the reaction to Abraham Lincoln by one ornery Democrat, who pounded the earth with his cane as he listened. "He's a dangerous man, sir! A damned dangerous man!" the Democrat exploded. "He makes you believe what he says, in spite of yourself." Passing time before one rally, Brooks sauntered with the Illinois lawyer in a grove, talking politics. "We crawled under the pendulous branches of a tree, and Lincoln, lying flat on the ground, with his chin in his hands, talked on, rather gloomily as to the present, but absolutely confident as to the future," the reporter recounted.

Lincoln did not forget his friend. When the president learned that Brooks had arrived in Washington, "he immediately sent word that he would like to see me, 'for old times' sake'; and nothing could have been more gratifying than the cordiality and bonhomie of his greeting when I called at the White House." The journalist was touched and surprised. "Do you suppose I ever forget an old acquaintance? I reckon not," Lincoln said. But the reporter was startled by the change that had come over Lincoln. "There was over his whole face an expression of sadness, and a far-away look in the eyes, which were utterly unlike the Lincoln of other days," he recalled. "I confess that I was so pained that I could almost have shed tears."

Soon enough, Brooks discovered that Lincoln could still laugh, and that "his face was often full of mirth and enjoyment." Brooks became a virtual member of the family, frequently dining with the Lincolns. By 1865, Mary Lincoln was lobbying for his appointment in the second term as presidential secretary, in place of John Nicolay and John Hay, who had defied her orders to snub Kate Chase. Brooks had achieved such stature that he was among the honorary managers of Monday night's inaugural ball, along with Senate secretary John W. Forney, Kate's husband William Sprague, General Ulysses S. Grant, and other luminaries from the world of politics, journalism, and the military.

On this busy night, the reporter was struck by the thousands of visitors admiring the newly expanded Capitol. "The great rotunda was a sight to behold, the flood of gaslights from its airy heights pouring down upon the vast throng of well-dressed people slowly circulating around the pictured walls, many, no doubt, thus taking their first glimpse of the national capitol," Brooks wrote. An unabashed celebration of America was underway. "The Capitol is literally jammed tonight," the *Baltimore Sun* reported. "All is excitement, and there is scarcely standing room in the halls." By some estimates, no fewer than ten thousand people were crammed into the building. "The galleries of the House of Representatives were overflowing with people, and it was almost impossible to pass from the Senate to the House wing, the passages and halls were so full of strangers and citizens promenading, loitering and humming with curiosity," Brooks reported.

Women—"most beautiful to behold," the unmarried reporter observed—filled the ladies' galleries above the House and Senate chambers. They wore the latest in French fashion, great flowing dresses of silk in solid colors of red, blue, or green, some with elaborate trimmings and all supported beneath by hidden hoops, petticoats, and/or crinolines. Mary Lincoln held court in the House gallery, accepting as her due the fawning greetings of many well-wishers. She had enlisted the elegant, beautiful Elizabeth Blair Lee, forty-six, to join her, along with the daughters of former war secretary Simon Cameron. Mrs. Lee, dealing with an ill son, had thought of refusing, "but as a similar excuse had induced me to decline the Theatre" and "Mother insisted I must go," she put her boy to bed and went to the Capitol. She "had a stupid time," she confessed, even though Mrs. Lincoln "was kind & confidential." The First Lady must have been none too pleased to see the young and lovely Kate Sprague show up, "gay and festive in silk attire," as Brooks put it, and looking "conspicuous in the ladies' gallery," along with other "feminine notables."

Indeed, the gallery became so crowded with beautifully adorned women that many wives of noted politicians could not find room to sit. At around nine o'clock, on the motion of outgoing representative George Pendleton of Ohio—an antiwar Democrat who had been the party's failed candidate for vice president in November—the House suspended its rules and permitted family members onto the floor. Soon, Brooks noted, the chamber "exhibited the extraordinary spectacle of hosts of nicely dressed ladies cosily seated among the members, as at the opera, their gay attire and blandishing looks gleaming strangely among the old oaken desks and chairs of the members, who could not pay so rigid attention to the pressing business of the waning hours as was demanded of them." In a corner sat the Committee on the Enrolled Bills, its members feverishly reading and comparing "great sheets of parchment that were soon to be the laws of the land rushed through in this indecent manner." Brooks found it fitting that the final hours of the Congress's work "should be distinguished by the same reckless disregard" for duty that "characterized its course from the beginning."

The most consequential legislation passed that day created the Bureau of Refugees, Freedmen, and Abandoned Lands—better known as the Freedmen's Bureau—to assist "destitute and suffering" ex-slaves, including women and children, with clothing, food, temporary shelter, and other essential provisions. The nation had a huge humanitarian crisis on its hands, with millions of formerly enslaved people essentially on their own, untold thousands having fled from their masters and now desperate for food and shelter. These black Americans had to be educated somehow, connected with work, accorded civil rights—including equal justice under the law and perhaps the vote. The difficulties of all this were enormous. The bill passed the House in the afternoon, and obtained Lincoln's signature that night.

Just beyond the House floor were anxious lobbyists, newspaper men, Cabinet members, and curious onlookers. "Grave senators" sat down among the women, waiting to see whether their legislation survived in this chamber. But members could not hear the clerk, and Speaker Schuyler Colfax's emphatic hammering with his gavel could not silence the buzz. Some of the people's representatives steadied their nerves with frequent nips from personal flasks. In the chaos, Brooks observed, "bills, which were reckoned as dead, were somehow galvanized into life and lived as laws, while many a healthy child of legislation was nipped untimely and died for want of breath." Lincoln's secretaries fought through the crowds to the legislative chambers with rolls of parchment signed by the president, official notification that the bills had become law. Swarms of job seekers, looking for eleventh-hour congressional approval of appointments "to high as well as low positions," as one dispatch put it, crowded the halls, pleading their cause. Working to supplement their pay, the pages "did a thriving business" that night collecting signatures of famous senators and representatives, their "autograph albums selling well at all the bookstores," Brooks noted.

Making their way through the mob, Louis J. Weichmann, John Surratt, and John Wilkes Booth were ascending the marble stairs toward the House gallery when, Weichmann recalled, Booth suddenly stopped. "Who's that?" he said, staring at a statue in the corner of one of the landings. "That is Mr. Lincoln," Weichmann replied. In authoritarian regimes, statues were part of cultic deification of living leaders, but Capitol sculptures had always depicted men of the past who had helped secure freedom. "What's *he* doing in here before his time?" Booth snapped. Weichmann was struck by Booth's passionate hatred of Lincoln. The war clerk's memory of the scene was surely somewhat askew, since there is no record of a full statue of Lincoln standing in the Capitol before he became a national martyr. A painted portrait or a bust on a pedestal is possible, however, as Lincoln had posed for such works in Washington and even before leaving Springfield, Illinois. But statue or no, Booth had clearly had more than his fill of the public tributes and lavish ceremonies surrounding Lincoln's inauguration to a second term.

Abraham Lincoln was in the President's Room, just behind the Senate chamber, signing legislation before the session expired and holding court with his Cabinet members and cronies, including his longtime friend and self-appointed bodyguard Ward Hill Lamon, now the U.S. marshal of the District of Columbia. Released from the gloom of the White House, the president, always a political animal, seemed unusually happy as he chatted with visiting senators. His inaugural address, the fruit of years of deep reflection, was completed. Yet he treated none of this as a personal triumph. On Wednesday, a group of congressmen had come to the White House to notify Lincoln of Congress's certification of his election, based on its formal count of the votes of the electoral college. Lincoln had prepared a brief reply that drew widespread praise for its uncommon modesty. "Having served four years in the depths of a great, and yet unended national peril, I can view this call to a second term, in nowise more flatteringly to myself, than as an expression of the public judgment, that I may better finish a difficult work, in which I have labored from the first, than could any one less severely schooled to the task." He stressed his reliance on the "Almighty Ruler" to help him with the job's "yet onerous and perplexing duties and responsibilities." Trying to escape his perplexing duties in the President's Room this Friday night, he discussed the news and worked his visitors for laughs with his celebrated country stories. "As usual, the time passed very pleasantly," Gideon Welles wrote in his diary.

Like the nation that had expanded beyond recognition in power and wealth since 1789, the lusciously ornate President's Room seemed an exotic hothouse outgrowth of the republican simplicity of America's founding. In a city of muddy roads, grubby neighborhoods, and a stinking canal, Lincoln and his friends sat on red velvet chairs under an arched ceiling ornamented with glittering gold, beneath a gleaming, eighteen-arm gas-fired chandelier that was embellished with figures of George Washington and Benjamin Franklin. The chamber was festooned with bright, warmly colored frescoes by the Italian-born artist Constantino Brumidi, who, drawing inspiration from Raphael's ceiling of the Stanza della Segnatura in the Vatican Palace, had created a weird mixture of Roman Catholic iconography and republican hero worship. Above two sets of doors, a mural on the room's south side depicted the nation's father, George Washington, flanked by young and pretty female figures representing Peace and her essential companion, Victory. The ceiling displayed four circular paintings that seemed to open to the blue heavens, each containing a female figure symbolizing a crucial aspect of governance. One portrayed Religion, her Madonna-like face veiled, a cross on her breast, a Bible in her hands. Another symbolized Liberty, who wore a sword while a cherub unsheathed her ax—expressing the common understanding that freedom must constantly be defended with military might or at least the threat of it.

One later visitor was almost overwhelmed by it all. "Gilding, frescoes, arabesques, glitter and glow above and around," she wrote. "There is not one quiet hue on which the tired sight may rest. Gazing, I feel an indescribable desire to pluck a few of Signor Brumidi's red legged babies and pug-nosed cupids from their precarious perches on the lofty ceilings, to commit them to nurses or to anybody who will smooth out their rumpled little legs and make them look comfortable." Walt Whitman found "the incredible gorgeousness" of such rooms in the Capitol to be "beyond one's flightiest dreams. Costly frescos in the style of Taylor's saloon in Broadway, only really the best and choicest of their sort, done by imported French and Italian artists, are the prevailing sorts." An advocate for robust democracy and the common man, Whitman rated this workmanship "the richest and gayest, and most un-American and inappropriate" imaginable for a building that stood for the rugged American people.

These gorgeous rooms were part of a dramatic expansion and renovation of the Capitol, its lavishness boasting to all comers that America was now the equal of any European power. During the 1850s, the project had been brilliantly championed by, of all people, the man who was at that moment trying with all his might to tear asunder the nation that this mighty building symbolized. Jefferson Davis, then secretary of war, had secured funding for the building's extraordinary transformation, a great national undertaking, and had overseen plans to replace its old copper dome, deemed too small for the massive new proportions of the Capitol, with a towering iron one. At its summit would stand a nineteen-and-a-half-foot-tall, nearly fifteen-thousand-pound statue designed by Thomas Crawford, representing *Freedom Triumphant in War and Peace*. Davis had exploded when he saw the original design, which had Freedom wearing a liberty cap, symbol of a freed slave in Rome. It was an unsuitable emblem for a nation of white citizens "who were born free and would not be enslaved," he argued. More to the point, the Mississippi slaveholder surely knew that a gigantic dark bronze statue of a freed slave would appall the South. The artist dutifully replaced the cap with a helmet clumsily adorned with eagle feathers. Ever since, visitors have mistaken the figure for a Native American.

In yet another irony, this statue symbolizing American freedom had been forged under the leadership of an enslaved black man named

Philip Reid, who had learned the difficult craft in a South Carolina foundry run by his owner, the self-taught sculptor Clark Mills. As a huge derrick helped workmen assemble the dome, Whitman often saw the statue "standing in the mud, west of the Capitol; I saw her there all Winter" in 1862–63, "looking very harmless and innocent, although holding a huge sword." Well before she was completed and installed, Salmon P. Chase, confident of America's future, put her on the five-dollar greenback, "making her twenty times brighter in expression" than the real thing, Whitman quipped. On the cold and windy afternoon of December 2, 1863, the giant statue's head, effectively the last piece of the new dome's exterior, was finally lifted into place before cheering thousands, to the thunder of cannons firing a thirty-five-gun salute, one blast for each state, North and South. Cannons at forts ringing the city answered with their own booming tributes.

Whitman stood in awe of the new dome, this "huge and delicate towering bulge of pure white" set on a hill. "There is no place in the city, or for miles and miles off, or down or up the river, but you see this tiara-like dome quietly rising out of the foliage," he wrote. "A vast eggshell, built of iron and glass, this dome—a beauteous bubble, caught and put in permanent form." By the time *Freedom Triumphant* ascended, the bronzeworker Philip Reid had won his liberation, along with his fellow slave laborers in the District of Columbia, through the Compensated Emancipation Act, which Lincoln signed into law in April 1862.

A group of New Yorkers visiting this Friday night showed up at the President's Room to serenade Lincoln with patriotic music. The players, from Poughkeepsie's Eastman Business College Band, were adorned with scarlet pants, blue overcoats trimmed with gold lace and large silver epaulets, and hats with large, flowing white and red plumes. Someone called out to Lincoln with a question about General William Tecumseh Sherman, who was somewhere in the Carolinas. As everyone knew, Sherman had left behind a ruined Atlanta, boldly cut off his line of communications, and marched through Georgia, living off the land

and sowing terror as he went. In early December, Lincoln had color-fully compared him to a hedgehog. "We know what hole he went in at, but we do not know what hole he will come out of," he quipped to the general's brother John, the senator. Late that month, General Sherman suddenly restored contact with Lincoln, from Savannah, Georgia—"I beg to present you, as a Christmas gift, the city of Savannah, with 150 heavy guns and plenty of ammunition, and also about 25,000 bales of cotton," he famously informed him—then quickly plunged into the dark heart of South Carolina. Lincoln revived the hedgehog image for his inauguration eve serenaders: "Sherman went in at Atlanta and came out right. He has gone in at Savannah and I propose three cheers for his coming out gloriously!" The president was in a holiday spirit.

Even the sudden appearance of a former political rival could not spoil the mood. Salmon P. Chase spent half an hour in the President's Room chatting with Lincoln and former Cabinet colleagues. Lincoln's men found the chief justice and his rabid supporters intensely annoying, particularly the ones who refused to concede that the president had done Chase a remarkable kindness. "There are some people in this world who never will have the manliness to be satisfied with any concession, however graceful, nor any object attained, however desirable," Brooks fumed in one dispatch. "Of this class are some of the over-zealous and indiscreet friends of the new Chief Justice, who, now that Chase has been appointed, gleefully claim that the President was coerced into making the appointment . . . that it was a popular choice forced upon the President by men who control confirmations in the Senate." Brooks found it "a pity that when the President has paid a noble and willing compliment" to a man who had actively campaigned against him, "he cannot have the poor satisfaction of knowing that his own purity of motive and fixity of intention are appreciated by those who made Chase and Chase's ambitions the excuse for injuring and conspiring against the good name of the President." Lincoln's reelection had not smoothed over the party's divisions.

After the chief justice left the President's Room, Welles spied him in the Senate conversing with members, for purposes Welles could only imagine. The new U.S. attorney general, James Speed, warned Welles that Chase habitually left the Supreme Court chamber in the Capitol every day to visit the Senate, "and is full of aspirations." Chase was also seen that night in the House chamber, "receiving the congratulations and greetings of his friends." Accompanying Chase on his rounds was Lincoln's former secretary of war, Simon Cameron. Though Lincoln had been forced to replace the Pennsylvania politician because of his lax management of a department rife with corruption ("I don't think that he would steal a red-hot stove," Congressman Thaddeus Stevens had advised the president, when asked about his fellow Pennsylvanian's honesty), Cameron remained close to Lincoln, advising him on the important matter of patronage in that key state, while his daughters remained close to the First Lady.

Inside the President's Room, much of the talk centered on the brightening military outlook, as messengers handed Lincoln reports from the front. "Every one appeared to be happy at the prospect of the early re-establishment of peace, General Grant having just telegraphed a glowing account of his successes and his control of the situation, and expressing the hope that a very few days would find Richmond in the hands of the national forces and the army of General Lee disbanded or captured," Ward Hill Lamon recalled of the scene. Sherman was busy chastising South Carolina, and General Philip Sheridan had burned and pillaged Virginia's Shenandoah Valley, stripping it of the food that was desperately needed to feed Lee's Army of Northern Virginia. Lee still defended the vital rail hub of Petersburg, the key to holding Richmond, and his ragged army—almost all that was left of the Confederacy's power—faced off against the Union's much larger and better provi- sioned Army of the Potomac. Occupying muddy, rat-infested trenches, they fired cannons and rifles at each other, but neither side had been able to gain an advantage during the fiercely cold winter. Lieutenant General Ulysses S. Grant, overseeing all the Union forces, was wary of sacrificing thousands more of his men in head-on attacks that stood little chance of killing many Confederates.

Yet the stalemate showed signs of breaking. In a dispatch written Thursday, *Philadelphia Inquirer* correspondent William H. Cunnington reported from the front about continuing desertions that were seriously weakening Lee. Many men—cold, hungry, and increasingly aware that their deaths would be futile—preferred to face the end of the war in Union hands. "Yesterday evening nearly two companies, tolerably well officered, entered our lines occupied by the Fifth Corps, and will rest hereafter from the war's alarms in the loyal North." A large steamer ferried them from Grant's headquarters at City Point to Washington, where they would be processed. "It has now got to be quite a business to receive, care for, and transport North the dissatisfied chivalry, that embrace every opportunity of entering our lines," Cunnington jeered. There were moments when Southern spirits lifted. At one point that week, Confederate soldiers on the line had let out a cheer. Deserters revealed to Union soldiers that they had heard rumors that disaster had befallen Sherman. But as "no Rebel salutes have been fired, and as the Rebel officials would not be slow in letting us know if they had any reliable intelligence" about Sherman's defeat, Cunnington noted, the story could be safely ignored.

The men on the Northern line struggled to keep up their spirits, too. Baseball helped. "We have had several good games of ball which serve to pass the time very agreeably," Warren S. Gurney, a band member with the Fifty-Sixth Massachusetts regiment, wrote to his mother on the same day as Cunnington's dispatch. But now it was pouring rain. "It is very true that I get blue at times. The same can be said of almost any soldier in the army," Gurney wrote to his uncle. "The men that can stand this kind of life and be perfectly contented should be classed with gorillas and mules." Gurney did receive an extraordinary pick-me-up in the form of a care package from home. "The box was elegantly packed, the pies, cakes, ginger snaps, syrup, tomato ketchup, white & brown bread & butter, apples everything was just as good as new," he wrote to his mother. They were a delightful substitute for the rock-hard crackers that formed the staple of the soldier's diet. "No more hard tack at present," Gurney enthused. Certainly, very few such boxes were going to Southern soldiers, as Lincoln's hard hand of war began to starve out civilians. Gurney wrote about the large number of "Johnnies" deserting every day, "quite discouraged at the prospect before them." They "are generally very poorly clothed" and "must have suffered severely the last winter." Confederate forces still hoped that their brilliant commander might somehow strike at Sherman, but "I think Sherman will get through all right in spite of him," Gurney reflected. Meanwhile, the Union forces expected Lee to evacuate Petersburg soon, and orders had come down to the entire line to be ready to move at a moment's notice in light marching order, as unencumbered as possible. As eager as he was to see the end of this hateful war, Gurney hoped "we shall not move until I have eaten up the contents of the box."

The armies' leaders also sensed the end was near. On February 20, fewer than two weeks before this night in the Capitol, Union general Edward Ord, a Grant favorite and confidant, sent a note to Confederate general James Longstreet, asking to discuss the illicit bartering going on between Northern and Southern soldiers on the line. What he really wanted to talk about, he soon made clear, was peace. Longstreet was a practical man who knew Grant from earlier days, having stood up for him at his wedding in 1848. When the generals met between the lines, Ord brought up the Hampton Roads peace conference, the summit days earlier between Lincoln and three Confederate delegates, which Grant had quietly advanced in the face of opposition from such hardliners as Secretary of War Edwin Stanton. Talks stalled when Lincoln spelled out his nonnegotiable terms, which were anathema to Jefferson Davis: a united country and the end of slavery. Ord had concluded that politicians would never have the guts to strike a peace bargain, but military men might lead the way, forcing the politicians to come along. Those on his side, he told Longstreet, thought "the war had gone on long enough; that we should come together as former comrades and friends and talk a little." The Confederate general, in turn, suggested that he and Lee knew the war was lost, even though President Davis could not accept reality, and it would be a "great crime" to sacrifice more men to it.

Ord proposed that war be suspended while Grant and Lee met, and suggested that it might help to involve the generals' wives. Longstreet's spouse, Louise, was an old friend of Mrs. Grant. Louise could pay a visit to Union headquarters at City Point, Ord suggested, and "bring as many Confederate officers as should choose to be with her." Julia Grant, escorted by Union officers, could then return the visit in Richmond. In short, "while General Lee and General Grant were arranging for better feeling between the armies, they could be aided by intercourse between the ladies and officers until terms honorable to both sides could be found." Julia, staying with her husband at City Point, was utterly charmed by the idea. "Oh! How enchanting, how thrilling! Oh, Ulys, I may go, may I not?" Grant did not like that part of the plan. "No, you must not. It is simply absurd. The men have fought this war and the men will finish it," he told her. Still, he was willing to set the peace plan in motion quietly under Lincoln's nose, usurping the authority that belonged to the commander in chief.

Longstreet brought the scheme back to Lee, and the two rushed off to Richmond, meeting at night in the president's mansion with Davis and Secretary of War John Breckinridge, who "expressed especial approval of the part assigned for the ladies." A telegram went to Lynchburg, Virginia, urging Mrs. Longstreet to come to Richmond quickly. In a second meeting between Ord and Longstreet, the Union general revealed that Grant was "prepared to receive" a letter from Lee requesting a summit. On Thursday, March 2, as Cunnington reported about desertions, Lee wrote to Grant a stiffly dignified letter, offering to meet, in the hope that a "military convention" might end the bloodshed. "Sincerely desiring to leave nothing untried which may put an end to the calamities of war, I propose to meet you at such convenient time and place as you may designate, with the hope that upon an interchange of views it may be found practicable to submit the subjects of controversy between the belligerents to a convention of the kind mentioned."

Only at that point did Grant feel he must involve the president. Up until then, he and Lincoln had enjoyed a warm relationship. Unlike other military leaders, Grant had fully grasped Lincoln's war aims—to extinguish the Confederacy's capacity to fight. This war was not about reclaiming territory or preserving the lives of young Americans or protecting civilians. It was about killing Confederate soldiers as quickly as possible, destroying the South's farms and factories, and forcing the rebels to quit. The hideous math guiding Lincoln and Grant was irrefutable: the South was far less capable than the North of feeding fresh young men into the lines to replace those who had been slaughtered.

Earlier in the war, Lincoln had been forced to deal with interminable delays as General George B. McClellan, a Democrat who yearned to return America to its prewar state, had maneuvered to minimize casualties and limit destruction. Lincoln grew exasperated at McClellan's endless calls for more troops to outflank the enemy with a minimum of bloodshed. Grant, by contrast, waged war without complaint and with almost unimaginable ferocity. When a politician urged Lincoln to replace Grant earlier in the war, Lincoln could not accede to the request: "I can't spare this man; he fights." He did not look like much: a slim and stooping forty-two-year-old standing five foot eight and weighing only 135 pounds, he had a ragged brown beard, a face lined by a lifetime of stress and failure, and a modest and even gentle demeanor. But Grant was relentless. His spring campaign of 1864 proved an extended study in mass carnage, as masses of young men were blown to pieces or riddled with agonizing wounds—Selden Connor among them, at the Battle of the Wilderness. Over a mere four weeks, the two sides had suffered some sixty-nine thousand casualties. In the Battle of Cold Harbor, on June 3, 1864, Grant had ordered a frontal assault on dug-in Confederates, and in little more than one hour, thousands more Union men had been killed or wounded. Even those gunning down waves of nameless men were horrified. "It was not war, but murder," Confederate general Evander Law observed. But the butchery continued all summer and fall, until Grant was finally slowed by winter's arrival, as the ground became muddy, then frozen, slippery and unpassable.

Through it all, Grant impressed Lincoln with his lack of pretension, his tact, his businesslike approach, and his fondness for dry humor. One of the three Confederate peace envoys Grant had permitted to

cross his lines in February 1865 was Alexander Stephens, the diminu-
tive vice president of the Confederacy. "I had always supposed that he
was a very small man, but when I saw him in the dusk of evening I was
very much surprised to find so large a man as he seemed to be," Grant
recalled. It turned out he was wearing a coarse gray woolen overcoat,
"so large that it gave him the appearance of being an average-sized
man. He took this off when he reached the cabin of the boat, and I
was struck with the apparent change in size in the coat and out of it."
Lincoln, who later joined the negotiations with Stephens, asked Grant
confidentially whether he had seen Stephens's overcoat. Grant replied
that he had. "Well," Lincoln said, "did you see him take it off?" Grant
said yes. "Well," Lincoln said, "didn't you think it was the biggest shuck
and the littlest ear that ever you did see?"

On the eve of the inauguration, a messenger interrupted the pleasant chatter in the President's Room with a stunning transmission from
Grant, handing it to Secretary of War Stanton. The secretary, Lamon
recalled, "having read it, handed it to the president and became absorbed
in thought." The message disclosed that Robert E. Lee had requested
an immediate interview to discuss terms of peace. As it was read to the
group, "Mr. Lincoln's spirits rose to a height rarely witnessed since the
outbreak of the war. All the better and kindlier impulses of his nature
were aroused," Lamon recounted. Suddenly, the end of the nation's
agony seemed near. "He was unable to restrain himself from giving
expression to the natural impulses of his heart," or from revealing "the
magnanimity with which the Confederates were now to be treated. He
did not hesitate to express himself as favorably disposed towards grant-
ing the most lenient and generous terms to a defeated foe."

Sitting there, getting redder by the minute, was Stanton. Like
many who had to deal with him, Noah Brooks found the war secretary a
"coarse, abusive and arbitrary" bully, who "abuses people like a fish-wife
when he gets mad, which is very frequent." On this night, according to
Lamon, Stanton turned his wrath on the president himself. In a "towering rage," with "his eyes flashing fire," Stanton lectured Lincoln: "Mr.
President, are you losing sight of the paramount consideration at this

juncture, namely, how and by whom is this war to be closed? Tomorrow is Inauguration Day; you will then enter upon your second term of office. Read again this dispatch: don't you appreciate its significance? If you are not to be President of an obedient, loyal, and united people, you ought not to take the oath of office,—you are not a proper person to be empowered with so high and responsible a trust." Lincoln, in Stanton's view, should not let his generals make a peace deal, when he himself had spelled out his conditions just days earlier. The president should control the terms of reconstruction, and no one else, certainly not his military officers.

It was Lincoln's turn to lapse into thoughtful silence, his joy at the prospect of peace fading from his face. "Stanton, you are right; this dispatch did not, at first sight, strike me as I now consider it," the president said. Lincoln took up a pen and paper and wrote a dispatch, asking Stanton to send it in his name: "The President directs me to say that he wishes you to have no conference with General Lee, unless it be for the capitulation of Lee's army, or on some minor and purely military matter. He instructs me to say that you are not to decide, discuss, or confer on any political questions; the President, holding the decision of questions in his own hands, will submit them to no military conference or convention. In the mean time you are to press, to the utmost of your ability, your military advantage." Stanton provided a stinging note of his own: "I will add that General Ord's conduct in holding intercourse with General Longstreet upon political questions not committed to his charge is not approved. . . . You will please in future instruct officers appointed to meet rebel officers to confine themselves to matters specifically committed to them."

Back at City Point, Grant read these curt responses with dismay. He considered this rebuke unjust, and he thought Lincoln was "unduly anxious" about how the talks could go, the general's aide-de-camp, Horace Porter, recalled. Always calm under fire, however, Grant moved immediately to minimize the damage, rushing off a response to Stanton: "I can assure you that no act of the enemy will prevent me from pressing all advantages gained to the utmost of my ability; neither will I, under any circumstances, exceed my authority or in any way embarrass the government. It was because I had no right to meet General Lee on the subject proposed by him that I referred the matter for instructions." Yet Stanton was basically right. The generals had plainly tried to go around the president to strike the peace deal that had eluded Lincoln. The following morning, no doubt with a pang of regret, Grant sent a letter to Lee. "I have no authority to accede to your proposition for a conference on the subject proposed," he wrote. "Such authority is vested in the President of the United States alone." For now, there would be no meetings of pragmatic military men, no efforts by "the ladies" to smooth things over. Cold, hard war would continue.

That point settled, and with the clock approaching midnight, Lincoln left the Capitol for his carriage ride in the wind and rain to the White House, a little more than a mile away, passing revelers on the way. Navy Secretary Welles shared his own carriage with Secretary of State Seward for the trip to their lovely brick homes surrounding Lafayette Square, where Welles lived on the north side and Seward on the east, both in sight of the White House. As Welles noted in his diary, their topic of conversation was neither Grant's message nor the inauguration; rather, Seward seemed obsessed with the plots being laid against the administration by some of its former friends. As their carriage sluiced through the mud in the drizzling night, Seward, Welles wrote, "expressed himself more unreservedly and warmly against Chase than I have ever heard him before." Lincoln would be challenged yet again to employ his political skills to keep the members of his own party in line, never mind the Confederates.

CHAPTER 4

THE REAL PRECIOUS AND ROYAL ONES

Saturday morning, March 4, 1865

Darkness gave way to a feeble dawn in Washington, an inauspicious day for Abraham Lincoln's second inauguration, "everything dim, leaden, and soaking," wrote one of the reporters seated in the House gallery. Even among the oddballs that the newspaper trade attracted, this journalist stood out: a towering, six-foot-tall forty-five-year-old with a cheery red face, long and tousled hair, and a wild, fleecy beard. William D. O'Connor, an admiring friend, described the writer as "serene, proud, cheerful, florid, grave; the brow seamed with noble wrinkles; the features, massive and handsome, with firm blue eyes." Looking more like a tradesman than a literary grandee, he wore clothing that was "cheap and plain, but spotless, from snowy falling collar to burnished boot, and exhaling faint fragrance." He "is so large & strong—so pure, proud, & tender, with such an ineffable *bonhommie* & wholesome sweetness of presence [that] all the young men and women are in love with him." The subject of O'Connor's unabashed admiration employed simpler terms about himself, claiming he made a good impression on the young wounded soldiers he liked to visit in the Washington hospitals because he was "so large and well—indeed like a great buffalo, with much hair."

This big, hairy, rambunctious buffalo of a man had worked on and off for decades as a journalist, mainly in Brooklyn. He had become notorious in literary circles, though, as the author of *Leaves of Grass*, a wildly original volume of poems that had shocked and appalled large numbers of his readers. This day, he was covering Lincoln's inauguration as a special correspondent for the *New York Times*. Readers knew his name so well that the newspaper had accorded him the rare journalistic distinction of a byline: "Walt Whitman."

His *Leaves of Grass* was like nothing in American literature. In a Victorian society that defined civilization by severe standards of restraint, the little book of twelve rambling poems offered uninhibited declarations of delight in life and in its author's own self, including open celebrations of sexual love and the physical body, in free verse untrammeled by accepted rules of rhythm or rhyme. It created a sensation from the moment of its publication in 1855, on the Fourth of July, of all days. The book's title was evidently a wry and self-deprecating pun—*leaves* being pages of a book, *grass* being publishing slang for second-rate material, something he well understood as a former printer and editor. A spirit of audacious joy, even fun, permeated the work, as its author defied convention with unabashed gusto. "I sound my barbaric yawp over the roofs of the world," he declared.

America's celebrated transcendental philosopher Ralph Waldo Emerson praised the book in a personal letter, using words that the publicity-mongering Whitman printed in gold leaf on the spine of a later edition: "I Greet You at the Beginning of a Great Career." But others had a decidedly different reaction. "Walt Whitman is as unacquainted with art, as a hog is with mathematics," *The Critic* of London informed its readers. For the book's indecency, it said, the author "deserves nothing so richly as the public executioner's whip." Critic Rufus Wilmot Griswold called the volume a "mass of stupid filth," while Boston-area minister and abolitionist Thomas Wentworth Higginson observed, "It is no discredit to Walt Whitman that he wrote *Leaves of Grass*, only that he did not burn it afterwards." The *Boston Intelligencer* deemed the book a "heterogeneous mass of bombast, egotism, vulgarity, and nonsense," and strongly recommended that the author "be kicked from all decent society as below the level of a brute." Griswold sought a more severe punishment than that, calling for criminal prosecution for obscenity. "The records of crime show that many monsters have gone on in impunity, because the exposure of their vileness was attended with too great indelicacy," he warned. Yet a few critics saw Whitman bravely striking a blow for honesty and sanity. "Nothing can more clearly demonstrate the innate vulgarity of our American people, their radical immodesty, their internal licentiousness, their unchastity of heart, their foulness of feeling, than the tabooing of Walt Whitman's *Leaves of Grass*," wrote William Porter Ray, a Harvard- and Heidelberg-educated journalist. "The atmosphere of *Leaves of Grass* is as sweet as that of a hayfield. . . . It is the healthiest book, morally, this century has produced."

Those who saw themselves in the liberal vanguard of change, such as Lincoln's Springfield law partner, William Herndon, made a point of reading it. Years later, their clerk Henry Rankin recalled that Herndon left a copy on a shared office table, and that Lincoln, in one of his glum moods, picked it up. He studied it silently for a while before "reading aloud a dozen or more pages in his amusing way." Lincoln liked the freshness and virility of the writing, Rankin recalled, and took the book home. The next morning Lincoln brought it back and laid it on the table, "remarking in a grim way that he had 'barely saved it from being purified in fire by the woman.'" Not surprisingly, the rigid and proper Salmon P. Chase leaned more toward Mary Lincoln's view of the book than her husband's. When Chase visited the home of a special treasury agent in 1862 and saw a copy of *Leaves of Grass* on the table, he asked, "How is it possible you can have this nasty book here?"

Whitman had another prominent friend in Washington who championed its virtues, though—a great, red-bearded, forty-three-year-old Scottish immigrant named Alexander Gardner. "He went strong for *Leaves of Grass*—believed in it, fought for it," Whitman recalled. "Gardner was large, strong—a man with a big head full of ideas: a splendid neck: a man you would like to know, to meet." Gardner was a fellow artist, though he was usually regarded as little more than an expert technician, as one of the men who handled the magical heavy box on a tripod—a photographer.

With his big frame and his air of ease and confidence, Gardner looked as solid, boxy, and unblinking as his machine. He had become fascinated with this new art form in 1851 while attending the Great Exhibition at Hyde Park in London, where he came across a display of the American photographer Mathew Brady's work. After emigrating to the United States in 1856, Gardner found work with Brady in New York before taking over Brady's Washington studio in 1858. During the war, Gardner captured images of the capital's elite—including the strikingly homely new president—under upper-story skylights that let in the beaming sun. In 1863, he took a beautiful portrait of Whitman in a white shirt, with a snowy beard and faraway look. It was the poet's favorite. "Gardner was a real artist—had the feel of his work—the inner feel, if I may say it so: he was not . . . only a workman (which God knows is a lot in itself, too!)—but he was also beyond his craft—saw farther than his camera—saw more: his pictures are an evidence of his endowment," Whitman later said.

Gardner's cameras were bulky things, with a single glass plate in a container that slid into the back. The plate was coated with a solution called collodion that the photographer mixed himself, using such dangerous chemicals as ethyl ether and acetic or sulfuric acid. In a darkroom, the photographer then submerged the plate in silver nitrite in a box that let in no light. To imprint a good image on this scrupulously prepared plate, a photographer removed a lens cap, took an exposure of two or three seconds while his carefully posed, unsmiling subject rigidly held his position lest he become a blur, and replaced the cap. He then rushed the fragile plate, still in its container, to his darkroom to develop it in a vat of pyrogallic acid. That produced the glass negative that could be used to print images. It was a demanding process that admitted no error.

In 1862, Gardner embarked on an extraordinary mission. He made this trying technology portable, so that he could record the scenes of the battlefields and campgrounds for people on the home front, who were desperate to see them. Transporting his chemicals and darkroom on a horse-drawn cart, he braved the overpowering stench of death and the risk of capture by roving Confederates to take shots of the dead, still unburied, at Antietam, where twelve hours of savage combat had killed more men in one day than in any battle ever waged on the continent. The exhibition of Gardner's photos in New York City under Brady's name created a sensation. The sight of the bloated bodies of dead men sprawled on the ground was like nothing else the public had ever witnessed, habituated as it was to lithographs that showed heroic charges rather than the macabre and grisly residue of battle. "The living that throng Broadway care little perhaps for the Dead at Antietam, but we fancy they would jostle less carelessly down the great thoroughfare, saunter less at their ease, were a few dripping bodies, fresh from the field, laid along the pavement. There would be a gathering up of skirts and a careful picking of way; conversation would be less lively, and the general air of pedestrians more subdued," a critic for the *New York Times* wrote. "As it is, the dead of the battle-field come up to us very rarely, even in dreams. We see the list in the morning paper at breakfast, but dismiss its recollection with the coffee." These grim photographs had changed that. "Mr. Brady has done something to bring home to us the terrible reality and earnestness of war. If he has not brought bodies and laid them in our dooryards and along the streets, he has done something very like it."

After a series of disputes with Brady, Gardner set off on his own, opening his own shop to make his own fame. On February 5, a month before Lincoln's second inauguration, Gardner took perhaps the most moving formal portrait of the suffering president. Lincoln looked wrinkled, haggard, terribly aged by the war, as Gardner's ruthlessly sharp lens captured the crosshatches in the dark pouches under his eyes. Yet it is the only photograph of Lincoln showing an enigmatic half smile, which invests it with an odd aura of warmth and compassion. When the large glass plate cracked, Gardner managed to salvage one print of the extraordinary image, rescuing this last great portrait of the president for posterity. On this rainy Inauguration Day, Gardner planned to haul his portable equipment to the Capitol, to secure images that artists could use as guides to produce lithographs of the scene for the enormously popular *Harper's Weekly* magazine, which did not yet have the technology to readily reproduce news photographs of the great national celebration. He hoped to take a picture of Lincoln reading his much-anticipated inaugural address to the thousands.

Already at the Capitol on this stormy dawn, capturing impressions with his equipment of vivid words, Whitman carefully studied the emotionally and physically drained lawmakers. They had been at work round the clock, trying to wrap up legislation before a new Congress took over at noon. "The members were nervous, from long drawn duty, exhausted, some asleep, and many half asleep," Whitman observed. "The gas-light, mixed with dingy day-break, produced an unearthly effect. The poor little sleepy, stumbling pages, the smell of the Hall, the members with heads leaning on their desks asleep, the sounds of the voices speaking, with unusual intonations, the general moral atmosphere also of the close of this important session, the grandeur of the Hall itself, with its effect of vast shadows up toward the panels and spaces over the galleries, all made a marked combination." Whitman was not a great admirer of congressmen. He once described them as "little mannikins, shrewd, gabby, drest in black, hopping about, making motions, amendments." Still, the writer had not lost faith in the cause of America, "even here amid all this huge mess of traitors, loafers, hospitals, axe-grinders, & incompetencies & officials that goes by the name of Washington."

Since January, he had rented a room in a house at 468 M Street, a little more than a mile away from the Capitol. Though Whitman was a staunch Union man, his landlords, Edward and Juliet Grayson, were Southern sympathizers, and their oldest son, Spence Monroe Grayson, was a private in the Second Maryland Infantry, now stationed in the Petersburg trenches, part of the ragged, evaporating army of General Robert E. Lee. Still, Whitman was fond of his landlady, who was "different from any I have found yet here, is very obliging, starts my fire for me at 5 o'clock every afternoon, & lights the gas, even & then turns it down to be ready for me when I come home." She also kept him well fed. "Mrs. Grayson gives me plenty of good vegetables, peas, string beans, squash & new potatoes, with fruit now & then, which is better than too much meat," Whitman wrote to his mother the following year. And he liked his neighborhood, which he called "the healthiest sweetest part of Washington," in sharp contrast with his last abode in the city, at 502 Pennsylvania Avenue, on swampy ground within smelling distance of the canal, with "very bad air" that he blamed for his spells of faintness and headaches. Whitman liked to visit the Capitol, which had been so beautifully renovated through the efforts of Jefferson Davis. On the previous Wednesday night, in addition to admiring the rotunda, he had peeked in on the House and Senate, then meandered through the building. "I wander'd through the long and rich corridors and apartments under the Senate; an old habit of mine, former winters, and now more satisfaction than ever. Not many persons down there, occasionally a flitting figure in the distance."

On Saturday morning, the quiet of the sleepy House chamber was suddenly, shockingly smashed. At about six thirty a.m., a crashing explosion of wind, hail, and rain lashed the building. "It beat like a deluge on the heavy glass roof of the hall, and the wind literally howled and roared. For a moment, (and no wonder) the nervous and sleeping Representatives were thrown into confusion," Whitman wrote. "The slumberers waked with fear, some started for the doors, some looked up with blanched cheeks and lips to the roof, and the little pages began to cry; it was a scene." To his fellow reporter Noah Brooks, writing for the *Sacramento Daily Union*, it seemed as if "a tornado had overwhelmed the building; the wind roared and shrieked among the columns; the glass roof thundered with a rattling storm of hail, and the growing daylight was extinguished in a black pall of cloud which covered the angry sky." The members ran "panic-stricken" from the chamber into the lobbies, "and for a moment the confusion was dire." The Washington *National Republican* reported that the sleeping members leapt to their feet "as if Lee's batteries had opened on the city from Arlington Heights." The House quickly recessed until nine a.m. By then, Whitman wrote, the lawmakers "recovered themselves; the storm raged on, beating, dashing, and with loud noises at times. But the House went ahead with its business then, I think, as calmly and with as much deliberation as at any time in its career. Perhaps the shock did it good."

The shock reverberated throughout Washington. "Rained—almost a hurricane. I had to wash the mud off," Clara Barton wrote in her diary. In the pounding rain and wind that morning, Miss Barton had a visitor: a Dr. Richardson, evidently Samuel A. Richardson, the thirty-four-year-old surgeon of the Thirteenth New Hampshire regiment, who was on a twenty-day leave from the front lines at Petersburg. Raised on a hardscrabble farm in the Granite State, a slender man with curly hair, a small mustache, and a little goatee, "Dr. Rich" was a beloved figure in the ranks. "He was as a father to all of the 'boys,' and his interest in them never wavered nor abated," wrote the steward of the regiment's hospital. "The sick looked forward to his visits with pleasure, and took fresh hope and courage from his inspiring words; his expansive smile was in itself sufficient to light up the entire hospital. He was universally beloved for his deep and ready sympathy, and his boundless charity and generosity." On this morning, Richardson had come out in the howling storm to look in on a tired and frazzled woman whose work he greatly admired. The doctor was sent up to Barton's room. He invited her "to return to the front with him" when his furlough was over and solicitously ordered her to rest during her own break from the constant stress and danger of her service.

A determined woman from Massachusetts, Barton was revered for her extraordinary efforts on behalf of soldiers, risking her life during a series of major battles to bring support and medical supplies to them. At the Battle of Antietam she had braved showers of bullets and shells that sent the medical orderlies diving for cover. While she was tending to one young man, a bullet tore through her dress and killed him. Pennsylvania surgeon James Dunn wrote to his wife of her courage there: "In my feeble estimation, General McClellan, with all his laurels, sinks into insignificance beside the true heroine of the age, the angel of the battlefield."

Still possessing a trim figure at forty-three, the petite, five-foot-two-inch-tall Barton had come up to Washington from Grant's headquarters at City Point to care for her dying brother, Stephen, and to enlist President Lincoln's endorsement of her new project: to find out what had happened to the vast number of missing American soldiers. In the wake of nearly four years of battle, there were hundreds of thousands of unmarked graves. Countless families, waiting in dread for a letter, had never learned what happened to a son, a brother, or a father. The government kept no comprehensive lists of prisoners and did not try to determine what had become of all those who had disappeared. Barton's own brother Stephen, living in North Carolina, had been picked up as a Confederate spy and for a time vanished into a Union prison, where his health had broken down, while his anguished family had no idea what had become of him. Barton hoped to enlist a team to interview returning prisoners of war to learn what had happened to some of their comrades. She expected that Lincoln, whose "care worn face" was "very dear" to her, would warmly embrace a mission that would mean so much to America's suffering families.

Barton had made extensive preparations to meet the great man, brightening her appearance with a new dress skirt a friend had bought her, having her rich brown hair pulled back into a silk net, and adorning herself with a fine fur coat and hat on loan from another friend. At four o'clock the past Monday afternoon, February 27, she arrived at the White House to lobby the president. One of her state's Republican senators, Henry Wilson, accompanied her, bearing a letter: "Miss Barton calls on you for a business object and I hope you will grant my request. It will cost nothing. She has given three years to the cause of our soldiers and is worthy of *entire* confidence." A guard told the pair they had shown up too late in the day to meet with the president. The next morning, Massachusetts congressman William B. Washburn accompanied Barton, with a letter that introduced her as "one of the most useful, devoted, *valuable* ladies in the country." But Lincoln was meeting with his Cabinet that day and had no time. On Wednesday, March 1, she waited again at the White House, with scores of supplicants. Inside

his office, Lincoln met with members of Congress, who formally noti-
fied him of his election, and took the time to write a glowing letter
of appreciation to Thomas W. Conway, superintendent of freedmen
for the Department of the Gulf, the Union military command that
oversaw the states along the Gulf of Mexico. Lincoln wrote that news
of Conway's "success" in elevating the "moral and physical" condition
of former slaves "has reached me, and given me much pleasure." This
was crucial work toward integrating those once held in bondage into a
free America. "The blessing of God and the efforts of good and faithful
men will bring us an earlier and happier consummation than the most
sanguine friends of the freedmen could reasonably expect," Lincoln
wrote. But he never called Barton into his office that day. The crush
of business leading up to the inauguration was simply too great. After
three days of frustration, Barton managed to hold back her tears until
she got back to her room and was alone. "I . . . do not feel it my duty
to bring myself to public mortification in order to do a public charity,"
she wrote bitterly. Though she would stubbornly persist in trying to
meet the president, any help from Lincoln would have to wait until
after the inauguration.

Whitman shared Barton's intense yearning to alleviate the misery this
war had caused. The poet had given up his bohemian life in New
York, his beloved late nights with friends at Charlie Pfaff's beer cellar
on Broadway near Bleecker Street, to stay in the nation's capital and
attend to the shattered, traumatized, and suffering men dragged back
from the battlefields to Washington hospitals. "I was always between
two loves at that time—I wanted to be in New York; I had to be in
Washington," he wrote. His visits to Washington hospitals had become
"a religion with me. A religion? Well, every man has a religion; has
something in heaven and earth which he will give up everything else
for—something which absorbs him, possesses itself of him, makes him
over in its image—something. It may be regarded by others as being
very paltry, inadequate, useless, yet it is his dream; it is his lodestar; it

is his master. That, whatever it is, seized upon me; made me its servant, slave; induced me to set aside other ambitions—a trail of glory in the heavens, which I followed, followed with a full heart." By the end of the war, he estimated, he would have made more than six hundred visits to hospitals and tended to eighty thousand to one hundred thousand sick and wounded men.

Whitman's great mission began in December 1862, when he left his home in Brooklyn in a panic to seek out his beloved brother George, a soldier in the Fifty-First New York Infantry regiment, after the newspapers reported he had been wounded in the murderous battle at Fredericksburg, Virginia. Securing a pass to the front, Whitman arrived to find grim evidence of surgeons working frantically to save lives. "Out doors, at the foot of a tree . . . I notice a heap of amputated feet, legs, arms, hands, & c., a full load for a one-horse cart," he later wrote, in a piece for the *New York Times*. Clara Barton was there, helping at the Lacy House, an elegant eighteenth-century brick mansion, just across the Rappahannock River from the city, that had been turned into a makeshift hospital, while bullets pierced its trees, windows, and doors. "I cannot tell you the number, but some hundreds of the worst wounded men I have ever seen were lying on a little hay on floors or in tents," Barton wrote. Some twelve hundred men were jammed into its twelve rooms. "They covered every foot of the floors and porticos and even lay on the stair landings!" she continued. "A man who could find opportunity to lie between the legs of a table thought himself lucky. He was not likely to be stepped on." Five men were jammed into a common four-shelf cupboard, where she fed and attended to them. "Three lived to be removed, and two died of their wounds," she recalled. "Think of trying to lie still and die quietly, lest you fall out of a bed six feet high!"

It turned out that George Whitman was faring well, having suffered a relatively minor wound through the cheek. But the poet was drawn to the Lacy mansion and to the wretched, untended men dying on blankets on the ground outdoors. He did the best he could to help and then ventured inside the house of horrors. "The large mansion is quite crowded, upstairs and down, everything impromptu, no system, all bad enough, but I have no doubt the best that can be done; all the wounds pretty bad, some frightful, the men in their old clothes, unclean and bloody," Whitman wrote. "I went through the rooms, downstairs and up. Some of the men were dying. I had nothing to give at that visit, but wrote a few letters to folks home, mothers, &c. Also talked to three or four, who seem'd most susceptible to it, and needing it."

That jarring experience had revealed to Whitman his mission in this war. He would tend to the wounded young men, beautiful in his eyes, who had given their all to save the nation. Washington was the place for it, filled with hospitals where the suffering soldiers went if they survived their treatment at the battlefield. The poet turned to his old friend Ralph Waldo Emerson for help securing a cushy government job that might cover his meager living expenses while he performed his real work. Emerson kindly wrote a letter of recommendation addressed to Chase, of all people, perhaps even dictated by Whitman himself: "Permit me to say that he is known to me as a man of strong original genius, combining, with marked eccentricities, great powers & valuable traits of character: a self-relying large-hearted man, much beloved by his friends; entirely patriotic & benevolent in his theory, tastes, & practice." The letter, of course, had to gingerly address the controversy surrounding Whitman. "If his writings are in certain points open to criticism, they show extraordinary power, & are more deeply American, democratic, & in the interest of political liberty, than those of any other poet." If the government could find this man work, "it may easily find that it has called to its side more valuable aid than it bargained for." As much of an understatement as that would turn out to be, the treasury secretary was unmoved when novelist, poet, and antislavery advocate John Townsend Trowbridge presented him the letter. Chase, according to Whitman, told Trowbridge, "he considered Leaves of Grass a very bad book, & he did not know how he could possibly bring its author into the government service, especially if he put him in contact with gentlemen employed in the beaureaus [sic]."

Whitman wound up finding work as a lowly copyist at the Army's paymaster's office, in the Corcoran Building near Chase's Treasury headquarters. He supplemented his income by writing occasional dispatches for the *New York Times* and other newspapers but used most of his free time to visit Washington-area hospitals. They were far from antiseptic places, reeking of feces, vomit, and putrid flesh. Many of the men suffered from severe typhoid fever, diarrhea, bronchitis, rheumatism, and pneumonia. "There are twice as many sick as wounded," Whitman noted.

Whitman let friends know that he was visiting the hospitals. "Who is there in Brooklyn who doesn't know Walt Whitman? Rough and ready, kind and considerate, generous and good, he was ever a friend in need, which is, after all, the only friend indeed," the *Brooklyn Daily Eagle* reported in December 1863. "Walt is now in Washington, a volunteer nurse, going from hospital to hospital, and doing good every moment of his life. We hear of him at the bedside of the sick, the pallet of the wounded, the cot of the dying, and the pestilent ward. He writes letters home for disabled men, bathes the feverish brow of half crazed soldiers, refreshes the parched lips of neglected sufferers, and attends with fidelity and tact to the thousand and one necessities of those who approach the gate of death. Surely such as he will find their reward here and hereafter." Yet some who detested *Leaves of Grass* could not resist joking about his work. Richmond's *Daily Dispatch* reprinted the observation of British literary critic George Augustus Sale that Whitman "is considered by many of his brethren to be himself as mad as a March hare," while the *Memphis Daily Appeal* noted that "Walt Whitman is now in Washington making gruel for the wounded soldiers. The *Saturday Evening Gazette* says: 'We dare say his gruel is better than his poetry': and we may add, if it is 'warmer' than 'Leaves of Grass,' there must be some scalded throats in the Washington hospitals."

In truth, most patients had no idea this bearded visitor was the author of a notoriously salacious book. "I can't recall a single case in which I gave away *Leaves of Grass*," Whitman wrote. That was his way with the young men he came to know, many of them from the working class and distinctly unliterary. After the war, when abolitionist Moncure Conway followed Whitman through Brooklyn while working on a piece for the London-based *Fortnightly Review*, he asked a man if he knew the bearded figure. "That be Walt Whitman." "What sort of man is he?" "A fustrate man is Walt. Nobody knows Walt but likes him; nearly everybody knows him, and—*loves* him." "He has written a book—hasn't he?" "Not as I ever hearn on," the man answered. What the young men in the hospitals liked about Whitman was his attention and warmth— and, the poet believed, his robust and unfussy appearance. "Many of the soldiers are from the west, and far north, " Whitman wrote, "and they take to a man that has not the bleached shiny & shaved cut of the cities and the east." The proprietor of a Washington army supply store, Elijah M. Allen, wrote to one of Whitman's admirers on a hot May afternoon in 1863: "Walt just passed [outside the store] with his arms full of bottles and lemons, going to some hospitals . . . to give the boys a good time. He was sweating finely; his collar and shirt were thrown open, showing his great hairy throat and breast."

On his rounds, Whitman brought with him gifts of candy, fruit, tobacco, stationery, stamped envelopes, newspapers, small amounts of money—all materials the hospitals did not provide. But his greatest gifts were surely his sympathy, his encouragement, and his presence. "I went sometimes at night to soothe and relieve particular cases; some, I found, needed a little cheering up and friendly consolation at that time, for they went to sleep better afterwards," he wrote, in February 1863. Michigan journalist Lois Bryan Adams, who dutifully visited wounded soldiers from her state in these hospitals, was struck by the men's intense yearning for human interaction. Initially she feared she was intruding, but she soon discovered otherwise. "O, ma'am, before I say another word, I want to thank you for coming to speak to me!" one "large-featured, bronzed complexioned" soldier told her. He had suffered a dangerous wound through his shoulder, and part of his lungs had been cut away to remove the ball. "You are the first, except the nurse, since I came here, and that is two days. Some pass through and speak to nobody; some talk to all others around me, but none to me before. I thank you; it makes me almost well." A Michigan soldier also recalled the effect of a visitor on him.

The brightest memory I took away with me was that of the face and voice of a beautiful lady who came several times while I was there. Her presence was like a gleam of sunlight in a darkened room. Courage and cheerfulness, strength and healing, seemed to follow in her train. She brought me some little delicacies to eat and drink, but better than that, she would sit down by the side of my cot and talk about home and mother, and the great cause in which we were engaged. That lady put new life in my veins, and I believe now but that for her I never would have left that hospital alive.

The boisterous Whitman was no beautiful lady, but the wounded men appreciated his kindness and interest. To the youngest soldiers, especially, he found, "there is something in personal love, caresses and the magnetic flood of sympathy and friendship that does, in its way, more good than all the medicine in the world." Many of them touched his heart. He wrote of a visit to Oscar F. Wilber of Company G of the 154th New York Infantry regiment, badly weakened by diarrhea and a wound that discharged pus and would not heal. Tears came to the young man's eyes when Whitman agreed to read to him from the New Testament about Jesus's crucifixion and resurrection. Wilber asked Whitman if he enjoyed religion. "Perhaps not, my dear, in the way you mean, and yet maybe it is the same thing," he responded. Wilber said that it was his "chief reliance"—and that he did not fear death. "Why, Oscar, don't you think you will get well?" Wilber answered: "I may, but it is not probable." He died a few days later.

Whitman was able to rally others. "I have the consciousness of saving quite a little number of lives by saving them from giving up," he wrote to his mother. Yet the experience drained him. "It is curious," he jotted into his notebook. "When I am present at the most appalling things—deaths, operations, sickening wounds (perhaps full of maggots)—I keep cool and do not give out of budge, although my sympathies are very much excited; but often, hours afterward, perhaps when I am home, or out walking alone, I feel sick and actually tremble when I recall the case again before me." He wondered about the future: "I see such awful things. I expect one of these days, if I live, I shall have awful thoughts and dreams—but it is such a great thing to be able to do some real good; assuage these horrible pains and wounds, and save life even—that's the only thing that keeps a fellow up."

The soldiers that came up from the battles of the spring of 1864— men such as Selden Connor—were in particularly bad shape, as the carnage badly outstripped the army's capacity to deal with it. "We receive them here with their wounds full of worms—some all swelled up and inflamed. Many of the amputations have to be done over again," Whitman wrote in another letter to his mother. There was a new horror unfolding: Lincoln and Grant's relentless push was exposing young men to such ceaseless terror that they were losing their sanity under the trauma and stress. "One new feature," Whitman continued, "is that many of the poor afflicted young men are crazy. Every ward has some in it that are wandering. They have suffered too much, and it is perhaps a privilege that they are out of their senses." He added, "Mother, it is most too much for a fellow, & I sometimes wish I was out of it."

Around him, young men died, bravely, and little fuss was made of the loss. Yet, in Whitman's eyes, they were "the real precious and royal ones of this land, giving up—aye even their young and precious lives—in the country's cause." He wondered whether it was worth it. "My opinion is *to stop the war now*," he wrote in one of his notebooks. "Mother, one's heart grows sick of war, after all, when you see what it really is," he wrote, three days after the Battle of Gettysburg, as maimed young men poured into the hospitals. "Every once in a while I feel so horrified and disgusted—it seems to me like a great slaughterhouse and the men mutually butchering each other." Even so, Whitman maintained that was it impossible to quit until the United States had vanquished a rebellion that sought to tear his beloved America to pieces. Writing to Thomas P. Sawyer, a soldier from Cambridge, Massachusetts, he had met in one of the hospitals, Whitman insisted: "This country can't be broken up by Jeff Davis, & all his damned crew."

* * *

While earnest in his devotion to the young men, Whitman had a powerful impetus for his fondness. Unmarried and unattached, he had long enjoyed the company of working-class men in their teens and twenties, recording dozens of sexually charged interactions with them in his notebooks ("fresh and affectionate," he wrote of one boyish acquaintance). It was not that women were uninterested. The sensual wordplay and glowing passion of *Leaves of Grass* stirred the romantic yearning of some of his female readers. In July 1860 Whitman received a letter from a Connecticut woman named Susan Garnet Smith, a total stranger who was so moved by his poems that she invited him to impregnate her. "My womb is clean and pure. It is ready for thy child my love," she wrote. "Angels guard the vestibule until thou comest to deposit our and the world's precious treasure. . . . Our boy my love! Do you not already love him? He must be begotten on a mountain top, in the open air. Not in *lust*, not in mere gratification of sensual passion, but in ennobling pure strong deep glorious passionate broad universal love. I charge you to prepare my love." Whitman scrawled on the envelope: "? Insane asylum." He preferred affectionate letters from the young men he had tended in the hospitals, such as the playful Alonzo S. Bush, a Union soldier with Company A of the First Indiana Cavalry, who was pleased to learn in December 1863 that Whitman was "once more in the hotbed City of Washington" and could tend to their mutual friend Lewis K. Brown, who had been wounded in the leg near Rappahannock Station, Virginia, in August 1862, and had suffered since, the leg becoming so infected that it would have to be amputated soon. "I wished that I could See him this evening and go in the Ward Master's Room and have Some fun for he is a gay boy," Bush wrote.

One night in late January or early February 1865, as a winter storm whipped Washington, Whitman had climbed aboard an empty streetcar on rails that ran up and down Pennsylvania Avenue between Georgetown and the navy yard. The slender, blue-eyed, fair-haired conductor, four inches shorter and twenty-four years younger than Whitman, was struck by the great red-faced, white-bearded figure in the passenger section. "Walt had his blanket—it was thrown around his shoulders—he seemed like an old sea captain," the young man recalled. "He was the only passenger, it was a lonely night, so I thought I would go in and talk with him. Something in me made me do it and something in him drew me that way."

The conductor's name was Peter Doyle, and he was far from home. Born in Limerick, Ireland, he had emigrated to the South and enlisted at seventeen to serve in the Confederate Army's Richmond Fayette Artillery. Surviving a series of hellish battles against the Army of the Potomac, the boy had been wounded at Antietam, where Whitman's own brother George had fought for the other side, on another part of the battlefield. Doyle recovered in a Richmond hospital, where he evidently concluded he had had enough of service to the Confederacy. He headed north for a new life, only to be apprehended by Union agents and clapped into an annex to Washington's Old Capitol Prison. Securing release by pledging not to serve the rebellion again, he found a job as a conductor on the horse-drawn trolleys.

On that cold night, moving from the platform into the coach, he made a friend for life. "We were familiar at once—I put my hand on his knee—we understood," Doyle remembered. "He did not get out at the end of the trip—in fact went all the way back with me. . . . From that time on we were the biggest sort of friends." The ardent Unionist opened his heart to the former Confederate. Peter Doyle would be the love of his life.

Whitman's low-level copying work and unpaid hours at the hospitals left him scant means to provide for himself. For a time, he wore ragged shirts and lived in what his admirer Trowbridge called a "bare and desolate back room" in an "old wooden tenement" at 456 Sixth Street. The building was just across the street from the splendid mansion that attracted many rich and powerful visitors—the home of Salmon P. Chase. Chase probably had no idea that the author of *Leaves of Grass* was his neighbor.

A longtime Democrat and man of the people, Whitman had little admiration for most of the noted Washington politicians trooping to Chase's handsome house. But one man he revered. On the streets of Washington, he had often seen Abraham Lincoln out in his carriage and on horseback, sometimes with his boy Tad alongside him on a pony, passing to and from his cottage at the Soldiers' Home, the president's summer retreat, three miles from the White House. Lincoln even came to recognize Whitman's face, though evidently he did not know who he was. "We have got so that we exchange bows, and very cordial ones," Whitman wrote in his notebook after seeing Lincoln on the morning of August 12, 1863.

"I love the President personally," Whitman wrote late that year. "He has a face like a Hoosier Michelangelo—so awful ugly it becomes beautiful—with its strange mouth, its deep-cut, crisscross lines, and its doughnut complexion." He had heard of Lincoln's uncouth behavior but had come to believe "that underneath his outside smutched mannerism, and stories from third-class country barrooms (it is his humor), Mr. Lincoln keeps a fountain of first-class practical telling wisdom." Time after time, Whitman thought, Lincoln had proved the experts wrong by sticking to his political instincts. "I more and more rely upon his idiomatic western genius, careless of court dress or court decorum." The president left Whitman feeling, despite seemingly endless military reverses, that the Union would prevail. "I have finally made up my mind that Mr. Lincoln has done as good as a human man could do—I still think him a pretty big President—I realize here in Washington that it has been a big thing to have just kept the United States from being thrown down & having its throat cut—and now I have no doubt it will throw down secession and cut its throat," he wrote to his mother, on October 27, 1863. The White House knew of Whitman's admiration. Two days after Whitman wrote that letter, John Hay noted in his own diary that "the poet" had been given a round-trip ticket to New York "to electioneer and vote for the Union ticket." And now, on March 4, 1865, Whitman had the privilege of covering Lincoln's second inauguration for the *New York Times*.

At the same time, Whitman was obsessed with another writing task. At the end of 1864, his friend William O'Connor had urged him to apply for a job opening: clerk in the Bureau of Indian Affairs, Department of the Interior. "Now, dear Walt, do this without delay. . . . I have every confidence that you will get a good and an easy berth, a regular income, &c., leaving you time to attend to the soldiers, to your poems, &c—in a word, what Archimedes wanted, a place on which to rest the lever." Whitman won the job and took advantage of his early quitting time to visit his beloved soldiers in the hospitals for seven or eight hours a day, six or more days a week. While sitting at bedsides of men comforted by his presence, he took out his pencil and filled little notebooks, some stained with the blood of the patients he served, with thoughts and sketches, mined for poems that he was now gathering into a new book, to be called *Drum-Taps*.

Whitman came to believe that future Americans would never truly understand "the seething hell" and "the black infernal background" of his times. "The real war will never get in the books," he concluded. Yet his new poems—drawn from his work in the hospitals, his intimacy with the wounded, his letters to their loved ones back home, and the passing of America's true royalty—did touch on the infernal cost of this war:

> *Come up from the fields father, here's a letter from our Pete,*
> *And come to the front door mother, here's a letter from thy dear*
> *   son . . .*
>
> *Down in the fields all prospers well,*
> *But now from the fields come father, come at the daughter's call,*
> *And come to the entry mother, to the front door come right away.*
>
> *Fast as she can she hurries, something ominous, her steps trembling,*
> *She does not tarry to smooth her hair nor adjust her cap.*
>
> *Open the envelope quickly,*
> *O this is not our son's writing, yet his name is sign'd,*

O a strange hand writes for our dear son, O stricken mother's soul!
All swims before her eyes, flashes with black, she catches the main
 words only,
Sentences broken, gunshot wound in the breast, cavalry skirmish,
 taken to hospital,
At present low, but will soon be better.

Ah now the single figure to me,
Amid all teeming and wealthy Ohio with all its cities and farms,
Sickly white in the face and dull in the head, very faint,
By the jamb of a door leans.

Grieve not so, dear mother, (the just-grown daughter speaks through
 her sobs,
The little sisters huddle around speechless and dismay'd,)
See, dearest mother, the letter says Pete will soon be better.
Alas poor boy, he will never be better, (nor may-be needs to be better,
 that brave and simple soul,)
While they stand at home at the door he is dead already,
The only son is dead.

But the mother needs to be better,
She with thin form presently drest in black,
By day her meals untouch'd, then at night fitfully sleeping, often
 waking,
In the midnight waking, weeping, longing with one deep longing,
O that she might withdraw unnoticed, silent from life escape and
 withdraw,
To follow, to seek, to be with her dear dead son.

CHAPTER 5

MEDITATION ON THE DIVINE WILL

Saturday, March 4, 1865

As a shrieking windstorm startled the members of Congress and tore through Washington, rattling its rain-streaked windows, the White House staff prepared for a long day of fuss and ceremony. Abraham Lincoln was generally up by seven o'clock each morning. He worked quietly in his White House office for a while before taking breakfast at around eight. He usually had a cup of coffee and an egg, maybe a piece of toast. He might eat an apple. "He was very abstemious—ate less than any one I know," his secretary John Hay noted. In a country notorious for its heavy drinking, Lincoln never touched liquor and did not seem to care all that much about food. He suffered from poor digestion and frequent constipation, and for a time treated the problem by taking "blue mass" pills—a laxative laced with mercury—which seem to have made him irritable and unable to sleep at night. He told a friend he quit the medicine early into his presidency "because it made him cross." He also skipped meals unintentionally. Prone to get lost in thought, he could forget to eat.

On this distracting day, he had to dress for the inauguration—in a new suit courtesy of the New York men's clothier Brooks Brothers, with a waistcoat, trousers, and its showpiece: a long, black double-breasted frock coat made of wool said to be finer than cashmere. The coat was no standard piece of clothing. In honor of the occasion, a Brooks Brothers seamstress named Agnes Breckenridge had embroidered its black lining with an intricate design of an eagle clutching in its beak two streamers bearing words from Massachusetts senator Daniel Webster's ringing defense of the Union in an 1837 speech: "One country, one destiny."

Lincoln was known to stuff into his pockets a watch fob, a brown wallet, an Irish linen handkerchief, and gold-rimmed spectacles that he now needed for reading. He wore polished calfskin boots that were custom-made by the New York shoemaker Peter Kahler, who during a trip to Washington had traced Lincoln's feet onto long sheets of cardboard—a whopping size fourteen. "Let this man come right in," Lincoln had scrawled on the business card Kahler had sent into his office, perhaps a testament to his difficulties in finding footwear that fit properly.

It was a handsome outfit, but somehow clothing on Lincoln's slouching frame always seemed ill-fitting. His collar looked several sizes too large for his scrawny neck, and his black hair, though freshly cut for today's ceremonies, was prone to stick up in several directions. His African American butler, William Slade, said to be "a Virginian of distinguished Southern ancestry," with an "olive" complexion and "straight chestnut-brown hair," assisted him. A black servant Lincoln had brought with him from Springfield in 1861, William Johnson, had been effectively driven out of the White House by the proud, light-skinned African Americans on the staff, who abided no such interlopers and considered him their social inferior because of his darker hue. Lincoln had Johnson work in the basement running the White House furnace until he could get him a job in Chase's Treasury Department.

In the mirror that morning were the ravages of a fifty-six-year-old face that had aged drastically in four years and was now deeply lined, with dark circles under the eyes and thinning chin whiskers flecked with gray. John Hay, who had worked at the president's side almost every day at the White House, was struck by the transformation. Lincoln had entered the office as one of the youngest presidents, but "his demeanor and disposition changed—so gradually that it would be impossible to say when the change began; but he was in mind, body, and nerves a very different man at the second inauguration from the one who had taken the oath in 1861," Hay wrote. "He continued always the same kindly, genial, and cordial spirit he had been at first; but the boisterous laughter became less frequent year by year; the eye grew veiled by constant meditation on momentous subjects; the air of reserve and detachment from his surroundings increased. He aged with great rapidity."

The intense pressure of the previous four years had followed a life of suffering and severe depression—possibly linked to the mental illness that blighted the paternal side of his family, including a great uncle who had once informed a court that he had "a deranged mind." Lincoln's tendency toward anxiety was so fierce that, when he was in his twenties, some of his friends were afraid to leave him alone with sharp objects lest he take the opportunity to kill himself. After temporarily breaking up with Mary Todd, before later marrying her, the thirty-one-year-old confessed to a friend, "I am now the most miserable man living. If what I feel were equally distributed to the whole human family, there would not be one cheerful face on the earth." Throughout his adult life, he struggled with despair, surviving through moments of laughter and his escape into hard intellectual labor. "His melancholy dripped from him as he walked," his law partner, William Herndon, said.

Childhood trauma had scarred Lincoln. When he was only nine, he lost his mother, Nancy, to a sudden, ghastly illness, from what seems purest fate—her drinking the milk of a cow that had happened to chew on a plant that was toxic to humans. "All that I am or hope ever to be I got from my mother," Lincoln had written of her, according to Herndon. She was "intellectual, sensitive and somewhat sad." In an act of gross irresponsibility, his father, Thomas, almost immediately thereafter left young Abe and his older sister, Sarah, in their log cabin in the wilderness of Indiana, putting them under the care of an inept teenage relative so that he could return to Kentucky to find a new wife. The children were soon filthy and on the edge of starvation. During the many months their father was gone, they survived on the dried berries that Nancy had put aside and on whatever they could find or kill nearby. "It was a wild region, with many bears and other animals still in the woods," Abraham remembered. Sarah, who endeavored to cook and keep house, often sat by the fire and cried. Later in life, Lincoln wrote of "the sad, if not pitiful condition" of the two. When he revisited the place of his childhood in his late thirties, he did not indulge in fond nostalgia but rather recalled the little boy's abject terror, in a stanza of the poem he felt stirred to write, "The Bear Hunt":

> *When my father settled here,*
> *'Twas then the frontier line.*
> *The panther's scream, filled the night with fear,*
> *And bears preyed on the swine.*

Some of the most damaging ordeals any child could suffer—the loss of a mother, abandonment, nights filled with fear, loneliness, filth, cold, and hunger—were among Lincoln's formative experiences. And when he was nineteen, his beloved sister, Sarah, died in the agonies of childbirth. In an 1862 letter to a grieving child, he wrote: "In this sad world of ours, sorrow comes to all; and, to the young, it comes with bitterest agony, because it takes them unawares. . . . I have had experience enough to know what I say." The sorrow never left him. "Lincoln's melancholy never failed to impress any man who ever saw or knew him. The perpetual look of sadness was his most prominent feature," Herndon said.

An unusually bright child, Lincoln escaped into books. He detested his crude origins and formed a lifelong resentment against his father, who frowned on his reading and his obvious dissatisfaction with the hard life of a farmer. The boy bitterly resented being loaned out to neighboring farms as a laborer and forced to turn over the ten to thirty-one cents a day he earned, an experience that sharpened his empathy for those who labored incessantly, without the prospect of freedom, for other men. "I used to be a slave," he asserted later in life. He was speaking metaphorically, of course, because when a white man reached the age of manhood at twenty-one, he was free to set off on his own— something Lincoln eagerly did, never returning. His resentment of his father cut so deep that he ignored repeated letters from family members reporting that his father was mortally ill before finally making it clear that he would not visit the old man on his deathbed in 1851. "Say to him that if we could meet now, it is doubtful whether it would not be more painful than pleasant," Lincoln instructed a relative. In lieu of a son's love, Lincoln offered religious bromides, icily advising the relative to tell Thomas to turn to his "merciful Maker, who will not turn away from him in any extremity. He notes the fall of a sparrow, and numbers the hairs of our heads; and He will not forget the dying man, who puts his trust in Him." When his impoverished father did die, Lincoln declined to attend the funeral, and he bothered to buy a stone to mark the grave only when he was preparing to depart for Washington as president-elect. Some who knew the family in Kentucky claimed that Abraham's paternity was in question—that his beloved young mother had been unfaithful, and the harsh and ignorant Thomas was not, in truth, his biological father. Abraham did, however, name his fourth son Thomas—the boy everyone called Tad.

From these bleak beginnings Lincoln's extraordinary drive lifted him above poverty and awkwardness to become an Illinois state representative, a respectable Whig, and a well-paid lawyer. Yet in his very first published piece, requesting the votes of his friends and neighbors for state representative at twenty-three, Lincoln already sounded his characteristic note of sadness. If he should lose, he wrote, "I have been too familiar with disappointments to be very much chagrined." He did, in fact, lose, but he won the next time. Having escaped a difficult father, he married a difficult woman, given to fits of rage and abuse. He took to riding the judicial circuit, traveling from court to court, staying away from his wife and boys for up to six months a year, three in the spring and three in the fall, while other lawyers hastened home on weekends. Determined to become an admired and powerful man, he tried again and again to break through in politics. "His ambition was a little engine that knew no rest," Herndon recalled. But Lincoln suffered defeat after defeat—making a poor impression as a one-term congressman with what was widely regarded as a laughable attack on a president, James Polk, fighting a war against Mexico; failing to win political appointments he earnestly sought and thought he had earned;

losing two serious bids for a U.S. Senate seat. His was a mediocre political career, at best, until his mastery of the English language—his rare ability to speak with great clarity and moral force about slavery, using the language and rhythms of the King James Bible and the precision of a lawyer's argument—captured national recognition. Through newspapers, Republicans around the country followed his brilliantly argued debates with Stephen A. Douglas, held during the 1858 Illinois senatorial campaign, and read his remarkable speeches, most notably his address to the Cooper Union in New York City on February 27, 1860. Lincoln's standing as a moderate weighed heavily with delegates at the 1860 Republican convention, but it was his words that attracted the party's notice and propelled him to the presidential nomination.

For all of this, Lincoln was regarded as a gentle, genial, good man. But though he was kind and gregarious, happy to tell funny stories and shake hands, and genuinely fond of the company of others, Lincoln kept his feelings to himself, shielding them even from those who knew him intimately. He was reluctant to reveal his heart, as if he feared giving anyone another opportunity to hurt him. One of his friends, David Davis, a judge who spent years on the circuit with him, called him "the most reticent—Secretive man I Ever Saw—or Expect to See."

Lincoln's hard life had left him with thick scar tissue over his psychic wounds, an expectation of disappointment, given the long futility of his struggle to shine in a world that seemed to be against him, and an unflinchingly pragmatic view of human nature. But it also had prepared him peculiarly well to wage increasingly brutal warfare in the face of constant heartache and nerve-racking setbacks, issuing orders that inevitably led to immense death and misery, all the time knowing his failure would lead to the country's annihilation and earn him the condemnation and ridicule of history.

However tenacious and resilient Lincoln was, this war had changed him. In February 1863, Benjamin B. French, the U.S. commissioner of buildings, noticed that the president was "growing feeble," with a hand that "trembled as I never saw it before." When French pleaded with Lincoln to rest, the president conceded that "it was a pretty hard life for him." His old Illinois friend Joshua Speed, who visited him at the White House, once asked him when he slept. "Just when everybody else is tired out," Lincoln responded glumly. He complained that his hands and feet felt cold all the time now. Longtime associates were "shocked in the change of his appearance," Congressman Isaac Arnold noted. "They had known him at his home, and at the courts in Illinois. . . . Now they saw the wrinkles on his face and forehead deepen into furrows; the laugh of old days was less frequent, and it did not seem to come from the heart. Anxiety, responsibility, care, thought, disasters, defeats, the injustice of friends, wore on his giant frame, and his nerves of steel became at times irritable." Lincoln told Arnold one day, "with a pathos which language cannot describe, 'I feel as though I shall *never be glad again*.'" One of his friends from the old days, journalist Noah Brooks, lamented that few who knew "the hearty, blithesome, genial, and wiry Abraham Lincoln" of the 1850s would recognize him in 1865, "with his stooping figure, dull eyes, care-worn face, and languid frame. The old, clear laugh never came back; the even temper was sometimes disturbed; and his natural charity for all was often turned into an unwonted suspicion of the motives of men, whose selfishness cost him so much wear of mind."

The war had altered more than Lincoln's appearance. It had reawakened his thoughts about God's role in this world of suffering. He had been raised in a religious home, steeped in the belief that the divine being, although an impenetrable mystery, acted from infinite love and guided the universe toward righteousness. Nancy and Thomas were Hard-Shell, or Separatist, Baptists who attended the antislavery Little Mount Separate Baptist Church, its meeting place three miles east of the Lincoln farmstead in Hodgenville, Kentucky. The Separatists, striving to reconnect with Christian belief in its most fundamental form, carefully studied the words of the Bible for guidance in all matters of faith, and embraced the doctrine of predestination, the certainty that everything that exists or occurs does so through the will of an all-knowing God. Their teaching held that each Christian—though inevitably acting out God's will—had a grave responsibility to study the Bible and follow its precepts. As stories about the ancient Israelites made clear, people invited greater suffering—on themselves, their children, and their children's children—when they veered from righteousness, the path of safety their ancestors had discovered at great cost. About a mile west of the Lincoln farm in southern Indiana, where young Abe lived from age seven to twenty-one, the family attended the Little Pigeon Creek Baptist Church. The bright young boy spent hours in that little log church, studying the services closely. When out playing, Abe liked to amuse his friends by climbing up on a stump and imitating the preacher's exalted language and heightened mannerisms.

The lessons he learned stayed with Lincoln. He believed good people forgave the failings of others, but that, under the laws of existence, grave wrongs inevitably rebounded on sinners and their society. "Lincoln maintained that God could not forgive; that punishment has to follow the sin," Herndon wrote. Lincoln was struck by a chilling passage from Thomas Jefferson's 1787 book *Notes on the State of Virginia* that spoke of the miseries Americans were preparing for themselves by surrendering to the temptations of evil in the form of slavery: "Indeed I tremble for my country when I reflect that God is just: that his justice cannot sleep forever: that considering numbers, nature and natural means only, a revolution of the wheel of fortune, an exchange of situation, is among possible events: that it may become probable by supernatural interference! The Almighty has no attribute which can side with us in such a contest." Marking Jefferson's birthday in 1859, Lincoln boiled down his warning: "Those who deny freedom to others, deserve it not for themselves; and, under a just God, can not long retain it."

Once he was free from his father's control, Lincoln wanted little to do with organized religion. Abraham professed a belief in "cold, calculating, unimpassioned reason," as he had put it in an address he delivered in Springfield at twenty-eight. His law partner thought that Lincoln was an outright religious skeptic, rejecting the literal truth of stories about Jesus, including miracles, and many other articles of the Christian faith. Lincoln told Herndon that his beliefs were like those that he had heard an old man express at a church meeting back in Indiana: "When I do good I feel good, when I do bad I feel bad, and that's my religion." Herndon wrote: "Mr. Lincoln had not much hope and no faith in things that lie outside the domain of demonstration; he was so constituted—so organized—that he could believe nothing unless his sense or logic could reach it." As a young man, Lincoln for a time had enjoyed the company of freethinkers in the town of New Salem, Illinois. A Springfield lawyer who had known him in the 1830s reported that Lincoln privately called Jesus Christ a bastard and wrote a little book on infidelity, questioning his divinity. A friend, fearing for Lincoln's career, supposedly grabbed the manuscript from him and thrust it into the fire. Throughout his life, Lincoln never seemed to regard Jesus as anything like his personal savior.

Yet, while religious doctrine did not move him, Lincoln never shook the strong sense that some power far beyond human understanding controlled the universe and that free will took humans only so far. Herndon argued that Lincoln "believed in predestination, foreordination, that all things were fixed, doomed one way or the other, from which there was no appeal." Given his notorious absence from church services, Lincoln was forced to address the question of his own "infidelity" during his run for Congress in 1846. He admitted that, early in life, he had believed in something known as "the Doctrine of Necessity," which was becoming unpopular as the culture shifted toward less gloomy, more hopeful Evangelical notions of individual moral agency. Describing the older doctrine as the idea "that the human mind is impelled to action, or held in rest by some power, over which the mind itself has no control," he assured voters that he had "entirely left off" arguing for the theory for the previous five years. But, as that careful lawyer surely knew, that was not the same thing as saying he did not *believe* in it. Certainly, the scarring events of his life—his harrowing childhood, his bouts with severe depression, the death of two of his children, his wife's cruel mood swings, his political failures in the face of strenuous efforts and superior intelligence—argued that he was not ultimately in control, that he did not even fully control his mental states.

Lincoln repeatedly returned to this fatalistic idea of existence. While it seemed clear that the universe was constructed in such a way that human beings fared best when they worked hard to lift their condition and treat each other with kindness, their most strenuous efforts were often overridden by mysterious circumstances, which he characterized as the Almighty's will. People had to live with physical conditions and innate abilities they did not choose, in a harsh world not of their making, enduring the inevitable blows of sickness, death, and human malevolence the best they could. "Things were to be, and they came, irresistibly came, doomed to come; men were made as they are made by superior conditions over which they had no control; the fates settled things as by the doom of the powers, and laws, universal, absolute, and eternal, ruled the universe of matter and mind," Herndon wrote, in trying to explain Lincoln's philosophy. "[Man] is simply a *simple tool*, a mere cog in the wheel, a part, a small part, of this vast iron machine, that strikes and cuts, grinds and mashes, all things, including man, that resist it."

Like a good liberal, Herndon contended that human beings had free will and could choose to act purely, without self-interest. Lincoln "smiled at my philosophy, and answered that it was impossible, because the motive was born before the man," Herndon recalled. "He defied me to act without motive and unselfishly; and when I did the act and told him of it, he analyzed and sifted it to the last grain. After he had concluded, I could not avoid the admission that he had demonstrated the absolute selfishness of the entire act." Lincoln admired the Founders for creating a system that fully recognized humans as they were—selfish, infused with the survival instinct, prone to step on each other in ruthlessly jostling for status—and accordingly limited the ability of the powerful to prey on individuals.

Lincoln was thus wary of idealists who thought human beings or political systems were perfectible. At twenty-nine, in an 1838 address before the Young Men's Lyceum in Springfield, Lincoln observed that "jealousy, envy, and avarice" were "incident to our natures" and that humans harbored "deep rooted principles of hate, and the powerful motive of revenge." The most moral thing to do, Lincoln believed, was to take people as they are—basically the same, North or South, whatever their politics. "Southern slaveholders," he said in an 1854 speech, were "neither better, nor worse than we of the North," and people of the North were "no better than they. If we were situated as they are, we should act and feel as they do; and if they were situated as we are, they should act and feel as we do; and we never ought to lose sight of this fact in discussing the subject." This view of human nature is why, however brutally he executed his powers, Lincoln was a poor hater; he could hardly hate people for simply being human.

Predestination was one of the pillars of his family's Hard-Shell Baptist faith; the Bible was the other. The King James version, with its rich and resonant language, was the one book readily available to the young Abraham, a copy to be found in almost every poor farmer's home. Lincoln kept reading the Bible all his life. He regarded it as something other than a document of faith. To him, it was a practical source of enlightenment, a moving, beautifully written, profoundly wise book, a distillation of millennia of hard-earned human experience about justice, morality, and self-advancement. He could quote entire chapters of it by heart—from Isaiah, the Psalms, the New Testament. His letters and speeches were accordingly rich with biblical allusions, perhaps most famously his 1858 declaration that "A house divided against itself cannot stand," culled from the Gospel of Matthew. "I believe this government cannot endure, permanently, half slave and half free," Lincoln explained. He seemed particularly drawn to God's admonition to Adam before expelling him from the Garden of Eden, in Genesis: "In the sweat of thy face shalt thou eat bread, until thou return to the ground." At the core of Lincoln's moral beliefs—forming both his hatred of slavery and his fierce love of the republic—was the idea that each person had a right to get ahead; to keep what he had earned from the sweat of his brow, free from its being snatched away by an aristocracy or a slaveholder. During his celebrated debates in 1858 against Senator Stephen Douglas,

Lincoln spoke of the "real issue" that would continue to grip America long after he and Douglas were gone.

> It is the eternal struggle between these two principles—right and wrong—throughout the world. They are the two principles that have stood face to face from beginning of time; and will ever continue to struggle. The one is the common right of humanity and the other the divine right of kings. It is the same principle in whatever shape it develops itself. It is the same spirit that says, "You work and toil and earn bread, and I'll eat it." No matter what shape it comes, whether from the mouth of a king who seeks to bestride the people of his nation and live by the fruit of their labor, or from one race of men as an apology for enslaving another race, it is the same tyrannical principle.

One of his children's friends, Julia Taft, noticed that Mr. Lincoln seemed to read the great book in a different way from many. "I have a notion, without knowing exactly why I have it, that at the beginning of the war he read the Bible quite as much for its literary style as he did for its religious or spiritual content," she recalled. "He read it in the relaxed, almost lazy attitude of a man enjoying a good book." When Tad once asked him why he had to go to Sunday school, Lincoln offered a more cultural than religious answer. "Every educated person should know something about the Bible and the Bible stories, Tad." Mary Lincoln's servant and seamstress, Elizabeth Keckley, remembered Lincoln appearing in the First Lady's room while she was being fitted for a dress. The war news was shattering, and Lincoln seemed completely dejected. "He reached forth one of his long arms, and took a small Bible from a stand near the head of the sofa, opened the pages of the holy book, and soon was absorbed in reading them." After a quarter of an hour, she looked at Lincoln and saw that "the dejected look was gone, and the countenance was lighted up with new resolution and hope." When a group of African Americans from Baltimore presented him with an expensive gift copy of the Bible in September 1864, bound in royal purple velvet with an eighteen-karat-gold shield on the front, in gratitude for his service to their people, Lincoln observed: "In regard to this Great Book, I have but to say, it is the best gift God has given to men. All the good the Savior gave to the world was communicated through this book. But for it we could not know right from wrong. All things most desirable for man's welfare, here and hereafter, are to be found portrayed in it." He often referred to the Bible in such terms of its utility.

Mary Lincoln was the conventionally religious member of the family, and she made sure the children went to church. She frequently attended Sunday services at the New York Avenue Presbyterian Church, a six-minute walk or a briefer carriage ride away, where the family rented a pew, eight rows from the front, for fifty dollars a year. But, as at the First Presbyterian Church in Springfield, where he had rented a pew earlier, Lincoln never became a member. He seemed uninterested in whether one denomination's form of worship was superior to another's. "President Lincoln was deeply and genuinely religious, without being in any way what may be called a religionist," recalled White House secretary William O. Stoddard. He maintained that Lincoln's religion was expressed "in his faith and in his life" rather than through any church. "That he had an abiding faith in the overruling providence of God, in His active interference in the affairs of men and nations, is beyond possible question," Stoddard added. As a Baptist and faithful churchgoer who revered the president, Stoddard may have been inclined to see him in that light. But others agreed.

As a careful politician, Lincoln could be expected to court the support of deeply Christian Americans by reciting religious platitudes. Even so, it is striking how obsessively he returned to the question of God's overruling will. He told a group of Quakers visiting him in 1863 that no one was more aware than he that without God's favor, "our highest wisdom is but as foolishness," and "that our most strenuous efforts would avail nothing in the shadow of His displeasure." Months later, he repeated the theme in comments to Presbyterians brought to the White House by his wife's pastor. "I have often wished that I was a more devout man than I am. Nevertheless, amid the greatest difficulties of my Administration, when I could not see any other resort, I would place my whole reliance in God, knowing that all would go well, and that He would decide for the right." The former rail-splitter, who found great pleasure in rereading a handful of Shakespeare's plays, particularly loved a line from *Hamlet*: "There's a divinity that shapes our ends / rough-hew them how we will."

Mary Lincoln believed her husband became more overtly religious after their three-year-old, Eddie, died in 1850. After his election as president, she said, "with the care of a great Nation upon his shoulders—when devastating war was upon us—then indeed to my knowledge—did his great heart go up daily, hourly, in prayer to God—for his sustaining power." She may have been exaggerating her martyred husband's piety, but Noah Brooks reported that, after Lincoln went to the White House, "he kept up the habit of daily prayer. Sometimes he said it was only ten words but those ten words he had." John Nicolay concurred: "Lincoln was a praying man. I know that to be a fact and I have heard him request people to pray for him, which he would never have done had he not believed that prayer is answered." If he prayed, though, Lincoln did not make much of a show of it. "There is a good deal on record about his being a man of prayer but I never heard him pray or saw him in the attitude of prayer," Julia Taft noted, "although I have seen him in moods when he might well have been struggling in silent prayer."

Whatever strength Lincoln drew from faith was called to the test in 1862, when he endured perhaps the most crushing loss of his life. His delightful and clever eleven-year-old son, Willie—"the most lovable boy I ever knew, bright, sensible, sweet-tempered and gentle-mannered," Julia Taft said—fell ill from typhoid fever, evidently contracted from drinking polluted water drawn from the Potomac, and died in the White House on February 20, at five p.m. A little letter that Willie had written at the age of eight after visiting Chicago with his father offers a hint of his charm and his dearness to Lincoln. "This town is a very beautiful place. Me and father have a nice little room to ourselves. We have two little pitchers on a washstand. The smallest one for me the

largest one for father. We have two little towels on top of both pitchers. The smallest one for me, the largest one for father. Me and father
had gone to two theaters the other night." He was the one of Lincoln's
four children most like him.

Perhaps in reaction to his own father, Lincoln was utterly indulgent to his children, refusing to punish them or even restrain their
behavior in company. Joseph Gillespie, a fellow member of the Illinois
House of Representatives, remarked that Lincoln's "children literally
ran over him and he was powerless to stop their importunities." Lincoln
could sit with visitors, another man observed, "and all the while, his two
little boys, his sons, clambered over [his] legs, patted his cheeks, pulled
his nose, and poked their fingers in his eyes, without causing reprimand
or even notice." Herndon, who had to deal with the children tearing
through the law office, knocking over inkstands and scattering papers,
found Lincoln's indulgence sickening. He complained that had the
boys "s[hi]t in Lincoln's hat and rubbed it on his boots, he would have
thought it smart." In Springfield, one Illinois man accompanied stuffy
U.S. senator Lyman Trumbull to Lincoln's office to discuss political
business. "We were sitting in the office talking to Mr. Lincoln, when
the door opened and a boy dashed in, running as hard as he could.
He was Tad. His father stood up and opened wide his arms. Tad came
running. When he was about 6 feet away he jumped and caught his
father around the neck. Lincoln wrapped his arms around the boy and
spanked him good, both of them laughing and carrying on as if there
was nobody looking at them." As president, Lincoln let Tad's pet goats
have the run of the White House. At one point, Tad hooked one of
the animals to a chair and rode around, shouting at visitors, "Get out
of the way there!" Lincoln explained his philosophy of parenting. "It
is my pleasure that my children are free—happy, and unrestrained by
parental tyranny," he said. "Love is the chain whereby to lock a child
to its parent."

After Willie died, his brother Tad cried on and off for a month, and
the raving of his mother, Mary, led the president to fear for her sanity.
Forced to maintain his composure in public and to keep his focus on

the crucial prosecution of the war, Lincoln set aside time each Thursday afternoon, the day of Willie's death, for private grieving. Elizabeth Keckley heard him pacing in his room, asking over and over why it had happened. There was no answer except God's inscrutable will.

Both Lincoln and his counterpart on the Confederate side, Jefferson Davis, urged their people to turn to God for strength and support. In his inaugural address, Davis recalled Providence's role in the grim and bloody struggle of the American Revolution and the establishment of freedom. "Reverently let us invoke the God of our fathers to guide and protect us in our efforts to perpetuate the principles which by his blessing they were able to vindicate, establish and transmit to their posterity," he said. "With the continuance of his favor ever gratefully acknowledged, we may hopefully look forward to success, to peace, and to prosperity." But neither success, nor peace, nor prosperity came to either North or South. Many read the ongoing slaughter as God's condemnation of their side in the struggle for its moral failings. In the style of seventeenth-century Puritan ministers, both presidents issued jeremiads. Named after the prophet Jeremiah, these statements lamented society's sins and called on the people to mend their ways.

Abraham Lincoln's 1861 proclamation setting aside a day of "public humiliation, prayer and fasting" noted that America "united, prosperous and happy" had been blessed by God but now suffered "faction and civil war." He called on Americans to "recognize the hand of God in this terrible visitation, and in sorrowful remembrance of our own faults and crimes as a nation and as individuals, to humble ourselves before Him, and to pray for His mercy, to pray that we may be spared further punishment, though most justly deserved."

Two years later, Lincoln returned to the theme with another dark proclamation calling for a day of fasting. In it, he suggested that "the awful calamity of civil war which now desolates the land may be but a punishment inflicted upon us for our presumptuous sins," requiring that the whole nation redeem itself.

We have been the recipients of the choicest bounties of Heaven; we have been preserved these many years in peace and prosperity; we have grown in numbers, wealth and power as no other nation has ever grown. But we have forgotten God. We have forgotten the gracious hand which has preserved us in peace and multiplied and enriched and strengthened us, and we have vainly imagined, in the deceitfulness of our hearts, that all these blessings were produced by some superior wisdom and virtue of our own. Intoxicated with unbroken success, we have become too self-sufficient to feel the necessity of redeeming and preserving grace, too proud to pray to the God that made us. It behooves us, then, to humble ourselves before the offended power, to confess our national sins and to pray for clemency and forgiveness.

This may have been boilerplate religious sentiment, but Lincoln seemed genuinely haunted by the question of what this hellish war meant. Given his belief in predestination, Lincoln could not accept— or, at least, he could not tell his people—that the carnage and chaos the nation had endured for the last four years was devoid of a deeper, even sacred meaning. If the world was ordered in a way to make justice superior to injustice, how could such suffering go on and on? The Union, after all, was struggling bravely to prevent a conspiracy from destroying this great nation conceived in liberty—a conspiracy mounted by men who clapped their fellow human beings in chains and refused to accept the people's judgment, as expressed in a free and fair election.

Lincoln did what he often did when presented with a thorny problem. Evidently, in the late summer of 1862, during some of the darkest days of the war, perhaps in advance of a politically touchy White House visit by a delegation of Chicago ministers who thought he was moving too slowly on eradicating slavery, Lincoln sat down and scribbled his thoughts onto a foolscap sheet of paper, lining up the arguments against one another. John Hay, who discovered the undated fragment after the president's death, titled it "Meditation on the Divine

Will." Hay considered it a rare look "into the most secret recesses" of Lincoln's soul. "Perplexed and afflicted beyond the power of human help, by the disasters of war, the wrangling of parties, and the inexorable and constraining logic of his own mind, he shut out the world one day, and tried to put into form his double sense of responsibility to human duty and Divine Power; and this was the result," Hay said of the little patch of writing.

Lincoln presented his arguments as a series of truths. "The will of God prevails," he wrote, starting with what to him was an elemental belief. "In great contests each party claims to act in accordance with the will of God. Both *may* be, and one *must* be, wrong. God cannot be *for* and *against* the same thing at the same time." That being the case, there must be a reason that God had permitted this war to continue, a reason neither North nor South could fully comprehend. "In the present civil war it is quite possible that God's purpose is something different from the purpose of either party—and yet the human instrumentalities, working just as they do, are of the best adaptation to effect His purpose," Lincoln wrote. "I am almost ready to say that this is probably true—that God wills this contest, and wills that it shall not end yet." Through His power, God "could have either *saved* or *destroyed* the Union without a human contest. Yet the contest began. And, having begun He could give the final victory to either side any day. Yet the contest proceeds."

This conundrum stuck with him. At the request of Albert Hodges, editor of the *Frankfort* (Kentucky) *Commonwealth*, Lincoln wrote a letter in April 1864 summarizing his conversation at the White House with Hodges and two other Kentuckians: Governor Thomas E. Bramlette and former Whig Senator Archibald Dixon, both of whom bitterly opposed Lincoln's recruitment of black men in the Union Army. As Lincoln told the small group, God's plan for this war had been different from his own. Revolutionary change had been forced on him. "In telling this tale I attempt no compliment to my own sagacity. I claim not to have controlled events, but confess plainly that events have controlled me," Lincoln wrote. "Now, at the end of three years struggle the nation's condition is not what either party, or any man devised, or expected. God alone can claim it. Whither it is tending seems plain. If God now wills the removal of a great wrong, and wills also that we of the North as well as you of the South, shall pay fairly for our complicity in that wrong, impartial history will find therein new cause to attest and revere the justice and goodness of God." That great wrong—the sin that had to be punished, the evil that had to be torn from the country at a horrifying cost—was slavery.

Five months later, Lincoln returned to the theme in a note to Eliza P. Gurney, thanking the Quaker widow for her prayers and her kind sentiments in a letter. "The purposes of the Almighty are perfect, and must prevail, though we erring mortals may fail to accurately perceive them in advance," Lincoln wrote. "We hoped for a happy termination of this terrible war long before this; but God knows best, and has ruled otherwise. We shall yet acknowledge His wisdom, and our own error therein. Meanwhile we must work earnestly in the best lights He gives us, trusting that so working still conduces to the great ends He ordains. Surely He intends some great good to follow this mighty convulsion, which no mortal could make, and no mortal could stay."

And still the slaughter had continued. Lincoln had survived an election that, for a time, few thought he could win. As his second term approached, the president seemed to feel he owed the country an explanation for the agonies it had endured under his watch. Having tested his strikingly religious ideas in both his private and public communications, Lincoln had worked them into the inaugural address he would deliver in a few hours. It would be like no other in American history. He would not bask in the glory of recent, hard-fought military victories, or present a detailed plan for reconstruction. He would speak about human depravity, about the hideous sin committed by both sides, and about the justice of God's infallible, implacable, inescapable will.

CHAPTER 6

PUBLIC SENTIMENT IS EVERYTHING

Saturday morning, March 4, 1865

Lincoln had labored hard—in a sense, for years—on the remarkably brief address he had in hand to carry to the Capitol that morning. He had all but finished it by the previous Sunday night, February 26, according to Francis Bicknell Carpenter, an ambitious portrait painter from upstate New York. Carpenter had been a special guest in Lincoln's White House office that night, along with two of the president's loyal political cronies, George Burt Lincoln (no relation) and John A. Bingham.

The previous year, Lincoln had given Carpenter permission to work in the White House for months on a project designed to celebrate the president as a major historical figure. Carpenter effectively became a fly on the wall for much of 1864, closely observing the president in action, while toiling on what he believed would be his masterpiece: a nine-by-fifteen-foot painting of Lincoln's presentation of his Emancipation Proclamation to the members of his Cabinet on July 22, 1862. The executive order, which declared that all enslaved people residing in territory controlled by the rebels were henceforth free, was "an act unparalleled for moral grandeur in the history of mankind," Carpenter asserted, and worthy of a great historical canvas of the sort that brought riches and fame to nineteenth-century artists. Sure enough, the finished work, put on exhibit in the White House's East Room exactly two years after the event it depicted, attracted large crowds before being crated up and taken on tour to other cities. Thousands of Americans bought copies of a meticulously detailed engraving of the painting by Alexander Hay Ritchie to display in their own homes.

While Lincoln was the painting's central figure and focal point, it featured detailed life-size portraits of each of the Cabinet members, including such celebrated men as Treasury Secretary Salmon P. Chase and his Cabinet counterweight, Secretary of State William H. Seward. With heavy symbolism, Carpenter grouped the radicals—Chase and Secretary of War Edwin Stanton—on the left of the painting, and clustered the more moderate members on the right, behind the seated Seward. Chase stood cross-armed and glowering, his head higher than anyone else's. One amused viewer said Chase seemed to be saying, "look at and admire me, for I am the handsomest man in this crowd, and I challenge anybody to deny it," journalist Lois Bryan Adams reported. Women generally gushed over the depiction, she noted, praising Chase's "fine form," "his full handsome face," the "sweet expression of his lips," and "his noble brow." One young woman declared, "there is nothing so beautiful in the whole picture as Mr. C's plum-colored coat!" The touchy Chase himself, by contrast, interpreted the painting as a tribute to his Cabinet rival. The "whole picture," Chase complained, was "subsidiary to Seward who is talking while every one either listens or stares into vacancy." Mary Lincoln acidly labeled it "the happy family."

The second guest in the president's office that Sunday night, G. B. Lincoln, was a grateful officeholder and that rarest of men, a Massachusetts-born abolitionist with a sense of humor. He had supported Lincoln in 1860 and had consequently received a prized appointment, in 1861, as postmaster of Brooklyn. In 1864, like many men the president had carefully rewarded with public posts, G. B. Lincoln loyally served as a Lincoln delegate to the National Union Party convention in Baltimore. He liked to tell the story of meeting Lincoln in Springfield in 1860, after the lawyer had won the Republican nomination and was headed for the presidency. G. B. Lincoln had brought with him a new stovepipe hat fashioned by a Brooklyn hatter who had obtained the nominee's measurements. Abraham Lincoln put it on his head and walked to the mirror, glancing over to Mary with a twinkle in his eye. "Well, wife, there is one thing likely to come out of this scrape, any how," he said. "We are going to have some *new clothes!*" The third man, John Bingham, had been thrown out of Congress in the 1862 election, when war-weary voters turned against radical Republicans and their Emancipation Proclamation. Lincoln had sustained Bingham, a brilliant Ohio lawyer and former Chase supporter, by appointing him judge advocate of the Union Army. Bingham greatly admired Lincoln for his way of expressing wisdom in his funny but pointed stories, though he found the president, he told a reporter, "the saddest man I ever met."

As Carpenter recalled, Lincoln came down a side corridor—one he had ordered built to help him get from the second-floor library directly to his office without having to make his way through the petitioners who crowded the waiting room during working hours—and entered the office "holding in his hand a roll of manuscripts." The president identified the roll as his inaugural address. He was in good spirits. "Lots of wisdom in that document, I suspect," he said. "I will put it away here in this drawer until I need it."

With the speech set aside for the moment, Lincoln sat by the fire and "commenced conversation in a familiar and cheerful mood." The talk turned to his early days in Illinois, and the immense satisfaction he took in his first election to the state legislature, a Whig in a district dominated by Democrats. "Nothing, he said, ever gratified him as much," Carpenter recalled. That was a turning point in his life from his painfully poor upbringing and extreme social awkwardness toward the people's acceptance. And now he was to be inaugurated president of the United States for a second time.

Lincoln had taken each step of his astonishing rise, striking even to Americans of the time, through his remarkable use of language— first as a skilled storyteller to charm an audience and win friends, and later as a distinctive writer, using plain and pointed language sparkling with idiosyncratic phrases. From his earliest days, he was fascinated by words, according to his loving stepmother, Sarah Bush Lincoln. "Abe read all the books he could lay his hands on—and when he came across a passage that Struck him he would write it down on boards if he had no paper & keep it there till he did get paper—then he would re-write it—look at it repeat it—He had a copy book—a kind of scrap book in which he put down all things and this preserved them," she recalled. For the rest of his life, Lincoln jotted down striking phrases and thoughts—increasingly including his own—often stowing them away in the cubbyholes of his law office's tall desk and even in the lining of his stovepipe hat. He refined his ideas, sometimes over the course of years, as they slowly emerged in his speeches and letters.

Sarah Bush Lincoln recalled Abraham's yearning as a boy to express himself plainly and extract clear meanings from the adults around him. "Sometimes he seemed pestered to give Expression to his ideas and got mad almost at one who couldn't Explain plainly what he wanted to convey." When the Reverend John P. Gulliver praised him in 1860 for the clarity of his speeches, Lincoln explained: "Among my earliest recollections I remember how, when a mere child, I used to get irritated when any body talked to me in a way I could not understand." After he clambered into bed at night in his family's little cabin, he recalled, he listened closely to the "dark sayings" of the adults, trying to make out their meaning. "I could not sleep, though I often tried to, when I got on such a hunt after an idea, until I had caught it; and when I thought I had got it, I was not satisfied until I had repeated it over and over, until I had put it in language plain enough, as I thought, for any boy I knew to comprehend." He used that approach throughout his life. "This was a kind of passion with me, and it has stuck by me," Lincoln said.

Lincoln began his writing career with attempts to mimic the florid oratory popular in the nineteenth century. But as his confidence grew, his language became more urgently direct, plain, infused with moral power. He peppered his speeches with colloquialisms that were distinctly out of fashion with the literary set, finding that they helped him get his message across. In expressing the best way to move juries, he advised his law partner, William Herndon: "Don't shoot too high; aim lower, and the common people will understand you. They are the ones you want to reach—at least the ones you ought to reach. The educated and refined people will understand you anyway. If you aim too high, your ideas will go over the heads of the masses, and only hit those who need no hitting." Herndon found the approach frustrating at times. In his quest to "see the thing or idea exactly and to express that idea in such language as to convey that idea precisely," Lincoln "used to bore me terribly by his methods—processes—manner &c. &c. Mr. Lincoln would doubly explain things to me that needed no explanation," Herndon recalled. "Lincoln's ambition in this line was this—he wanted to be distinctly understood by the Common people."

Lincoln's style was more than plain; he had a finely tuned ear for the rhythm of sentences and the boom and whisper of words. To Herndon's intense annoyance, Lincoln typically came into the office each morning, threw himself on the sofa, and began reading aloud from the newspapers. "I catch the idea by two senses," he told Herndon, "for when I hear what is said and also see it, I remember it better even if I do not understand it better." Lacking formal training in rhetoric and writing, he surely used this means to give himself a lengthy self-education in the power of pacing and the use of such rhetorical devices as balanced phrases, alliteration, and probing questions, until he could almost intuitively make his own writing flow and ring. "I write by ear," Lincoln told a law student named Gibson William Harris. "When I have got my thoughts on paper, I read it aloud, and if it sounds all right I just let it pass."

America presented Lincoln with an issue worthy of his pen. During the 1850s, in hope of saving the Union, the political establishment mounted an increasingly desperate defense of slavery. Lincoln, a passionate believer in the nation's founding ideals, feared that the entire country, North as well as South, was being conditioned to accept slavery as a permanent feature of American life, something that could not help but corrode freedom everywhere. In 1854, when the Democrats in Congress tried to quell the storm by passing Illinois senator Stephen Douglas's Kansas-Nebraska Act, permitting slavery's possible spread into northern territories, Lincoln by his own admission was "aroused . . . as he had never been before." He regarded the Democrats' efforts to placate the slave states as something more than merely political; the spread of slavery was an assault on the integrity of the United States that would destroy liberty. From then on, he fervently labored over his speeches until they were clear in their logic, easy for his audience to follow, with arguments those listeners could take home and share with others.

The crowds found him a different kind of speaker. He did not attempt to score points through the politician's art of stoking the people's self-righteousness and vindictiveness. Rather, he stressed Americans' shared values and the moral power of the ideals enunciated in the Declaration of Independence. Inclined to treat others decently, he had long understood that the best way to persuade people was to respect their humanity and recognize that they might have just reasons for disagreeing. "If you would win a man to your cause, first convince him that you are his sincere friend," he had observed in a speech back in 1842. A man who is admonished by a speaker "will retreat within himself, close all the avenues to his head and his heart; and tho' your cause be naked truth itself, transformed to the heaviest lance, harder than steel, and sharper than steel can be made, and tho' you throw it with more than Herculean force and precision, you shall no more be able to pierce him, than to penetrate the hard shell of a tortoise with a rye straw." Sure enough, his decency appealed to listeners and influenced the national debate. He lost two Senate elections along the way but won a national reputation as a man who could bravely and eloquently make the case for blocking the spread of slavery.

Lincoln believed that the ability to frame an argument and sway minds was the essence of power in a representative democracy. "Our government rests in public opinion. Whoever can change public opinion, can change the government, practically just so much," Lincoln said in an 1856 speech. At the first of his celebrated seven Senate campaign debates against Stephen Douglas, on August 21, 1858, in Ottawa, Illinois, he said: "In this and like communities, public sentiment is everything. With public sentiment, nothing can fail; without it nothing can succeed. Consequently he who molds public sentiment, goes deeper than he who enacts statutes or pronounces decisions."

In their later biography of Lincoln, his secretaries John Nicolay and John Hay noted, "Nothing would have more amazed him while he lived than to hear himself called a man of letters." Yet Lincoln clearly understood that his words would be immensely important in leading the nation through its darkest hours. Through them, he would rally the North to endure the war's horrible costs, signal his firm intentions to the enemy and to the world, and make the case, as stirringly as possible, for the survival of this extraordinary young republic and the cause of freedom that it embodied.

In his first inaugural address, Lincoln tried to soothe the fears of the South but made it plain that he intended to preserve the Union, in sharp contrast to outgoing president James Buchanan. In his closing, in a passage conceived by William Seward but reworked by Lincoln, with his beautiful ear for language, to lift the phrases into perfect pitch, the president movingly appealed to his listeners' emotions: "I am loth to close," Lincoln said. "We are not enemies, but friends. We must not be enemies. Though passion may have strained, it must not break our bonds of affection. The mystic chords of memory, stretching from every battle-field and patriot grave to every living heart and hearthstone all over this broad land, will yet swell the chorus of the Union when again touched, as surely they will be, by the better angels of our nature." Years of inconceivable carnage followed, but Lincoln never lost hope that the love Americans once had for their country might be revived.

He continued to shape the public's perception of what this war meant. In his message to Congress on July 4, 1861, Lincoln explained what was at stake for humanity. "It presents to the whole family of man, the question, whether a constitutional republic, or a democracy—a government of the people, by the same people—can, or cannot, maintain its territorial integrity, against its own domestic foes." This war would test whether a minority, defeated at the polls, could simply ignore the majority by breaking up the country, "and thus practically put an end to free government upon the earth. It forces us to ask: 'Is there, in all republics, this inherent, and fatal weakness?' 'Must a government, of necessity, be too strong for the liberties of its own people, or too weak to maintain its own existence?'"

These were questions Lincoln asked again, more succinctly and memorably, in his Gettysburg address more than two years later, on November 19, 1863. In a brief speech of only 272 words, commemorating the Union soldiers slaughtered on that battlefield, Lincoln noted that the United States, a mere eighty-seven years earlier, had been "conceived in liberty, and dedicated to the proposition that all men are created equal." The war was a test of whether this young nation, or any country that invests so much power in the people, "can long endure." He urged the American people, through their gratitude and respect for the immense sacrifices men had made at Gettysburg, to rededicate themselves to the cause—"that this nation, under God, shall have a new birth of freedom—and that government of the people, by the people, for the people, shall not perish from the earth." As he demonstrated with the questions he asked in his "Meditation on the Divine Will," which he would hone and perfect in the second inaugural address, Lincoln had a way of refining his ideas until he could express them with simplicity, poetic beauty, and immense power.

Lincoln's speeches and state papers seemed puzzling to their readers at first because, unlike the works of more systematically educated presidents, they popped with catchy phrases and homely ideas. The July 4, 1861, message, for example, included the phrase "sugar-coated," which a government editor and seasoned newspaperman named John D. Defrees urged Lincoln to remove, noting the use of such a term was undignified and unworthy of a state paper of lasting historic importance. "Defrees," Lincoln responded, "that word expressed precisely my idea, and I am not going to change it. The time will never come in this country when people won't know exactly what *sugar-coated* means." Many highly educated Americans found Lincoln's folksiness embarrassing and ungentlemanly.

Unlike other presidents, Lincoln had not spent years in boarding schools or colleges becoming immersed in the proper way of saying things. During his days on the court circuit in Illinois, lawyer Henry

C. Whitney had been struck by Lincoln's absurdly indiscriminate taste in literature. He seemed to love with equal passion the Bible, Shakespeare, and the crude humorists Petroleum V. Nasby, Artemus Ward, and Joseph Glover Baldwin. "Was there ever such a curious *mélange* of almost supreme greatness and boyish vacuity as was compressed in this unique, uneven and incomprehensible man?" Whitney wondered. Ralph Waldo Emerson, the great philosopher from the Harvard Divinity School, was appalled and embarrassed by Lincoln's ungentlemanly way of expressing his ideas. "You cannot refine Mr. Lincoln's taste, extend his horizon, or clear his Judgements; he will not walk dignifiedly through the traditional role of the President of America, but will pop out his head at each railway station and make a little speech, and get into an argument with Squire A and Judge B. He will write letters to Horace Greeley, and any editor or reporter or saucy party committee that writes to him, and cheapen himself."

Many found his style clunky and uninspiring. The editor of the Jersey City *American Standard* rated the first inaugural address, with its lyrical conclusion, as "involved, coarse, colloquial, devoid of ease and grace, and bristling with obscurities and outrages against the simplest rules of syntax." The *Clearfield Republican* in Pennsylvania thought little of Lincoln's offering at Gettysburg: "We pass over the silly remarks of the President. For the credit of the nation we are willing that the veil of oblivion shall be dropped over them, and that they shall be no more repeated or thought of." A *Times* of London correspondent agreed: "The Gettysburg ceremony was rendered ludicrous by some of the sallies of that poor President Lincoln," he wrote. "Anything more dull and commonplace it wouldn't be easy to produce."

Yet Lincoln's words stuck in the mind. As the war ground on, even members of the literary set noticed that there was something wonderful about the way he wrote. Harriet Beecher Stowe, the author of the best-selling, immensely influential antislavery novel *Uncle Tom's Cabin*, marveled that "there are passages in his state-papers that could not be better put; they are absolutely perfect. They are brief, condensed, intense, and with a power of insight and expression that make them worthy to be inscribed in letters of gold." John Hay, educated at Brown University, admitted that he found "some hideously bad rhetoric—some indecorums that are infamous" in the president's public August 26, 1863, letter to his friend James C. Conkling, effectively a speech to be read aloud at a rally back in Springfield, Illinois. It described naval vessels as "Uncle Sam's web-feet"—"as if the government were a goose," the *Illinois State Register* sneered—and referred to the Mississippi River as "the Father of Waters." Yet Hay believed that the letter would take "its solid place in history, as a great utterance of a great man. The whole cabinet could not have tinkered a letter which could have been compared with it. He can snake a sophism out of its hole, better than all the trained logicians of all schools." New York lawyer George Templeton Strong noted in his diary, somewhat condescendingly, that "there are sentences that a critic would like to eliminate, but they are delightfully characteristic of the 'plain man' who wrote it and will appeal directly to the 'plain men' from Maine to Minnesota."

As the war continued, even some of Lincoln's persistent critics began to appreciate his style. In April 1864, *New York Tribune* editor Horace Greeley almost grudgingly conceded that the man had some talent for expression: "The President is not generally esteemed a man of signal ability; yet he has no adviser, and (since Jefferson) has had no predecessor, who surpasses him in that rare quality, the ability to make a statement which appeals at once, and irresistibly, to the popular apprehension—what we may call the shrewdly homely way of 'putting things.'" An Oxford professor named Goldwin Smith, writing in Britain's *Macmillan's Magazine* in early 1865, assured his erudite readers that Lincoln was "something more than a boor" in his Gettysburg Address. While some of the phrases "betray a hand untrained in fine writing," the professor wrote, "it may be doubted whether any king in Europe would have expressed himself more royally than the peasant's son." Journalist Noah Brooks, in a private letter in December 1864, argued that Lincoln had become a more forceful writer since taking office: "It is interesting and curious to observe how the President has grown morally and intellectually since he has been at the White House; take his messages and read them through *ad seriatim* and you will see his advancement in ability, logic and rhetoric, as evident as in the letters of a youth at school."

Lincoln impressed many Americans with his unvarnished statements of devotion to the Union's preservation and the cause of freedom, and his humble admissions that he saw himself as the agent of God's unknowable will. At one point, General Ethan Allen Hitchcock saw Lincoln enter a back room at the War Office absorbed in thought. Looking into Lincoln's sad eyes, Hitchcock observed, "You have a very trying position, Sir." "Yes," Lincoln responded, and "did I not see the hand of God in the crisis—I could not sustain it." The general was moved by the simplicity and earnestness of the statement, and by the "devout intelligence of the man." As the war went on, he never saw Lincoln write or do anything that was not in line with his deep sense of "devout responsibility." Elizabeth Palmer Peabody, an educator and abolitionist who was friendly with Ralph Waldo Emerson and his liberal set, discussed Lincoln with General Hitchcock after she met with the president at the White House in February 1865. "The General thinks his abilities are very great—& his integrity & love of his country most profound—& that we have had no greater President—& depend upon it he says bye and bye this will be seen & acknowledged."

Many newspapers on that Inauguration Day—hawked on street corners, dropped on doorsteps, and read over breakfast tables—expressed a newfound appreciation for the president. The pro-Republican *New York Times* saw victory nearing in the nation's struggle for survival. "But for the great practical wisdom of Mr. Lincoln, not only in shaping his action, but in recognizing the appropriate time for his action, the result would have been very different." Any historian later studying the war "will be astonished as he scans Mr. Lincoln's path through all the immense difficulties of his Presidential term, that he has traversed it with such forecast, such firmness and such success." For all the complaints about Lincoln's dictatorial tendencies, the nation had duly held a presidential election on schedule—in the middle of its crisis—that he might well have lost, and he was still robustly attacked in hundreds of newspapers. Through his actions, Washington, D.C., which the Union's enemies had threatened to overrun, remained the nation's capital. The border states, essential to the Union's survival, had not fallen to the rebels. The institution of slavery had been fatally wounded without destroying all support for the war in the North. The economy somehow kept sputtering on.

The *Pittsburgh Commercial* that morning noted that Lincoln was "not a new man now, but versed in the affairs of government, and familiar with the combinations and details of war; more honored and better loved, than at first, by the people who called him to his high position." On December 20, 1860, the *Charleston Mercury* had famously shouted on its front page, "The UNION is DISSOLVED!" as if the matter were settled. But for four long years, Lincoln had refused to give in. "With pleased and grateful eye, he looks on the setting sun of the rebellion, as it goes down amid its own blood-red clouds. The awards of sorrow and desolation have been meted out to the whole area of the rebellion. The guilty conspirators have had blood, to their fill; but *the Union is NOT dissolved*," the *Commercial* proclaimed.

Democratic-leaning newspapers, to be sure, still voiced fears about the immense powers Lincoln had seized. "Mr. Lincoln commences, to-day, a second term unfettered by constitutional restraint as if he were the Czar of Russia, or the Sultan of Turkey," the *Cincinnati Enquirer* asserted. "We have exchanged moral purity for the most terrible corruption. We have parted with everything that makes a nation desirable, in order to maintain a bloody supremacy over a certain portion of the land. Where is the public liberty that was handed to Mr. Lincoln four years ago for preservation? It lies bleeding and prostrate at the feet of a ruined and violated Constitution." But James Gordon Bennett's *New York Herald*, which for years had sharply criticized Lincoln for his evident waffling and what it considered his boneheaded decisions, seemed to be waking up to a new impression. "He is a most remarkable man," the paper observed. "He may seem to be the most credulous, docile and pliable of backwoodsmen, and yet when he 'puts his foot down he puts it down firmly,' and cannot be budged. He has proved himself, in his quiet way, the keenest of politicians and more than a match for his wiliest antagonist in the arts of diplomacy." Lincoln's nature, the editor thought, had much to do with it. "Plain common sense, a kindly disposition, a straight forward purpose and a shrewd perception of the ins and outs of poor, weak human nature, have enabled him to master difficulties which would have swamped almost any other man. Thus, to-day, with the most cheering prospects before him, this extraordinary rail-splitter enters upon his second term the unquestioned master" of American politics.

And he would enter it with a speech of profound power. The writing had never been easy for Lincoln. It required painstaking effort—during his presidency amid constant distractions and demands for his time. He took the work extremely seriously, knowing that his words had to be chosen scrupulously to have the most powerful effect, and that a careless phrase might be misconstrued and used against him. During the 1864 campaign, when a Republican club in Buffalo asked him for a letter that could be read aloud at a rally, Lincoln dutifully wrote a draft—then decided against finishing it. He explained to the club's president that "a public letter must be written with some care, and at some expense of time." Lincoln often worked out his ideas this way, writing thoughtful and occasionally pointed letters that he set aside, as impolitic to send. Writing developed his command of a topic and supplied him with ideas he later mined for speeches and public letters.

Lincoln liked to have stiff slips of pasteboard or boxboard handy to write on—an approach he used when he wrote "anything requiring thought," according to his friend Noah Brooks. He gathered together the ideas jotted on these slips later when composing a speech or paper. "Seated at ease in his armchair, he lays the slip on his knee, and writes and rewrites in pencil what is afterward copied in his own hand with new changes and interlineations," Brooks explained. Lincoln's whole approach centered on meticulous refinement of ideas that had struck him earlier and that he had written down for later use. In printed proofs of his works in progress, he had the compositors set up spaces of a half inch between each line. "More corrections and interlineations are made,"

Brooks noted, "and from this patchwork, the document is finally set up and printed." Lincoln's son Robert similarly recalled this laborious process. "He was a very deliberate writer, anything but rapid. I cannot remember any peculiarity about his posture; he wrote sitting at a table and, as I remember, in an ordinary posture. . . . He seemed to think nothing of the labor of writing personally and was accustomed to many scraps of notes and memoranda. In writing a careful letter, he first wrote it himself, then corrected it, and then rewrote the corrected version himself." None of this involved dictation or professional speechwriters.

After his pleasant Sunday night chat with Carpenter, G. B. Lincoln, and Bingham, the president sent the "clean copy" of his speech off to the printer, who produced a text Lincoln could read from in delivering the speech and one that could be distributed to the masses. But even after getting the printed version back, Lincoln tinkered with it, crossing out the very last phrase in the speech—"the world"—and substituting the more poetic, more lyrical "all nations." It was a typical tweak by Lincoln. In this very short address, every word counted.

The president took the printed version of his four-paragraph speech and cut the text into twenty-seven scraps. He heated up a wad of the smelly animal glue of the time—typically made of the hide and bones of cattle and horses, it gave off the odor of a wet dog—and meticulously pasted the pieces onto a sheet of paper in two columns. All this was to produce a reading copy that would help him deliver the speech to best effect. The short chunks of text would guide Lincoln to pauses for dramatic impact, helping his listeners follow what he was saying. With a pen, he added commas, again to finesse his pacing.

With that pasted-up and perfected reading copy in his hand, Abraham Lincoln exited the White House in his fine new Brooks Brothers suit and stovepipe hat, climbed up into a small carriage and, in the wind-driven rain of the early morning, before the massive crowds could block the streets, splashed through the mud of Pennsylvania Avenue to the Capitol.

CHAPTER 7

INDEFINABLE FASCINATION

Saturday morning, March 4, 1865

John McCullough, a tall, roughly handsome, thirty-two-year-old Irish-born actor, had been up and about that stormy morning and was returning to the room at the National Hotel that he shared with a dear friend, John Wilkes Booth. The fellow actors loved to go out together, drinking, laughing, and womanizing, notwithstanding the fact that McCullough had a wife and two sons in Philadelphia. When McCullough was in Washington, Booth put him up at the hotel. With no space available in the inauguration crush, Booth had generously shared his room with another man too: John Parker Hale Wentworth, a visitor from California who was the cousin of Booth's secret fiancée.

As usual, McCullough burst into Booth's room without knocking. This time, he got a shock. His friend was sitting alone, "booted, spurred, gauntlets on his hands, and a great revolver before him, and his mouth was working and his eyes staring on vacancy." For the rest of Inauguration Day, Booth continued to act strangely. "All that day he was saying queer, luney things," McCullough said.

His friends had become increasingly concerned about Booth's strange behavior in recent months. He had some new obsession that McCullough could not quite fathom. McCullough had returned to their room several times to find Booth, for example, conversing with "ill-dressed, lowering fellows." On those occasions, Booth had quickly hustled McCullough out, telling him, "John, you don't want to know those country operators in oil." To be sure, Booth had invested some of the proceeds of his lucrative acting career in the extremely risky enterprise of oil exploration, teaming up with three men—the manager of the Cleveland Academy of Music, John Ellsler; a Cleveland capitalist named George Paunell; and a gambler and former prizefighter, Thomas Mears—to form the Dramatic Oil Company. Booth had even gone out to Pennsylvania in 1864 to work the field himself, in overalls and boots. But the grubby and downcast men around him in Washington of late, federal authorities later discovered, had nothing to do with oil.

Sometime before the inauguration, Booth had also "imposed on my good nature," McCullough recounted, "by making me get on a horse" and join him for a lengthy ride around the city, closely investigating its forts, ferries, and bridges. For some reason, Booth was looking for a way to make a quick escape from Washington. "Now, Johnny, if a man was to get in a tight place and have to break out of this city, *there* would be one opportunity," Booth pointed out excitedly. "What do I want to see that for, Booth? I prefer to leave by the cars," McCullough joked. A comfortable seat in a railroad car did not skin his backside as riding around on a truculent horse did. Booth, by contrast, was in hardened riding form—in excellent shape altogether. He had a membership at Brady's Gymnasium on Louisiana Avenue near the Canterbury Theatre and "was always practicing gymnastics," McCullough recalled.

Other friends had found Booth behaving oddly that winter, charming and kind one moment, fierce and churlish the next. Any political discussion was certain to set him off into a tirade against the tyrannical Lincoln and his brutal destruction of the Founders' America. An acquaintance from oil country in Pennsylvania long remembered the snarling statement Booth made there before the November election: "I would rather have my right arm cut off at the shoulder than see Lincoln president again." Booth seemed no happier months later, as Lincoln's second inauguration approached. In late February, Booth's friend and business adviser Joe Simonds wrote to him, "I hardly know what to make of you this winter, so different from your usual self. What is the matter?" Was a degenerative disease wasting his brain and changing his personality, making him snappish and turning him into a megalomaniac? His development of a large neck tumor that had to be painfully removed, rashes over his right elbow, pain in the chest, growing hoarseness, and stark mood shifts were all possible symptoms of syphilis, rampant in the nineteenth century, particularly among men who frequented prostitutes. But no one really knew what was wrong with him. For some time, Booth had been telling his friends he was "going to do something that would bring his name forward in history." Just what dramatic act he had planned for Inauguration Day remained a secret to all but a small circle. Whatever it was, he was determined that it would propel him into the history books. "Booth was crazy for fame," said his friend John T. Ford, the owner of Ford's Theatre.

By March 1865, John Wilkes Booth already enjoyed far greater fame than most men would ever see. A man of no more than average height, he struck the public as amazingly good-looking, and his looks put him in stark contrast to the gangling, haggard, slouching president he detested. Many had spoken of Booth as a god. Ford asserted that Booth had "Apollo's own grace about him," and when Booth walked down the street, four out of five people "would turn to look at him again." At his hotel, Ford recalled, women guests gathered at the foot of the staircase in the dining room "just to see him come down stairs." When Booth approached the theater on Tenth Street near F Street, a short walk from the National Hotel, Ford's younger brother Harry liked to call out: "There comes the handsomest man in Washington!" But he was more than that. Harry found him to be "one of the simplest, sweetest-dispositioned, and most lovable men" he ever knew, a sentiment echoed by actor John Mathews, who called Booth "a most winning, captivating man." He was "a marvelously clever and amusing demigod," according to theater callboy and sometime actor William J. Ferguson. Booth adored children, and they loved him. His sister Asia wrote that John poked fun at her for having so many "little trotters," but Booth greatly enjoyed his visits with children. "He lies on the floor and rolls over with them like a child," she noted. Booth went out of his way to make Joseph Hazelton, the eleven-year-old program boy at Ford's Theatre, feel special. He liked to tousle his hair and slip him money for a stick of candy. Finding the boy to be a bit ragged, Booth took him to a nearby shop to buy him a new cloth cap "more befitting his professional duties" than the one he was wearing.

He was fond of stopping in at John Deery's billiards saloon, located above the lobby of Grover's Theatre in Washington, to enjoy male camaraderie and the game that Lincoln also found engaging—"the only non-utilitarian thing that I know of Lincoln indulging in," said the president's lawyer friend Henry C. Whitney. Like countless others, the proprietor adored Booth. "He was as handsome as a young God," Deery said, "but his appearance was not more seductive than his manners." Booth was devoid of the "artificiality and staginess" common to actors. "In his ways with his intimates he was as simple and affectionate as a child," Deery said. He "cast a spell over most men with whom he came in contact, and I believe all women without exception." Moreover, Booth "could absorb an astonishing quantity of liquor and still retain the bearings of a gentleman." He was particularly fond of the popular drink known as a brandy smash, mixed with sugar syrup, fresh mint leaves, and a slice of fruit. Deery saw him consume a quart of brandy at his bar in less than two hours. "He frequently remarked that he never got drunk in his legs, that he never staggered," said James Shettel, a friend and boarding-school classmate.

Booth's looks and charisma proved immensely lucrative. He boasted of earning $20,000 a year on the stage, a staggering sum in the 1860s, when a carpenter might make $625 annually. He dressed in the most expensive clothing, fashionably cut, with colorful ties, high silk hats, and kid gloves. He spent money in top photographic studios, posing in his costly attire and having the images printed up as *cartes de visite*, little cards, two by three and a half inches, to be distributed to his many friends. In the slang of the time he was a "spad"—a dandy or ladies' man—"and he was a matinee idol," Shettel said. "Seldom has the stage seen a more impressive, or a more handsome, or a more impassioned actor," actor Charles Wyndham recalled. "Picture to yourself Adonis, with high forehead, ascetic face corrected by rather full lips, sweeping black hair, a figure of perfect youthful proportions and the most wonderful black eyes in the world. . . . At all times his eyes were his striking features but when his emotions were aroused they were like living jewels. Flames shot from them."

At the time, American theaters provided entertainment-starved city dwellers with a full night of drama, comedy, adventure, and, often, fetching female dancers. Critic, writer, and director Augustin Daly, who introduced the legendary plot device of a villain tying a damsel to railroad tracks, described the extensive bill of Booth's day. For twenty-five cents, theatergoers could take in a "five-act tragedy, then a *pas seul* by a favorite danseuse, perhaps a comic song, and the whole to conclude with a rattling farce or a gorgeous extravaganza."

Acting was in Booth's blood. He was the son of an even more famous thespian, one of America's legendary actors, English-born Junius Booth, a mentally troubled man whose manic performances at New York's Bowery Theatre captivated, among thousands, Walt Whitman. The quirky Brooklyn poet and journalist considered Junius an inspired genius, "by far the greatest histrion I have ever seen in my life." The elder Booth introduced an intense style of acting—"electric personal idiosyncrasy," Whitman called it. "The words fire, energy, *abandon*, found in him unprecedented meanings," the poet wrote, leading crowds to erupt in "those long-kept-up tempests of hand-clapping peculiar to the Bowery." Whitman drew inspiration from Booth's vitality for his own exuberant, histrionic poetry in *Leaves of Grass*.

After Junius Booth's death in 1852, John's older brother Edwin became arguably the most successful actor in the United States, outshining even John. Edwin had spent much of his boyhood traveling from city to city with his father, learning the acting trade. He grew up to be a Union man and a strong Lincoln supporter. John, by contrast, had spent much of his youth on the family's rural Maryland farm, working with black slaves and steeping himself in Southern culture. When John set out to be an actor himself, he relied more on his aura and his name than his acting skills. While Edwin squeezed the brilliance out of Shakespeare's complex characters, John was bold, impulsive, untutored, so fond of swashbuckling action scenes that he sometimes injured his fellow actors with his sword and even knocked them off the stage. His fellow oil investor Ellsler thought John the more dynamic actor. "John has more of the old man's power in one performance than Edwin can show in a year. He has the fire, the dash, the touch of *strangeness*." After watching one of Booth's wild bits one night, Ellsler asked whether he had rehearsed it. "No, I didn't rehearse it," Booth replied. "It just came to me in the scene, and I couldn't help doing it. But it went all right, didn't it?"

Whitman, hearing John Wilkes Booth's acting praised, checked out his Richard III performance at his New York debut on March 17, 1862. He was dismayed. "It is about as much like his father's, as the wax bust of Henry Clay, in the window down near Howard street, a few blocks below the theatre, is like the genuine orator in the Capitol, when his best electricity was flashing alive in him and out of him," the poet lamented. Lincoln's secretary John Hay believed the young Booth's appeal "lay rather in his romantic beauty of person, than in any talent or industry he possessed." Another unimpressed theatergoer reported to his wife: "Did not like him at all. He rants & his face has no more expression than a board fence." Shettel concluded that John was too impulsive to work at his craft. "In truth, he would not study, would not exert himself, would not apply himself, but he would skim over a part and improvise," causing confusion onstage because other actors would miss their cues. In 1864, Shettel recounted, the great Shakespearean actor Edwin Forrest, an ornery perfectionist, was performing in Baltimore when a supporting player fell ill. When someone suggested sending for Booth in nearby Washington, Forrest exploded, insisting he would not "tread the boards with that G— d— spad!"

Forrest had a point. Booth's craving for constant excitement often overwhelmed his devotion to acting. While performing in Richmond before the war, for example, he left his company in the lurch after a thunderous political development. In October 1859, abolitionist John Brown and a small band of supporters raided a federal arsenal at Harpers Ferry, Virginia (now West Virginia), intending to distribute rifles and pikes to slaves to ignite a race war and win their freedom. Brown, who saw himself as the agent of God's avenging justice, was a friend and longtime confidant of Frederick Douglass, and Northern abolitionists had secretly funded the ludicrous plot. Though the episode ended quickly after a company of marines led by Robert E. Lee surrounded the arsenal, a nation already on edge exploded with rage at the act of terrorism. Douglass ardently denied any role but, fearing his arrest as a co-conspirator, fled to Canada hastily and sailed for England. Meanwhile, the Virginia governor, having been warned that abolitionist vigilantes might attempt to thwart Brown's trial and punishment, called up local militia units to protect the rule of law. Booth, frantic to play a role in the unfolding drama, threw off his acting commitments and impulsively climbed aboard a train carrying militia members. Putting together a uniform from pieces he could buy or borrow, he was among the men standing guard on a lawn in Charles Town, Virginia, just up the hill from the courthouse, on December 2, 1859, watching Brown's execution. Though the abolitionist's act against the South infuriated him, Booth never forgot Brown's stoicism and courage on the gallows. "He was a brave old man," Booth told his sister Asia; "his heart must have broken when he felt himself deserted." Many were similarly struck by Brown's demeanor at the hour of his death. The *Brooklyn Daily Eagle* contrasted the "Roman firmness" of the stern abolitionist with "the flight of the skulking and cowardly negro, Douglass, who promised to stand by him." Whether Douglass had made such a promise or not, he survived the mob's flaring lust for revenge to carry on his fight for freedom.

For all his passion, Booth declined to enlist with the rebels after war broke out, unlike thousands of pro-Confederacy men from his border state of Maryland. He did not see himself as front-line cannon fodder. Rather, Booth believed he could use his wealth, position, and personality to advance the South's cause in more significant ways. "My brains are worth twenty men, my money worth a hundred," he told his sister. "I have a free pass everywhere; my profession, my name, is my passport." For a long time, though, he did not seem to do much more to serve the South than to reap the rewards of acting and castigate Lincoln.

In November 1863, after more than two years of slaughter and misery had thinned the South's armies, Booth was safely in Washington, starring with Clara Morris in the play *The Marble Heart* at Ford's Theatre. The stunningly attractive and vivacious teenager was utterly smitten with her costar. "He was so young, so bright, so gay, so kind," Morris recalled, marveling over "the ivory pallor of his skin, the inky blackness of his densely thick hair, the heavy lids of his glowing eyes . . . [that] gave a touch of mystery to his face." He was "truly beautiful." The critics were almost as effusive. Booth brought "many of his best qualities as an artist" to the role of "romantic young sculptor," the *National Republican* reported. "The part is exceedingly picturesque and engaging, but Mr. Booth, by his earnestness, his vigorous grasp of genius, and his fervor of style, invests it with an interest beyond the author's ideal, and claims in the result the most brilliant honors of his art. The role is peculiarly well fitted to Booth, and it is not to be wondered at that he has achieved in its embodiment his richest distinctions." Washington's *Evening Star* praised Booth's "fine, expressive face . . . and a voice both forcible and musical." On November 9, 1863, three days before Kate Chase's wedding and ten days before the delivery of the Gettysburg Address, a White House party made up of Abraham and Mary Lincoln and aides John Nicolay and John Hay set out to Ford's Theatre to see what all the fuss was about. Lincoln tended to find Shakespeare's harrowing explorations of human nature far more diverting than such light modern plays. Hay panned Booth's performance in his diary. "Rather tame than otherwise," he wrote.

Women were far less prone to dismiss Booth's qualities. In restaurants, waitresses crowded "round him like doves about a grain basket," Morris recounted. Hotel maids were "known to enter his room and tear asunder the already made-up bed, that the 'turn-over' might be broader by a thread or two, and both pillows slant at the perfectly correct angle. At the theater, good heaven! As the sunflowers turn upon their stalks to follow the beloved sun, so old and young, our faces smiling, turned to him." In sum, she said, "It is scarcely an exaggeration to say the sex was in love with John Booth." Julia Ward Howe, the middle-aged author of

"The Battle Hymn of the Republic," spied him in the chapel at Mount Auburn Cemetery in Cambridge, Massachusetts, at the funeral of his sister-in-law, and described him as "a young man of remarkable beauty." He received piles of passionate letters from grown women—"and, alas! girls, you may well believe were legion," Morris noted. While he saved the letters, Booth chivalrously cut their authors' names from the bottom and destroyed those scraps, to shield the women's reputations. "They are harmless now, little one," he told Morris, pointing to the pile of letters. "Their sting lies in the tail!" When one actor jovially picked up one of the letters to read aloud the titillating details of the writer's desire, noting that the identity was safely gone, Booth interceded. "The woman's folly is no excuse for our knavery—lay the letter down, please!"

Booth's endless affairs with dazzled young women complicated his life to no end. In late 1860, in Montgomery, Alabama, he took up with Louise Catherine Wooster, a "strikingly handsome" eighteen-year-old who had been busily working as a prostitute for three years. "I was young, rather pretty and had a sweet disposition. Soon, I became quite a favorite," she explained. Still, Louise hoped to escape the trade, with John's help. "Oh! How I loved him," she recalled. "We were never to part, he said. He had advised me to adopt a theatrical career. Then we would always be together." But as the war approached, Booth packed his bags and headed north alone. In April 1861, in Albany, a young actress, Henrietta Irving, slashed his forehead with a knife during a quarrel about his philandering. He bandaged his head and returned to his mother's home to heal. Luckily for the actor, the resulting scar was near his hairline. In wartime Washington, Booth regularly visited the upscale house of prostitution at 62 Ohio Avenue in the heart of Hooker's Division, a small Class 1 operation owned by an established Baltimore madam named Mrs. Starr. The actor grew found of her daughter, a pretty and petite blonde named Nellie, who also went by the names Ella Turner and Fannie Harrison. Born to an unknown father, Ella claimed to be nineteen or twenty years old in 1865 and said that Booth had been visiting her for three years. A pleading note from her was found in his trunk:

My Darling Baby

Please call this evening or as soon as you receive this note. I will not detain you five minutes—for gods sake.

Yours Truly,

E.T.

If you will not come write a note the reason why

Washington Feb. 7th

While dealing with the desperate entreaties of a prostitute, Booth was cultivating what he considered a much more serious attachment. Lucy Lambert Hale was a young woman of high social status, seemingly above a common actor. But Booth employed his looks, wealth, and charm to infiltrate her world, for purposes that initially may have had little to do with romance. "He was a welcome guest in the highest circles of society and ingratiated himself with ladies of distinction," his sister Asia Booth Clarke proudly declared. "From them he gathered much to serve his purpose," she said. While engaged in his schemes to aid the South, he was, typically, swept up by passion and "undesignedly fell in love with a senator's daughter."

Lucy's father, John Parker Hale—"well-looking elderly gentleman, tall and portly, of ruddy countenance, pleasing and intellectual features, and a particularly fine head," according to John Hay—held views that could not have been further removed from Booth's. Feisty and opinionated, Hale was an outright abolitionist. He had persevered through years of struggle in New Hampshire over the issue of slavery, finding an implacable foe in Franklin Pierce, who resolutely supported the South's cause on the pragmatic grounds of keeping the Democratic Party—and the country—from tearing itself apart. When the Democrats decided to eliminate Hale for his heretical views, he refused to go quietly, instead embarking on what the press dubbed "the Hale Storm of 1845," addressing meetings in every city and town in New Hampshire about the grave wrong of enslaving human beings. A. P. Putnam, a student at Pembroke Academy, long remembered Hale's courage in championing freedom against the Democratic establishment. "To all human seeming, it meant political ostracism and ruin. Few would have ventured the contest, even for dear Liberty's sake, so proud and tyrannous and fierce was the power which was then in rule," Putnam recalled. "It thrills me, even now, to recall the lofty and courageous spirit with which he threw down the gauntlet, and went before the people with his magnificent appeal." Hale improbably won so many hearts and minds that, in 1846, the legislature elected him to the U.S. Senate. Decades later, Frederick Douglass described Hale's "moral heroism" as "more sublime" than that of virtually any "patriot, statesman, or philanthropist of our times."

Among the senator's greatest admirers was Walt Whitman, who marveled over Hale's talent for connecting with people. Even as an old man, Whitman remembered Hale's powerful voice. "There is a mysterious, wonderful, quality in the human voice which no plummet has yet sounded—to which literature has not done any sort of justice—as it could not, I suppose," he said. He cited three speakers in his lifetime who possessed an astounding ability to move listeners: the poet Alfred, Lord Tennyson, the Kentucky abolitionist Cassius Clay, and John P. Hale.

In 1852, antislavery Democrats, organizing as the Free Democrats Party, asked Hale to be their presidential candidate. He was prepared to decline, when he received a letter from Whitman. The journalist-poet argued that Hale could create a "real live Democratic party . . . a renewed and vital party, fit to triumph over the effete and lethargic organization now so powerful and so unworthy." While Whitman admitted that he did not know the great men of Washington, "I know the people." In particular, he knew the "real heart of this mighty city" of New York, where he spent much of his time—"the tens of thousands of young men, the mechanics, the writers, &c. &c." Beneath "all the bosh of the regular politicians, there burns, almost with fierceness, the divine fire which more or less, during all ages, has only waited a chance to leap forth and confound the calculations of tyrants, hunkers, and all their tribe."

Hale did decide to run, winning the endorsement of Douglass, among other leading abolitionists. But the divine fire did not catch. He captured only 5 percent of the national vote, while his nemesis, Pierce, was handily elected president. Yet Hale was not finished. Two years later, he won back his Senate seat, then joined the new Republican Party, rising to prominence with antislavery senators Salmon P. Chase, William Seward, and Charles Sumner. The South regarded Hale as an agitator bent on destroying the United States. On the Senate floor, Henry S. Foote of Mississippi openly advocated his lynching. "I invite him to Mississippi," Foote said, "and will tell him beforehand, in all honesty, that he could not go ten miles into the interior before he would grace one of the tallest trees of the forest with a rope around his neck, with the approbation of every honest and patriotic citizen; and that, if necessary, I should myself assist in the operation." But he was not safe even in New Hampshire. Arriving at the depot in his town of Dover in August 1861, he was set upon by a drunk, who was furious that the abolitionists had precipitated the horrors of civil war. "You are one of the men who have brought all this trouble upon us," the man said, punching Hale in the face and knocking off his hat. "Get out of my way," Hale said, walking away without returning the blow. John Hay noted that Hale built a reputation in the Senate for "ceaseless and merciless attacks" on those in power. "He has been fighting so long for the rights of the down trodden minority, that he has fallen in love with the very idea of hopeless championship."

Leading up to this day of Lincoln's second inauguration, Hale had suffered through some particularly stormy months, including the loss of his Senate seat when the New Hampshire legislature turned against him. He antagonized the party's establishment by accusing Navy Secretary Gideon Welles of nepotism in awarding contracts. When the press broke a story that Hale had used his own navy contacts to improperly help a legal client, Welles gloated with bitter satisfaction: "This loud-mouthed paragon, whose boisterous professions of purity, and whose immense indignation against a corrupt world were so great that he delighted to misrepresent and belie them in order that his virtuous light might shine distinctly, is beginning to be exposed and rightly understood. But the whole is not told and never will be—he is a mass of corruption." Having lost his election, Hale lobbied Lincoln for the $12,000-a-year job of minister to Spain, as a reward for his years of service to the Republican Party and the cause of freedom. At the same time, Booth, another man in love with the idea of hopeless championship, was lobbying Hale's daughter Lucy for her love.

For years, Senator Hale had been living in hotels in Washington with his two high-spirited and attractive older daughters. They often stayed at the National Hotel, a crowded and noisy house that was not always to Hale's liking. In early October 1863, the National afforded the senator the use of its best chamber, the President's Room, about which he complained: "Although it was a very nice room . . . there was no mosquito net over the bed & the mosquitoes annoyed me all night till broad day light." Hale decided to grab his valise and march up to Rebecca Scott's boardinghouse at the corner of Seventh and G, where he "had a very nice room & a bed entirely encompassed by a spacious net suspended from the ceiling overhead." Though he returned to the big hotel later, he still seemed of two minds, warning his wife: "I do not believe we shall be satisfied with the National Hotel. . . . The House is very full and a great proportion of the guests seem rowdies. I think I shall be looking out for new quarters but shall not make any change until I hear from you." Fatefully, the family decided to stay. With its excellent kitchen, superb stock of wine, prominent clientele, and many rooms, it seemed a better place for the Hales than a cramped boardinghouse.

From this home base, Lucy Lambert Hale emerged as one of the leading ladies of Washington, popular at parties and dances and celebrated in the press. "An unusually large number of brilliant belles, who seem to have been born for the ball-room, flutter and flirt nightly amid showers of smiles and full ranks of bright buttons," wrote one society reporter in early 1862, leading off with the presence of "John P. Hale, with his accomplished lady" and "two handsome daughters" at one of the "pleasant hops" at the National Hotel. The party included the president's son Robert Lincoln, representing "the White House and Harvard College." These were more than dances, the reporter added. "Plots are planned, schemes are scented, offices are obtained, matches made and money won . . . and, as in former courts in old countries so in this—the paramount influences of our women are most eagerly sought—and most effective when obtained." When not attending parties, Lucy did what she could to support the U.S. Sanitary Commission, which was striving to improve the ghastly conditions for wounded soldiers, whom she visited near the front lines in Virginia with her mother, escorted at one point by an old beau, Captain Oliver Wendell Holmes Jr. She became close with the unmarried offspring of two other Republican senators who lived at the hotel—Mary Eunice Harlan, daughter of James Harlan of Iowa; and Mary Douglas Chandler, daughter of Zachariah Chandler of Michigan. In January 1864, the Hale women dazzled at a ball held at the National Hotel celebrating the thirty-seventh anniversary of the admission of the Chandlers' home state of Michigan into the Union, according to the Washington *Evening Star*: "Among the ladies present specially notable for elegance of costume or attractiveness of person, were Mrs. Senator Hale, and the Miss Hales." While the "pretty women were not all of Michigan," the reporter quipped, they had an obvious affinity for the state "and especially for her young men." The hotel's ballroom was festooned with the "gloriously and honorably tattered" battle flags of the Fourth and Twenty-Fourth Michigan regiments, which had done "sharp work" early in the war at the Gettysburg bloodbath. General Alfred Pleasonton, a dashing cavalry officer, "led off the first dance with Miss [Lucy] Hale, youngest daughter of Senator Hale; and the dancing was kept up from thence with spirit until the morning hours."

Lucy had spent much of her youth teasing, tantalizing, and torturing a series of young men, seemingly enticing the opposite sex with an ease, skill, and fascination comparable to Booth's. Holmes, later a justice of the U.S. Supreme Court, had been among the smitten. He wrote to the teenage Lucy, confessing to "a slightly jealous disposition" and expressing his relief that moral standards in her New Hampshire hometown prevented her from "riding with young gentlemen" in his absence. "Please give my respects to all the young ladies at Dover & thereabouts but to none of the male species," Holmes wrote. When Lucy noted in a response that she had several "correspondents," he protested: "How many young gentlemen do you keep going at once on an average? It is not so agreeable to reflect on the various rivals who are at the same time receiving as great or greater ? share of the imperial favor." Holmes urged her to remember their times together—"the baths the walks the night on the piazza & the last night, & more than all the [railroad] cars."

Two years later, another ardent young lover foundered on the rocks of her indifference. After Lucy expressed dismay over his confession of romantic feelings for her, the suitor thanked the nineteen-year-old for "the kind tone" of her words, "characteristic of a lovely woman." He further spouted: "My vocabulary is wanting in expressions to make known the intense gratification it afforded me to be the recipient of a letter penned by the fairest hand imaginable." With heavy-handed wit, he wished the daughter of an abolitionist senator a happy anniversary of John Brown's execution. His excessive attention got him nowhere, though she carefully preserved his letter and similar attestations of desire.

Late in 1862, a soldier stationed in Houston undertook the "charming privilege" of asking her a question: "Do you still cast a thought on your friends in the South? I am anxious to learn whether you entertain in regard to us the same kindly feelings, as in days of yore." A recruiting officer in Augusta, Maine, gushed over seeing her during a visit to Boston in late 1864: "I am passionately fond of the beauties of art (and nature) and I assure you that two of the most delightful hours I passed in Boston, and indeed two of the most charming I've known for months, were those passed in admiration of that beautiful picture at which I gazed so attentively as to almost cause it to blush." Years later, John Hay—always susceptible to the charms of Washington's young women—wrote to Lucy, wondering aloud whether

> there were anyone else in the world just like you; one of equal charm, equal power of gaining hearts, and equal disdain of the hearts you gain. The last glance of those mysterious blue-gray eyes fell upon a dozen or so of us and everybody but me thought the last glance was for him. I have known you too long. Since

you were a school-girl—yet even in those early days you were as puzzling in your apparent frankness and real reserve as you are today. . . . You know how I love and admire you. I do not understand you, nor hope to, nor even wish to. You would lose to me something of your indefinable fascination if I knew exactly what you meant.

Even Robert Lincoln, the president's oldest son, seemed drawn to Lucy. An 1878 newspaper article, supposedly based on the recollections of an anonymous socialite who had resided at the National Hotel, claimed that he became infatuated with her, stirring Booth's jealousy and inflaming his anger at Robert's father. The article seems far-fetched in any number of ways—it even got Lucy's first name wrong—and Robert Lincoln was quick to deny it. But, in truth, he did know Lucy and her circle at the hotel. He sent Miss Hale fragrant bouquets of flowers from the White House conservancy and inscribed a book of patriotic poetry for her. One can imagine that Senator Hale would have far preferred that his daughter take up with the president's son rather than an impulsive actor of bad reputation. But by the second inauguration, young Lincoln had fallen in love—not with Lucy but with her flirtatious friend Mary Harlan, the beautiful, blond, and blue-eyed daughter of the Iowa senator, a match Mary Lincoln had aggressively encouraged by planning outings that brought the two together.

John Wilkes Booth, on the other hand, shared the "indefinable fascination" for Lucy that Hay, Holmes, and numerous other men had felt. On Valentine's Day, 1862, the young lady received a thrilling letter from an anonymous admirer:

You resemble in a most remarkable degree a lady, very dear to me, now dead and your close resemblance to her surprised me the first time I saw you.

This must be my apology for any apparent rudeness noticable. —To see you has indeed afforded me a melancholly pleasure, if you can conceive of such, and should we never meet nor I see you again—believe me, I shall always associate you in my memory, with her, who was very beautiful, and whose face, like your own I trust, was a faithful index of gentleness and amiability.

With a Thousand kind wishes for your future happiness I am, to you—

A Stranger

It was, some analysts believe, from the pen of Booth. If he did not write that one to Lucy, he evidently wrote another. Booth's brother Junius reported, in a letter to their sister Asia, that John had kept him up until three thirty one night in February 1865 while struggling over a long Valentine's Day letter to Lucy, "every now and then using me as a Dictionary." During the winter of 1864–65, the *Springfield* (Massachusetts) *Republican*'s Washington reporter noted, it was well known that Booth "was very intimate with wives and daughters of prominent Republican Senators and Representatives at the National Hotel. . . . They must have known that he was not only a secessionist, but a gamester and whoremonger. Such was his general reputation, but because he was handsome, and could spout Shakespeare by the hour, these ladies permitted intimacies." A letter from Lucy to her mother on New Year's Day, 1864, her twenty-third birthday, suggests the whirlwind of her social activities. "Last evening, the ladies of this Hotel had a dancing party in the parlors and it was a pleasant affair. Tonight there is to be a reception at the Speaker's, Mr. [Schuyler] Colfax. . . . We are invited to dine at Becca Scott's tomorrow (Saturday)—and I shall probably attend Mrs. Lincoln's reception [at the White House] before going. Today, we are invited to take a drive with a lady friend. . . . I have just returned from my ride and enjoyed it very much. We rode five or six miles out of town."

At some point, Lucy began riding out with Booth. They fell deeply in love, an "attachment," Booth's sister Asia wrote, that "resulted in a secret and conditional engagement." Later, Booth's friend John McCullough revealed that "there were two young women in Washington who were enamored of Booth and myself," of such "high connections" that "their names required to be protected." Lucy seems a plausible identification for one of the women. Whether her sister Lizzie was the other, as some have alleged, is unclear. "We used to meet them in Baltimore," McCullough disclosed, using the code names "Jack" and "Bob" in their telegrams: "Jack and Bob are here; come over." Booth could not help gushing about his beloved. That spring, while visiting with a friend, actor Sam Chester, he had boasted that he was engaged to be married to a young woman from a good family and had fervently kissed a ring on his little finger that she had given him. By March 1865, word was getting out about their relationship. When Junius asked his brother why he was in Washington instead of focusing on his oil investments, Booth answered "that he was in love with a lady in Washington & that was worth more to him than all the money he could make." Booth's mother, Mary Ann, wrote to him: "The secret you have told me, is not exactly a secret, as Edwin was told by someone, you were paying great attention to a young lady in Washington . . . and if the lady in question is all you desire—I see no cause why you should not try to secure her. Her father . . . would he give his consent?"

The answer is not clear. What does seem probable, though, is that Senator Hale yielded to Lucy's entreaties for treasured VIP passes to Lincoln's second inauguration, one of which she gave to Booth, providing him a precious opportunity to draw close to the president on that day. (The senator also requested from John Nicolay, on March 2, the president's autograph on two pictures at the request of an unnamed "lady friend of mine.")

Booth's friends later heard stories that might explain why the actor was in a frenzied state on the morning of March 4. "He . . . meditated seizing [President Lincoln] in his own carriage as he returned from the second inauguration, and driving that carriage off pell-mell," John Ford said. John McCullough had a similar impression: "It was the day, as afterwards appeared, when he had designed to abduct Mr. Lincoln."

CHAPTER 8

THE BLIGHTING PESTILENCE

Saturday, March 4, 1865

Nearly two hundred miles away from Washington, at a venerable plantation named Vaucluse in Campbell County, Virginia, the Reverend John Blair Dabney toiled quietly on the passionate sermon he would deliver on Sunday. The great old house, "although far removed from railroads, stage-coaches and public conveyances," overflowed with company before the war, a neighborhood girl named Letitia M. Burwell recalled fondly. "For the Vaucluse girls were so bright, so fascinating, and so bewitching pretty, that they attracted a concourse of visitors, and were sure to be belles wherever they went." Dabney, who had graduated first in his class at Princeton, became a lawyer and tried his hand at literature, his elegant writing appearing alongside Edgar Allan Poe's in the *Southern Literary Messenger*. In 1856, he turned to a life of God. Since then, this "pure-hearted Christian" had traveled weary miles on horseback in the county's Moore Parish to tend to four country churches as an Episcopal priest. He served "without money and without price," Burwell noted, quoting the Book of Isaiah: "Surely his reward is in Heaven." Dabney's bright and dashing son, Chiswell, had quit the University of Virginia in 1861, at seventeen, to enlist in the Confederate forces and had risen to captain and aide-de-camp to flamboyant cavalry general James Ewell Brown "Jeb" Stuart before being wounded in the right arm. Regarded as "the Adonis of the staff . . . remarkably handsome," the boy still served the cause. For the past four years, the

Reverend John Blair Dabney had urged his flock to remain steadfast as Northern invaders slaughtered their sons and tried to force them back into the Union rather than let them live in peace in the new republic they had created.

But the minister's prayers had come to naught. Abraham Lincoln, backed by the enormous wealth and power of the North, was drawing closer to victory, and the sixty-nine-year-old Dabney conceded that God might let the enemy win—a turn of events so painful and incomprehensible that he thought it might prefigure the Second Coming. Whatever misery awaited his people, Dabney could not accept that the brutal conquest of the South meant God had blessed Lincoln's diabolical work—his destruction of the last vestige of the Founders' America on the continent and his raising of a new federal behemoth in its place. Surely, the Almighty would ultimately punish the Northern oppressors for their crimes. "They may succeed in extirpating or subduing us by their superior power in giving peace to the South by reducing it to a desert," the priest sermonized. "They may be permitted by a righteous providence to inflict on us unspeakable calamities; [but] when the victims of their savage warfare shall have vanished from the earth, they may be made to suffer untold evils for their cruelty, intolerance, and pride in the destruction of their government, [with] the dissipation of their vaunted wealth."

On this same Saturday, Emma Holmes, twenty-six, sat down with her diary and pen in devastated Camden, South Carolina, and filled page after page with fresh memories of the last two weeks of anguish, an experience so otherworldly that it now seemed "like a dream or a nightmare." The daughter of a once wealthy plantation owner and physician, she had left her beautiful seaside city of Charleston in 1862 after a fire had consumed the family mansion, and now taught eight children in the wealthy household of John Mickle. In recent days, General William Tecumseh Sherman's troops had rampaged through Camden, and waves of soldiers had ransacked the Mickle mansion for two harrowing days.

"Not the smallest box even of children's baby clothes or toys escaped their hands, save the top of my hat box," Holmes wrote. Soldiers rolled cartloads of meat, turkey, and chickens away from the estate, along with eighty bales of cotton. The troops could not get their hands on the family silver, however; it had been buried in the woods.

Lincoln had resolved, through Sherman, to drive the war deep into the South, a psychological as well as geographical invasion, demonstrating to Confederate leaders and the civilians who supported them that Union forces could now freely enter their homes, ransack their goods, burn their mills and factories, abuse their slaves, and terrorize their wives and children. "Thousands of people may perish," Sherman admitted, but Southerners would finally realize "that war means something else than vain glory and boasting. If Peace ever falls to their lot they will never again invite War." General Philip Sheridan had done much the same in devastating Virginia's once-fertile Shenandoah Valley, the main source of food for General Robert E. Lee's tattered army. Lincoln wanted to make it clear that further resistance was futile, and that this horrible war must end. Dexter Horton, an Indiana soldier in Sherman's army, wrote to his wife: "Our march over the country has been like the blighting pestilence, for we have taken or turned upside down everything before us."

The army's advance was teaching the South a hard lesson, but at a price of almost intractable bitterness. After Sherman's forces had looted her plantation in Covington, Georgia, Dolly Sumner wrote in her diary: "This ended the passing of Sherman's army by my place, leaving me thirty thousand dollars poorer than I was yesterday morning. And a much stronger Rebel!" While Lee remained a powerful symbol of virtuous manhood to Southerners, Sherman had become the indelible emblem of Northern cruelty. After taking Atlanta in September 1864, Sherman issued an order to civilians to leave their homes, whether they had anywhere to go or not. "If the people raise a howl against my barbarity and cruelty, I will answer that war is war, and not popularity-seeking," he explained to Major General Henry Halleck. "If they want peace, they and their relatives must stop the war."

Sherman's lean, hard veteran army of sixty thousand men—thinned out through medical examinations to leave only the strongest to march deep into a hostile South—was, in his view, "the bravest and best army that ever trod American soil." Confederate general Joseph E. Johnston conceded, "there had been no such army since the days of Julius Caesar." After breaking from its supply line and communications and marching through Georgia, destroying railroad tracks, mills, crops, repair shops—virtually anything that might sustain the South's war effort—Sherman's army had turned toward South Carolina, a target for special punishment, as the cradle of the rebellion. By then, Sherman's very name was enough to inspire terror. As his forces approached the capital city of Columbia, panicked people flooded the railroad station, desperate to escape. In the frenzy, train "car windows were smashed in, women and children pushed through, some head foremost, others feet foremost." Those left on the platform begged tearfully to be taken aboard cars already "jammed to suffocation," terrified they would be left to the savagery of the enemy.

When Sherman's men arrived, they broke into Columbia's stores and distributed the goods among themselves "right and left," a woman wrote to her daughter. Then they "found liquor and all became heartily drunk." Fires caught in several areas and, fed by a strong wind, turned the city into an inferno that night. Many families found themselves burned out of their homes in the cold of winter. One soldier, with tears in his eyes, told a family: "If I saw any rebels burning down my home as all of you are seeing us burning down yours, I would hate them all my lifetime." A Columbia girl, seventeen-year-old Emma LeConte, wrote in her diary that the word "Yankees" had now become "a synonym for *all* that is *mean*, despicable and abhorrent." She pondered their fate in a world ruled by a just God. "I wonder if the vengeance of heaven will not pursue such fiends! Before they came here I thought I hated them as much as was possible—now I know there are no limits to the feeling of hatred," she declared. "The fiends acted as if they were a deputation sent from Hell to destroy the Earth," reported the *Fairfield Courier*, published in Winnsboro, twenty-eight miles away. "Barbarians could not have completed their work with more satisfaction than did the *United States troops*—fighting under a flag that we once honored and loved but now made more cursed to us than the vilest reptile that inhabits this globe." Bent on revenge, Confederate guerillas who found any Union soldiers wandering away from the army were quick to force them to their knees and shoot them, slit their throats, or hang them in nearby trees. Yet Sherman marched on.

He was having an effect. South Carolina governor Andrew Magrath warned Jefferson Davis in early 1865 that the people's attitudes toward the war were changing. "It is not an unwillingness to oppose the enemy, but a chilling apprehension of the futility of doing so, which affects the people." Soldiers were peeling away from Lee's ranks outside Petersburg and heading home to defend their families. "The state of despondency that now prevails among our people is producing a bad effect upon the troops," Lee wrote to North Carolina governor Zebulon B. Vance in late February. "Desertions are becoming very frequent, and there is good reason to believe that they are occasioned to a considerable extent by letters written to the soldiers by their friends at home."

All the same, many Southern white women refused to concede that continued resistance was useless. Fiercely protective of their homes and culture, they would not accept that years of misery—all the destruction, deprivation, dismemberment, death—had been in vain. "With General Lee at our head," a mother wrote hopefully to her son, "we shall not be made slaves to these wretches." Near the end of Sherman's terrifying occupation of Camden, Emma Holmes let loose her frustration and fury when two reasonably well-behaved young soldiers entered her house, one from Illinois, one from Pennsylvania. "I fired volley after volley of rebel shot at them," she wrote. "In fact, I hurled so many keen sarcasms, such home thrusts, that the Pennsylvanian said 'I was the best rebel he had met, and that it was such women as I who kept up this war by urging on our brothers and friends.'"

After Sherman's scavengers departed, heading for fresh fields to destroy, Holmes hotly debated about the South's weak response with her neighbors and a young Confederate soldier named Crouch, who had been hiding from Sherman's men, knowing that they would either kill or imprison him. When the others told her that there were no men left to impede Sherman's march, she fumed: "If all the men who had taken to the woods to save themselves had formed bands & bushwhacked and harassed them at every step, the Yankees would not have walked like masters through the land." A man named Dr. Pickett explained that such action would only encourage Sherman to burn more houses. "Every boy capable of bearing a gun" ought to have turned out, Holmes shot back, insisting, "it was better they should die in the defense of their country than live under Yankee rule." Among the items the Yankee soldiers had stolen for no seeming purpose was a photograph of Emma and her friend Dora Furman, "taken . . . in the days of 'auld lang syne' & a memento of many happy hours." She found it "in the yard with the mark of a heel, where some Yankees had ground it under foot, crushing both ambrotype & outer glass of course into fragments—doubtless, with the Nero-like wish that Hydra headed secession might have been then & there crushed out."

By the time Holmes sat down to write her scornful assessment, the crusty Sherman, with his wrinkled, pockmarked face and patchy red beard, was fifty-five miles northeast, in Cheraw, South Carolina, the last town of any size south of the North Carolina border. In a drenching cold rain on Thursday, March 2, Union soldiers had driven back a thin force of Confederate defenders straight through Cheraw and then across the Pee Dee River. The Southern forces managed to burn the covered bridge behind them just as the Union men arrived. While Sherman's engineers were building pontoon bridges over the swift-running river, swollen from weeks of rain, his soldiers lingered in Cheraw for several days, throwing up tents in open spaces near the homes of well-to-do Southerners and making big fires out of nearby fences and carriages, while terrified women looked out of their windows. The little riverport town of a few thousand people, with convenient transportation on the wide Pee Dee River and the railroad line into Charleston, was important to the Confederate cause as "a manufacturing center for the rebel army," one soldier wrote in his diary. Sherman's efficient destroyers quickly put an end to Cheraw's days of supplying the Confederacy.

The forty-five-year-old general, beloved by his troops as "Uncle Billy," rode toward Cheraw on his handsome Lexington, Kentucky, horse in the drizzling rain on March 3, displaying none of the pomp of his high position. "His dress is as unassuming as the man. A field officer's coat without rank, low canvassed belt, hat with cord and none on his pants," noted one lieutenant. "There's not a thing of the military in his appearance." Another soldier, undeterred by the rules of spelling, observed colorfully in a letter home that when "you se him a riding a long you would think that he was somb oald plow jogger his head bent a little to one side with an oald stub of a sigar in his mouth." Though he was tough and bold, Sherman was given to terrible anxiety and had suffered a mental breakdown early in the war. He had formed a bond with Ulysses Grant, who preceded him in the command of the army. Both men shared a lack of pretension and a keen ability to think strategically, and both struggled with personal imperfections that had threatened their careers. "He stood by me when I was crazy and I stood by him when he was drunk," Sherman would say.

As he approached Cheraw, Sherman questioned a slave about the muddy road into the town, asking whether any guerrillas—the bushwackers Miss Holmes so yearned for—were around. "Oh! no, master, dey is gone two days ago," the man said, quipping, "you could have played cards on their coat-tails, dey was in such a hurry!" Shortly after the chat, another general came along, demanding that the black man explain what he was doing there. "Dey say Massa Sherman will be along soon!" he exclaimed. Amazed to discover that the battered man he had been chatting with was in fact the famous, fearsome general, the slave trotted alongside him into town, though Sherman observed, "he seemed to admire the horse more than the rider."

African Americans were closely studying the progress of this predatory army, which was inflicting great misery on their people while simultaneously advancing the cause of their freedom. Henry D. Jenkins, a slave on a South Carolina plantation, watched Union soldiers seize "money, silver, gold, jewelry, watches, rings, brooches, knives and forks, butter-dishes, waters, goblets and cups," as well as horses, sheep, cows, chickens and geese, corn in the crib, meat in the smokehouse—even the fishnet and the fish it had caught. All in all, he observed sardonically, Sherman's men "seemed more concerned 'bout stealin', than they was 'bout de Holy War for de liberation of de poor African slave people." Not that such stealing was official Union policy. Sherman and his command staff repeatedly stressed that looting of private homes or abuse of private citizens was not permitted. "I want the foragers . . . to be kept within reasonable bounds for the sake of discipline," Sherman emphasized in an order on February 23. "I will not protect them when they enter dwellings and commit common waste—as women's apparel, jewelry, and such things are not needed by our army; but they may destroy cotton and tobacco," which sustained the Confederate government. Still, the army had to live off the land to survive, and the seizure of provisions by groups of foragers inevitably led to other depredations. Moreover, soldiers who had suffered miserably for years and watched their brothers die in agony felt little sympathy for this proud population that had brought on secession and war. "South Carolina has commenced to pay an installment long overdue on her debt of justice and humanity," one soldier wrote in his journal.

Some members of the avenging army descended to rape. A doctor who observed the destruction of Columbia wrote that an "old negro woman" was "subjected to the most brutal indecency" by seven Union soldiers, who decided to "finish the old Bitch" by wrestling her into a ditch and holding her head underwater until she drowned. Another slave was raped in front of her white mistress. Naked bodies of black women who had been violated and killed were left around the city. Few soldiers seemed to engage in such conduct, and Southern propaganda may have exaggerated the horrors. Still, Union general Oliver O. Howard chided the army for disgraceful conduct that included "the robbing of some negroes and abusing their women." At the same time, some former slaves did brisk business as prostitutes. One soldier complained that "nothing but these damn negro wenches" were available for paid sex, and "I can't get it hard to go to them." Later he gave in, because all the white prostitutes along the march were dangerously diseased. Yet many of Sherman's men were sympathetic to black people and disgusted by what they saw of slavery in South Carolina. "We could not resist the conviction that a civilization in which a score of lives are impoverished and embittered, are blasted and debased and damned, in order that one life may be made sweeter, is a system of wrong that no language can properly condemn," an Ohio officer wrote.

As the soldiers marched through Georgia and South Carolina, thousands of hungry black men, women, and children, many clad in patched rags, abandoned their masters and their homes and followed the Union Army. In Sherman's eyes, they were nothing but a hindrance. The gruff general, in truth, regarded blacks as inferior to whites and resisted heavy pressure from President Lincoln, through his secretary of war, to enlist slaves as soldiers. "I like niggers well enough as niggers," Sherman wrote in a private letter, "but when fools & idiots try & make niggers better than ourselves, I have an opinion." David Conyngham, a *New York Herald* correspondent who had taken up a gun to fight with Sherman's men, offered a white soldier's impression of the "swarms of negroes" marching in front of, behind, and beside the great army. "All ages, sizes, and both sexes, were either mounted on broken-down mules or horses, or crammed into some rheumatic old coach, or were laboriously toiling along, faint and sweating, rendering the air not very pleasant to the olfactory nerves." Yet many African Americans embraced this army, however destructive or indifferent to their fate, as the instrument of their deliverance. Some pitched in with military intelligence, giving the army directions, explaining where the Southern forces were, and pointing out where goods were hidden. One veteran under Sherman saw an elderly couple insist on joining the throng, though both the soldiers and their master begged them to stay. "We must go," they said. "Freedom is as sweet to us as it is to you."

On March 3, as Congress scrambled to finish its business for the session, Sherman sought out one of Cheraw's finest houses, the property of a blockade-runner, which one of his generals, Frank Blair, had selected for his headquarters. The day before, Blair—a former congressman and a close political ally of Lincoln—had meted out rough justice in retaliation for a guerilla's shooting of one of his foragers. Blair intended to send a message to the Southern populace. A rebel prisoner was chosen by lot and, despite his protests that he had a large family of small children, stood up against a tree and shot to death by twelve men of the Thirtieth Illinois regiment. Now Blair himself was foraging in Cheraw. That Friday was "so wet that we all kept in-doors," Sherman recalled. Around noon he sat down for lunch with Blair in a basement dining room, where "the regular family table was spread with an excellent meal; and during its progress I was asked to take some wine, which stood upon the table in venerable bottles." It was so good, Sherman asked Blair where he got it. Blair jovially refused to tell him, asking only, "Do you like it?" After dinner, he sent to Sherman's tent, the general remembered, a case of "a dozen bottles of the finest madeira I ever tasted." Blair had "captured, in Cheraw, the wine of some of the old aristocratic families of Charleston, who had sent it up to Cheraw for safety." Before he was through with the town, Blair had collected some eight wagonloads of bottles intended for the South's most educated palates and distributed them "to the army generally, in very fair proportion," Sherman noted approvingly. He also provided Sherman with fine rugs taken from upper-crust homes to be used in tents or cut up as saddle blankets. It was all part of sending a message to the South.

That night, the general visited with a family, the Woodwards, whose home had been taken over for a regimental headquarters. Sherman laughed and talked easily with the Southerners, one officer who was present noted, but with every word he revealed "his implacable hatred of the rebel cause." When the head of the house asked the general where he would go next, Sherman answered, "I have about sixty thousand men out there, and I intend to go pretty much where I please."

Arriving in Cheraw the following day, Brigadier General William B. Hazen set up his headquarters in the fine home of a judge, an "amiable and respected citizen." It was equipped with "a very good library," Hazen recalled. Understandably nervous about its fate, the judge wanted to move the books to safety, "but I assured him that there was no occasion for doing so, as no one at my headquarters ever disturbed property in the houses we occupied, and that books would especially be held sacred." A few minutes after the judge left the room, Sherman arrived to greet his general. "He is a rapid and constant reader, and his eyes at once fell upon the library," Hazen recounted. At the time, Sherman was "taking a course" of the swashbuckling historical novels of Sir Walter Scott. After examining the shelves closely, Sherman "ended by appropriating such volumes of Scott's novels as he just then happened to want." Given his promise, Hazen was mortified, but Sherman "remarked in a pleasant way that it made no difference," since he would leave behind in Cheraw as many books as he took. While Hazen pondered how he would reimburse the judge, his orderly appeared with "a fine-looking, well-dressed young man" he had found hidden in the garret of the house, though the judge had insisted earlier that no one was concealed. He turned out to be the magistrate's son, a customs officer from Charleston. The sudden appearance of the prisoner "completely nonplussed" the judge, who might well have been executed for the cover-up. When Hazen informed him about the requisitioned books "and proposed that we should call it even," the judge "felt perfectly satisfied." On reflection, Hazen also gave his commander a pass. "No man ever lived who was more thoroughly free from venal taint than General Sherman; but he claimed, and perhaps rightly, that reading-matter was necessary food, and that we had a right to forage for it."

The soldiers sweeping through town also found a huge store of weapons: twenty-four cannons, two thousand muskets, and thirty-six barrels of gunpowder. One of the big guns bore a brass plate claiming it to be the cannon that started the war: FIRST GUN FIRED ON FORT SUMTER. That afternoon, Sherman devised a memorable way to celebrate Lincoln's inauguration. He ordered the big guns overloaded with powder. Calibrating the festivities to the minute Lincoln was to take the oath, Sherman had twenty-three of the cannons detonated, one by one, rattling the windows of Cheraw and sending the smell of exploded gunpower wafting over the town. The earsplitting, ground-shaking destruction was one more symbol of the Confederacy's enfeebled state and impending death. George N. Compton, an Illinois chaplain with Sherman's army, noted in his diary: "Old honest Abe is inaugurated today—God bless him & spare his life to see the close of the war." Jenkin Lloyd Jones, stationed hundreds of miles west in Chattanooga, Tennessee, with the Sixth Battery of the Wisconsin Artillery, sounded a similar note in his diary: "This is the day on which Abraham Lincoln is to be inaugurated. President for the second time. After four years tempestuous sailing 'mid terrible breakers he has carried the good old ship of state through. May his second voyage know more sunshine, and be as successful as before."

Two days later in Cheraw, in one of the freakish accidents incident to warfare, soldiers making their morning coffee carelessly ignited a little trail of gunpowder that led to an immense pile. The Confederate magazine blew up spectacularly, throwing dirt, rocks, and shot high into the sky in a mushroom cloud and setting the business district on fire. "The explosion shattered the windows of many houses and killed several Yankees," recalled Charles L. Prince, a boy of eleven at the time. One woman recalled that every window of her house was shattered, the shutters torn from their hinges, and plaster broken inside. "I was cooking our breakfast at the time, the pan I had on the fire was knocked out of my hand, things were hurled from one side of the room to the other. My poor child clung to me screaming."

It was all a fearful ordeal for the residents. "Those five days were my idea of hell," one woman remembered. "We were all helpless and in the power of an immense body of soldiers." Outside of town, both Pine Grove, the plantation of the Prince family, and the Woodlands, that of Charles Prince's uncle John A. Inglis, were destroyed. Inglis may have been a target; he had served as chairman of the committee that had drawn up South Carolina's ordinance of secession in December 1860. "Nothing left but ashes and chimneys," his daughter Laura Prince Inglis wrote. "My father's library of over four thousand volumes reduced to ashes. My five hundred dollar Steinway piano cut to pieces with axes, before starting the fire. The family portraits slit into ribbons with bayonets." Many years later, she told lurid stories of the occupation in private discussions, among them the tale that Yankee soldiers had ordered two young women to strip naked and play piano for them. "You'll never hear about that because Southern ladies would never disclose such public humiliation," she confided to a male friend.

Six miles outside of Cheraw, at a plantation named Cash's Depot, the Reverend John Bachman got a taste of Sherman's campaign, witnessing "the barbarities inflicted on the aged, the widow, the young and delicate females," as he put it in a letter to Jefferson Davis. Although then hiding in an obscure corner of the South, Dr. Bachman was an extraordinary and widely admired man, a transplanted New Yorker consumed by intellectual curiosity. He had made himself an expert in natural science, priding himself on following empirical evidence wherever it led, under the motto "Nature, Truth and No Humbug." His work contributed to the development of the then-radical theory of evolution. Elected to the American Academy of Arts and Sciences in 1845, Bachman founded South Carolina's Newberry College and befriended the famous bird expert John James Audubon. He sent Audubon the skin of a small bird he had discovered, which the ornithologist duly named Bachman's warbler. Since 1815, Bachman had earned his living as pastor of Saint John's Lutheran Church in Charleston. His parishioners loved and revered him for his tireless service to their needs. Yet this richly fulfilling life was haunted by constant illnesses and the death of loved ones. Bachman suffered from recurrent tuberculosis, cholera, malaria, and possibly yellow fever. Five of his fourteen children died in infancy. Three of his grown daughters died of tuberculosis, as did both his first and second wives, who were sisters.

The owner of a few household slaves, Dr. Bachman vehemently argued that, whatever race theorists might think, humans were a single species, a unified family. But not all humans were equal. Like John Wilkes Booth and many other advocates of the Southern way of life, the minister believed slavery was a humane means of sustaining an intellectually inferior race and that whites had a solemn responsibility to care for blacks, rather than leave them to fend for themselves. He laid out these beliefs in his writings: "That the negro will remain as he is, unless his form is changed by an amalgamation—which latter is revolting to us. That his intellect, although underrated, is greatly inferior to that of the Caucasian, and that he is therefore, as far as our experience goes, incapable of self-government. That he is thrown on our protection. That our defense of slavery is contained in the holy scriptures. That the scriptures teach the rights and duties of masters to rule their servants with justice and kindness, and enjoin the obedience of servants." Yet these views did not deter him from inviting a free black man, Daniel Payne, to his house frequently to discuss zoology and study his collections.

Bachman was so deeply admired by South Carolina's elites that he was accorded the high honor of delivering the invocation at the Charleston secession convention in 1860. While the men planning their momentous break from the United States bowed their heads, the minister prayed that God's wisdom would inspire Southern whites to serve the needs of blacks, to "enable us to protect & bless the humble race, that has been confided to our care; so that we may save them from corruption & ruin, so that while we teach them duty to those who are their protectors, we may also train them up under all the hallowed influences of the religion of thy dead Son, our Savior." He prayed too that God would move Northern hearts to let the South go in peace, "so that our Southern Union may not be cemented by the blood of those who were once our brethren."

Despite Bachman's devotions, the war had come, and the blood that had been shed seemed more likely now to cement the national Union than the Southern one. After Union guns began bombarding Charleston, the pastor packed up his priceless and irreplaceable books and papers and fled the city. Sherman's men found them in Columbia and destroyed them. Bachman made his way to Cash's Depot, the great plantation of Confederate colonel Ellerbe Cash. With its two hundred slaves and eight thousand acres of land, it made an inviting target. Dr. Bachman, as a leading figure at the secession convention, surely made another. Cash was not at home, and rather than flee, the frail, seventy-five-year-old Bachman remained at the mansion to provide the women any protection he could as the sole white male left.

The minister had been appalled by reports that Sherman's soldiers had been forcing slaves, through threats or outright torture—blacks were hung by their thumbs or even lynched—to reveal where plantations' valuables had been hidden. At Cash's Depot that Saturday, the first group of soldiers to arrive asked for all firearms, promising nothing else would be touched. After the residents complied, a second party soon arrived, demanding that the now defenseless inhabitants turn over keys to the women's chests of drawers. The soldiers took away any items they wanted: watches, earrings, wedding rings, even daguerreotypes of loved ones. One woman came in for special humiliation. "A lady of delicacy and refinement, a personal friend, was compelled to strip before them, that they might find concealed watches and other valuables under her dress," the pastor wrote. The soldiers emptied the smokehouses, filling up the plantation's fine carriages with bacon and hams, and made off with every head of poultry on the place. A third party took away every last mule, horse, and carriage.

On Sunday, Sherman's men continued their work. The black people on the plantation were kicked, knocked down, and stripped of their church clothing, their best, Bachman reported. Soldiers successfully forced them to reveal the location of items hidden in the woods. Then they "cut open the trunks, threw my manuscripts and devotional books into a mud-hole, stole the ladies' jewelry, hair ornaments, etc., tore many garments into tatters, or gave the rest to the negro women to bribe them into criminal intercourse." A fourth group of soldiers—the worst of the bunch—arrived. "They came, they said, in the name of the great General Sherman, who was next to God Almighty. They came to burn and lay in ashes all that was left" of the plantation—bridges and depots, cotton gins, mills, barns, and stables. The soldiers ignited the outbuildings surrounding the Cash mansion, and the flames threatened to leap to the large and noble house. It was spared, barely, when the wind shifted. The "trembling females thanked God for their deliverance." A hundred mounted men looked on, refusing to help the residents and laughing at their efforts to save their house.

Then the troubles really started for Bachman. Soldiers stripped him of his watch. And, having heard that $100,000 in gold and silver was buried on the grounds, they demanded that he disclose where. "Coolly and deliberately they prepared to inflict torture on a defenseless, gray-headed old man," Bachman informed the Confederate president. They took him out behind a stable, cocking their pistols at his head, kicking him in the stomach and knocking him down seven or eight times, while the minister insisted he did not know. A lieutenant announced a new plan, Bachman recounted: "'How would you like to have both your arms cut off?' He did not wait for an answer, but, with his heavy sheathed sword, struck me on my left arm, near the shoulder. I heard it crack; it hung powerless by my side, and I supposed it was broken. He then repeated the blow on the other arm. The pain was most excruciating, and it was several days before I could carve my food or take my arm out of a sling, and it was black and blue for weeks." Bachman's daughter rushed out of the house, frantically warning the soldiers that her father had been minister of the same church for fifty years and that God would protect him. The interrogation ended. Leaving the mansion that evening, the aged scientist saw the night sky lit up from fires burning in hundreds of places in the neighborhood. That evening, Dr. E. P. Burton, surgeon of the Seventh Illinois regiment, described the scene at Cheraw, where factories, warehouses, and other structures of use to the Confederacy had been set on fire. "Vast clouds of dense smoke were arising from burning buildings and hung around the town in a mournful grandeur," he wrote, adding later, "I am getting about satiated with burning."

With the vanguard of his forces already across the border into North Carolina, Sherman planned to bid farewell to South Carolina. His men were leaving behind a path of destruction fifty miles wide, the landscape stripped so clean that, according to a Confederate prisoner, "a crow could not fly across it without a haversack." A few days later, a young woman left her family's rice plantation on the Pee Dee River and traveled along the road the Union forces had taken. "Dead horses all along the way," she recalled, "and, here and there, a leg or an arm sticking out of a hastily made too-shallow grave." The stench was almost unbearable.

South Carolina richly deserved this treatment, Union chaplain George Whitfield Pepper insisted: "The thousands of homes she has filled with mourning, the unnumbered hearts she has wrung with anguish, are all witnesses of the justice of her punishment. Let her drink the cup she has brewed, and lie on the bed she has made." Sherman's goal was to reach Virginia, where, acting in concert with Grant, he would surround and crush Lee's Army of Northern Virginia, ending the war. The Northern papers had already been filled with rumors that Lee was about to abandon Petersburg, exposing Richmond to be seized.

How much Lincoln knew of the horrors of Sherman's march is not clear, however strongly he supported the general's mission of crushing the Confederacy's will to fight. The president had often expressed his determination to prosecute the war to the fullest of his powers, perhaps most colorfully in a July 28, 1862, letter to Union loyalist Cuthbert Bullitt of Louisiana, who had passed along complaints that Union forces in the state were stoking resentment by interfering with slavery, then protected by the Constitution. "What would you do in my position? Would you drop the war where it is? Or, would you prosecute it in future, with elder-stalk squirts, charged with rose water? Would you deal lighter blows rather than heavier ones?" Lincoln asked. "I shall not do *more* than I can, and I shall do *all* I can to save the government, which is my sworn duty as well as my personal inclination. I shall do nothing in malice. What I deal with is too vast for malicious dealing." In 1863 Lincoln approved the Lieber Code, a set of rules for fighting the war devised by Columbia College law professor Francis Lieber. While it prohibited certain war crimes and served as a model for later international conventions of war, it authorized the destruction of civilian property, the summary execution of guerrillas, and the starvation of noncombatants. "To save the country," Lieber stated, "is paramount to all other considerations."

While the horrors of total war left deep scars on America, the Northern and Southern armies set aside their hatreds to exchange some prisoners, a program that had started up again after a long interruption. The March 4 edition of the *Wheeling Intelligencer*, of West Virginia, reported that about one hundred wretched figures had passed through town, many barely able to drag themselves along. They were Union soldiers, newly released from Confederate prisons, "enroute from the pens of the south" to Camp Chase, in Columbus, Ohio, 125 miles west, for food, shelter, and medical care. "The most of them look like walking skeletons, and can move about with the assistance of a heavy staff or crutches. They all agree as to the horribly inhuman treatment received at the hands of those in charge of the rebel prisons." Many men had not survived their brutal captivity. On that day, the *Spirit of the Times*, of Batavia, New York, wrote about one of them, Lieutenant Joseph Willert, of the Eighth New York Heavy Artillery, who had been "allowed, as have thousands of others of our best men, to suffer and starve and die, in the loathsome prisons of a cruel and barbarous foe." The newspaper did not blame the barbarous foe alone; it also faulted Abraham Lincoln.

Lincoln had halted the prisoner exchanges in April 1864, in retaliation for the Confederates' treatment of black prisoners of war, whom they executed or re-enslaved, regarding such men as engaged in servile insurrection and the property of their one-time masters. But many believed Lincoln had a hidden reason for halting the exchanges: a war of attrition plainly favored the North. The populous Union could replace the men and matériel taken out of action, while the ravaged South could not. Immigrants kept on flooding into the North, including Irishmen willing to fight in return for handsome bounties, and hundreds of thousands of former slaves had stepped in to fill the ranks.

There was good reason for the Union to stop giving the Confederacy its soldiers back.

But the policy carried horrific costs. The South's prisoner-of-war pens, such as the infamous stockade in Andersonville, Georgia, quickly filled beyond the capacity of officials to provide adequate food and shelter. Union soldiers, deprived of enough to eat and tortured by lice, fleas, flies, and mosquitoes, died in agony, starving to death, perishing from the cold, and wasting away from diarrhea and disease. The stalemate continued, for the most part, until January 1865, when Lincoln, yielding to a furious public backlash, renewed the trades. For men like Lieutenant Willert, Lincoln's reversal came too late. The *Spirit of the Times* predicted that "the impartial historian" of the future would surely send the name of Jefferson Davis down "in infamy" to posterity for rebelling against his country and brutally mistreating prisoners. But "within the same volume shall be found a stain and blotch upon the name of Abraham Lincoln, which all the tears of the widows and orphan Children, whose husbands and fathers have perished in southern prisons, could never wash away."

One of the ex-prisoners on the move on this Saturday was a young man on his way to his mother's house in Brooklyn. George Whitman, seized outside Petersburg in September 1864, had been locked up in a complex of tobacco warehouses in Danville, Virginia, sleeping on floors encrusted with the excrement of sick fellow prisoners, fending off starvation and scurvy while suffering a serious illness. A Confederate prison inspector found the buildings "dirty, filled with vermin," and lacking sufficient fireplaces. "The prisoners have almost no clothing, no blankets," and high mortality "is caused, no doubt, by the insufficiency of food." Fewer than half of the 333 men captured with Whitman survived.

George Whitman's brother Walt was outraged. In his roles as a journalist and a loyal brother, he bitterly criticized the Lincoln administration's shutdown of prisoner exchanges, excoriating Secretary of War Edwin Stanton in a *New York Times* piece in late 1864 for a "cold-blooded policy" that is "more cruel than anything done by the Secessionists." The policy was a gross betrayal of fifty thousand of the Union's "bravest young men—soldiers faithful to it in its hours of extremest peril." Whitman wrote of the "helpless and most wretched men" who had died by the thousands, with "their last hours passed in the thought that they were abandoned by their Government, and left to their fate." They were "exchanged," at last, by "starvation, (Mr. Editor, or you, reader, do you know what a death by starvation actually is?)." Those still alive were suffering from "mental and physical atrophy" and "cannot long tarry behind" the dead. Unbeknownst to Walt, who had been working behind the scenes in Washington for his brother's release, George was a free man on this day of Lincoln's inauguration, having traveled to Annapolis before making his way north.

Southern sympathizers were at least as outraged as Whitman over the halt in exchanges. One articulated the threat to the South well. "We cannot spare one man, whereas the United States Government is willing to let their own soldiers remain in our prisons because she has no need of them," John Wilkes Booth seethed. In 1864, Booth entered a plot to change all that. Spending thousands of his own dollars, the actor enlisted co-conspirators in a plan to kidnap Lincoln, spirit him to Richmond, and offer him in exchange for thousands of Southern men held in Northern prisons. Booth had met with Confederate agents in Montreal, perhaps receiving encouragement and support. By March 1865, the renewal of exchanges had made the scheme moot. Yet Booth was not prepared to give up his dream of combating Lincoln's cruelty, intolerance, and pride.

CHAPTER 9

THERE WAS MURDER IN THE AIR

Saturday morning, March 4, 1865

It was an ominous morning for an inauguration parade. "The dawn came slowly, with cold, black, angry clouds shutting out every particle of sky," journalist Lois Bryan Adams noted. "The wind howled viciously. The rain poured in torrents. The streets were transmuted into beds of rivulets," the *New York Herald* reported. Those who looked out from their rain-streaked windows saw "mud, mud everywhere, and not a dry spot to set foot upon. A pretty prospect, indeed, for a grand procession." The tens of thousands of Americans here for a celebration "were doomed to seek it by trudging through a sea of mud and a torrent of rain."

The hardier spectators braced themselves for the elements. Men tucked their pant legs into long boots, women looped up their skirts. People who had older clothes to wear put them on, knowing their hats and coats would get soaked and stained, probably ruined. But many people, of course, had brought only their best. "What a dawn it was for the thousands upon thousands who have gathered here from all parts of our still great country, thousands who never saw the Capital before, and probably never will again," Adams wrote. Even by Washington standards, it was a mess. "Such a wet, dirty morning as this . . . hardly ever dawned upon Washington," another reporter noted. "Rain had been falling all day yesterday and last night, making the proverbial filthy streets of the political metropolis filthier and more unpleasant than ever."

After watching congressmen at work in the Capitol that morning, Walt Whitman ventured out in the rain to report on the inaugural parade that would slosh down Pennsylvania Avenue, the wide boulevard that led in a straight line for 1.2 miles from the pillared front of the Treasury Building, next to the White House, all the way to the Capitol. Though the great avenue was paved, it was often hard to tell, since horse manure and Washington's notorious dust constantly built up on it, covering the stones. Authorities might have swept and shoveled it before the grand inauguration, but days of rain hit first, and traffic had churned the avenue into a river of muck. The poet's overwhelming impression was of "mud, (and such mud!) amid and upon which streaming crowds of citizens" poured. The Washington *Evening Star* joked that the Army Corps of Engineers had taken soundings of the street with the idea of building one of its famous pontoon bridges to the Capitol, "but it was found the bottom was too soft to hold the anchors of the boats, and the project was abandoned." Police made sure that all "who could not swim" were kept on the sidewalks. The *New York Herald* described "a vile yellow fluid, not thick enough to walk on, not thin enough to swim in," coating the avenue. Those venturing out that morning got flecked with the liquid from head to heel. "All the hacks were yellow with it," the *Herald* observed, "and all the horses, and all the little boys, all the world floundered about in it, and swore at it, and laughed at it."

Despite it all, the broad sidewalks for the whole length of Pennsylvania Avenue filled quickly with Union soldiers and pedestrians, perhaps half of them African Americans. No one had ever seen so many black people on Washington's streets at one time. This day seemed to symbolize for African Americans "the triumph of their race over a fast fading social prejudice and political injustice," the *Times* of London observed. The reporter found clear manifestations of black pride, remarkable in a culture that had propped up slavery by relentlessly portraying African Americans as subhuman. "The negroes held their heads high, as if they thoroughly understood that, under the beneficent sway of Abraham Lincoln," they were suddenly the equals of any men or women. Buoyantly happy black women wore their best dresses, willing to let their hems become caked in mud, effectively ruined, for the sake of honoring the president who had issued the Emancipation Proclamation and, on January 31, 1865, had pushed through a recalcitrant U.S. House of Representatives the Thirteenth Amendment, which would abolish slavery permanently. Having passed the Senate in 1864, it was now making its way through the states for ratification. The approval of twenty-seven of the thirty-six states was required to make it part of the U.S. Constitution, and in little more than a month it had already been ratified in eighteen.

Philadelphia abolitionist J. M. McKim, writing from Washington to a friend in Edinburgh, Scotland, recalled that defenders of slavery had ruled the nation's capital before the start of the war. "Now, what do I see to-day? Freedom, Freedom, Freedom everywhere! In the presidential mansion, in both houses of Congress, in the Supreme Court (the author of the Dred Scott decision is dead and the court is anti-slavery), in the hotels, in the public parks, on the streets, everywhere is freedom, and everybody free! Not nominally and abstractedly, but really and actually. I tell you, my friend, slavery has received its death-wound. . . . The snake is killed. Though it still wriggles, it is cut into pieces." One man above all had led the nation to this consummation. "If Mr. Lincoln were to die now, the impartial historian would write him down—a fearless and sagacious statesman, an incorruptible chief magistrate, and an honest man. The best measure of ability is success; the best test of fidelity, in a popular government, is the continued and increasing confidence of the people. Judged by these tests, Mr. Lincoln's ability and trust are beyond question."

On Pennsylvania Avenue, the "surging tide was augmented by the constant streams of life pouring from every street and byway," Adams wrote. Soon the intersections were clogged up with carriages fighting to get around each other, "horrid perpetual entanglements . . . sometimes a dead lock," Whitman observed. "Clattering groups of cavalrymen" thundered by on "a gallop," putting everyone at risk. Though some pedestrians dashed into the streets "in the most reckless manner," the *Evening Star* noted, "fortunately no one is believed to have been lost."

After all that the nation had suffered for the last four years, few seemed inclined to let some soggy weather spoil their day. "It is a long time since we have had reinauguration"—Andrew Jackson had been the last president to take the oath of office for a second time, on March 4, 1833—"and the weather would have to prove as tempestuous and sulphureous as it unfortunately did in the time of Sodom and Gomorrah, for the procession to forbear turning out, or the populace to forbear looking on," one reporter quipped. From windows and balconies, women waved white handkerchiefs, "and the ribbons waved and the bonnets and dresses all contributed their quota of color and decoration to the scene." The United States' red, white, and blue flag was everywhere, "mammoth or miniature," covering almost every open space of every building along the street, and on carriages, railroad cars, and horse harnesses, "giving an exceedingly lively appearance to the scene." The State Department was decked out in flags, the War Department adorned with flags and evergreens. Fife and drum corps started playing early that morning, brightening everyone's mood, and brass bands belted out patriotic tunes. "Windows and doors were full from cellar to attic, and thousands of anxious eyes looked down from balconies and housetops. Flags were everywhere, but dripping and drooping," Adams wrote.

An excited little boy looked out from the handsome Federal-style brick house of Elizabeth Blair Lee, who had reluctantly joined Mary Lincoln at the Capitol the night before. Her father, Francis Preston Blair, an adviser to a series of presidents, including Lincoln, had built her Pennsylvania Avenue home snug against his own, just across the street from the White House. (Joined, they would become today's Blair House.) Elizabeth, who had put on a splendid silk dress for the inauguration, was relieved that her seven-year-old, Blair, recovering from an illness that produced eruptions on "his dear little face," had been "very bright" that morning. The boy often played with the rambunctious Tad Lincoln at the executive mansion just two hundred yards away, and in time would be given Tad's beloved pet goats. This morning, Blair was so excited about the music and marching that he slid out of his sick bed and stood in a large upstairs window—"closed," Elizabeth assured her husband in a letter—to watch what was transpiring down on the avenue. By half past ten, the rain seemed to be stopping, and thousands of people poured out of homes and hotels to join in the fun. Ten minutes later, the rain poured down again, soaking everyone. But by eleven, a thin streak of light appeared on the western horizon.

A sodden crowd had assembled in front of the White House, some gathering there since nine a.m. At precisely five minutes before eleven, Lincoln's friend Ward Hill Lamon, officiously enacting his role as U.S. marshal of the District of Columbia, entered the east gate of the White House to escort the president to the Capitol. He discovered to his dismay that Lincoln was already gone, having left the morning's pomp and circumstance to Mary. Hours earlier, the president had "very quietly" ridden "down to the Capitol in his own carriage, by himself, on a sharp trot," Whitman reported. Lincoln, the *New York Herald* noted, turned up "unseen by anybody and ungreeted by a cheer, and proceeded at once to his room, near the Senate Chamber," to get to work signing legislation, so thoroughly immersed in the task that he did not stop to remove his stovepipe hat. Among the bills he made law that morning was one related to the nation's earlier struggle for survival, providing increased pensions for the last five survivors of the Revolutionary War. Lamon, who was used to Lincoln's recklessness by now but was by no means inured to it, assigned two marshals to escort Mrs. Lincoln, and rushed to the Capitol to protect the president.

Mrs. Lincoln proudly stepped up into the presidential carriage. Accompanying the First Lady were two distinguished Republican senators: Henry B. Anthony, a former editor of the *Providence Journal*, who had become governor of Rhode Island and, later, a U.S. senator, as well as one of President Lincoln's staunchest allies; and James Harlan of Iowa, like Lincoln a Whig turned Republican in a Democratic state. Harlan, who had urged Lincoln before he became president to name the brilliant Salmon P. Chase as his treasury secretary, had become a family friend. His lovely daughter Mary joined the official procession that day, escorted by the president's attentive son, twenty-one-year-old

Robert, who had been given leave from his duties as an aide to General Grant to attend his father's inauguration. The president's bodyguard, the Union Light Guard of Ohio, protected the carriages.

The parade to the Capitol began. Confident, athletic young firemen in black or brightly colored shirts, some with axes slung over their shoulders, walked alongside their prized, polished steam engines drawn by teams of horses. Four companies of the Forty-Fifth U.S. Colored Infantry regiment—the first black soldiers ever to take part in an inauguration parade—stepped out into the mud with precision. Bands filled the air with sprightly marches, one approaching as another passed by. "The mingled noises are blended together harmoniously by the subdued thunder of the countless drums," one reporter noted. Floats made their appearance—a "muslin Temple of Liberty" and a "pasteboard Monitor," after the famous ironclad ship, Whitman noted wryly. It was all "characterized by a charming looseness and independence. Each went up and down the Avenue in the way and at the time which seemed convenient, and was a law unto itself." A float sponsored by the *Washington Chronicle* carried a small press, and employees were "printing off a *Chronicle Junior* by hundreds," tossing them to the crowd.

The Temple of Liberty float, drawn by four large bay horses, was supposed to be adorned with pretty girls in white dresses, one representing each state. But in the wake of the raging storm that morning, their places under the red, white, and blue tenting had been taken by boys, black and white, deemed to be of sturdier stuff than the females. As the horses pulled the float along, the boisterous boys belted out two war songs, "Rally round the Flag" and "The Battle Cry of Freedom." The ersatz *Monitor* was the work of the Lincoln and Johnson Club of Washington. Pulled by four white horses, the *Monitor*—the phrase "The Union: Our Home" emblazoned on its bow—fired off shots at intervals from two guns mounted in the turret. The marchers primarily waved American flags, though green flags of Erin held aloft by proud Irish immigrants ran a close second.

It all suggested a forward-looking, confident, fun-loving America, unbowed by four years of bloody war, never mind a little mud and rain.

"Everybody felt that they were taking part in a holiday pageant, and every one felt also that the clouds that had so long lowered over our Union house were in the deep bosom of the ocean buried, and that the rainbow of peace, resting upon the shoulders of Grant and Sherman, was shedding its rays of splendor over the whole country," the *New York Herald* observed. At Lincoln's first inauguration, Confederate sympathizers had been plentiful in what was still essentially a Southern city. "The city was filled with rebels who proclaimed their sentiments boldly in the streets, and hinted violence to the Executive," the *Evening Star* recalled. At theaters, patriotic songs were "hissed down," while "loyal men were assaulted in the avenue, and cheers for Jeff. Davis were of common occurrence." Sharpshooters had to be posted along the avenue and on rooftops. The aged leader of America's military at the time, General Winfield Scott, had sent scouts into the crowd, looking for any signs of trouble. While that day had passed off quietly, "the feverish anxiety of that morning, and the certainty of terrible bloodshed following any riotous demonstration, created impressions on the minds of those who were present that probably will never be erased." This day seemed different. Though Lamon and the nervous General Henry Halleck were on edge, and the guards at the Capitol had been instructed to look for trouble, there seemed to be nothing transpiring on Pennsylvania Avenue but a celebration. Among the tens of thousands was teenager Virgil Connor, who had left his bedridden brother Selden behind in room six at the Douglas Hospital and was watching the fun with his friend Cal. He marveled at the "crowd almost innumerable assembled in an[d] about the Capitol and on Pa. Avenue."

As the parade passed, the throng lustily cheered the closed presidential carriage, unaware that Abraham Lincoln was not inside. "It was a play of Hamlet with Hamlet left out," one reporter quipped. Frederick Douglass, standing along the parade route, was one of the people deceived. But he was not as hopeful as the newspapers about the rainbow of peace. Having endured a lifetime of threats and contempt for his unyielding insistence on freedom for all human beings, Douglass knew that Abraham Lincoln had stoked savage hatreds by breaking the

South and effectively destroying the institution of slavery—hatreds on full display during the presidential campaign several months earlier.

At the 1864 Democratic National Convention in Chicago, delegates had spoken out fervently against a despot they believed was extinguishing America and its precious liberties. Ohio congressman S. S. Cox thundered that Lincoln had heedlessly "deluged the country in blood" and "filled the land with grief and mourning." ("God damn him!" a listener shouted out.) "For less offenses than Mr. Lincoln had been guilty of," Cox said, "the English people had chopped off the head of the first Charles." New York editor C. Chauncey Burr thought it a "wonder" that Lincoln could even find Cabinet members willing to carry out "the infamous orders of the gorilla tyrant that usurped the Presidential chair." He referred to Lincoln as "Abraham Africanus," the king of the blacks, a man obsessively advancing abolition at the cost of the Constitution and the nation's precious blood. Benjamin Allen of New York predicted: "The people will soon rise, and if they cannot put Lincoln out of power by the ballot they will by the bullet." Other speakers expressed the hope that, after the Democrats took over, Lincoln would be arrested, prosecuted, and hanged for his brazen assaults on the Constitution. "The man who votes for Lincoln now is a traitor and murderer," the *La Crosse Democrat*, in Wisconsin, editorialized. "And if he is elected to misgovern for another four years, we trust some bold hand will pierce his heart with dagger point for the public good."

His victory had left many Americans, North and South, disgusted. As the *Times* of London noted, "fully one-third of the States took no part in his re-election and considered him a foreigner, and the bitter enemy of their liberty and independence," while a majority of the other two-thirds found Lincoln "fit to carry on to its close the fearful war of which his first election had been the signal." Emma Holmes, the young woman in demolished Camden, South Carolina, recorded angrily in her diary after the November election that the "vulgar, uncouth animal" had been "again chosen to desecrate the office once filled by Washington—the immortal." On December 1, the *Selma* (Alabama) *Morning Dispatch* openly published an advertisement by a man seeking

$1 million in financial backing "to cause the lives of ABRAHAM LINCOLN, WILLIAM SEWARD and ANDREW JOHNSON to be taken by the first of March next. This will give us peace, and satisfy the world that CRUEL TYRANTS cannot live in a 'land of liberty.'"

Even in the overwhelmingly Republican state of Massachusetts, Boston abolitionist and women's rights activist Lydia Maria Child admitted that the president stirred little admiration. "There was no enthusiasm for honest old Abe," she observed. "There is no beauty in him, that men should desire him; there is no insinuating, polished manner, to beguile the senses of the people; there is no dazzling renown; no silver flow of rhetoric; in fact, no glittering prestige of any kind surrounds him; yet the people triumphantly elected him, and notwithstanding the long, long drag upon their patience and their resources which this war has produced." In Lincoln's hometown of Springfield, the Democratic *Illinois State Register* called his reelection "the heaviest calamity that ever befell the nation." It signaled "the farewell to civil liberty, to a republican form of government, and to the unity of these states."

Virulently racist anti-Lincoln songs had sprung up, including a popular campaign tune called "All for the Nigger!" that was still making the rounds in 1865. It lamented Lincoln's election and voiced sympathy for the working men who had been forced to die in the Union Army, unable even to buy their way out permanently by paying the government $300, a life's savings for such men:

> *Now boys will you tell me just what it has cost,*
> *To elect old Abe Lincoln, and all his black host?*
> *Just eight hundred thousand—our country's best blood—*
> *Have been slain, and their bodies lie under the sod.*
> *And it's all for the nigger, great God can it be,*
> *The home of the brave, and the land of the free. . . .*
>
> *Three hundred won't save you, you must yield them up your life,*
> *In this fiend excited slaughter, this fratricidal strife,*
> *The land is filled with orphans—the nation groans with debt,*

The heart of the great Gorilla would sink us deeper yet.
And it's all for the nigger, great God can it be,
That this was once a land of the brave and the free.

Another song, "Fight for the Nigger," sung to the tune of the popular folk song "Wait for the Wagon," was, if anything, even more brutally racist:

Three cheers for Honest Abe, he will be a great man yet,
Though he's loaded us with taxes, and burdened us with debt;
He often tells us little jokes while pocketing our pelf,
And the last he made the nigger the equal of himself.
Fight for the Nigger,
The wooly-headed Nigger,
The sweet-scented Nigger,
And the Abolition crew.

Some white people feared that, because of Lincoln's extraordinary transformation of America, black men would next have their way with white women, a disgusting thought to many who had been acculturated to view African Americans as subhuman. One L. Seaman, the author of a mocking, bitterly racist 1864 pamphlet, *What Miscegenation Is! And What We Are to Expect Now That Mr. Lincoln Is Re-elected*, lingered over the image of a pretty white girl of sixteen kissing a black man. "The thick tufts of wool of the one lends beauty to the long, waving auburn hair of the other, and the sweet, delicate little roman nose of the one does not detract from the beauty of the broad, flat nose, with expanded nostrils of the other," he wrote. "Since the re-election of Mr. Lincoln, the Royal Blood of Africa—the *crème de la crème* of colored society have been extremely jubilant." Seaman noted with contempt that the Reverend Henry Ward Beecher, the abolitionist, believed that the war was about just one thing: ending slavery. In Beecher's words, "every drop of blood spilt without accomplishing that" was "certainty squandered." Seaman also quoted Frederick Douglass: "My friends, this is an age of progress; we are growing wiser every day; those who, a few years ago, would not recognize the colored man as their equal, now begin to see that he is, in some instances possessed of superior qualities." In this topsy-turvy world, the author reflected, anything was now imaginable. "Congress will soon pass a law making the colored man a legal voter, and declaring him eligible to office; he will occupy public positions, from policeman up to President." The prospect of white men losing power, status, and women to once debased blacks through Lincoln's infernal war was edging some Americans toward explosive rage.

The president's appearance in public, even on this glorious day of his inauguration, made Douglass nervous. "I felt then that there was murder in the air, and I kept close to his carriage on the way to the Capitol, for I felt that I might see him fall that day. It was a vague presentiment," he recalled. As the parade passed the crowd, thousands joined Douglass in following it toward the Capitol with its "milky bulging dome," as Whitman earthily put it, topped by "the Maternal Figure over all"—the statue of *Freedom Triumphant*. Another who believed Abraham Lincoln was part of the parade was John Wilkes Booth, who watched intently for the carriage from an embankment near the north wing of the Capitol, a position it would necessarily pass as it turned into the grounds. He seemed strangely obsessed. When a friend pushed through the crowd to greet him, Booth completely ignored him and kept his eyes fixed on the procession. Through the day, "he was gruff and moody to all who addressed him," the *Philadelphia Inquirer* later reported. This was the day, the newspaper added darkly, "fixed . . . for the assassination."

Lincoln had received warnings that he was in danger many times. Before his first inauguration on March 4, 1861, alerted to plausible evidence of a plot to kill him, Lincoln had scrapped some of his scheduled public appearances and entered Washington secretly, accompanied by Lamon, who was armed with a brace of pistols and a bowie knife. The diversion had earned Lincoln sneers from the opposition press, which excoriated him for skulking into town like a coward. Sobered by that experience, Lincoln decided to ignore the death warnings. In March

1864, Francis Bicknell Carpenter, while painting Lincoln's face into his grand work, asked the president about rumors of a plot to kidnap him. "Well, even if true, I do not see what the Rebels would gain by killing or getting possession of me. I am but a single individual, and it would not help their cause or make the least difference in the progress of the war. Everything would go right on just the same," Lincoln replied. The barrage of menacing letters began when he was propelled into national prominence as the Republicans' presidential candidate in 1860. "Soon after I was nominated at Chicago, I began to receive letters threatening my life. The first one or two made me a little uncomfortable, but I came at length to look for a regular instalment of this kind of correspondence in every week's mail, and up to inauguration day I was in constant receipt of such letters. It is no uncommon thing to receive them now; but they have ceased to give me any apprehension." When Carpenter expressed surprise, Lincoln replied, "Oh, there is nothing like getting used to things!"

The presidential secretaries John Nicolay and John Hay confirmed that "his mail was infested with brutal and vulgar menace, mostly anonymous, the proper expression of vile and cowardly minds." Some contained crude drawings of Lincoln being hanged. Some were splashed with red ink depicting blood. When John W. Forney—the newspaper editor and Senate secretary who threw the stag party for Andrew Johnson on the eve of his inauguration—was visiting Lincoln in his office in 1865, the president acknowledged that he constantly received death threats. Lincoln simply stuck them into a pigeonhole in his desk. "In that place I have filed eighty just such things as these. I know I am in danger; but I am not going to worry over threats like these," he said.

Lincoln's indifference to it all no doubt contributed to his weak security. For much of the war, people could simply walk into the White House, virtually at will, sometimes getting all the way to his personal secretary's office without being stopped. One tourist from Dubuque, Iowa, pushed her way into a Cabinet meeting, determined to get a look at the president. Lincoln let her in. "Well, in the matter of looking at one another," the president said, laughing, "I have altogether the advantage." Oblivious to the notion that he was an open target, Lincoln wandered out of the White House at almost any hour, day or night, and walked "across the lawn to the War Department for a consultation or to seek some news," journalist William A. Croffut recalled. The president had a particularly unnerving habit of going to the theater unguarded, accompanied only by Mary or one or two friends. "To-night, as you have done on several previous occasions, you went unattended to the theater," an exasperated Lamon lectured the president in December 1864. "When I say unattended, I mean that you went alone with Charles Sumner and a foreign minister, neither of whom could defend himself against an assault from any able-bodied woman in this city. And you know, or ought to know, that your life is sought after, and will be taken unless you and your friends are cautious; for you have many enemies within our lines."

Growing more fearful for Lincoln's life as the war went on, Lamon asked that four or five men from the District of Columbia's Metropolitan Police Department be assigned to guard the White House. William Crook, who took up the guard position in January 1865, noted that Lincoln accepted the threats stoically. "He believed that if anybody was bad enough to kill him there was nothing on earth to prevent it," Crook said. Secretary of State William Seward, perhaps Lincoln's closest adviser, scoffed at reports of assassination plans. In a letter to John Bigelow, the American consul in Paris, he argued that they "furnish no ground for anxiety. Assassination is not an American practice or habit, and one so vicious and desperate cannot be engrafted into our political system." While a would-be assassin had fired twice at Andrew Jackson three decades earlier—the irascible sixty-seven-year-old Jackson beat him with his cane after both guns misfired, while Congressman Davy Crockett wrestled the man to the ground—no one had ever killed a president.

Lincoln loved to escape the intense pressures of the White House when he could. In hot weather, he regularly departed the stifling mansion late in the afternoon to stay overnight at a cottage on the breezy, sloping green grounds of the Soldiers' Home, a retirement home for veterans just outside the city. For Seward, that mere fact confirmed there was no cause for alarm. "He goes to and fro from that place on horseback, night and morning, unguarded. I go there unattended at all hours, by daylight and moonlight, by starlight and without any light," the secretary of state wrote. All the same, Mary Lincoln fretted about her husband's safety, and Secretary of War Edwin Stanton assigned a cavalry guard to accompany him to and from the cottage, while a permanent detachment of armed guards oversaw the house. Lincoln complained that "he and Mrs. Lincoln couldn't hear themselves talk for the clatter of their sabres and spurs"—and, given that so many of the guards were new soldiers, "he was more afraid of being shot by the accidental discharge of one of their carbines or revolvers, than of any attempt on his life." A drummer boy named Harry M. Kieffer, serving with the guards at the Soldiers' Home, noted that Lincoln liked to take off on his own, just as he had this Inauguration Day. "Often did I see him enter his carriage before the hour appointed for his morning departure for the White House, and drive away in haste, as if to escape from the irksome escort of a dozen cavalry-men, whose duty it was to guard his carriage between our camp and the city." When the escort arrived, ten or fifteen minutes later, and it "found that the carriage had already gone, wasn't there a clattering of hoofs and a rattling of scab-bards as they dashed out past the gate and down the road to overtake the great and good President," Kieffer wrote with amusement.

Lincoln's trips back and forth were so regular that Whitman often paused to watch him go by. "I see the President almost every day, as I happen to live where he passes to or from his lodgings out of town," the poet wrote.

> Mr. Lincoln on the saddle generally rides a good-sized, easy-going gray horse, is dress'd in plain black, somewhat rusty and dusty, wears a black stiff hat, and looks about as ordinary in attire, &c., as the commonest man. A lieutenant, with yellow straps, rides at his left, and following behind, two by two, come the cavalry men, in their yellow-striped jackets. They are

generally going at a slow trot, as that is the pace set them by the one they wait upon. The sabres and accoutrements clank, and the entirely unornamental *cortège* as it trots towards Lafayette square arouses no sensation, only some curious stranger stops and gazes.

Like others, Whitman worried that the president was taking needless risks. "The reb cavalry come quite near us, dash in & steal wagon trains, &c—It would be funny if they should come some night to the President's country house, (soldier's home,) where he goes out to sleep every night—it is in the same direction as their saucy raid last Sunday," Walt wrote, on July 30, 1863, to his mother. "I really think it would be safer for him just now to stop at the White House, but I expect he is too proud to abandon the former custom." For all of Seward's absence of concern, the possibility of Lincoln's abduction or killing seemed plain enough to journalist Noah Brooks, who noted: "To my unsophisticated judgment nothing seems easier than a sudden cavalry raid from the Maryland side of the fortifications, past the few small forts, to seize the President of the United States, lug him from his 'chased couch,' and carry him off as a hostage worth having." That, indeed, was one of John Wilkes Booth's plans.

One night in August 1864, around eleven o'clock, Lincoln, deep in thought, was traveling to the cottage alone on his horse, "jogging along at a slow gait," when a gun went off, and a bullet whizzed near the president's ear. The horse, panicked, bolted. "At a break-neck speed we soon arrived in a haven of safety," Lincoln recounted to Lamon, noting he lost his hat. "I was left in doubt whether death was more desirable from being thrown from a runaway federal horse, or as the tragic result of a rifle-ball fired by a disloyal bushwacker in the middle of the night," Lincoln laughed. A private on duty named John W. Nichols confirmed the incident, recalling that he heard a shot at eleven p.m. and saw Lincoln, bareheaded, dash up to the gate on horseback soon thereafter. Nichols and a corporal investigated. At the intersection of the driveway and the main road, they found the president's silk hat—with a bullet hole through the crown. "The shot had been fired upward, and it was evident that the person who fired the shot had secreted himself close by the roadside," Nichols said.

The next day Nichols handed President Lincoln his hat and pointed out the hole. "He remarked rather unconcernedly, that it was put there by some foolish gunner and was not intended for him." Nonetheless, Lincoln admonished the soldiers to keep the matter secret. "We felt confident that it was an attempt to kill him, and a well nigh successful one, too. The affair was, of course, kept quiet in compliance with the President's request," Nichols recalled. "After that the President never rode alone."

But even surrounded by others, the president would never be perfectly safe from a determined assassin. As the presidential carriage passed Booth, the *Philadelphia Inquirer* later reported, the actor turned from his friend without a farewell and hurried away. He intended to get inside the Capitol.

CHAPTER 10

A FUTURE WITH HOPE IN IT

Saturday, noon, March 4, 1865

By noon, thirty to forty thousand people had gathered on the muddy ground on the eastern side of the great Capitol building, murmuring and looking toward the wooden platform erected on the great central steps below the magnificent new dome. "The ladies giggled at being squeezed so tightly in the press, and whispered with each other about crushed crinolines," the *New York Herald* reported. Perhaps because of his celebrity status, Frederick Douglass somehow had managed to make his way from the parade route to the very front of the crowd. He did not have a coveted pass to get indoors. But whites and African Americans mixed freely outside, the smell of their damp woolen clothing permeating the air. The *Herald* continued: "Colored persons innumerable flocked around, though none were admitted to the Capitol. Soldiers off duty were present in large numbers." The crowd waited stoically for the ceremonies to begin, the paper noted: "There was no noise, no confusion, no enthusiasm, no comfort. Men, women and children soaked about quietly, caught colds, and waited for something to see. Either they were moved by no stronger feeling than curiosity, or else the rain had taken all the starch out of them."

Some African Americans in the crowd, though, were animated, the *Herald* reported. They chatted and joked, wondering when Lincoln would arrive. "Ya! Ya! Linkum allus slow an' sure," one reportedly proclaimed, to laughter. It was an astute observation. Though Lincoln had not moved toward liberating the race as quickly or as boldly as many had hoped, he had done so steadily and surely. Many black people had come to see this prairie lawyer as something much greater than a politician. He was an extraordinary, even divinely inspired figure—raised up from poverty and sent by Providence to lead their people out of centuries of darkness and misery to the light of freedom, much as the Bible stories had told of exodus and salvation in ancient days, miraculous events that altered the path of human existence. On November 28, 1862, a day of Thanksgiving proclaimed by the president, more than one thousand escaped slaves living in a muddy refugee camp in the nation's capital, thrilled by the prospect of Lincoln's emancipation of their brethren, gathered to pray. Harriet Beecher Stowe, the author of *Uncle Tom's Cabin*, attended the service and "heard the sound of that strange rhythmic chant which is now forbidden to be sung on Southern plantations," a Negro spiritual:

> *Oh, go down, Moses,*
> *'Way down into Egypt's land*
> *Tell King Pharaoh*
> *To let my people go!*

As she was leaving the ceremony, Stowe saw an old woman lift her hands. "Bressed be de Lord dat brought me to see dis first happy day of my life! Bressed be de Lord!" she said, according to Stowe's transcription. She and other black Americans believed that God had broken their chains through his instrument of a tall, ungainly, country-bred lawyer with scruffy whiskers.

Douglass himself was warming to this idea, though he had viewed Lincoln for much of the war as a cautious, even craven politician who sadly lacked the moral fiber of such men as the august Salmon P. Chase, now readying himself to administer the oath as chief justice. Lincoln had certainly entered office in 1861 as no abolitionist. He initially hoped to keep America essentially as it was—united, with the monstrous injustice of slavery intact, shielded by the Constitution.

On these very steps four years earlier to the day, as president of the Southern slave states as well as the free states of the North, Lincoln had plainly declared, "I have no purpose, directly or indirectly, to interfere with the institution of slavery in the States where it exists. I believe I have no lawful right to do so, and I have no inclination to do so." He merely hoped to set slavery on the path of ultimate extinction through a policy of containment, by blocking its spread to new territories, and by asserting from the highest office in the land that this institution, though deeply embedded in American culture, was morally unjust. He quickly had to abandon this approach when the Southerners insisted on going their own way.

To save the Union—and his right to be president over all the states—Lincoln, moderate by nature, embraced increasingly radical measures. He refused to return the thousands of slaves who had flocked to Union lines, whatever the Constitution might say; indeed, he began encouraging them to flee their owners. He proclaimed the freedom of all slaves under rebel control through the Emancipation Proclamation and tried to persuade the slave states that remained loyal to the Union to emancipate their slaves in exchange for compensation. He introduced African Americans into the Union military. He championed a constitutional amendment barring slavery in every state. After Lincoln's four years in office, the revolution that the Union and its reckless enemies had wrought was on full display this day. Black troops were massed by the hundreds outside a Capitol built by black labor, representing the more than 150,000 African Americans who had enlisted to fight for the Union, helping to turn the tide of the war. Thousands of black women wearing bright dresses of yellow, orange, and blue blended with the thousands of whites waiting to watch Lincoln take the oath. Former slaves, long kept ignorant of the wider world, had poured in from the countryside. "The Yankee soldiers had told them they were free, and they intended to see the man who had given freedom to them. Nobody dared to stop them either," wrote John W. Washington, an amateur historian who interviewed one woman who made the journey from southern Maryland. "They traveled all night in an old ox-cart with straw all over the floor, had bags of food and arrived in Washington the next day in time to see the parade go up the Avenue."

While the great abolitionist Douglass waited outside the Capitol in the elements, the actor John Wilkes Booth used his VIP ticket to penetrate the majestic building. Holding the view that white men created this extraordinary country for the benefit of white men, Booth could not share the joy of the black people flooding the city and filling the Capitol grounds. Raised on his father's estate, Tudor Hall, amid slavery in Bel Air, Maryland, he had fully embraced the code of the Southern aristocracy, with its boldness and courage, racial and class superiority, devotion to property rights, and readiness to punish insults and pusillanimous troublemakers. Booth believed "the noble framers of our Constitution" had preserved slavery as "one of the greatest blessings"—for both blacks and whites—"that God ever bestowed upon a favored nation." In an interview with a Northern reporter, a white woman in Washington raised amid slavery in Virginia discussed the common belief that slavery was God's will, his way of bringing black people from Africa to a more enriching life in America, where they were exposed to the Bible and the bounty of Western civilization. But it seemed that black people had taken another great step in their journey, toward freedom. "If God's design in bringing the niggers over here has been accomplished we ought to let them go," the Southern woman said. Nonetheless, she bitterly resented the moral preening of Northern liberals. Virginians lived with slaves "just as we do with our families and think as much of them. If these abolition Yankees get them free now they ought to be made to take every one of them to the North and take care of them. But they won't do it, you'll see."

Less than one hundred miles southeast of the Booths' Tudor Hall, in rural Talbot County on the Eastern Shore of Chesapeake Bay, Douglass had grown up with a distinctly grimmer impression of an institution that, for the enslaved, meant a life of unceasing toil for others, enforced by the agony of the lash, and the constant terror of being separated from everyone dear to them. Though slaveholders and their human chattel often expressed genuine affection and concern for one another, and many slaveholders believed themselves to be deeply compassionate, the system's dependence on corporal punishment and a virtual police state—with passes, roving guards, informants, bloodhounds, and slave catchers—suggested to its many critics that it was not nearly as benign as its proponents claimed.

Douglass was born—exactly when, he could not learn—to an enslaved woman named Harriet Bailey. Named Frederick Augustus Washington Bailey at birth, he never knew who his father was, though he was certain it was a white man. The "whispered" rumor was that her master had impregnated Harriet, a common enough occurrence in slavery. Mary Chesnut, a bright and witty diarist married to a former U.S. senator from South Carolina, noted that Southern men "seem to think themselves patterns—models of husbands and fathers." But like "the patriarchs of old," she said, "our men live all in one house with their wives & their concubines, & the Mulattoes one sees in every family exactly resemble the white children." Indeed, most slaves by the mid-nineteenth century had light brown skin, rather than the darker hue of Africa, hinting at an unstated reason that slaveholders fought so desperately to preserve the institution. Thomas Jefferson, author of the Declaration of Independence and himself a slaveholder, had warned of the corruption, not only sexual, that follows having complete power over fellow human beings. "The man must be a prodigy who can retain his morals and manners undepraved by such circumstance," he wrote in his *Notes on the State of Virginia*.

Separated from his mother in infancy, Frederick was eventually sent to a Baltimore household, where his mistress—a tenderhearted woman who treated him as she "supposed one human being ought to treat another"—taught him the rudiments of reading. That outraged her husband, who not unreasonably feared that literacy would only fuel his slaves' aspirations for freedom. "If you give a nigger an inch, he will take an ell," Douglass recalled him saying, using an old English adage (an ell measured about forty-five inches). "A nigger should know nothing but to obey his master—to do as he is told to do. Learning would *spoil* the best nigger in the world," he added. Douglass set himself to

Abraham Lincoln's earliest known photograph, taken in 1846 or 1847, when he was thirty-seven and a Congressman-elect.

Mary Todd Lincoln, in 1861.

Selden Connor,
of the Nineteenth
Maine Voluntary
Infantry Regiment.

Self-portrait of Alexander Gardner.

Stephen Douglas.

Dead at Antietam, negative by Timothy H. O'Sullivan, positive by Alexander Gardner.

Detective Allan Pinkerton, Abraham Lincoln, and Major General John A. McClernand at the Antietam battlefield.

Willie and Tad Lincoln, two of the sons of Abraham and Mary Lincoln, with their cousin Lockwood Todd.

Salmon P. Chase.

Kate Chase Sprague.

The White House during the Lincoln administration.

The National Hotel in 1860, drawing by A. Meyer showing the Capitol dome under construction in the distance.

Edwin Stanton.

Clara Barton.

Abraham Lincoln with his secretaries John G. Nicolay (left) and John Hay, in a photograph taken by Alexander Gardner on November 8, 1863, one day before Lincoln and Hay saw John Wilkes Booth perform at Ford's Theatre.

The Capitol dome under construction, with the stinking canal in the foreground.

A member of the Perseverance Fire Company of Philadelphia.

Benjamin Brown French.

Ulysses S. Grant.

General William Tecumseh Sherman on his horse outside Atlanta, 1864.

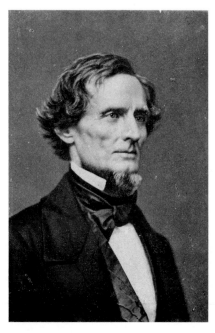

Jefferson Davis.

Robert E. Lee.

The front steps of the Douglas Hospital in Washington, where Selden Connor was treated, with Sister Mary Collette and staff.

Ward at Armory Square hospital in Washington.

Frederick Douglass,
in January 1863.

Lithograph by A.H. Ritchie of Francis Bicknell Carpenter's painting,
The First Reading of the Emancipation Proclamation.

Walt Whitman,
photographed by
Alexander Gardner.

Walt Whitman
with his longtime
companion
Peter Doyle.

John Wilkes Booth, photographed by Alexander Gardner.

John Surratt.

Lucy Hale, photograph found in John Wilkes Booth's pocket when he died.

Alexander Gardner's Washington studio, at the corner of Seventh and D streets.

Ford's Theatre (center) on Tenth Street.

Andrew Johnson.

Abraham Lincoln takes the oath on March 4, 1865, administered by Supreme Court Chief Justice Salmon P. Chase, in an engraving based on an Alexander Gardner photograph.

Andrew Johnson and Abraham Lincoln before Lincoln delivers his inaugural address, detail of a photograph by Alexander Gardner.

Abraham Lincoln delivers his second inaugural address, photographed by Alexander Gardner.

Spectators stand in the mud on the outskirts of the Capitol grounds waiting to see Abraham Lincoln take the oath.

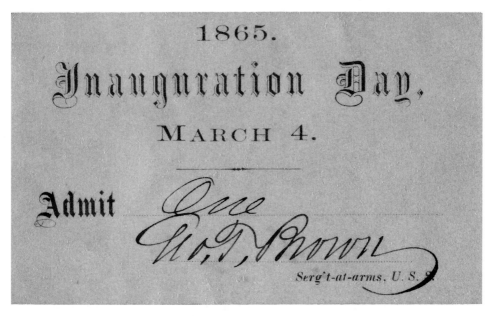

1865.

Inauguration Day.

MARCH 4.

Admit One

Geo. T. Brown

Serg't-at-arms, U.S.

Ticket for admission to the Capitol on Inauguration Day.

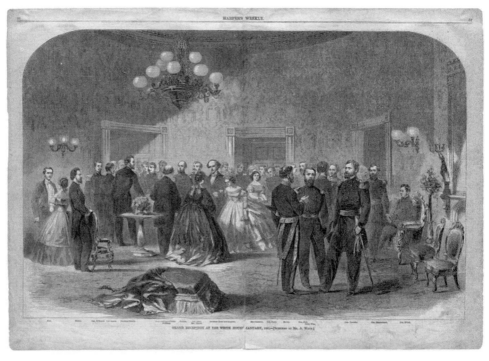

Lincoln greets well-wishers in the White House's Blue Room in 1862, the same room where he greeted thousands of Americans on the night of March 4, 1865.

doing the very things the master advised against—immersing himself in reading and gaining knowledge, the key to freedom. "I now understood what had been to me a most perplexing difficulty—to wit, the white man's power to enslave the black man. It was a grand achievement, and I prized it highly. From that moment, I understood the pathway from slavery to freedom." He called the man's argument with his wife the "first decidedly antislavery lecture" he ever heard.

The clever boy managed to get his hands on a book called *The Columbian Orator*, a reader and elocution manual for students, packed with poetry, plays, and political speeches, many tending toward opposition to slavery. "Every opportunity I got, I used to read this book," he recalled. Reading changed Frederick. Assigned to field labor as a young man, he bitterly hated the beastlike stupor he fell into after unrelenting physical toil from sunup to sunset, and he was haunted by the prospect of a life without the promise of anything better. "The thought of only being a creature of the *present* and the *past*, troubled me, and I longed to have a *future*—a future with hope in it," he wrote. Beaten by an overseer who sought to crush his will, Douglass refused to break. He attempted to escape, but his plan was foiled when a fellow slave betrayed him. He was jailed, then sent to Baltimore, hired out to work in the city's shipyards. On September 3, 1838, dressed in a sailor's outfit, bearing a sailor's protective pass and posing as a free black mariner, Douglass made his way to the railroad station. "I felt assured that if I failed in this attempt, my case would be a hopeless one," he recalled. "It would seal my fate as a slave forever." But he got away safely to the free North. To help escape detection, he changed his name from Bailey to Douglass. A friend who had just read Walter Scott's narrative poem "The Lady of the Lake," centered on the Scottish Douglas clan, suggested the moniker.

Douglass found his way into abolitionist circles and onto speaking platforms. The leaders of the movement quickly recognized that a stern, bright, articulate former slave was invaluable to their cause. A reporter for the *Christian Recorder* marveled at "the magnetism and melody of his wonderfully elastic voice." A printed text could convey his ideas, but not "the manner, the tone of voice, the gesticulation, the action, the round, soft, swelling pronunciation with which Frederick Douglass spoke, and which no orator we have ever heard can use with such grace, eloquence and effect as he." Audiences were enthralled by Douglass's story and struck by his noble bearing, itself a powerful argument for shared humanity in a culture that relentlessly propagandized the inferiority of African Americans. Elizabeth Cady Stanton, the women's rights activist, recalled that Douglass "stood there like an African prince, conscious of his dignity and power, grand in his physical proportions, majestic in his wrath," possessed of "keen wit, satire and indignation." Douglass did more than condemn slavery; he struck at the lie that a black man was less than fully human. "He stands erect," Douglass insisted. "Upon his brow he bears the seal of manhood, from the hand of the living God. Adopt any mode of reasoning you please with respect to him, he is a man, possessing an immortal soul, illuminated by intellect, capable of heavenly aspirations, and in all things pertaining to manhood, he is at once self-evidently a man, and therefore entitled to all the rights and privileges which belong to human nature."

In straightforward prose simmering with moral outrage, the famous orator brought his experiences to life in a book, *Narrative of the Life of Frederick Douglass, a Slave*, published in 1845. It quickly became a best seller. "We wish that everyone may read his book, and see what a mind might have been stifled in bondage—what a man may be subjected to the insults of spendthrift dandies, or the blows of mercenary brutes, in whom there is no whiteness except of the skin, no humanity in the outward form," the critic Margaret Fuller wrote in the *New York Tribune*. "Frederick is a strong man, and will not fail to arouse the sympathies of his readers in behalf of the oppressed," *The Practical Christian* of Hopedale, Massachusetts, opined. "May he long live with his burning eloquence, to pour truth on the naked conscience of this wicked nation."

Yet Douglass discovered in the North, no less than the South, a culture that was far from ready to treat African Americans as equals. In his adopted city of New Bedford, Massachusetts, he watched congregants stalk out of a church rather than share a cup of Communion wine from which a black man had drunk. He was stunned to discover that parents in town coaxed their children to behave by warning that a "black man" would come to get them if they were naughty. Knowing millions of people still trapped in slavery were suffering as he had, he felt a fierce urgency to end the institution that many Northerners did not seem to share. "While we are here speaking in their behalf, saying noble words and doing noble deeds," Douglass declared in an 1848 speech before the American Anti-Slavery Society in New York City, "they are under the yoke, smarting beneath the lash, sundered from each other, trafficked in and brutally treated." He lamented "that the American nation, to keep them in their present condition, stands ready with its ten thousand bayonets, to plunge them into their hearts." He called on Northern men to remember "that you are not only guilty of withholding your influence, but that you are the positive enemies of the slave, the positive holders of the slave, and that in your right arm rests the power that keeps them under the yoke." Many white people considered him a self-serving agitator intent on stirring up racial hatred and sectional rivalries that might provoke civil war or a slave uprising, like the one led by Nat Turner in 1831, in which some sixty white men, women, and children were slaughtered.

It is not clear when Abraham Lincoln first learned of Frederick Douglass, but by 1858 the abolitionist was so well known that Senator Stephen Douglas could exploit his unpopularity in the famous Lincoln-Douglas debates, during the Illinois senatorial race (which Lincoln would lose). Illinois was a Democratic state, hostile not only to abolitionists but to black people themselves. Only ten years earlier, more than 70 percent of the electorate had voted to make it illegal for black Americans, free or not, to settle in Illinois. In his quest for reelection, the Democratic senator readily played the race card, tying his Republican opponent to the fiery black leader. For years, Lincoln had carefully explained that, though he considered slavery immoral and adamantly opposed its extension to the territories, he was no abolitionist; he thought trying to abolish slavery at once would not only violate the Constitution but tear the country apart. Senator Douglas, blowing through such fine distinctions, declared that Lincoln deserved a medal from "Fred Douglass for his Abolitionism." Playing on the voters' fears that black males might gain ascendency over whites—and make free use of their women—the politician told a story: "I have reason to recollect that some people in this country think that Fred Douglass is a very good man. The last time I came here to make a speech . . . I saw a carriage, and a magnificent one it was, drive up and take a position on the outside of the crowd; a beautiful young lady was sitting on the box seat, whilst Fred Douglass and her mother reclined inside, and the owner of the carriage acted as a driver." The black abolitionist was in town to speak "for his friend Lincoln as the champion of the black man." Senator Douglas made clear to Illinois voters where he stood on the racial divide: with them.

Douglas's tall and ungainly opponent regarded slavery as "a blot upon our civilization" and a "standing menace to our peace and liberties," as Lincoln would put it later. Lincoln believed the Founders had been forced to accept slavery as one of the compromises necessary to create the United States, though they set it on the path of ultimate extinction, something that probably would have happened had the Yankee Eli Whitney not invented the cotton gin, a labor-saving device that increased cotton exports tenfold in two years and suddenly made slavery vastly more profitable. It was obviously incompatible with the self-evident truths the Founders had laid out in the Declaration of Independence, that "all men are created equal" and endowed with rights no government could justly take away. In this extraordinary country, Lincoln held, each person was to be treated as a sovereign, free to make the most of his life on the strength of his own merits—to have, as Douglass had put it, a future with hope in it. No group or class had the right to dominate another or to steal the fruits of anyone's labor.

The senator saw America differently. "I do not question Mr. Lincoln's conscientious belief that the negro was made his equal, and hence is his brother; but for my own part, I do not regard the negro as my equal, and positively deny that he is my brother or any kin to me whatever," Douglas said. "Now, I do not believe that the Almighty ever intended the negro to be the equal of the white man. If He did,

He has been a long time demonstrating the fact," the senator quipped. "For thousands of years the negro has been a race upon the earth, and during all that time, in all latitudes and climates, wherever he has wandered or been taken, he has been inferior to the race which he has there met. He belongs to an inferior race, and must always occupy an inferior position." That whites were innately superior to blacks seemed common sense to nineteenth-century Americans, North and South, including many of those who opposed slavery.

Recognizing that this line of attack put him in considerable political danger, Lincoln protested that he never considered blacks the social equals of whites. "I am not nor ever have been in favor of making voters or jurors of negroes, nor of qualifying them to hold office, nor to intermarry with white people," Lincoln insisted. He asserted that there is "a physical difference between the white and black races which I believe will forever prevent the races living together on terms of social and political equality." Insofar as the two races must live together, with one claiming superiority, Lincoln added, "I as much as any other man am in favor of having the superior position assigned to the white race." Still, he added, with a twist of Lincolnian wit: "I do not understand that because I do not want a negro woman for a slave I must necessarily want her for a wife."

For all his detestation of slavery, Lincoln genuinely feared that freed blacks might never get ahead in American society. Prejudice was so pervasive in the culture, he thought, that the races would find it impossible to coexist. For years, Lincoln had supported the idea of offering owners compensation if they gave up their slaves; this was to be closely followed by the shipping of freed blacks off to their own country in Africa (Liberia) or Central America, leaving the United States to the whites. "What I would most desire would be the separation of the white and black races," Lincoln flatly declared in a political speech in his home city of Springfield, Illinois, in July 1858.

Even as president, while unprecedented slaughter was working to extinguish slavery, Lincoln continued to strive for separation and colonization. At the White House in August 1862, after he had already resolved to announce the Emancipation Proclamation—sure to anger many voters, upend slavery, and inflict enormous pressures on society —Lincoln almost desperately pleaded with a group of distinguished African Americans to use their influence to persuade black people to the leave the country. "You and we are different races. We have between us a broader difference than exists between almost any other two races," Lincoln explained, knowing that a reporter in the room would disseminate his monologue to Northern voters. Even when black Americans "cease to be slaves, you are yet far removed from being placed on an equality with the white race. You are cut off from many of the advantages which the other race enjoy." Free men aspire "to enjoy equality with the best," Lincoln noted, "but on this broad continent, not a single man of your race is made the equal of a single man of ours." He did not want to debate the matter. This was the plain "fact with which we have to deal. I cannot alter it," he said. Bitter feelings about blacks had already inflamed civil war, he observed: "See our present condition—the country engaged in war!—our white men cutting one another's throats, none knowing how far it will extend; and then consider what we know to be the truth. But for your race among us there could not be war, although many men engaged on either side do not care for you one way or the other. Nevertheless, I repeat, without the institution of Slavery and the colored race as a basis, the war could not have an existence."

Frederick Douglass found Lincoln's scheme of deporting millions of black people as preposterous as it was despicable. The United States was the only country his people knew; it was as much their country as anyone's. He compared Lincoln to "an itinerant Colonization lecturer" and accused the president of "showing all his inconstancies, his pride of race and blood, his contempt for Negroes and his canting hypocrisy." He found his notion of blaming black Americans for the Civil War particularly repulsive. "Mr. President," he wrote, "it is not the innocent horse that makes the horse thief, not the traveler's purse that makes the highway robber, and it is not the presence of the Negro that causes this foul and unnatural war, but the cruel and brutal cupidity of those who wish to possess horses, money, and Negroes by means of theft, robbery, and rebellion."

Lincoln surely could grasp that the cost of transporting millions of people from the United States would be staggering, the logistics nightmarish if not impossible. With the midterm elections approaching, Lincoln might have delivered his demagogic soliloquy to reassure white voters that he was on their side. An adviser to the administration around that time spelled out the full-blown fear in the Midwest in the wake of Lincoln's Emancipation Proclamation: "Ohio will be overrun with negroes, they will compete with you and bring down your wages, *you* will have to work with them, your *wives* and *children* must associate with theirs and you and your families will be degraded to their level." Lincoln, a cautious student of public opinion, read such reports with care.

Yet, if only through his steely determination to win the war and prevent the nation's destruction, Lincoln was unquestionably doing more for Douglass's people than any man ever had. Neither Lincoln nor most Americans had embarked on war with the idea of eradicating slavery anytime soon. But the president knew full well that slavery sustained the rebellion. With his mastery of political timing, Lincoln had kept the crucial border states of Missouri, Kentucky, and Maryland from breaking free and had retained the American people's support for the war while steadily, painstakingly undermining the institution. In July 1862, Lincoln had convened his Cabinet to discuss a momentous wartime measure: The U.S. government would recognize all the slaves of Southern insurgents as free, unless the rebels laid down their arms. After issuing the warning in September, the president formally signed the Emancipation Proclamation on January 1, 1863.

Despised by voters in much of the North, who opposed transforming the war into an abolition crusade and flooding their states with free blacks, Lincoln's warning of emancipation led to a Republican bloodbath in the November 1862 House elections, forcing Republicans to join with National Union Party moderates to barely retain control of the chamber. Critics argued that the proclamation would have little meaning, since it would free people only in those places where the Union had no power to free them. But, as both Lincoln and his opponents realized, it would have a profound psychological impact, strengthening the Union cause and weakening the South. With the war clearly defined as a powerful moral crusade of freedom versus slavery, France and England could no longer consider lending aid to the Confederates. And word would spread through the Southern grapevine to African Americans that the president in faraway Washington, D.C., had declared they were free, inspiring many to abandon their masters, crippling the South's ability to feed its people and sustain its armies. "It is my last card, and I will play it and may win the trick," Lincoln said.

The president's enemies branded the proclamation an act of barbarism, a call for an insurrection by slaves, an evil incitement to millions of blacks to slaughter Southern whites, notably helpless women, with only the elderly and infirm to defend them while their men were off bravely fighting for their independence. Eleven days after Lincoln signed the proclamation, Jefferson Davis expressed his outrage to the Confederate Congress. Certain that blacks would never be able to provide for themselves outside of slavery, Davis called it "a measure by which several millions of human beings of an inferior race, peaceful and contented laborers in their sphere, are doomed to extermination." At the same time, Davis believed that the proclamation's "insidious recommendation" that slaves "abstain from violence unless in necessary self-defense" was, in truth, an encouragement "to a general assassination of their masters." While he sneered that Lincoln was motivated by "impotent rage," since the Union was plainly losing the war, Davis proposed that the South retaliate by executing Union officers taken as prisoners of war—or, as he put it, treating them "in accordance with the laws of those States providing for the punishment of criminals engaged in exciting servile insurrection."

Lincoln hoped that many thousands of Southern slaves inspired by the proclamation to abandon their masters would take up arms for their freedom. In 1863, the United States began to enlist as soldiers those who had fled. While the president admitted that this gave "serious offense" to many white Americans, he believed enough now grasped the difficulty, if not impossibility, of crushing the rebellion without such radical actions. To soften the outrage and opposition of those who flatly refused to accept African Americans as the equals of whites, Lincoln supported paying the black soldiers less. Though Douglass was outraged at this blatant injustice, he played a leading role in urging members of his race to enlist, arguing that the moment had arrived for African Americans to smash slavery at last and free their race. "There is no time for delay. The tide is at its flood that leads on to fortune. From East to West, from North to South, the sky is written all over, 'Now or never,'" Douglass declared in March 1863. "The iron gate of our prison stands half-open. One gallant rush from the North will fling it wide open, while four millions of our brothers and sisters shall march out into Liberty!"

Five months later, seeking to get black enlistees equal pay, Douglass arranged to meet with Lincoln in person. Given the fierce racial prejudice of the times and the bitterness of his invectives against the president, Douglass approached the session with some trepidation. At the White House, he found that "the stairway was crowded with applicants . . . and as I was the only dark spot among them, I expected to have to wait at least half a day." But within two minutes, he was ushered into Lincoln's office, finding the president seated "in a low armchair with his feet extended on the floor, surrounded by a large number of documents and several busy secretaries."

Lincoln immediately put Douglass at ease. "I know who you are, Mr. Douglass; Mr. Seward has told me all about you," the president said. "Sit down. I am glad to see you." Douglass was surprised. He later related: "In his company, I was never in any way reminded of my humble origin, or my unpopular color"—a remarkable thing at the time. Nonetheless, Douglass pulled no punches. When Lincoln asked him his views of the political and military situation, Douglass said he was most disheartened by "the tardy, hesitating, vacillating policy of the President of the United States." Lincoln allowed that he might seem slow, but he did not vacillate. "I think it cannot be shown that when I have once taken a position, I have ever retreated from it."

On the question of equal pay, Lincoln argued, with typical pragmatism, that black men "had larger motives for being soldiers than white men" and "ought to be willing to enter the service upon any condition." He knew that African Americans' service in saving the Union would make a powerful case for the final destruction of slavery and the recognition of their rights. While the inequality of pay was a "necessary concession to smooth the way," Lincoln promised that it would be corrected over time. "We had to make some concessions to prejudice," he said. "I assure you, Mr. Douglass, that in the end they shall have the same pay as white soldiers." Douglass was "not entirely satisfied with his views," but left the meeting with a new appreciation of the president. At the very least, Lincoln clearly respected him and seemed to be genuinely interested in his perspective.

Douglass continued urging black men to fight, despite their lower pay, few to no opportunities for advancement in the ranks, and a far grimmer disadvantage: the serious risk of being executed or sold back into slavery if captured by the Confederates. He recognized that if black men fought to save the nation they would be making an almost unanswerable argument for full citizenship. "Shall colored men enlist notwithstanding this unjust and ungenerous barrier raised against them? We answer yes. Go into the army and go with a will and a determination to blot out this and all other means of discrimination against us," Douglass implored. "Once in the United States uniform and the colored man has a springing board under him by which he can jump to loftier heights."

Douglass's own son Lewis fought as a sergeant in the famous Fifty-Fourth Massachusetts regiment, joining in the almost suicidal assault on Fort Wagner near Charleston, South Carolina, in July 1863—a battle in which the regiment sustained 50 percent casualties. The black enlisted men were led by colonel Robert Gould Shaw, a white Boston scion and son of prominent abolitionists. An educated black woman from Massachusetts, Charlotte Forten, while teaching freed slaves at Port Royal, South Carolina, had met the "noble little" Shaw days before the battle. "What purity, what nobleness of soul, what exquisite gentleness in that beautiful face! As I look at it, I think 'The bravest are the tenderest.' I can imagine what he must be to his mother. May his life be spared to her!" Forten wrote. Leading his men to the fort's parapet, Shaw was shot through the chest three times and killed. "Men fell all around me. . . . How I got out of that fight I cannot tell, but I am here," Lewis Douglass wrote to his future wife. "My Dear girl I hope again to see you. I bid you farewell should I be killed. Remember if I die I die in a good cause."

The South's attitude toward black Union soldiers was made brutally clear at Fort Pillow, Tennessee, in April 1864, when former slave trader Nathan Bedford Forrest led a vastly larger Confederate force against the defenders, quickly forcing their surrender. "No quarter! No quarter! Kill the damn niggers; shoot them down!" Forrest's men shouted. In cold blood, they gunned down all African Americans who surrendered. "The slaughter was awful—words cannot describe the scene," Confederate sergeant Achilles Clark wrote home after the battle. "The poor deluded Negroes would run up to our men, fall upon their knees, and with uplifted hands scream for mercy, but they were ordered to their feet and then shot down."

Still, as Douglass expected, the mere existence of black soldiers fighting bravely worked a profound and irreversible change in America. Many had doubted blacks would display the same courage and initiative as whites in combat. Journalist Lois Bryan Adams, interviewing wounded soldiers in Washington in May 1864, reported that one white officer who had initially opposed fighting alongside blacks had changed his mind in recent days. Black regiments under General Ambrose Burnside—shouting "Fort Pillow and revenge!"—had used bullets and bayonets to kill every rebel within their reach, including a number who had surrendered. "Some officers undertook to reprove them for cruelty, when the dusky warriors excused themselves by saying the rebels got in the bushes and there was no other way to get them out. They were excused," Adams wrote. "On all hands are heard praises of their valor and intrepid daring." The following month, after African American soldiers charged Confederate troops straight uphill outside

Petersburg, Virginia, a white officer wrote: "The problem is solved. The negro is a man, a soldier, a hero."

That August, one year after their first meeting, Douglass returned to the White House to see Lincoln again. He was shocked by the president's appearance. "The dimmed light in his eye, and the deep lines in his strong American face, told plainly the story of the heavy burden of care that weighed upon his spirit," Douglass recalled. In the meeting, Lincoln revealed that he stood little to no chance of winning reelection in November. He explained that voters believed that he had become obsessed with waging an abolitionist war, letting America's finest young men be slaughtered for a political cause many whites did not support. The powerful peace movement that was sweeping the North, he believed, would lead to the election of Democrats, followed by the rapid end of the war and the country's perpetual division.

Fearing the permanent enslavement of millions of black people as a result, Lincoln asked Douglass whether he would consider organizing "a band of scouts, composed of colored men, whose business should be somewhat after the original plan of John Brown, to go into the rebel States, beyond the lines of our armies, and carry the news of emancipation, and urge the slaves to come within our boundaries." The president wanted as many slaves as possible separated from their masters before the end of his term on March 4, 1865. "He saw the danger of premature peace, and, like the thoughtful and sagacious man as he was, he wished to provide means of rendering such consummation as harmless as possible," Douglass observed. It was incumbent on slaves to act immediately, Lincoln said. "He thought that now was their time—and *that only such of them as succeeded in getting within our lines would be free after the war is over*," Douglass recalled. This impassioned plea struck Douglass forcefully. Lincoln had declared repeatedly that his only object was to save the Union, with or without slavery, a position Douglass had criticized as immoral and unfeeling. But in this hour of desperation, Lincoln revealed something more: "What he said on this day showed a deeper moral conviction against slavery than I had ever seen before in anything spoken or written by him."

In that moment, it struck Douglass that he may have been wrong about the man he had denounced weeks earlier as an evil prevaricator. Instead, the president seemed to be guided by a profound desire to free the enslaved. Lincoln's anguish over their suffering and his fears for their future were all too plain. After visiting Lincoln, Douglass privately tested this newfound impression of the president with the "gloomy" secretary of war, his friend and fellow radical Edwin Stanton. Stanton confessed that he saw Lincoln more in the light of a calculating politician who said things for effect. "He thinks far less of the President's honesty than I do, and far less of his antislavery than I do," Douglass wrote to his friend Theodore Tilton, a poet, editor, and abolitionist. But Douglass could not believe that Lincoln's passion was just an act. The president did care—intensely, he was certain. "I have not yet come to think that honesty and politics are incompatible," Douglass wrote. Years later, Douglass admitted that, from the perspective of abolitionists, "Lincoln seemed tardy, cold, dull, and indifferent." But there was another side he had come to consider. "Measure him by the sentiment of his country, a sentiment he was bound as a statesman to consult," Douglass said, and Lincoln "was swift, zealous, radical, and determined."

Douglass was struck, too, when the president, not long after the August meeting, invited him to tea at his beloved retreat at the Soldiers' Home. Though the abolitionist had another engagement, the purely social invitation was further evidence of Lincoln's genuine fondness for his company and his striking absence of racial feeling. In a speech that fall, Douglass still faulted Lincoln for his sluggishness in moving against slavery, in enlisting black soldiers, and in stopping discrimination against them. But Douglass warned his audience that a Democratic victory would be disastrous. He also heeded the pleas of Republican strategists to lie low until the campaign was over. "I am not doing much in this Presidential Canvass for the reason that Republican committees do not wish to expose themselves to the charge of being the 'Nigger' party," he wrote to Tilton. "The negro is the deformed child which is put out of the room when company comes."

A sudden, dramatic shift in the North's military fortunes—most notably Sherman's conquest of Atlanta—changed everything. Swing voters decided to back Lincoln for a second term, however weak his leadership seemed, rather than risk losing what had been finally gained at such terrible cost. With the president safely reelected on November 8, 1864, Douglass could abandon his mission to infiltrate the South, and Lincoln could focus on a far more effective approach: an amendment to the Constitution forever abolishing slavery, removing forever the danger it posed to the republic and ensuring that his proclamation's promise that former slaves would be "forever free" would be kept. Lincoln was deeply worried that the end of the war—now in sight— would leave large numbers of African Americans trapped in chains, since the Emancipation Proclamation, merely an executive order issued as a war measure, would lose all constitutional force as soon as the hostilities ended. The Senate had already approved the amendment, and the president, concerned that many long months would pass until a new Congress took over, resolved to get it through the lame-duck House. It was a tough go. By mid-January, House Speaker Schuyler Colfax warned that he was still five votes short of the two-thirds margin required. Insisting that the amendment's passage was a vital war measure, Lincoln resorted to personal appeals to House members and employed surrogates to engage in some rank horse trading. When members heard of peace negotiations, which would dampen ardor for such a momentous war measure, he reassured Congress there were no negotiations taking place in Washington. (He failed to reveal they were taking place in Virginia.) The campaign worked. To his intense relief, the House passed the measure on January 31, 1865, sending it off to the states for their expected ratification. It now appeared certain that the slaves would be free, even if the war was to end precipitously.

Douglass, characteristically, insisted the effort fell short. "Slavery is not abolished until the black man has the ballot," he said. Still, everything was moving in his direction. In February, the Reverend Henry Highland Garnet became the first black minister to preach to the U.S. House of Representatives—he spoke about the end of slavery while

Congress weighed the integration of the city's horsecar lines. Journalist Adams mused that "the day may not be far off when mind and soul, and not the color of his skin, shall mark the measure of a man."

In an August 1863 letter, Lincoln had looked forward to a time when the war might end. When that day finally came, he noted, some black Americans would know that, "with silent tongue, and clenched teeth, and steady eye, and well-poised bayonnet, they have helped mankind on to this great consummation." In the many months since, the dedication and courage of African American soldiers had led Lincoln to set aside his grim conviction that racial conflict would continue to tear at the nation in a postwar America. Lincoln would make no more appeals for colonization of blacks in Africa or elsewhere. In July 1864, his aide John Hay noted that Lincoln had finally "sloughed off" the idea. As the war neared its end, Lincoln cautiously supported something that Booth and other critics would deride as "nigger citizenship"—the voting franchise for African Americans. "I would myself prefer that it were now conferred on the very intelligent, and on those who serve our cause as soldiers," Lincoln would say a month into his second term. While fierce prejudice persisted, black soldiers had made a compelling case through their service that, in courage and devotion to country, they were the equals of white men and had earned the right to be treated as such.

As the Union's chances strengthened, dramatic changes in racial relations reached even to the South. On this Inauguration Day, Northerners read in their morning newspapers stunning reports that the Confederate House of Representatives had passed a measure calling for the enlistment of three hundred thousand black troops. Though the Confederacy could not bring itself, even in this dire hour, to promise slaves emancipation in return for their service, such a move could not help but profoundly alter Southern society. Georgia's Howell Cobb, one of the leading men of the Confederacy—General Sherman had ordered his troops to loot and burn down Cobb's plantation in retribution ("spare nothing," Sherman said)—was appalled. "The day you make soldiers of them is the beginning of the end of the revolution," Cobb warned. "If slaves will make good soldiers our whole theory of slavery is wrong." While Lincoln noted that it was "their business, not mine," he was struck by the Confederates' decision to enlist black men. "I have in my lifetime heard many arguments why the negroes ought to be slaves; but if they fight for those who would keep them in slavery it will be a better argument than any I have yet heard," he quipped.

As Lincoln and Douglass both understood, the nation's future would depend greatly on how Americans came to interpret the meaning of this terrible war. North and South could not unite around the mere conquest of one section by another, leaving fratricidal hatreds hardened in place for generations. For more than a year, Douglass had been giving a speech called "The Mission of the War," in which he argued that something vastly greater than military conquest was at the heart of the Civil War. "What we now want is a country—a free country—a country not saddened by the footprints of a single slave—and nowhere cursed by the presence of a slaveholder. We want a country which shall not brand the Declaration of Independence as a lie," he said. The "manifest destiny" of the war, he now believed, was "to unify and reorganize the institutions of the country" around the equality of blacks. That was "the secret of the strength, the fortitude, the persistent energy—in a word, the sacred significance—of this war. Strike out the high ends and aims thus indicated, and the war would appear to the impartial eye of an onlooking world like little better than a gigantic enterprise for shedding human blood."

The president's voice, of course, would carry much more weight than Douglass's. At Gettysburg, Lincoln had maintained that the meaning of this war was the preservation of an extraordinary nation, yielding "a new birth of freedom." After another year and a half of death and dismemberment, revolutionary change, and mounting hatreds, with Union forces at last crushing the dwindling armies of Southern men, Americans turned to Lincoln's second inauguration for any insights he might have about what the nation had achieved through this monstrous bloodbath.

A cold, stiff March breeze blew through the milling crowd in front of the Capitol. Douglass stood in the mud under a cloudy sky, waiting for Lincoln to speak.

CHAPTER 11

ANDY AIN'T A DRUNKARD

Saturday, noon, March 4, 1865

Well-dressed white men and women, eager to get out of the rain and the muck, swarmed to the doors at the northern end of the Capitol building, the only access that morning. Union soldiers were guarding the doors, and only those who bore a VIP ticket— the "talismanic pass," as the newspapers put it—could gain entrance. An "oratorical captain" bellowed at the crowd: "Ladies and gentlemen, my orders from the Sergeant-at-Arms are to let no more in at present, and those orders I shall obey." At intervals, the line moved, and the captain spoke again: "Ah, ladies and gentlemen, this restriction is only temporary. The Sergeant-at-Arms now says that you may pass in. But allow me to say that under no circumstances can anybody enter without a ticket. Move on. Please to move on." Even illustrious guests found it exceedingly difficult to get in. Between nine and ten a.m., former Massachusetts governor John H. Clifford found "such a crowd" of people "of very distinguished consideration" on the Capitol steps "as I never before encountered." After his friend Samuel Hooper, a congressman from his state, somehow made it inside, Clifford had to clamber into the building through a window—doing so "with a degree of ability that would . . . surprise you," he informed his wife.

At a quarter to noon, the procession featuring the presidential carriage—minus the president—was still not yet in sight, and people began to feel uneasy. "If Old Abe don't arrive here soon, we won't have any President," one man in the crowd said. "Beg your pardon, Andy Johnson will be President until Lincoln's sworn in," another jested. With time running out, the closed carriage broke free from a parade that seemed to be going at its own speed and "dashed through the mud" to the eastern front of the Capitol, trailed by a squad of dragoons and the mounted parade marshals, bedecked in yellow scarfs. "This was all the simple pageant which accompanied the President's wife to the door. It was more than republican in its simplicity. It was really democratic," the *New York Herald* declared.

Other carriages had been driving up in rapid succession, dropping off passengers as close as they could get. As noon approached, Noah Brooks wrote, "flocks of women streamed around the Capitol, in most wretched, wretched plight; crinoline was smashed, skirts bedaubed, and moire antique, velvet, laces and such dry goods were streaked with mud from end to end." With his VIP pass, the actor John Wilkes Booth slid indoors, walking among women who had found the weather exceedingly annoying. "The mud in the city of Washington on that day," Brooks marveled, "certainly excelled all the other varieties I have ever seen before or since, and the greatest test of feminine heroism—the spoiling of their clothes—redounded amply to the credit of the women who were so bedraggled and drenched on that memorable day." The *Herald* reporter savored the "grand national display" of women's ankles as they lifted their skirts to ascend the stairs. "Representative ankles were exhibited by the fair dames and lasses of every State in the Union. The variety of shape and size and hose was perfectly bewildering; but every foot was muddy and every skirt bedraggled."

The French diplomat Adolphe Pineton, the Marquis de Chambrun, had arrived at eleven a.m., in the rain, possessing not only a ticket to get inside the Capitol but also a special pass to the floor of the Senate. The crowd inside was so thick as it flowed toward the Senate chamber that "an individual was swept along like a stick in a freshet," the *Herald* reported. Still, everyone seemed to be in a good mood. "The ladies chatted about friends and fashions and ruined finery, for every dress was spoiled," the paper noted. Few seemed to be discussing the key figure of the day, Abraham Lincoln, who was still out of sight in the President's Room, wearing his new Brooks Brothers suit, signing bills before the congressional session ended at high noon. Pages came and went constantly with messages for the president. Just outside that room, Chambrun faced the challenge of forcing his way through the mob in the lobby and onto the Senate floor. "I pushed with some difficulty through the crowd which besieged all doors and penetrated at last into the Senate chamber," he noted. When he arrived, the "assembly had but three-quarters of an hour more of life." The Senate was still discussing its business, while the clock ticked toward noon, the hard end of the session. Navy Secretary Gideon Welles found the scene appallingly chaotic. "There was great want of arrangement and completeness in the ceremonies," he grumbled in his diary. "All was confusion and without order,—a jumble."

Never one to see ladies treated unchivalrously, Senator Lazarus W. Powell, an aristocratic fifty-two-year-old Democrat from Lincoln's birth state of Kentucky, took note of the swelling cacophony of women's voices outside the chamber. A pro-Union slaveholder and respected former governor, Powell had often criticized the president's war measures as dangerous intrusions on constitutional liberty, including Chase's creation of a national bank and a national currency, which shifted enormous power from the states to the central government. He found the administration's crudeness and belligerence hard to take. On the Senate floor, he had denounced Secretary of War Edwin Stanton and General Benjamin Butler as "heartless ruffians" who were "strangers to kindness, gentleness, benevolence, and those elevated manly virtues that gracefully adorn the life of a Christian gentleman." On this day, noting that women who were here for the inauguration had nowhere to sit, the senator moved that the gallery doors be opened now, well before the appointed hour of noon.

Several senators objected to this full-scale invasion of the seats above their chamber when much work remained to be done, but the majority voted to let the women in, for better or worse. "The rush and scramble for the stairs was characteristic of the gentler sex," the

Chicago Tribune noted sarcastically, "and from that time until the Senate adjourned, the confusion rendered proceedings inaudible." Women poured into the gallery, quickly filling any space not reserved for reporters and diplomats. "Their elegant costumes, glittering diamonds, charming countenances . . . produced a scene enchanting in the extreme. It was a sight that can never be forgotten by those who were favored with a view," the *New York Herald* marveled. "They were the wives of foreign noblemen, wives and daughters of members of the Cabinet, Senators and Representatives, butterflies of fashion, and others whom position secured for them admittance to this gay scene—presenting, altogether, the talent, beauty and grace of the fair sex of America in numbers seldom gathered in one building." Their "gay attire," one witness said, resembled "the gorgeous hues of a vast tulip bed." Not more than fifty men were able to get a seat. "The ladies monopolized everything," the *Herald* noted. "It used to be considered that McClellan was the favorite with the fair sex; but the manner in which they flocked after Mr. Lincoln on Saturday showed that they are as fickle in their political likings as in everything else. If a thing of beauty be a joy forever, certainly a thing of so many beauties as the inauguration must live forever." The men, dressed in their best suits but crowded out of the cermonies, occupied themselves by "roaming restlessly about the Capitol building, and looking out every possible window."

Solomon Foot of Vermont, who for the past four years had served as chairman of the Committee on Public Buildings and Grounds, overseeing the reconstruction of the Capitol, was presiding over the Senate. A hefty sixty-two-year-old with stringy white hair, a prominent beaklike nose, and tired eyes, Foot was "greatly discomfited to find that the fair ladies in the gallery had not the slightest idea that they were invading a session of the Senate," Brooks noted. "They chattered and clattered like zephyrs among the reeds of a water-side." Another reporter observed that the sound was just like the nesting of a flock of pigeons in some wilderness. Senators complained they could not even hear what was going on in the chamber, while Foot violently banged his gavel to no effect. "The gay people in the galleries talked on just as though there was no Senate in session in the United States." The chamber did quiet a little "when the attention of the fair mob was diverted by the arrival of eminent personages," who took seats below them in the extra chairs and couches set out on the Senate floor.

Joseph Hooker—the dashing Massachusetts general known as "Fighting Joe," an inveterate gambler, drinker, and womanizer, who bore a thick mane of blond, wavy hair—arrived, looking "handsome, rosy, and gorgeous in full uniform." Hooker, fifty, had once held command of the Army of the Potomac, a post that a desperate Lincoln had given him in 1863 after the army had suffered defeat after defeat, even though the general had disparaged his fellow officers and suggested a dictatorship might be needed to save the country. "Of course it was not *for* this, but in spite of it, that I have given you the command," Lincoln wrote to Hooker at the time. "Only those generals who gain successes, can set up dictators. What I now ask of you is military success, and I will risk the dictatorship." Under the leadership of the hard-partying Hooker, the headquarters of the Army of the Potomac quickly became "a place no self-respecting man liked to go, and no decent woman could go. It was a combination barroom and brothel," groused Charles Francis Adams Jr., an upstanding cavalry officer who was a grandson of President John Quincy Adams and son of the U.S. ambassador to Britain. In the end, Hooker proved to be one more painful disappointment to Lincoln and the country. He lost his nerve at the Battle of Chancellorsville and had to be replaced. While Hooker redeemed himself with bold service at Chattanooga, General Sherman did not trust him with high command, so he was available for such ceremonial duties as attending this day's inauguration. Vice Admiral David Farragut entered the Senate chamber in splendid dress uniform. After Farragut had captured Mobile Bay, the Confederacy's last major open port on the Gulf of Mexico, Lincoln had made him the nation's first three-star naval officer. The two famous military chiefs led in a large delegation of navy and army brass, "brilliant in gold lace and epaulets." First Lady Mary Lincoln, having been escorted from the presidential carriage and into the Capitol, entered the gallery, attended by Senator Anthony. Wearing a black velvet robe trimmed with ermine, Mrs. Lincoln was greeted with respect, "not any more from the fact of her being the wife of the president than the fact of the elegance and exceeding good taste of her dress and general queen like bearing," the *New York Herald* gushed.

The Supreme Court justices appeared on the Senate floor, led by the "manly form" of Salmon P. Chase, "looking very young and also very queer," Brooks noted, "carrying a 'stove-pipe' hat and wearing his long black silk gown"—the one his daughter, Kate, and Frederick Douglass had helped him try on the night before. In his other hand, the chief justice grasped two essential items: the Bible on which Lincoln would take the oath and a copy of the Constitution. He looked "every inch like a judge," the *Times* of London reported.

If girth was the standard, one of the most imposing justices was a three-hundred-pounder from Illinois. In addition to being arguably the fattest man in the chamber that morning, he was also the one most responsible for Lincoln's presidency. David Davis knew Lincoln from past days, when the prairie lawyer had traveled the Eighth Judicial Circuit through central Illinois, arguing his cases in front of Judge Davis. Lawyer Leonard Swett, who became close to both men, first encountered Davis at a country inn in Danville, Illinois. Told he could meet the judge upstairs, Swett climbed the stairs, knocked on the door, heard two voices tell him to enter, and beheld an enormously rotund man and a grotesquely tall one, "engaged in a lively battle with pillows, tossing them at each other's heads." Suspending the fight, the tall man—wearing an immense saffron-yellow nightshirt under which protruded two enormously large feet—crossed the room and held out his big hand. "My name is Lincoln," he said. He struck Swett as beyond question "the ungodliest figure I had ever seen."

Later, Davis, with Swett's help, brilliantly managed the Lincoln forces at the 1860 convention in Chicago, somehow yanking the nomination from Senator William Seward, a far more prominent figure backed by the powerful machine of Albany editor Thurlow Weed. When a position opened on the Supreme Court in 1862, Lincoln came under heavy pressure to appoint his old friend, the corpulent country judge.

Hawkins Taylor, a prominent Republican from Iowa, had to remind Lincoln that "but for the extraordinary effort of Judge Davis, you would not have received the nomination at the Chicago Convention. . . . I feel that it is due to yourself as well as to Judge Davis that you should tender him the appointment of Supreme Judge." Swett joined in the lobbying blitz, going so far as to confront Lincoln at the White House at seven o'clock one morning, before the president could turn to other business. "If Judge Davis, with his tact and force, had not lived, and all other things had been as they were, I believe you would not now be sitting where you are," Swett had lectured him. Lincoln replied gravely, "Yes, that is so." Lincoln finally gave Davis the job, though grudgingly, given the fierce competition for the lifetime post and his need to parcel out prized appointments to secure vital political alliances.

Though a Republican, Davis tended to reflect the conservative values of the people of his state. In January 1863, he confronted Lincoln about the disastrous condition of the country and the failure of his war policy, advising him to shake up his Cabinet and back out of the deeply unpopular Emancipation Proclamation. "Lincoln was a peculiar man; he never asked my advice on any question—sometimes I would talk to him & advise him; he would listen," Davis later reflected. Listen, but not always heed.

The Cabinet members entered the Senate chamber, with the man whom Davis had maneuvered out of the presidency leading the procession—Secretary of State Seward—followed by War Secretary Stanton, Navy Secretary Welles, Attorney General James Speed, and Postmaster William Dennison, a former Ohio governor, who had done Lincoln loyal service as the chairman of the convention that nominated him in 1864. House Speaker Schuyler Colfax of Indiana then led a number of his representatives in, having adjourned his chamber with a little speech: "We go hence, with our official labors ended, to the Senate chamber, and the portico of the Capitol; there, with the statue of the Goddess of Liberty looking down, for the first time, from her lofty pedestal, on such a scene, to witness and participate in the inauguration of the elect of the American people."

All eyes turned to a hubbub up above as the "gorgeous array of foreign ministers in full court costume" and their families took their seats in the diplomatic section of the gallery. They "lit up the place with a radiance agreeable enough to my European eyes," the *Times* of London correspondent noted approvingly, though a New Englander standing next to him in the press gallery dismissed their finery as "gimcrack" and "flunkeyism," the "kind of thing that did not suit a free country." The strict spirit of decorum was broken momentarily when a minister from South America, entangling his feet in the "massive crinoline" of a woman's hoop dress, lost his balance and rolled down the aisle. The ministers seemed to be outdoing each other in gaudy displays. "Mr. Edward De Stoeckl, Envoy Extraordinary of Russia, was prominent among these delegations, distinguished by numerous medals, insignia of rank and orders of nobility which covered and decorated his breast," the *New York Herald* observed. Two years later, De Stoeckl would negotiate with William Seward the sale of Alaska to the United States for $7.2 million—an incredible bargain for America, though it was initially disparaged as "Seward's folly." Italian minister Joseph Bertinatti, meanwhile, renowned for entertaining the powerful of Washington at his three-hour, eleven-course, six-wine dinners, "displayed himself in light colored pants, white vest and dress coat, with the entire breast and tails covered with heavy gold lace, making it difficult and awkward for him to take a seat. His performances in this line were exceedingly amusing."

Shortly before noon, as the Senate ended its session "under the weight of weariness," as Chambrun put it, and the chatter became so loud the senators could not discuss anything, outgoing vice president Hannibal Hamlin of Maine stepped to the podium. As the crowd fell silent, he offered a brief valedictory farewell. Hamlin was a respected man, a powerful orator and radical Republican—a fierce opponent of slavery and an advocate for black civil rights. Like many men before and after him, he found the vice presidency to be a "nullity." Lincoln would sometimes listen to Hamlin, as a longtime politician who knew what was going on in New England, and he was characteristically gracious to the vice president. "[Lincoln's] treatment of me was on his part that of kindness and consideration," Hamlin recalled. But Lincoln declined to invite him to Cabinet meetings and showed little need for his guidance. Troubled by the "slow and unsatisfactory movement of the Government" during the grim year of 1862, the vice president complained with some bitterness: "Of course I am not consulted at all, nor do I think there is much disposition in any quarter to regard any counsel I may give much if at all."

However unimportant the position was, the vice presidency was at least an honorable one that paid a salary. In June 1864, Hamlin had suffered the humiliation of being cast out of it. Lincoln's supporters, desperate to cobble together enough votes from pro-Union Democrats and Republicans to win the election, rebranded the Republicans as the National Union Party and chose the Democrat Andrew Johnson to balance the ticket. How much Lincoln had to do with that was not clear. His friend Brooks, who thought highly of Hamlin, asked Lincoln on the eve of the convention about his preference for a running mate, but the president "was craftily and rigidly non-committal." Years later, Lincoln's secretary John Nicolay assured Hamlin's grandson that the president never turned against his vice president and simply let the convention do as it pleased. But a Pennsylvania delegate, Judge S. Newton Pettis, claimed he visited Lincoln on the morning of the convention and asked him his preference. Lincoln "leaned forward and in a low but distinct tone of voice said, 'Governor Johnson of Tennessee.'" Such a whispered preference would, of course, carry great weight. After the convention duly chose the governor, Pettis informed Johnson: "I was with the President ten minutes after receiving the intelligence of your nomination—I need not tell you of the satisfaction felt and *expressed* by him at the result!" Lincoln's longtime friend George B. Lincoln also revealed to Johnson that the president voiced "the perfect accord of feeling and sympathy upon public questions between yourself and himself and his satisfaction at your nomination." The double-crossed Hamlin faced an immediate future without income. He resolved he would not beg for a government job, bitterly informing his wife that he did not "ask favor of the Administration to prevent from going to the poor house. So you see I have some pride."

In Washington on Friday, Johnson formally resigned as military governor of Tennessee, expressing his "high regard" for War Secretary Stanton and thanking him for "the uniform kindness which you have been pleased to extend to me personally and officially." Stanton replied with florid praise.

> In one of the darkest hours of the great struggle for national existence against rebellious foes, the Government called you from the Senate, and from the comparatively safe and easy duties of civil life, to place you in front of the enemy, and in a position of personal toil and danger, perhaps more hazardous than any encountered by any other citizen or military officer of the United States. With patriotic promptness, you assumed the post, and maintained it under circumstances of unparalleled trials, until recent events have brought safety and deliverance to your State, and to the integrity of that constitutional Union for which you so long and so gallantly periled all that is dear to man on earth.

That night, while Lincoln was at the Capitol signing bills and Chase was hosting Douglass, the weary Johnson attended the stag party thrown in his honor by his friend John W. Forney, who kept the liquor flowing.

At eight o'clock Saturday morning, Senator James R. Doolittle, a Wisconsin Republican and a member of the Committee of Arrangements for the Inauguration, sent a formal note to Johnson at Kirkwood House, a five-story hotel on Pennsylvania Avenue at Twelfth Street, where the vice-president-elect occupied a two-room suite on the second floor. "I have the honor to inform you that I will Call at your hotel at ½ past 10 O Clock," Doolittle wrote, to escort Johnson to his inauguration. As the two took their one-mile carriage ride through the rain to the Capitol, the vice-president-elect was out of sorts, evidently feeling achy and nervous. At the Vice President's Room, Johnson joined Hamlin and his twenty-seven-year-old son, Charles, a major in the Army of the Potomac who had fought at Gettysburg. Both greeted Johnson warmly and engaged in friendly conversation. Johnson asked for some whiskey to calm his jitters. Hamlin confessed he had none but sent out for a bottle. When it arrived, the vice-president-elect downed a glass, then had a second and even a third. "I need all the strength for the occasion I can have," Johnson said.

After Johnson had fortified himself, he and Hamlin were ready. Shortly before noon, with the eyes of the women in the gallery on them, they entered the crowded Senate chamber, arm in arm. The whiskey had settled Johnson's nerves, but it soon began to have a stronger effect. "The warmth of the Senate chamber, with possibly other physical conditions, had sent the fiery liquor to his brain," Brooks wrote. When Hamlin had finished his brief farewell, Johnson, "whose face was extremely red," sprang to his feet to speak before taking the oath of office.

He was supposed to make some brief, polite comments—seven minutes had been scheduled—acknowledging his assumption of the office. Instead, the new vice president launched into a maudlin diatribe. He mumbled at times, shrieked at others, wildly gesticulating while his audience whispered audibly. His theme was that, in this great republic, the mighty notables in Washington all owed their power to the people. "I'm a-goin' for to tell you—here today; yes, I'm a-goin' for to tell you all, that I'm a plebian!" Johnson proudly declared. "I glory in it; I am a plebian! The people—yes, the people of the United States have made me what I am; and I am a-goin' to tell you here today—yes, today, in this place—that the people are everything." He was slurring his words. "It might have been appropriate at some hustings in Tennessee; but it certainly was far from appropriate on this occasion," the *New York Herald* said. In coming east to Washington, the paper quipped, Johnson "evidently did not shun Bourbon county, Kentucky."

Johnson pointed accusingly at the Cabinet officers in the Senate chamber, asking them if they understood that their power derived from the people, addressing them without their titles: "Mr. Stanton," "Mr.

Seward," "And you too, Mr. —" He stopped, drawing a blank. Leaning over to his friend Forney, Johnson asked loudly, "Who is the secretary of the Navy?" Brooks saw Hamlin nudging Johnson to end his speech, but he continued. He had lost all sense of time. The Navy secretary whose name Johnson forgot, Gideon Welles, recorded in his diary that the speech was "a rambling and strange harangue, which was listened to with pain and mortification by all his friends." Welles noted that Johnson "has been sick and is feeble; perhaps he may have taken medicine, or stimulants, or his brain from sickness may have been overactive in these new responsibilities. Whatever the cause, it was all in very bad taste." Attorney General James Speed, sitting to Welles's left, agreed, whispering, "all this is in wretched bad taste," adding, "The man is certainly deranged." Seward, reticent to judge harshly, speculated that Johnson was merely overcome with emotion to be visiting the Senate and his friends again. "Johnson is either drunk or crazy," Welles told Stanton, who had lavished praise on Johnson the day before. Stanton replied, "There is evidently something wrong." The vice president's friend Forney tried in vain to persuade Johnson to take his seat, whispering that the time for the dissolution of the Thirty-Eighth Congress had come. Johnson ignored his advice.

If he were not the new vice president, the sergeant at arms would have had Johnson arrested for drunkenness in the Senate chamber, the *Times* of London remarked. Rising above one's station was one thing; bringing shame on it was another: "No one thinks the worse of Mr. Lincoln because in early life he was a rail-splitter and a boatman; but if, as President of the United States, he behaved liked a rail-splitter, spoke like one, drank like one, thought like one, and could not import into the higher sphere of his new life anything but the vulgar manners and gross habits of the old, it would be impossible for anyone to forget his origin, or not to lament that circumstances had lifted him out of a sphere in which it would have been better if he had remained."

The *New York Herald* reported that Republicans hung their heads and looked at one another as if to say: "Is he crazy, or what is the matter?" Finding their adversaries humiliated, Democratic senators leaned forward and appeared to be chuckling. "The speech was disconnected, the sentences so incoherent that it is impossible to give an accurate report," the *Herald* said. "It was not only a ninety-ninth rate stump speech, but disgraceful in the extreme." The crowd began to buzz: "What a shame." "Has he no friends?" "Is there no person who will have mercy upon him?" "Tell him to stop and save the country further disgrace." The official reporter was told to refrain from transcribing the speech and that Johnson would submit his remarks later. Chambrun, watching all of this with astonishment, assumed that Johnson had "acquired the wretched habit of drinking to excess" and had chosen to begin his new job "intoxicated." Senator Zachariah Chandler of Michigan confessed to his wife: "I was never so mortified in my life. Had I been able to find a small hole, I should have dropped through it out of sight." Former Massachusetts governor Clifford wrote to his spouse that "the new Vice president Andy Johnson disgraced himself and the Country by delivering the speech of a harlequin *so drunk he could not know what he said*. I never before felt so ashamed of my Country & this was the universal feeling."

In the President's Room, Lincoln continued signing bills until shortly after noon. He was expected in the Senate chamber after a brief speech by Johnson, but something had gone wrong. "The sound of a harsh, shrill voice was heard from the Senate chamber, and there seemed to be no end to this extraordinary and untimely oratory," the *Herald* noted. The reporter eavesdropped on the visitors crowded in the Senate lobby, listening to the rant emanating from inside: "There's a gas bag," one opined. "A pretty time to make a stump speech," another complained. "'Why can't he dry up, and let Old Abe be inaugurated?' was the general query." A personal acquaintance of Johnson standing outside the chamber refused to believe that the pontificating loudmouth was his friend. "Andy ain't no such man," he protested.

After waiting in vain for the speech to end, Lincoln was informed he could proceed into the chamber. He stepped from the President's Room into the hallway, quietly bowing to the thirty or forty people who crowded around the door. The *Herald* was struck by the crowd's respectful behavior. "Every head was uncovered as Mr. Lincoln passed, and no one attempted to rush him or crowd upon him. When he came to the door of the Senate a passage was made for him without any pushing or disturbance. Seldom have our people proved so polite upon any similar occasion." Lincoln passed into the Senate, escorted by Senators John Brooks Henderson of Missouri, one of the authors of the Thirteenth Amendment, and Lafayette S. Foster of Connecticut, president pro tempore of the Senate. Chambrun studied the president as he entered the room. "His bearing was modest. He walked with eyes inclined downward and took his seat in an armchair contiguous to, but below the bench occupied by the Senate clerks." But he was treated to another painful embarrassment, as the man he had allowed to become vice president in place of the elegant Hamlin was making a great fool of himself. As Johnson rambled on, Chambrun observed, "the President closed his eyes and seemed to retire into himself as if beset by melancholy reflections." Lincoln "totally ignored the many eyes which sought his own in the hope or perhaps expectation of a smile, nod or other sign of recognition on his part, while he, as overcome by the august solemnity of the occasion, remained absorbed."

Finally, after nineteen minutes, Hamlin managed to silence Johnson and administer the oath of office. "The effort of the Vice-President elect to go through with the form of repeating the sentences as read by Mr. Hamlin was painful in the extreme," the *New York Herald* reported. "He stumbled, stammered, repeated portions of it several times over." Johnson then flamboyantly planted his lips on the Bible or, as General Benjamin Butler put it, "slobbered the Holy Book with a drunken kiss." Then Johnson turned to the audience and tried to resume his speech. Hamlin distracted him and declared the old Senate adjourned.

Joseph B. McCullagh had seen much in this war that disgusted him, but nothing quite like this. The celebrated Washington correspondent of the *Cincinnati Commercial* under the well-known byline "MACK," he was a Dublin-born immigrant who had run away from home at eleven to the big city, New York, without friends or money, surviving by becoming an apprentice printer. Still brash at nineteen, he had climbed aboard the USS *Cincinnati*, the lead gunboat in the Union attack on Fort Donelson in Tennessee on Valentine's Day, 1862, braving fire as it pounded the stronghold. McCullagh was in the pilothouse when an exploding bombshell wounded flag officer Andrew Foote. Now, at twenty-two, he watched a Tennessee politician besmirch his adopted nation with the "most illiterate" speech ever uttered in the Senate. "But the subject is really too sickening to write about," McCullagh concluded. "All I have to say about the inauguration is, may He who controls the lives of men and the destinies of nations preserve the life of Abraham Lincoln, and spare the country the humiliation it would be made to feel in the contingency of Andrew Johnson's assumption of the reins of government."

The rain had stopped, and the inauguration planners had given the go-ahead to move outside for Lincoln's much-anticipated address and his oath of office. First the senators-elect had to be sworn in. The woozy Johnson, now officially presiding over the Senate, motioned them forward to touch a Bible and nod in assent, but he neglected to have them take the oath. Embarrassed, they returned to their seats. Forney called them back and swore them in. That ritual over, the presidential party flowed out of the chamber and toward the rotunda and the building's central exit, while women and dignitaries bolted from the Senate gallery, frantic to keep up, Mary Lincoln among them. Chambrun, accompanied by Massachusetts senator Charles Sumner, walked close behind the president, quite embarrassed to be in such a prominent place.

John Wilkes Booth hurried through the crowd toward the rotunda, the great, soaring heart of the Capitol, fed by arteries connected to the House and Senate chambers. The round room was 96 feet in diameter, filled with sculptures, and rose to the peak of the stunning dome, 180 feet overhead. Otis S. Buxton, the assistant doorkeeper of the House of Representatives, was walking from the Senate chamber with a friend when he saw Booth pass by "in great haste, going in the direction of the rotunda." "That man must be in a hurry," the friend observed. "That is Wilkes Booth," Buxton replied. He had "seen him often on the stage and off it, here and elsewhere." The friend said he did not know him but had seen his famous father, Junius, on the stage.

Outside, tens of thousands were stationed in front of the wooden platform built on the steps, eagerly awaiting the historic ceremony. As Lincoln walked through the building, he turned to Benjamin B. French, the marshal of ceremonies, and prudently instructed him, "Don't let Johnson speak outside."

Johnson's humiliating performance was yet another burden to bear, but Lincoln was not unduly worried. He later reassured the troubled treasury secretary, Hugh McCulloch: "I have known Andy Johnson for many years; he made a bad slip the other day, but you need not be scared; Andy ain't a drunkard."

Americans had to pray he was right.

CHAPTER 12

AN EXCELLENT CHANCE TO KILL THE PRESIDENT

Saturday afternoon, March 4, 1865

The man in charge of the inauguration festivities, sixty-three-year-old Benjamin Brown French, was exhausted by noon. Five years earlier, he had been spry enough to play the increasingly popular game of baseball, until he injured a tendon in his left leg while running. Now he had an expanding waistline, thinning white hair, graying, bristling sideburns, and deep rings under his eyes. He was weary, plagued by headaches and toothaches, and utterly fed up with the high life in Washington.

The previous Saturday, French had felt duty-bound to attend Mary Lincoln's dull reception at the White House from one to three p.m., then rush off to the party at the home of Kate Sprague and her father, Chief Justice Chase, which, though unquestionably "a very brilliant affair," was still just an irksome social responsibility. "Really I shall rejoice when Lent begins, for I am tired of gaiety," French confessed in his diary. He feared "the Inauguration and the Ball will about use me up." During the week since, as the U.S. commissioner of public buildings, he had been giving "all the aid in my power to perfecting the arrangements" of this day's inauguration ceremony. He had been on his feet since dawn, handling myriad details. The wild windstorm and drenching rain of the morning had added to his stress, forcing on French the decision of whether to keep Lincoln indoors, disappointing tens of thousands of visitors, or to risk sending him out into the elements. During a shower that morning, workers had hastily removed all the chairs from the temporary wooden platform outdoors where the swearing-in was to take place. "The hopes of the crowd again sunk," a reporter noted. Then patches of blue sky appeared in the west. "As the important time approached, the chairs were returned to their place on the platform—all eyes brightened, and were anxiously turned to the East front of the Capitol." Just before the fateful hour of one p.m., French stood by the massive east door of the rotunda, waiting to direct the president through it and into the open air.

The commissioner was already under fire from critics who said he should have removed all the dirt covering Pennsylvania Avenue before the festivities, which theoretically might have mitigated the rivers of mud that had splashed all over everyone and everything. In truth, there was little French could have done. The sluggish Congress had not approved appropriations to do the cleaning until the day before—much too late to get anything done in a rainstorm. Still, some wondered why he put the indoor events in the cramped Senate chamber instead of the much larger House of Representatives.

More than thirty years earlier, French had served in the New Hampshire legislature with two rising political stars, initially allies, later bitter enemies, both graduates of Bowdoin College: Franklin Pierce, who became a congressman, senator, and then president of the United States on the strength of being a Northern Democrat who was tolerant of slavery and intolerant of abolitionists; and John P. Hale, who became a zealous antislavery crusader.

As president of the Athenaean Society at Bowdoin, Pierce thoughtfully recruited Hale for membership in that Democratic club, though his friend came from a long line of Federalists. On March 3, 1832, shortly before Hale was elected to the New Hampshire House of Representatives, French wrote him a comically histrionic letter deploring the nature of politics and pitying the "poor devil" who worshiped at its shrine, as they both did. An American politician, he declared, "must discard conscience—bid farewell to truth—say adieu to virtue—and swear by all that's holy that he & his party are right and everybody else is wrong. He must submit his character to, that worse than fiery ordeal, the publick press. He must always be unhappy—always in a fever—his pulse never less than 120, and he can never hope to rest his head upon the pillow, for his *throbbing temples* forbid it."

French, a Democrat, moved to Washington to begin a stressful career of wrestling for appointed offices, rising or falling with his party's fortunes. For fourteen years, he worked as clerk for the Democratic-controlled House of Representatives, until a Whig-dominated Congress turned him out, one of the votes against him cast by an obscure Illinois politician named Abraham Lincoln. Fortunately, in 1853, French's friend Pierce, newly elected the fourteenth U.S. president, made him commissioner of public buildings—only to fire him two years later when he learned that French, increasingly troubled by the Democrats' bullying support of slavery, had flirted with joining the nativist American (or Know-Nothing) Party. By the end of the decade, French had become a full-fledged Republican and managed to win back the commissioner's job in 1861, several months after Lincoln's election as the sixteenth president.

Soon after Lincoln appointed him, French met with the First Couple. He was genuinely impressed. "She is evidently a smart, intelligent woman, and likes to have her own way pretty much. I was delighted with her independence and her lady-like reception of me. Afterwards I saw the President and he received me very cordially," French wrote in his diary on September 8, 1861. Like many in the president's circle, though, he quickly came to find Mary Lincoln exceedingly trying. The "Republican Queen plagues me half to death with wants with which it is impossible to comply," he complained later that fall, in a letter to his brother. When the First Lady wildly overspent a congressional appropriation for sprucing up the White House, French was forced to break the news to Lincoln, who was already harried by serious setbacks in the war and consequent political nightmares. French gently suggested that they seek a further infusion of cash from Congress. In a rare flash of temper, the president barked that he would never ask for more money "for flub dubs for that damned old house!" Lincoln knew what the public would make of such a request. "It would stink in the land to have it said that an appropriation for $20,000 for furnishing the house had been overrun by the President when the poor freezing soldiers could not have blankets." But eventually the president backed down and, under French's suave lobbying, Congress covered the overrun. Yet, through it all, French retained a grudging admiration for Mrs. Lincoln's endurance and pride, and he simply adored the president.

French accompanied Lincoln to the Gettysburg battlefield in November 1863, when the president famously delivered what French called "a few brief, but most appropriate remarks" in dedication of a national cemetery. In and around that Pennsylvania town, French discovered something remarkable that had eluded the Washington elites. However much Lincoln was disparaged by the sardonic radical Republicans and the shrill and sarcastic Democrats, the common people loved him. "Anyone who saw & heard as I did, the hurricane of applause that met his every moment at Gettysburg would know that he lived in every heart. It was no cold, faint, shadow of a kind reception—it was a tumultuous outpouring of exultation, from true and loving hearts, at the sight of a man whom everyone knew to be honest and true and sincere in every act of his life, and every pulsation of his heart. It was the spontaneous outburst of heartfelt confidence in *their own* President."

The day after the ceremonies, French had ridden his horse along the torn battlefield, where he found the white clapboard house, scarred with shot and shell, that the victorious Union general, George Meade, had made his headquarters four months earlier. The place was still haunted by the "very offensive" stench of the carcasses of two dead horses outside. A young man on the property explained he had burned fifteen others, but these last two were so close to the outbuildings that he did not dare. Trooping down the sloping field in front of the house to return to his tethered horse, French discovered two photographers— one of them, to his surprise, someone he knew well: Alexander Gardner. "At his urgent request I walked back to the house and took a position on the porch where I was, I suppose, photographed with the house." Two children posed on the porch with him. The next month, French visited Gardner's studio in Washington, at Seventh and D Streets, with its huge sign out front advertising "VIEWS of the WAR." He sat for a portrait to be used as a *carte de visite* and purchased a copy of the porch picture. While there, he took time to study Gardner's earlier photographs of Gettysburg, as harrowing as those of Antietam that had created such a stir in New York. "The carnage at Gettysburg, as shown by views taken by him while the field was strewn with the dead, gave me a most realizing sense of the concomitants of Battle," French reflected. "Oh the blood that has been needlessly shed during this awful war of rebellion!"

For the inauguration, French would need a ceremonial table up on the wooden platform to hold a tumbler of water for the president. He had one specially made, thirty inches high by twenty inches wide by twenty inches deep, with leftover iron parts from the construction of the Capitol's spectacular new dome. Its foot was fashioned from one of the leaflike parts of the inner dome, inverted; its pillar was one of the balusters of the iron railing around the opening of the eye of the dome; its top a square piece cut from the thin iron panels used, all painted white. "It is unique, and there probably will never be another like it in the world," French enthused. Lincoln would stand behind it when taking the oath—fragments of the Capitol bonded together, one more symbol of a country whose broken parts the president would somehow have to reunite. French told the president that he would give the table "to him to take to Illinois as a memento of the Capitol, when he should retire from the Presidency."

At half past noon Saturday, French was focused on getting the key players of the inauguration from the Senate chamber out to the platform and into the seats arrayed behind that table. It was chaos. Senator Henry B. Anthony of Rhode Island had been forced leave Mrs. Lincoln in the gallery while taking his oath of office down on the floor, handing over the responsibility of escorting her outside to Senator James Harlan of Iowa. But they got caught behind the mob that rushed from the Senate chamber and stuffed the hallways, and Harlan could not get Mrs. Lincoln into her assigned seat until her husband's speech and oath were over. The First Lady seemed an afterthought on this gala day. But she was not alone, as the *Times* of London reported:

"Every one was left to shift for himself, and the members of the Corps Diplomatique, with all their fine feathers and uniforms, sashes and ribands, stars and crosses, fared no better than the common crowd, and were left to fight their way into or out of the mass, as it best pleased them. Most of them were so displeased at the want of arrangement, or the want of courtesy, whichever it might have been, that they made no attempt to follow the President, and consequently took no part in the great celebration of the day."

But something far more ominous was unfolding in the bedlam. As Lincoln and his party passed through the Capitol rotunda at the head of a surging mob, French happened to see a man jump from the crowd into the procession behind the president, seemingly determined to get close to Lincoln. French called out in alarm to a Capitol officer standing nearby, Lieutenant John W. Westfall. The officer grabbed the man by the arm, stopping him, "when he began to wrangle & show fight," French recounted to his son, Francis, on April 24. French hurried over to the struggling man and told him he must fall back. The young man protested that he had every right to be there, and "looked very fierce & angry that we would not let him go on." He was handsome, with the diction of an educated man, and he did possess a signed pass for the inaugural events. "He asserted his right so strenuously, that I thought he was a new member of the House whom I did not know & I said to Westfall 'let him go,'" French recalled. While French and Westfall were questioning the man, Lincoln kept on walking, oblivious to the altercation. He passed through the door of the east portico and onto the platform. French had to turn his attention there.

Six weeks later, Westfall heard a gentleman recount that John Wilkes Booth "was in the crowd that day, & broke into the line & he saw a police man [grab] hold of him keeping him back." Remembering the half-crazed man he had seized by the arm, Westfall came to French and asked him whether he recalled the incident. "I told him I did," French wrote, "& should know the man again were I to see him." When French looked closely at a photograph of Booth that had been distributed by the authorities, "I recognized it at once as the face of the man with whom we had the trouble. He gave me such a fiendish stare as I was pushing him back, that I took particular notice of him & fixed his face in my mind, and I think I cannot be mistaken."

Some historians would come to question this memory, but Ward Hill Lamon, Lincoln's loyal bodyguard, was certain that Booth intended to follow the president outside and strike him down in front of tens of thousands at the inauguration—the perfect stage for an actor who yearned for historic fame and wished to demonstrate that the freedom-loving men of America would not endure tyranny. The setting might well have appealed to a man who had notably played the Shakespearean role of Marcus Brutus, the self-proclaimed defender of the Roman republic who assassinated the dictator Julius Caesar in the capital. "A tragedy was planned for that day which has no parallel in the history of criminal audacity," Lamon insisted. "Its consummation would have been immeasurably more tragical than the awful scene witnessed at Ford's Theater on the memorable 14th of April following." Given the immense crowds gathered for the event, Lamon reflected, it was "amazing that any human being could have seriously entertained the thought of assassinating Mr. Lincoln in the presence of such a concourse of citizens. And yet there was such a man in that assemblage. He was there for the single purpose of murdering the illustrious leader who for the second time was about to assume the burden of the Presidency. That man was John Wilkes Booth."

Several officers working that day later testified that they witnessed the scuffle. John Plants, stationed with French at the east door of the rotunda, swore in an affidavit that he saw Westfall seize a man "who seemed to be greatly excited." Policeman Charles J. Cleary, also in the rotunda, had "seen Booth often and states positively that the stranger who broke through the line on that occasion was no other person." Policeman William J. Belshan testified that "a severe struggle ensued" when Westfall seized Booth: "The east door was closed; assistance came to Westfall and the stranger was forced back into the crowd. The conduct of this man was much talked about by those who witnessed it." Calling Booth's plan one of "phenomenal audacity, Lamon later declared: "So frenzied was the assassin that he determined, if possible, to take the President's life at the certain sacrifice of his own; for nothing can be more certain than this, that the murder of Mr. Lincoln on that public occasion, in the presence of such a vast concourse of admiring citizens, would have been instantly avenged. The infuriated populace would have torn the assassin to pieces, and this the desperate man doubtless knew."

Long before Lamon publicly advanced this idea, French was privately certain that assassination was exactly Booth's plan. "My theory is that he meant to rush up behind the President & assassinate him, & in the confusion escape into the crowd again & get away," French wrote in his April 24 letter. "But, by stopping him as we did, the President got out of his reach. All this is mere surmise, but the man was in earnest, & had some errand, or he would not have so energetically sought to go forward." If police had dragged Booth away and searched him, they might have found a murder weapon, a hidden knife or derringer. He might have been arrested, tried, and imprisoned. Instead, after the altercation, the actor was evidently able to safely melt into the mob that was flooding out the rotunda's east door and onto the steps of the Capitol, near the platform where Lincoln was to make his speech.

Lincoln stepped out from the Capitol building, the first to appear on the wet planks of the walkway. "The appearance of the tall form produced an instantaneous effect," one reporter recounted. "The whole color of the vast mass of humanity which was gathered around the east end of the capitol was changed and transfixed as if by a magician's wand." Somber for the last hour, the tens of thousands were suddenly "all crying at once, and cheering for the man of the people's choice. The excitement and enthusiasm seemed likely never to subside." A "thunder of shouts, hand-clappings and wild hurrahs rent the air," wrote Adolphe Pineton, the Marquis de Chambrun, following close behind Lincoln. The U.S. Marine Band, which featured Antonio Sousa on trombone, father of the future "March King," John Philip Sousa, brayed out "Hail to the Chief." People everywhere waved flags, tossed hats into the air, flapped handkerchiefs, laughed and roared. Stretching out before Lincoln was a "sea of heads, tossing and surging, as far as the eye could reach, among the budding foliage of the park opposite," Noah Brooks wrote.

In the middle of that sea, rising up from the crowd, was an immense half-naked statue of George Washington, "with a monitory finger pointed to heaven," as the *New York Herald* put it. Twelve tons, extraordinarily difficult to transport to the Capitol, it originally had been stationed in the old rotunda, placed there in 1841, but had to be moved out onto the lawn when it threatened to bring the floor crashing down. French had been there when it was dedicated by President John Tyler and had recorded the crowd's derision and dismay: One viewer thought Washington "must have jumped out of bed in a hurry & taken the sheet with him." Another quipped, "But I don't believe the old General ever slept without his shirt on in all his life!" One man, struck by the footwear depicted, protested, "Sandals! General Washington with sandals on! Why the idea is ridiculous!" Once moved outside, the statue was fully exposed to scandalized passersby, who found it ludicrous that the artist, Boston-born, Harvard-educated sculptor Horatio Greenough, had turned the great republican leader—the exemplar of modesty, restraint, and civility—into a bare-chested Greek god. "Did anybody ever see Washington naked?" Nathaniel Hawthorne mused, reflecting on the statue. "It is inconceivable, he had no nakedness, but I imagine was born with his clothes on and his hair powdered, and made a stately bow on his first appearance in the world."

Beyond the statue, past the crowd, through the leafless trees, loomed the ominous brick walls and barred windows of the Old Capitol Prison, where enemies of the state were incarcerated, including female Confederate spies. Walt Whitman knew of a French professor imprisoned there in 1863 on spurious charges and condemned for a week to "a nasty, lousy dungeon without light—in it was a nigger with his wrist in manacles, and four white deserters." Whitman had been appalled that a boy of seven was also incarcerated at the time: "He and his father were taken as secesh guerillas in Virginia, and the government is holding onto the child," with hope of exchanging him for a Union prisoner in the South. "Mother, my heart bleeds [over] all sorts of such damnable things of one kind or another I meet with every day," Whitman wrote. Only the day before Lincoln's inauguration, a Union soldier, Sergeant Charles Sperry of Company E, Thirteenth New York Cavalry, had been freshly shaved, led outside the old prison's walls to an inner square, and told to kneel behind a coffin. He declined a blindfold; his hands were bound behind his back. A Catholic priest— Father Francis Edward Boyle, the pastor of Saint Peter's Church, who knew and served Mary Surratt, owner of the boardinghouse Booth liked to visit—heard Sperry's confession and prayed by his side. The previous June 18, Sperry had attempted to rape a fifteen-year-old girl, Anna M. Nelson, lifting her dress while she fought him desperately, preventing penetration.

The only real question had been whether Lincoln would save Sperry's life. The president often looked for grounds to pardon men convicted of capital offenses, including rape, seeking some reason to save a life. Indeed, he strove to make his mercy toward the condemned part of his public image, like his folksy storytelling, perhaps to soften the harshness attending his extraordinarily cruel prosecution of the war. A Philadelphia businessman and writer named Francis De Haes Janvier wrote a sentimental poem glorifying Lincoln for this trait, "The Sleeping Sentinel," which became so popular that the actor James Murdoch took to reciting it among other patriotic works to raise money for the Union cause. Lincoln had him deliver it before a gathered audience at the White House one afternoon in January 1863. In the poem, a young man—based on an actual soldier, twenty-two-year-old William Scott of Groton, Vermont—is sentenced to death for falling asleep at his post. The poet describes Lincoln in the White House:

> 'Twas night. In a secluded room, with measured tread and slow,
> A statesman of commanding mien paced gravely to and fro.
> Oppressed, he pondered on a land by civil discord rent;
> On brothers armed in deadly strife: it was the President!

The woes of thirty millions filled his burdened heart with grief;
Embattled hosts, on land and sea, acknowledged him their chief;
And yet, amid the din of war, he heard the plaintive cry
Of that poor soldier, as he lay in prison, doomed to die!

As the soldier is about to be executed, a "stately coach" hurtles to the scene "in a cloud of dust," and Lincoln emerges with his pardon to save the boy's life. Allowed to fight on, the soldier charges the enemy in a battle, and is the first among his company gunned down. As he lay on the field:

While yet his voice grew tremulous, and death bedimmed his eye—
He called his comrades to attest he had not feared to die!
And, in his last expiring breath, a prayer to heaven was sent,
That God, with his unfailing grace, would bless our President!

In the case of Sergeant Sperry, Lincoln had evidently found no grounds for mercy, and no stately coach would come hurtling in the dust. The firing squad duly shot several lead balls through Sperry's chest, one near his heart, killing him instantly. His body slumped to the right of the coffin.

The Frenchman Chambrun was thrilled by the spectacle spread out before him. "Thousands of colored folk, heretofore excluded from such reunions, were mingled for the first time with the white spectators," he wrote. "Further off, to right and the left, infantry troops were drawn up. Among them was a Negro battalion. Many uniforms were also distinguishable in the crowd." The audience was vastly bigger than the one at Lincoln's first inauguration. "I think there were at least twice as many at the Capitol as four years ago," reported Lincoln secretary John Nicolay, up on the platform with assistant secretary John Hay.

Hundreds of VIP spectators continued to pump out of the building behind the president's cortege. The *New York Herald* recorded the scene: "Ladies, senators, negroes, justices, secretaries, diplomats and people generally tumbled upon the platform pell mell." Secretary of State William Seward and Secretary of War Edwin Stanton took seats on the left, some distance from the president, and seemed unusually friendly. "Stanton had his arm around Seward's neck, and constantly whispered in his ear." The sour Gideon Welles sat on his own, speaking to no one. The well-lubricated new vice president talked to everyone. General Rufus Ingalls, in charge of supplying Grant's troops at City Point, Virginia, and Fighting Joe Hooker took their seats. "Colonels and captains were as plentiful as roses in June," the *Herald* observed, adding tartly, "Chief Justice Chase sat erect and dignified, evidently reflecting that he ought to be in Lincoln's place."

Having left her little boy back home, the graceful Elizabeth Blair Lee sat down next to Lincoln's first secretary of war, the well-connected Simon Cameron, who was still pulling wires even though he was out of office. This was Elizabeth's third inauguration, though her first in twenty-eight long years; in 1837, the eighteen-year-old had watched Democrat Martin Van Buren take the oath, a cheerful, animated little New Yorker whom her distinguished father, Francis Preston Blair, had served—as he did Lincoln—as an unofficial adviser. She did not seem especially interested in attending the present one, other than for the opportunity it afforded her to gather intelligence about the prospects of her husband, U.S. Navy rear admiral Samuel Phillips Lee, for a promotion. In fact, she talked right through Lincoln's inaugural address. "Whilst Mr. L was speaking I got a chance to ask Mr Cameron" about her husband's prospects, she would write. She had been "bitterly disappointed" to hear that Chase's allies, the radical Republicans on the House Committee on Military Affairs, had blocked her husband's military promotion because he was "linked in with the xxx Blairs." Detesting the Blairs for their political moderation and opposition to black civil rights, the radicals had already forced one of Elizabeth's brothers, Montgomery, out of Lincoln's Cabinet, and another, Frank, out of Congress and into the field with General Sherman, where he was serving this day in Cheraw, South Carolina, distributing Southerners' fine wine to the troops.

Many of those streaming from the building without assigned seats tried to get a better view from the platforms of the colossal statuary groups that rose from the Capitol's steps. On one side was *The Rescue*, by the same Horatio Greenough, a ten-ton work whose installation French had overseen in 1853. It depicted a massive white frontiersman thwarting a smaller, hatchet-wielding, naked Native American from committing an act of savagery, pulling back the Indian's arms to prevent his cruel and mindless slaughter of a young white woman, who is cowering in the background and trying to shield her baby. Greenough, a brazen race supremacist, designed it "to convey the idea of the triumph of the whites over the savage tribes," replacing Native Americans' barbaric violence with the graces of civilization—a tougher sell now, perhaps, during a fratricidal war that had already claimed more than a million casualties. Native Americans were not the only people the sculptor viewed as inferior. "I avoid a black man as I avoid a dirty, low white man," Greenough explained. "I turn my back on him, as all animals spurn their own ordure."

However blatant the triumphal message of *The Rescue* might have been, the humble masses visiting the Capitol seemed to have great difficulty deciphering it. They took the work literally and thought the sculptor was merely depicting the brave act of a famous pioneer. A lithograph based on the group of statues was labeled "Daniel Boone Protects His Family." Many settlers had friends and relatives who had been killed by Native Americans, including Lincoln, whose grandfather Abraham had been shot dead by an American Indian hidden in the forest near his Kentucky cabin. On the other side of these stairs was *Discovery of America*, by the Italian neoclassical sculptor Luigi Persico. It depicted Christopher Columbus, in the attire of a conquistador, thrusting a globe up in the air with his massive outstretched arm, eyes

straight ahead, ignoring a scowling Native American woman cringing
beside him, naked but for a loincloth sliding off her young body. Both
statuary groups were exuberant, if clumsy, images of America's prewar
confidence, the nation's belief in Manifest Destiny—the idea that it was
God's mission to conquer and civilize the weak and savage through the
power of white Americans and their culture of freedom.

John L. O'Sullivan, editor of the *United States Democratic Review*,
had written in 1839 of America's divine destiny—not to conquer lands
but "to establish on earth the moral dignity and salvation of man"
through the values expressed in the Declaration of Independence. While
the kings and nobles of Europe had led great armies that massacred
each other in the quest for land and power, America's great mission was
to develop and perfect the ideals of freedom—"freedom of conscience,
freedom of person, freedom of trade and business pursuits, universality
of freedom and equality." By demonstrating the tremendous force of
these ideas in unleashing human potential, America would change the
world. "We are the nation of human progress, and who will, what can,
set limits to our onward march? Providence is with us, and no earthly
power" could halt the United States, O'Sullivan asserted. These notions
were popular with many Americans, who were proud of their remarkable
heritage and disinclined to dwell on the darker side of the country's
stunning growth in power and influence, at least until the horrors of
civil war were shoved in their faces.

Some people at the time, including a gloomy young lawyer in
Springfield, Illinois, warned of dangers, even as they shared the common
faith in the might of a free America. "Shall we expect some transatlantic
military giant, to step the Ocean, and crush us at a blow? Never!—All
the armies of Europe, Asia and Africa combined, with all the treasure of
the earth (our own excepted) in their military chest; with a Buonaparte
for a commander, could not by force, take a drink from the Ohio, or
make a track on the Blue Ridge, in a trial of a thousand years," Abraham
Lincoln proclaimed in 1837, two years before O'Sullivan's manifesto.
"At what point then is the approach of danger to be expected? I answer,
if it ever reach us, it must spring up amongst us. It cannot come from

abroad. If destruction be our lot, we must ourselves be its author and finisher. As a nation of freemen, we must live through all time, or die by suicide."

Out on the grounds with the thousands, Walt Whitman studied the celebration, ready to jot notes with his pencil in his pocket notebook. The president he so loved—that odd, rough-hewn Westerner with the sad face—was up on the platform and would soon speak. Feeling euphoric, the poet sensed that something otherworldly was happening. Shortly before, as Whitman had flowed toward the Capitol with the crowd, he noticed people looking up to the sky, seeing something rare in a blue patch that had broken through the clouds. "Our heavenly neighbor Hesperus, the star of the West, was quite plain just after midday; it was right over head. I occasionally stopped with the crowds and looked up at it. Every corner had its little squad, thus engaged." Among those peering at the diamond above "were soldiers, often black, with raised faces." They were "well worth looking at themselves, as new styles of physiognomical pictures."

During the waning weeks of winter, Whitman had repeatedly spotted this celestial body, the planet Venus, unusually bright in the night sky. While many of the days had offered "leaden heaviness, fog, interstices of bitter cold, and some insane storms," some nights had been intensely beautiful, he wrote in the *New York Times*. To his eyes, the "star of the West" had "never been so large, so clear" in the evening sky. It seemed to be reaching out, "as if it held rapport indulgent with humanity, with us Americans." On recent nights, it had "hung close by the moon, then a little past its first quarter. The star was wonderful, the moon like a young mother." After so much suffering, Whitman found it strangely moving. "The sky, dark blue, the transparent night, the planets, the moderate west wind, the elastic temperature, the unsurpassable miracle of that great star, and the young and swelling moon swimming in the west, suffused the soul." A lonely sound had touched him, too, on these winter evenings. He had heard, "slow and clear, the deliberate notes of a bugle come up out of the silence, sounding so good through the night's mystery, no hurry, but firm and faithful, floating along, rising, falling leisurely, with here and there a long-drawn note." The bugler was playing a tattoo "in one of the army hospitals near here, where the wounded (some of them personally so dear to me) are lying in their cots, and many a sick boy, come down to the war from Ohio, Illinois, Wisconsin, and the rest."

It all lifted Whitman's spirits: the beauty of the heavens, his new-found affection for the horsecar conductor Peter Doyle, his work on a poignant book of poems about the war, and the launch of Lincoln's voyage into a second term. The journalist-poet had long shared in the people's faith in America's great destiny. He envisioned a mighty demo-cratic nation stretching from the Atlantic to the Pacific, from north to south, releasing the energy of every man and woman as no country ever had. "The United States themselves are essentially the greatest poem," he wrote in 1855, in his preface to *Leaves of Grass*, comparing the "largeness and stir" of America with the "tame and orderly" coun-tries that had preceded it. In his poem "Song of Myself," he declared: "I will make the continent indissoluble, I will make the most splendid race the sun ever shone upon, I will make divine magnetic lands." Lincoln, in his slow and stubborn way, was thwarting a stupendously powerful attempt to dissolve that continent and break that magnetic bond. Moreover, he was trying to bring forth a new nation that would expand its remarkable freedom.

Frederick Douglass, yearning too for a more perfect union, stood near the front of the crowd, just below the platform—so close that he caught Lincoln's eye. The president pointed him out to the woozy vice president, who flashed what Douglass took to be an expression of "bitter contempt and aversion." His memory perhaps distorted by what was to come, Douglass recalled turning to a friend and remarking, "Whatever Andrew Johnson may be, he certainly is no friend of our race." Looking back on the event years later, Douglass drew a contrast: "Mr. Lincoln was like one who was treading the hard and thorny path of duty and self-denial. Mr. Johnson was like one just from a drunken

EVERY DROP OF BLOOD

debauch. The face of one was of manly humility, although at the top-
most heights of power and pride; that of the other was full of pomp
and swaggering vanity."

An earnest young man among the elites up on the platform could
not see the manly humility in the face of Lincoln, only his arrogance
and tyranny. Several days later, John Wilkes Booth boasted to a friend,
the actor Sam Chester: "What an excellent chance I had to kill the
President, if I had wished, on Inauguration Day! I was on the stand, as
close to him nearly as I am to you." The appalled Chester asked "what
good it would do him to commit a crazy act like that."

Booth answered: "I could live in history."

CHAPTER 13

WITH MALICE TOWARD NONE

Saturday afternoon, March 4, 1865

To cheers, applause, and the sprightly notes of "Hail to the Chief," Abraham Lincoln ambled toward his seat. He had a "shambling, loose, irregular, almost unsteady gait," *Times* of London reporter William Howard Russell had observed back in 1861, and four years of grinding war had only exacerbated the president's tendency to stoop. When Lincoln sat down, his knees rose above his waist, making it apparent that his great height was in his protracted, bony legs, the mates of his long, pendulous arms, rather than in his slender upper torso. "A marble placed on his knee thus sitting would roll hipward," his former law partner, William Herndon, recounted. "It was only when he stood up that he towered above other men." As Lincoln sat waiting for his moment to speak, he "smiled to himself," the *New York Herald* reported. "He was dressed in black, with a plain frock coat. In his hand he held a printed copy of his inaugural address."

After a time, George T. Brown, the Senate's sergeant at arms, rose from his seat and stood before the massive crowd. Lincoln knew the forty-five-year-old Brown well. Both had been prominent lawyers in Illinois, and though they were originally from different parties—Lincoln a Whig, Brown a Democrat—they had found common cause in the 1850s in opposing the spread of slavery to the territories. Lincoln had pleaded for Brown's legislative vote in his quest for a U.S. Senate seat in 1854, but the Scottish-born lawyer and editor of the

Alton (Illinois) *Daily Morning Courier* spurned Lincoln to help elect Lyman Trumbull, a fellow Democrat turned Republican, under whom Brown had studied law. In 1856, Brown had presided over the state's first Republican convention, in Bloomington, where Lincoln's keynote address, an impassioned condemnation of slavery, thrilled the crowd. In 1861, when Republicans gained control of the U.S. Senate for the first time, Trumbull rewarded Brown for his loyalty with the prized patronage plum of sergeant at arms, letting him leave Illinois behind and come to the power center of Washington. In that role, Brown signed the passes—including one held by John Wilkes Booth—that permitted people access to the Capitol and then the platform.

Senator Trumbull, though a fellow Republican from Illinois, never really warmed to Lincoln. While he considered Lincoln a generally truthful and compassionate man, Trumbull also found him a shrewd and secretive politician—"as cunning as a fox"—who hid his nature behind a folksy image that duped his adversaries into underestimating him. Moreover, "Mr. Lincoln was a follower and not a leader in public affairs," careful to maintain his power by riding the strong current of public opinion. Trumbull found it confounding that Lincoln's slavish admirers, "instead of regarding his want of system, hesitancy, and irresolution as defects in his character," actually sought "to make them the subject of praise." While Lincoln did help end slavery and save the Union, Trumbull asserted that "a man of more positive character, prompt and systematic action, might have accomplished the same result in half the time, and with half the loss of blood and treasure."

Now, as Trumbull looked on, Brown ushered Lincoln—the man they had frozen out of the Senate—into the vastly more powerful and important job of president. At one p.m., the "historic Brown," as Noah Brooks put it, began bowing, "with his shining black hat in hand, in dumb-show before the crowd"—a nineteenth-century signal to an audience to be quiet. After Brown's exaggerated bowing gradually silenced the throng, "Abraham Lincoln, rising tall and gaunt" from his seat, stood behind the table with his inaugural address, pasted in two broad columns upon a single large page of paper. Brooks reported that a "roar of applause shook the air, and, again and again repeated, finally died far away on the outer fringe of the throng, like a sweeping wave upon the shore."

At that moment, the sun, hidden all day, "burst forth in its unclouded meridian splendor and flooded the spectacle with glory and light," Brooks noted. "Every heart beat quicker at the unexpected omen, and not a few mentally prayed that so might the darkness which has obscured the past four years be now dissipated by the sun of prosperity." Standing near the president, former Massachusetts governor John H. Clifford was moved. "The sun shone out just as the Pres. Commenced his address for the first time since I arrived here," he wrote. The "clouds were rolled away like a scroll," the Washington *National Republican* reported, "and the sun shone forth ominously—ominous of the bright future of the best Government the sun ever shone upon." Lincoln later spoke of the moment to Brooks: "Did you notice that sunburst? It made my heart jump." Walt Whitman certainly noticed it. The weather that morning had been "like whirling demons, dark, with slanting rain, full of rage; and then the afternoon, so calm, so bathed with flooding splendor from heaven's most excellent sun, with atmosphere of sweetness; so clear it showed the stars, long, long before they were due." The poet saw another omen: "As the President came out on the capitol portico, a curious little white cloud, the only one in that part of the sky, appeared like a hovering bird, right over him."

Walt Whitman's friend Alexander Gardner was ready with his cameras, their carefully coated glass plates slid into place, to capture images that would guide the artists of *Harper's Weekly* magazine in creating lithographs of the scene for its hundreds of thousands of readers. Before the speech, Gardner's cameras had recorded the soaked crowds, including African American soldiers standing with their boots in the mud and their rifles on their shoulders, pointed skyward. One of the magazine's published lithographs suggested that a member of Gardner's team had set up his camera off to the right, at the fringe of the enormous throng, securing an image of the distant platform, tiny beneath the massive Capitol, with its new dome topped by the statue of

Freedom. Tens of thousands of people could be seen massing in front
and taking up places on the stairs of the House and Senate wings, far
beyond earshot of the president, some chatting with each other since
there was nothing to be heard. A huge American flag flapped over the
House. In the distance, Benjamin B. French's unique table could be
made out, but the figures on the platform were tiny blurs. Even the
massive statuary groups, rising from the crowd with their thrusting
arms and exaggerated gestures, looked trivial from so far away.

Another photographer, probably Gardner himself, was off to the
left, shooting on a hard angle but much closer to the action. He collected
several images in brilliant detail. In one, Abraham Lincoln is seated next
to the flush-faced Andrew Johnson. Both men look forward instead of
engaging in conversation. Johnson has his legs crossed, a large stovepipe
hat in his hands. Lincoln is seemingly lost in thought, his head tilted
slightly, his expression halfway between a frown and a wry smile, his
hair cut short and reasonably under control, his long and bony legs
uncrossed, his hands pressed firmly in his lap. A later shot shows the
president in his new suit standing tall behind the table with the tumbler
of water on it, with his prominent nose, thin chin whiskers, neck too
scrawny for his gleaming white collar, and his head bent down to read
from the sheet of paper held firmly in both of his hands. Chief Justice
Salmon P. Chase can be seen seated to the right, holding what looks
like Lincoln's stovepipe hat, a hat he had been seen carrying earlier
in the Senate chamber. Four years earlier, before his first inaugural
address, the new president had fumbled with his hat until Stephen
Douglas, Lincoln's old adversary, who had met defeat as the Northern
Democratic nominee in the 1860 presidential campaign, sprang up and
said, "Permit me, sir." Douglas submissively held Lincoln's hat during
his address, something that many took as a noble gesture of solidarity,
at a time of national crisis, with the man who had once been his political enemy. "Doug must have reflected pretty seriously during that half
hour, that instead of delivering an inaugural address from the portico,
he was holding the hat of the man who was doing it," the *Cincinnati
Commercial* reported at the time. Gardner's photograph may well have

captured Chase, who had hoped to wrest the 1864 nomination from Lincoln, doing the same. Surrounding Lincoln in the photograph are hundreds of listeners, many crowded onto the platform around the dramatic poses of *The Rescue*. Some analysts have detected John Wilkes Booth in one face or another in that group, though the identifications seem to be guesswork. With his extraordinary photographs, Gardner had frozen in time one of the supreme moments in American history.

Before the silent crowd, the president, looking down on his sheet of paper, began to speak. "Every word was clear and audible as the ringing and somewhat shrill tones of Lincoln's voice sounded over the vast concourse," Brooks wrote. Though perhaps only several hundred out of the thousands gathered could hear Lincoln, the *New York Herald* reporter made note of the president's "loud, clear voice." Another man standing nearby recalled, "His voice was singularly clear and penetrating. It had a sort of metallic ring. His enunciation was perfect."

In an intensely compressed speech of some seven hundred words that took only five and a half minutes to deliver—the second shortest inaugural address, behind only George Washington's perfunctory 135 words at his second inauguration—Abraham Lincoln proceeded to share what he had learned from four years of horror and suffering; of sending young men to their deaths; of shattered limbs and amputations; of unleashing savagery, hunger, and disease; of irreparable loss, tears, and heartbreak in homes across America. No inaugural address had ever ventured into the mystery of suffering this way; none ever would again. It was all to the purpose of persuading Americans to set their hatreds aside.

With a crowd of men standing alongside and behind him, Lincoln loomed taller than any. "During the whole ceremony he looked unusually handsome," noted the *New York Herald*. "When delivering his speech his face glowed with enthusiasm, and he evidently felt every word that he uttered." Clifford, standing close by, informed his wife that evening, "The address is admirable, and was admirably delivered."

"Fellow countrymen," Lincoln piped, "At this second appearing to take the oath of the Presidential office, there is less occasion for an extended address than there was at the first. Then a statement, some-what in detail, of a course to be pursued, seemed fitting and proper."

He had given that first address in dire circumstances, after seven states had already seceded from the Union to form a Confederate government under President Jefferson Davis. Lincoln had appealed to Southerners for peace, laying out his policies in detail for upholding the Constitution, promising them that he would refrain from interfering with slavery where it existed and faithfully execute the laws for track-ing down escaped slaves. The pledge disgusted Frederick Douglass, who accused Lincoln of being "double-tongued" in both opposing and supporting slavery, branding him an "excellent slave hound" and the "most dangerous advocate of slave-hunting and slave-catching in the land." Douglass also had been dismayed by the new president's concil-iatory tone toward the arrogant secessionists who were threatening a treasonous war on behalf of slavery. "We are not enemies, but friends. We must not be enemies," Lincoln had implored. "Though passion may have strained it must not break our bonds of affection. The mystic chords of memory, stretching from every battlefield and patriot grave to every living heart and hearthstone all over this broad land, will yet swell the chorus of the Union, when again touched, as surely they will be, by the better angels of our nature."

The people of the Southern states had spurned this eloquent plea, concluding that the better angels of their nature found expres-sion in their own love for home, hearth, and the Southern way of life. In their eyes, the election of a slavery-hating Republican president without a single Southern electoral vote plainly indicated a fatal shift in power to the expanding North, its population swelled by immi-grants and factory workers, its burgeoning cities filled with grasping capitalists and crooked politicians who had no love or understanding for the South. A new America was coming into existence, leaving the South with the prospect of remaining in the Union as little more than an exploited colony. The Southerners' way of life could now be eroded, their wealth pillaged, and the Constitution's strict limits on federal authority loosened. Southerners had thus resolved to break free, form a new nation and, if need be, defend their independence with their blood.

This day's crowd—far more sympathetic to the Union cause than the mixed audience of Northerners and Southerners Lincoln had addressed four years earlier—surely expected the president to celebrate the hard-won successes of the war in recent months, to rally Americans to finish the job, and to explain how the war would be ended. The audience almost certainly thought he would offer details about the reconstruction of the country and the treatment of the Southern states, including the rights to the franchise of both freed slaves and former Confederates.

But the president's opening words were drab, uninspiring. He noted only that many public comments had been made about the issues raised by the war and that he could add little. "Now, at the expiration of four years, during which public declarations have been constantly called forth on every point and phase of the great contest which still absorbs the attention, and engrosses the energies of the nation, little that is new could be presented." The people, after all, had been anxiously reading about battlefield results in the newspapers, much as Lincoln had followed the shifting fortunes of battle from the War Department's telegraph room. "The progress of our arms, upon which all else chiefly depends, is as well known to the public as to myself, and it is, I trust, reasonably satisfactory and encouraging to all." Here Lincoln paused, as if expecting applause. But his flat statement produced none. He moved on. While everyone in the crowd knew the war was nearing its conclusion, Lincoln deliberately avoided saying so. "With high hope for the future, no prediction in regard to it is ventured."

Lincoln was failing to praise the nation for its bravery and resolve. He was not honoring the courageous Union soldiers who had all but won the war. He had sung the praises of such men with supreme eloquence at Gettysburg, but now he had something different to say. Stanton and Seward leaned forward, "remarkably attentive," and the crowd "kept pushing nearer and nearer the platform," the *New York Herald* noted. "Beyond this there was no cheering of any consequence. Even the soldiers did not hurrah much." Frederick Douglass, looking on, had the same impression. "The whole proceeding was wonderfully quiet, earnest, and solemn," he recalled. There "was a leaden stillness about the crowd." Lincoln, for some reason, was not seeking easy applause.

Instead, he reviewed some painful history, starting with the terrifying predicament he had encountered four years earlier, to the day, when "all thoughts were anxiously directed to an impending civil-war." Americans, for and against the preservation of the Union, had hoped for a different outcome than war. "All dreaded it—all sought to avert it. While the inaugural address was being delivered from this place, devoted altogether to *saving* the Union without war, insurgent agents were in the city seeking to *destroy* it without war—seeking to dissolve the Union, and divide effects, by negotiation." By using the word "all" three times in this short passage, Lincoln was emphasizing that Americans had been unified in their desire to avoid war.

Insurgent agents, Lincoln had said. From the start, he had refused to accept that the Union had been dissolved, refused to frame the struggle as a war between two countries or two governments. He had insisted throughout that only insurgents or rebels were fighting the United States—not the South and its people, since in his view many Southerners remained loyal and would patriotically embrace the United States once again when the war was over. He saw people in all parts of the country as fellow Americans.

Lincoln recalled that those opposing the Union had hoped that the government would let them go in peace. Those defending the Union had hoped that it could be kept intact without the necessity of violence. "Both parties deprecated war; but one of them would *make* war rather than let the nation survive; and the other would *accept* war rather than let it perish," Lincoln explained, a line that won a smattering of applause. Lincoln waited it out before finishing his point: "And the war came." Through this passive expression, he underscored his theme, stated repeatedly in his previous lines—that civil war had erupted despite the efforts and wishes of leaders on both sides. Something more than the will of the people was at work.

In his brief synopsis of the origins of this terrible war, Lincoln identified a cause. Whatever differences Americans had over theories of states' rights, federal power, and regional economics, one explosively emotional issue was at the heart of the dispute. The ownership of human beings by other human beings, particularly of a racial group deemed to be inferior, had led Americans to fiercely dispute the very meaning of America: whether the founding ideals articulated in the Declaration of Independence—that all men are created equal—should apply. "One eighth of the whole population were colored slaves, not distributed generally over the Union, but localized in the Southern part of it," Lincoln said. "These slaves constituted a peculiar and powerful interest. All knew that this interest was, somehow, the cause of the war." Going over his printed speech one last time, choosing every word with the utmost care, Lincoln had crossed out the word "half" in "southern half" and scrawled above it "part." Perhaps he wished to emphasize that equal sides were not at war with each other; only insurgents against the government. In fact, nowhere in the speech did Lincoln identify the South as the enemy. This speech was not about blaming one side or the other.

To be sure, Lincoln had, at many times, faulted the insurgents for seeking disunion and bringing on a war rather than give ground on slavery. In an 1860 speech at Cooper Union in New York that left people talking about him as a possible presidential candidate, he addressed the Southern firebrands who threatened to break up the Union: "Your purpose, then, plainly stated, is, that you will destroy the Government, unless you be allowed to construe and enforce the Constitution as you please, on all points in dispute between you and us. You will rule or ruin in all events." Yet Lincoln had also long held that the people of the North and the South were essentially the same, even if driven by circumstances to occupy different political ground. "I think I have no prejudice against the southern people. They are just what we would be in their situation. If slavery did not now exist amongst them, they would not introduce it. If it did now exist amongst us, we should not instantly give it up," he said during a speech in Peoria, Illinois, in 1854.

"When southern people tell us they are no more responsible for the origin of slavery, than we; I acknowledge the fact. When it is said that the institution exists; and that it is very difficult to get rid of it, in any satisfactory way, I can understand and appreciate the saying. I surely will not blame them for not doing what I should not know how to do myself." At Cooper Union, he addressed Southern citizens this way: "You consider yourselves a reasonable and a just people; and I consider that in the general qualities of reason and justice you are not inferior to any other people." Lincoln had the ability to step out of his own emotions and coldly assess the motives of others, a peculiar trait that helped him immensely as president. His goal had never been to punish the South.

The opposing sides had first tried to resolve their differences through politics, Lincoln continued in his second inaugural address. The insurgents were willing to go to war to make sure slavery was protected and nurtured, while those Americans who had elected a new government were determined to set it on a gradual path to extinction. "To strengthen, perpetuate, and extend this interest was the object for which the insurgents would rend the Union, even by war; while the government claimed no right to do more than to restrict the territorial enlargement of it." Here was blame for the insurgents and a defense of the Union position, but not a strident one. While both sides deprecated war, their years of political maneuvering to avoid it had come to naught. The American genius for compromise—essential to the creation of the Union in 1787 and to its perpetuation through the Missouri Compromise of 1820 and the Compromise of 1850—had lost its power. It could no longer bridge the gap over slavery. Men who thought they could avert a civil war through the political process—Lincoln included—had failed spectacularly.

That was not Americans' only misapprehension. The struggle that ensued—its length, its horrors, its revolutionary outcome—was beyond the capacity of anyone to predict. "Neither party expected for the war, the magnitude, or the duration, which it has already attained. Neither anticipated that the *cause* of the conflict might cease with, or even before, the conflict itself should cease. Each looked for an easier triumph, and a result less fundamental and astounding." Lincoln included. He had been as wrong as anyone. He did not know where America was going; no one did.

And here Lincoln introduced his theory for the war's hideous destruction. A force beyond human understanding was behind it. Almighty God was involved.

Lincoln's short speech now became a theological exploration, bristling with biblical quotes and allusions. Prior to Lincoln only one president had quoted even a single passage from the Bible in an inaugural address. Forty years earlier, John Quincy Adams had cited the 127th Psalm—"except the Lord keep the city the watchman waketh but in vain"—to stress that he could not succeed without God's support. Lincoln, a rationalist and freethinker who never joined a church, would deliver the most overtly religious address of any. A close reader of his well-worn Bible for its deep wisdom about human nature, he chose to cite three passages from the book, all essential to his argument about the meaning of this war.

Americans, overwhelmingly Christian, had prayed fervently to God during this conflict, North and South, hoping to sway the divine will through their devotions. As Lincoln put it, both sides "read the same Bible, and pray to the same God; and each invokes His aid against the other." For four years, pulpits North and South had rung out with denunciations of the enemy and eloquent defenses of the justice of their own cause, along with warnings that the tendency of sinful man to defy God would bring on fresh disasters. Both Northerners and Southerners earnestly believed that God was on their side.

The celebrity preacher Henry Ward Beecher, pastor of the Plymouth Church in Brooklyn, a friendly correspondent with Lincoln and the brother of the author of *Uncle Tom's Cabin*, certainly believed God embraced the cause of the North. Six weeks after the inauguration, he would be a celebrated guest of Stanton at a ceremony at Fort Sumter, in Charleston Harbor, as General Robert Anderson raised the American flag over the fort that Confederate guns had forced him to abandon almost exactly four years earlier. In his fiery speech commemorating the occasion, Beecher placed "the whole guilt of this war upon the ambitious, educated, plotting, political leaders of the South. They have shed an ocean of blood." He predicted that their day of trial and punishment, under a righteous God, would come. "And from a thousand battle-fields shall rise up armies of airy witnesses, who, with the memory of their awful sufferings, shall confront those miscreants with their words of fierce accusation; and every pale and starved prisoner shall raise his skinny hands in judgment." The Southern traitors then "shall be whirled aloft and plunged down forever and forever in an endless retribution," while God would say, "Thus shall it be to all who betray their country." On many Northern pulpits, preachers argued that the turning tide of the war signified that God opposed the South, and that those who had sought to bring down the Union merited God's severe punishment.

Southern preachers believed just as earnestly that their people were the ones who had acted in accordance with God's will. Before the war, they pointed out—whatever Northern fanatics might say—slavery had been a common feature of human societies for thousands of years, woven into life on earth and sanctified by God in the laws handed down by the patriarchs. Many preachers argued that slaveholders had a solemn responsibility as Christians to treat their laborers with compassion and generosity, a moral duty that the brutal factory owners of the North often eschewed. Under this system, its proponents argued, slaves had multiplied greatly. They arguably lived longer than blacks in Africa, facing less of a risk of war or starvation, while being introduced to Christian faith and salvation. "We cherish the institution not from avarice, but from principle," said noted theologian James Henley Thornwell, a Presbyterian minister in Columbia, South Carolina. Believing that God cared deeply about them, Southerners expressed their ardent faith in the preamble of the Constitution of the Confederate States, which invoked "the favor and guidance of Almighty God." The U.S. Constitution that had launched America in 1787, by contrast, was entirely secular, containing no such reference. "The American nation stood up before the world, a helpless orphan and entered upon a career without a God," Benjamin Morgan Palmer, the minister of the First Presbyterian Church of New Orleans, noted. When he read the preamble of the Confederate Constitution, Palmer's "heart swelled with unutterable emotions of gratitude and joy. . . . At length, the nation has a God: Alleluia!" Southern preachers argued throughout the war that their people had the right to self-determination and should have been allowed to leave the Union in peace. As John Adger recounted in 1866 in the *Southern Presbyterian Review*, they viewed Lincoln's terrifying coercion of the South as "a cruel, unjust, and wicked war of invasion upon free States, and they sisters States also, urged on, in great part, by an infidel fanaticism." Until the prospect of Northern victory stared at them, they "took it for granted that the Almighty would never allow such a cause to triumph. They prayed fervently for the success of the Confederacy, and they never doubted that their prayers would be heard."

In his second inaugural address, Lincoln cited a biblical passage that had always struck him forcefully: God's injunction to Adam after he had defied the divine will and eaten the apple from the Tree of Knowledge. Because of his disobedience, Adam—and all males who followed him throughout human history—would have to work to survive. "In the sweat of thy face shalt thou eat bread," God said. Lincoln believed it was the height of injustice for anyone—slaveholder or aristocrat—to steal the fruits of the labor of another man. It was thus hard for him to accept that people who supported such an injustice could pray to God for aid. As he put it in his inaugural address, "It may seem strange that any men should dare to ask a just God's assistance in wringing their bread from the sweat of other men's faces." The line, the *New York Herald* reported, "caused a half-laugh." Yet Lincoln quickly and emphatically backed off: "but let us judge not that we be not judged." He was quoting Jesus, in Matthew 7:1, one of the most widely cited sayings from the Bible. Just as Lincoln would refrain from celebrating the Union's impending victory this day, he would claim no moral superiority. Almost alone among the theological thinkers of his time, breaking with preachers of both the North and the South, Lincoln was questioning the righteousness of both sides. This speech would be a confession of grave national failure, not a celebration of victory.

Lincoln drew on his meditation of two and a half years earlier, when he first explored the sobering idea that God was somehow not fully on the Union's side, given the war's staggering losses and the immense suffering its people had endured. Now, addressing the nation on the brink of victory at last, Lincoln hypothesized that God's intentions in this terrible war had been different from those of either side. "The prayers of both could not be answered; that of neither has been answered fully. The Almighty has His own purposes."

Lincoln offered a theory about those purposes. He quoted the fiery passage of Matthew 18:7, in the ringing notes of the King James translation: "Woe unto the world because of offences! for it must needs be that offences come; but woe to that man by whom the offence cometh!" That passage comported with Lincoln's view of reality, one embedded in Americans' Christian culture—that God tests humans; that the evil they do thrives in this world, causing great pain for many; but that, under the Almighty, punishment eventually comes to those who defy God's will and mistreat others. This was not a God who gently loves—it was a mysterious force that punishes wayward human beings, whole groups of them who participate in sin. It was the God of Lincoln's Puritan forebears, of the Little Pigeon Creek Baptist Church he attended as a boy, the God who punished wrong in a manner that might seem enigmatic to mere mortals—"this vast iron machine, that strikes and cuts, grinds and mashes," as William Herndon put it—but turns out to foster justice in extraordinary and unforeseen ways.

Jesus had made this point while teaching a lesson about who is greatest in the kingdom of God. He pulled a child aside, arguing that no one could enter the kingdom unless he or she became a little child; and he warned of the suffering that would befall those who harmed the innocent. Was slavery, Lincoln now asked, one of those offenses that, "in the providence of God, must needs come" as a moral test of the beings he created, but that God now "wills to remove" from America? Had God given "both North and South, this terrible war, as the woe due to those by whom the offence came?" And if that was the case, wasn't the cruel suffering the nation had endured entirely just? Or, as Lincoln said, "Shall we discern therein any departure from those divine attributes which the believers in a Living God always ascribe to Him?"

Both sides in this war, he was arguing, shared responsibility for the grievous offense of slavery. Both sides had brought it to these shores, nurtured it, endured it, and sustained it. As a result, some four million black Americans had lived and worked under it, under brutal conditions, suffering the pain and indignity of the lash and, perhaps more agonizing, permanent separation from loved ones who had been sold away. The Founders had created a country that tolerated it, even if they hoped to set it on a path to extinction. Lincoln himself had declared on this very spot, four years earlier: "I have no purpose, directly or indirectly, to interfere with the institution of slavery in the States where it exists. I believe I have no lawful right to do so, and I have no inclination to do so." But God had a different plan.

Lincoln was freely stating that he had not been in control of the nation's fate, a confession of weakness rare for any politician. Nor could he say how much suffering the nation had yet to endure. "Fondly do we hope—fervently do we pray—that this mighty scourge of war may speedily pass away," he said. "Yet, if God wills that it continue until all the wealth piled by the bond-man's two hundred and fifty years of unrequited toil shall be sunk, and until every drop of blood drawn with the lash, shall be paid by another drawn with the sword, as was said three thousand years ago, so still it must be said 'the judgments of the Lord are true and righteous altogether.'" He was quoting here the Nineteenth Psalm, which calls on fallen man to humbly accept the will of the Almighty as beyond human understanding.

Salmon P. Chase, out on the hustings in 1863, had speculated that God wanted this war to continue until slavery was eradicated. But Lincoln was saying that God had done more than that. Humans had made grave mistakes of judgment that precipitated this war. But perhaps the war itself had been no mistake at all. Perhaps it was God's verdict on the dark sin that had stained America and its vaunted freedom.

What Lincoln was saying was astonishing. For the first time, an American president in an inaugural address was denouncing slavery as an unmitigated evil, speculating that God himself had rendered that judgment on it by punishing all Americans through this disastrous war. For the last four years, Lincoln had often repressed his hatred of slavery, keeping his focus on the political actions that would best advance the war effort and save the Union, carefully calibrating his actions to public opinion, to the intense irritation of such men as Chase and Douglass. Now Lincoln was, perhaps, revealing his heart. Slavery, he was proposing, was so grievous an abomination that God had willed this enormous catastrophe on the people of America to end it. African Americans were stunned to hear a president speak this way. "Negroes ejaculated 'bress de Lord' in a low murmur at the end of almost every sentence," the *Herald* reported. Many wept. "Looking down into the faces of the people, illuminated by the bright rays of the sun, one could see moist eyes and even tearful faces," Brooks wrote.

Moreover, Lincoln was suggesting that Americans had earned their terrible suffering—and any still to come. All the treasure sunk into the war had been justly lost. Every drop of blood in this ocean of carnage had been justly spilled.

In his annual message to Congress in December 1862, Lincoln had urged his people to rid themselves of slavery as a practical means of saving the Union. "Fellow-citizens, *we* cannot escape history. . . . The fiery trial through which we pass will light us down in honor or dishonor to the latest generation," he said. "We know how to save the Union. The world knows we do know how to save it. We, even *we here*, hold the power and bear the responsibility. In *giving* freedom to the *slave* we *assure* freedom to the *free*—honorable alike in what we give and what we preserve. We shall nobly save or meanly lose the last best hope of earth."

More than two years later, it appeared the people would indeed nobly save the Union. But Lincoln was not praising them for that. He was not giving a rousing patriotic speech that his Northern audience could cheer with wild enthusiasm. He was making a plea to all Americans, to the victors as well as the vanquished, to religious leaders on both sides, to the radical Republicans as well as the embittered Confederates, to the new Congress and to himself as president, to set aside their moral superiority and humbly accept God's will. All had sinned, all had failed miserably. After all of this—the forever forlorn mothers, the maimed men writhing on the battlefield and suffering in hospitals, the murder of black prisoners and the starvation of white ones, the brutal insult of Sherman's march, leaving a gaping wound across the South, the hunger and deprivation on the home front, the wretched refugee camps filled with escaped slaves with no means of support or education—it was time for Americans to stop thinking about self-righteousness. The only way forward was to recognize that all had been wrong and to treat each other with mercy.

An exhausted Lincoln hoped his fellow Northerners might interpret the ghastly events of the last four years as he had, instead of reveling in victory and seeking to punish the South. Though Americans had fought each other savagely for four years, they were still united by their trust in God and their faith in the Christian message that suffering must not murder love. Lincoln earnestly hoped they would reflect on the truth that God's harsh judgment had fallen on all, North and South. He was pleading for healing, not vengeance; reconciliation, not continued strife and division. The shattered people of this country had to put bitterness aside. There was no other way to end this nightmare.

"With malice toward none; with charity for all; with firmness in the right, as God gives us to see the right," Lincoln said, "let us strive on to finish the work we are in; to bind up the nation's wounds; to care for him who shall have borne the battle, and for his widow, and his orphan—to do all which may achieve and cherish a just, and lasting peace, among ourselves, and with all nations."

There was a long burst of applause as Lincoln stepped back. Those words, Brooks wrote, deserved to be "printed in letters of gold."

In his communications with Generals Ulysses Grant and William Sherman, Lincoln had been stressing that, when the final surrender came, reconciliation rather than vengeance must be the goal. Those savvy generals, reading this address by their commander in chief, could not have missed the point. When another general asked Lincoln several weeks later how he should treat the Confederates who had fallen under his charge, Lincoln declined to give specific orders but said, "If I were in your place, I'd let 'em up easy, let 'em up easy." While many Northerners demanded that Confederate leaders be hanged for treason and for the evils of the war, Lincoln privately hoped Jefferson Davis and other top officials might flee to Europe. In America, they could only be a focus of Southern identity and stir Northerners' lust for retaliation.

John Wilkes Booth, watching from a short distance away, had no interest in Lincoln's interpretation of the war as God's judgment on all. He clung to his ardent belief that Lincoln was a tyrant who merited retribution. As Brooks later recounted, no one who was there that day would ever forget "the tall, pathetic, melancholy figure of a man who, then inducted into office in the midst of the glad acclaim of thousands of people, and illuminated by the deceptive brilliance of a March sunburst, was already standing in the shadow of death."

CHAPTER 14

A TRUTH THAT NEEDED TO BE TOLD

Saturday afternoon, March 4, 1865

As the cheering faded, Abraham Lincoln returned to his seat. After a pause, he and Chief Justice Salmon P. Chase rose together, the new Capitol dome towering above them. The men in the crowd respectfully removed their hats. Clutching his copy of the Constitution, Chase read the oath of office, as Lincoln placed his right hand on the Bible. "I saw Mr. Lincoln bow his head and extend his right arm," wrote Adolphe Pineton, the Marquis de Chambrun. Chase's words were inaudible to the crowd, but not Lincoln's piping repetition of them. "I can swear that those who witnessed this act were convinced that never was an oath spoken more certain of being kept inviolate," Chambrun wrote. Lincoln recited the oath in "a clear, solemn voice," the *Philadelphia Inquirer* reported. After a firm declaration of "So help me God," he bent his tall frame and kissed an open page of the book.

That afternoon, Chase had the Bible delivered to Mary Lincoln at the White House, marking the passages Lincoln had kissed:

None shall be weary nor stumble among them; none shall slumber nor sleep; neither shall the girdle of their loins be loosed, nor the latchet of their shoes be broken:

Whose arrows are sharp, and all their bows bent, their horses' hoofs
shall be counted like flint, and their wheels like a whirlwind.

This passage, Isaiah 5:27–28, spoke of God's fierce vengeance, exacted through a war pursued to its pitiless conclusion. The terrifying army of Assyria, having conquered the kingdom of Israel, marches onward in perfect order. Its men decline to pause to relax and loosen their clothing. Their sandals are tied and in repair, their weapons are ready, the wheels of their engines of death are whirling. The verses' meaning seemed clear enough to Matthew Henry, a Welsh minister who wrote an influential six-volume analysis of the Bible in the early eighteenth century: "When God comes forth in wrath, the hills tremble, fear seizes even great men. When God designs the ruin of a provoking people, he can find instruments to be employed in it." This Old Testament warning marched in step with Lincoln's message that this catastrophic war was a judgment on America.

"I hope the sacred book will be to you an acceptable souvenir of a memorable day," Chase wrote to Mary, "and I most sincerely pray . . . that the beautiful sunshine, which, just at the time the oath was taken, dispersed the clouds that had previously darkened the sky, may prove an auspicious omen of the dispersion of the clouds of war, by the clear sunshine of prosperous peace, under the wise and just administration of him who took it." It was a generous note from a man who thought that he, not Lincoln, should have taken that oath, to a woman who still bitterly resented him and his daughter.

After the oath, Lincoln and Chase sat down for the final element of the ritual: a performance by the U.S. Marine Band and a chorus of "God Save the President," a hackneyed patriotic song by the Viennese-trained composer George Felix Benkert and the Philadelphia businessman and poet Francis De Haes Janvier, the author of "The Sleeping Sentinel," that famous tribute to Lincoln's mercy and justice. Since the song was more than four years old, Janvier's lyrics avoided such touchy matters as the near-dictatorial powers Lincoln had seized during the war. He portrayed the president as the humble representative of a united, free, and proud people who bowed only to God:

> *All hail! unfurl the stripes and stars!*
> *The banner of the free!*
> *Ten times ten thousand patriots greet*
> *The shrine of liberty!*
> *Come, with one heart, one hope, one aim,*
> *An undivided band,*
> *To elevate, with solemn rites,*
> *The ruler of our land . . .*
>
> *Not to invest a potentate*
> *With robes of majesty—*
> *Not to confer a kingly crown,*
> *Nor bend a subject knee.*
> *We bow beneath no sceptred sway—*
> *Obey no royal nod—*
> *Columbia's sons, erect and free,*
> *Kneel only to their God! . . .*
>
> *Our ruler boasts no titled rank,*
> *No ancient, princely line—*
> *No regal right to sov'reinty,*
> *Ancestral and divine.*
> *A patriot—at his country's call,*
> *Responding to her voice*
> *One of the people—he becomes*
> *A Sov'reign, by our choice! . . .*
>
> *And now, before the mighty pile*
> *We've reared to liberty,*
> *He swears to cherish and defend*
> *The charter of the free!*

God of our country! seal his oath
With thy supreme assent.
God save the Union of the States!
God save our President!

The formal ceremony completed, the tall figure in black briefly acknowledged the people's loud applause, bowing and smiling. Four years earlier he had struck many in the crowd as a third-tier hack politician whose meager abilities seemed absurdly ill-matched to the crisis overtaking the nation. The people's perception had changed. "I was very near Mr. Lincoln when he delivered his greatest address," recalled Elizabeth Bacon Custer, the twenty-two-year-old wife of daring Union cavalry general George Armstrong Custer. "And I saw how quietly he received the plaudits of the people who were much more aware of his greatness than when he came from the West, almost unknown, four years before." A Williams College student who had been determined to see the president take the oath, Hamilton Gay Howard, the son of Michigan Senator Jacob M. Howard, had "secured a coign of vantage in getting directly in front of the statue of Columbus holding a globe," a spot "less than one hundred feet of Mr. Lincoln." He too was struck by the president's demeanor. "During the entire proceedings he looked pale, thin, haggard, and worn out, but the smile was as benignant, the patriarchal mien was as majestic as ever glorified mortal. He seemed to tower above all his surrounding personalities, and to be chosen leader specially selected by the Divine Ruler for the occasion." James R. Doolittle Jr., the son of another senator—the Wisconsin Republican who had accompanied the aching, shaky Andrew Johnson to the Capitol that morning—already sensed something that would later become an article of faith in the United States. Lincoln "rivals the greatest statesmen of our country; he is surpassed by none, not even by Washington," the young man wrote in a letter that day to his brother. Far from being an awkward bumpkin, "Mr. Lincoln is possessed of great dignity. It is not the selfish, conceited, proud, imperial dignity which Mr. Chase assumes, but is kind, approachable and winning." Lincoln, he added, "is great mentally, and no less morally." In less exalted language, Virgil Connor wrote enthusiastically to his mother in Maine: "Heard Abe deliver his inaugural: saw Hamlin, Johnson and a score of other big bugs."

As the band played "Hail to the Chief," Virgil and the crowd bellowed their approval, and the startling booming of artillery began from scattered points. The *New York Herald* reported that some members of the crowd cried "speech, speech!" when Vice President Johnson appeared at the front. "He rubbed his red face with his hands, as if to clear up his ideas, but did not succeed, and said nothing." A path was cleared for the newly inaugurated president, and the party reentered the Capitol building before the thunder of one hundred guns had stopped.

The crowd began to disperse, and the doors of the Capitol were thrown open to hasten the process. "The crowd inside," the *Herald* noted, "rushed out with as much disorder as that which characterized the rush from the galleries as the procession left the Senate for the platform." Senators, struggling to pass in the opposite direction, returned to their chamber for the vice president's formal adjournment. After waiting for up to an hour for the sozzled Johnson to appear, the senators "slipped out one by one and disappeared without being adjourned."

Outside, people trudged along as the massive crowd began to move sluggishly. "Men, women and children were all mixed together and covered with mud," the *Herald* observed. "Everybody was knee-deep at least. Such pushing and crowding and jamming and damning was never seen before." The carriageway at the east gate quickly became clogged with people trying to squeeze through. "It is a wonder that nobody was killed there. Several ladies fainted and had to be carried off," the paper noted.

Frederick Douglass, trooping with the mob, was lost in thought. A man he had long considered a conniving politician, a poor inferior to Chase, had used his inaugural address to express the very idea that Douglass and his fellow abolitionists had embraced from the start: that this war was about ending the evil of slavery. In presenting the war as a just verdict on the American people, the president was effectively arguing for the humanity of all, white and black. As a superb writer and orator, Douglass could grasp the brilliance of Lincoln's prose. The words "struck me at the time, and have seemed to me ever since to contain more vital substance than I have ever seen compressed in a space so narrow," he recalled. "I clapped my hands in gladness and thanksgiving at their utterance."

Douglass conceded, however, that many in the crowd betrayed "expressions of widely different emotion." Many of the working-class soldiers directing the crowds that afternoon disdained racial equality and Lincoln's notion that God had punished America for the sin of slavery. "The darkeys suffered most. Soldiers knocked negro women roughly about and called them very uncomplimentary names," the *Herald* reported. "It seemed as if there was a reaction from the anti-slavery sentiments of the inaugural, and every negro boy got an extra push on account of his color." Lincoln's speech would not quickly change hearts.

In truth, the ugliness surrounding the war resumed the moment Lincoln's words faded. One belligerent Union officer, determined to make his getaway, demanded that the driver of a parked carriage take him and his friends to Willard's Hotel. The driver refused, saying he was waiting to transport a group of women who had hired his services. The officer shot back that the driver would take him whether he wanted to or not. When the driver still resisted, the officer and his friends roughed him up, seized the carriage, and drove off with it. Determined to regain his vehicle, the hackman hailed a guard, and a chase ensued. At Willard's the guard managed to take the officer and his underlings into custody and return the man's carriage. "Of course, the officers were exhilarated," the *Herald* noted, employing a euphemism for drunk. "As the phrase here is, they had inaugurated too often."

One hundred miles south, in the Confederate capital of Richmond, a weary General Robert E. Lee was conferring with Secretary of War John C. Breckinridge, no doubt discussing their shrinking military options and Ulysses S. Grant's peace gesture. Lee had already written to President Jefferson Davis that it seemed doubtful Grant would accept any terms "unless coupled with the condition of our return to the Union"—and "whether this will be acceptable to our people yet awhile I cannot say." The real question, of course, was whether this would be acceptable to Davis, who had pledged to thousands at a rally less than a month earlier that he would never accept reunification. The more pragmatic Lee seemed to appreciate the futility of fighting on. While rain fell on his camp at two o'clock that early morning, he had called for Major General John B. Gordon to look over some shocking reports he had received from his officers about continued desertions and the weakness of his forces. "The revelation was startling," Gordon recalled. He frankly advised Lee to seek peace terms, "the best we can get." Barring that, Gordon said, the army should either fight immediately or abandon Petersburg—and with it, Richmond—and try to link up with General Joseph E. Johnston's forces in North Carolina in the desperate hope of somehow beating Sherman before he could join Grant. By two p.m., rumors were racing through Richmond. "There is almost a panic among officials here who have their families with them, under the belief that the city may be suddenly evacuated, and the impossibility of getting transportation," Confederate war clerk John Beauchamp Jones recorded in his diary. Word spread that Lee's family was preparing to leave Richmond.

So much had changed since the bombardment of Fort Sumter in Charleston Harbor had brought down the American flag in April 1861. At the U.S. Capitol, War Secretary Edwin Stanton offered ex-governor John Clifford a lift to his next destination in his carriage. On their ride through the crowds, the two had "a nice talk" about Stanton's plans for the formal flag raising at Union-controlled Fort Sumter on April 14, almost exactly four years after the flag had come down and the Civil War was ignited. Stanton "has invited me to join the party—Isn't this a temptation," Clifford wrote proudly to his wife.

After Lincoln spent two hours inside the Capitol, presumably resting and having some lunch, the procession lined up once again for the journey down Pennsylvania Avenue, back to the White House. This time, the president would participate in his own inaugural parade. At three p.m., Mary Lincoln entered the closed presidential carriage with Senators Henry B. Anthony and James Harlan. The president climbed up in a separate carriage, an open barouche drawn by four gray horses. Accompanying him, bookending their earlier formality, were Lafayette S. Foster and John Brooks Henderson, the senators who had walked him into the Senate chamber. Lincoln affixed his stovepipe hat to his head. Just as they were setting off, his eleven-year-old son, Tad, came running out of the Capitol. The boy clambered up the carriage step and plopped himself in the seat next to his father.

Walt Whitman was able to size up the president before he departed. He "looked very much worn and tired; the lines, indeed, of vast responsibilities, intricate questions, and demands of life and death, cut deeper than ever upon his dark brown face; yet all the old goodness, tenderness, sadness, and canny shrewdness, underneath the furrows," Whitman wrote. Four years earlier, Lincoln had been protected by a phalanx of armed cavalrymen, with sabers drawn. This time, there were "no soldiers, only a lot of civilians on horseback"—the parade marshals—"with huge yellow scarfs over their shoulders, riding around the carriage."

The pasteboard *Monitor*, the Temple of Liberty, the fire companies and their engines, the black troops, and everyone else who had marched up muddy Pennsylvania Avenue in spitting rain four hours earlier marched back, this time under a clear sky and a glorious warm sun. "With all the bands playing inspiring airs, and the whole city like a rainbow with banners, the grand panorama is reversing itself," wrote journalist Lois Bryan Adams. Like Whitman, she marveled at the appearance of glittering Venus. "A stainless sky with sunlight, starlight and moonlight overhead, all at the same moment, and beneath them a pageant as emblematic of human freedom and equality as the broadest construction could require!" Yet it was as haphazard as before. "There were wide intervals between the different parts of the procession, which was as badly ordered as everything else on inauguration day," the *New York Herald* reported. The journalist was unimpressed with the crowd's reaction to Lincoln. "The President bowed right and left to the people but did not take off his hat. There was some clapping of hands, but no cheering, except in front of Willard's." Adams had almost the precisely opposite impression. She saw Lincoln ride by a boisterous crowd with his hat off, and instead of bowing right and left, "he seems not to see the thronging multitudes who wave flags and handkerchiefs and cheer him as he passes." In the wake of the president and his parade, the crowd came pouring down from the Capitol, onto muddy Pennsylvania Avenue.

"Laboring through the mire" half an hour after the event, the Washington correspondent of the *Times* of London ran into "a leading politician" on Pennsylvania Avenue. There was one topic: not Lincoln's address but Johnson's ludicrous speech. "He was drunk; very drunk," the politician disclosed. But it was not all Johnson's fault, he speculated. "His liquor was drugged by some Southern rebel, in order to throw disgrace on the Federal Government." If that were the case, the *Times* man asked skeptically, why didn't the agent drug Lincoln instead? "So he would have done, I have no doubt, only he could not get at Old Abe, who is besides, a sober man, and does not take drinks with strangers." Shortly after that, the journalist came across a Democratic senator. "The country is disgraced," the Democrat said. He had never prayed for Lincoln before, but he would start now. "Should he die within the next four years, which calamity may Heaven in its mercy avert, we should have Andrew Johnson for President, and sink to a lower level of degradation than was ever reached by any nation since the Roman Emperor [Caligula] made his horse a counsel." An editor of a Washington paper stopped by and joined the conversation. "Mark my words," he said, "Mr. Johnson will never recover from the disgrace he has brought upon himself. He is ruined as a public man forever."

Other reporters sprinted off to file dispatches. Some newspapers rushed the address into that evening's edition, printed on steam-powered rotary presses and sold damp on the street by bawling newsboys who feverishly handed over copies and pocketed copper pennies. The speech took up little space—merely half of a standard single column—making it easy for newspapers to print and for the public to read. The Washington *Evening Star* boasted that it was first of the city's papers to publish the speech, "and our power press was kept busy for a long time supplying the eager demand for it." Large metropolitan papers that obtained the speech by telegraph and had no Sunday edition transmitted it to their readers on Monday. "It speaks—through the flashing communications of the telegraph—to his millions of constituents—to a great, free republic," the *Boston Transcript* noted.

Editors had to digest this compact, oddly religious inaugural address and publish their opinions almost immediately. They made snap judgments without the benefit of hindsight, often reacting along party lines. Even editors at New York's largest newspapers seemed oblivious to the address's stronger points.

The *New York Herald*, in fact, found nothing at all of import in it, dismissing Lincoln's second inaugural address as "a little speech of 'glittering generalities' used only to fill in the program." It argued that the ever-calculating president had displayed a typical reluctance to venture into unsettled areas that might stir division and controversy. His address "was only an effort at best to avoid any commitment upon any question affecting our domestic or foreign affairs, excepting the abolition of slavery." The slavery issue "being practically settled, he was free to discuss" it, "and it has served the purpose of a tub to the whale." That popular saying was a reference that sailors would understand; a ship endangered by energetic gams of whales sometimes threw a tub into the water to divert the dangerously large creatures while it hoisted sail and moved on. Lincoln, in the *Herald*'s view, flung the issue of slavery out to Americans for them to toss around.

While distinctly more liberal than the *Herald*, Horace Greeley's influential *New York Tribune* faulted the speech as less "politic" and "humane" than Lincoln's first inaugural address—and emphasized the point by printing both. The mercurial editor, hot and cold toward Lincoln over the previous four years, seemed to miss the president's main point. Greeley read into Lincoln's references to the God of the Old Testament a promise of vengeance against the South, failing to be assuaged by his call for "malice toward none" and "charity for all." Almost incredibly, Greeley lamented that the speech lacked "manifestations of generosity, clemency, magnanimity."

Henry Raymond's loyally Republican *New York Times* admired the address's "calmness" and "modesty" and found it an expression of Lincoln's iron will. "We have a President who will be faithful to the end, let what betide. Let him be sustained with the same fidelity."

The *New York World*, long a bitter critic of Lincoln's policies and a past victim of his war censorship, found the address a painful embarrassment befitting a day of disasters. "It is with a blush of shame and wounded pride, as American citizens, that we lay before our readers to-day the inaugural addresses of President Lincoln and Vice-President Johnson," the paper stated. The editor accused Lincoln of failing to comfort or rally the nation. "The pity of it, that a divided nation should neither be sustained in this crisis of agony by words of wisdom nor cheered with words of hope." He regarded "Mr. Lincoln's substitution of religion for statesmanship" to be "not less gratuitous than it was absurd. The President's theology smacks as strongly of the dark ages as Pope Pius's politics." It was especially sad that Lincoln's lamentable life had now been made precious by the new vice president, "the person who defiled our chief council chamber . . . with the spewings of a drunken boor."

Across America's heartland, editors bent their heads over the president's brief and gloomy remarks and hastily scribbled out editorials to be set in type. In Columbus, the Democratic *Daily Ohio Statesman* found the address "as chilly and dreary as was the day on which it was delivered." The editor blasted Lincoln for betraying his promise in his first inaugural speech to refrain from interfering with slavery in the South, and insisted that it was time for peace, not continued war. In his view, "this infernal butchery should be brought to an end in the shortest space of time conceivable, and not, as Mr. Lincoln affects to believe, that 'God wills' the War shall 'continue until all the wealth piled by the bondmen's two hundred and fifty years of unrequited toil shall be sunk, and until every drop of blood drawn with the lash shall be paid with another drawn with the sword.'" The editor failed to grasp Lincoln's theory that the Almighty was punishing both North and South for the great wrong of slavery. "Are we to understand that a people can read the same bible, and pray fervently to the same God for enlightenment and direction, and yet one portion of them be suffered to pursue a course of life that shall lead to moral and spiritual damnation, while the other portion shall be made moral heirs of eternal glory? From such an opinion we dissent, most decidedly."

The *Chicago Times*, another opposition paper, was not inclined to take a dispassionate view of anything Lincoln did. In 1863, Union general Ambrose Burnside had ordered the *Times* padlocked and its editor, Wilbur Storey, thrown in jail. Twenty thousand citizens rallied in Chicago against the administration's heavy-handed attack on the First Amendment, and Lincoln, bombarded by complaints from both angry Democrats and worried Republicans, rescinded the order. Still disgusted with the president nearly two years later, the *Times* found his second inaugural address profoundly "Lincolnian"—in the sense of being utterly insipid. "We had looked for something thoroughly Lincolnian, but we did not foresee a thing so much more Lincolnian than anything that has gone before it. We did not conceive it possible that even Mr. Lincoln could produce a paper so slip-shod, so loose-joined, so puerile, not alone in literary construction, but in its ideas, its sentiments, its grasp. He has outdone himself. He has literally come out of the little end of his own horn. By the side of it, mediocrity is superb." The city's pro-Lincoln paper, the *Chicago Tribune*, praised the address as "an exceedingly brief, terse, Saxon document; strong in its naturalness and impressive in its simplicity, directness and force." Rather condescendingly, the editor opined that Lincoln's writing "exhibits a marked improvement" over his earlier speeches "in style and grace, without losing that originality not to say peculiarity of thought and expression which marks everything that comes from his hand."

In Michigan, the *Grand Haven News* dismissed the entire day's activities as an "abolition ceremony" that held little appeal to normal Americans. In terms of rallying the nation, the event "seems to have been a wretched failure in every part of the country." But, then, Lincoln's whole administration had been a disaster. His first inauguration had "proved the greatest calamity that ever befell this or any country under the light of the sun. Who then, could rationally rejoice in view of the second event of precisely the same character?" The *Holmes County Farmer* of Millersburg, Ohio, found it incredible that thousands of Americans even had the stomach to celebrate Lincoln's inauguration after the monstrous debacle of the previous four years.

> [The] administration that has caused the rivers to run red with blood and clad the people in the sable garments of sorrow—that has led to useless slaughter . . . of the vigorous and strong of our population—that has trampled upon laws, disregarded rights, and overthrown our system of government—that has covered the nation with debt and borne the people down with taxation— that has filled the land with spies, pimps and informers—that has substituted military despotism for popular government, and that secured another four years of power by force and fraud, did not want for those willing [to] rejoice, applaud and make merriment amidst the general gloom.

The government employees, contractors, and assorted Yankee "cormorants" who had made vast amounts of money from the war, the reporter observed, "were prompt to do honor to their master and rejoice over the hellish feast they expect to enjoy for the next four years."

The Age, in Philadelphia, thought that Lincoln, who had taken an oath to defend the Constitution, could have used the speech as an opportunity to explain his mass jailing of political enemies, his assaults on a free press, and his other violations of the people's essential rights. "In lieu of any such attempt, however, he has given us mere trash," the paper said. "He had nothing to say, and he has said it." The editor of Ohio's *Dayton Daily Journal*, shocked at the address's brevity, at first thought there had been some technical glitch and the telegraph had failed to transmit all of it. But "that was Old Abe's fault, and not the telegraph," the *Cincinnati Enquirer* explained.

The *Utica Telegraph* of New York found Lincoln's speech all but indecipherable. He "labors and stumbles, and soon flounders into a sea of twaddle," the paper opined. Whatever its political intentions, "as a literary performance it is one of the worst on record." That editor was not surprised: "Neither his cast of mind nor his educational experiences should lead us to expect anything else. He is neither by nature nor by opportunity a man of grace and accomplishment." Another upstate newspaper, the *Rochester Union and Advertiser*, dismissed the speech as the work of "an obscure village lawyer, elevated from the dregs of society to a position far beyond his deserts." Lincoln's supposed literary skill "has been puffed by the unremitting efforts of a partizan press and venal orators."

The *Ottawa Free Trader* in Illinois, reflecting widespread concerns about Lincoln's religion theme, asked, "Who has made Abraham Lincoln, or any mortal man, the interpreter of the decrees of God?" The *Cincinnati Enquirer* similarly branded the address "at once the most absurd, and the most blasphemous document that has ever emanated from a public man in America." To the extent any political meaning could be coaxed out of the address, the paper claimed, "it means war: a war of wrong under the pretense of right, a war of hatred under the pretense of justice, a war of revenge in the name of philanthropy—a war of extermination."

Several newspapers ran a piece called "The Inaugural with the Bark Off," a searing parody of the speech that mocked Lincoln's soaring oratory and his claims of bearing no malice while pushing on with the brutal conflict:

> All pray to the same God. He doesn't appear to be on either side. When He makes up His mind we will have to stand it.
>
> Meanwhile, without malice, let us charitably and firmly continue to cut each other's throats; taking care of such people as may be widowed and orphaned; in order that we may not injure or harm one another, but maintain a just and lasting peace among ourselves and other nations.

In the battered Confederacy, editors, not surprisingly, found little or nothing to admire. The *Daily Express* of Petersburg, Virginia, a city under siege by tens of thousands of Union troops, called it "a queer sort of a document, being a compound of philanthropy, fanaticism and scriptural morality." The editor bristled at Lincoln's attempt to "have the world believe that his bosom is overflowing with the most distressing emotions in contemplating [the war's] horrors, and that he used all his efforts and influence to prevent it breaking out." He sneered at Lincoln's references to God. "One would suppose that his knees were almost lacerated by his prayers and that his heart was the abode of all the Christian graces." Still, the editor insisted he would refrain from branding Lincoln a blatant hypocrite. "It is not for us to know any human heart, and still less such a heart as Lincoln's. God is the great searcher of this deceitful and most desperately wicked organ, and He alone knows whether it is always what the lips of its owner would represent it to be."

Twenty-five miles away, the *Daily Richmond Examiner* dismissed the "manifesto" of "Abraham the First" as "a harangue eminently fit to be made by Abraham Lincoln to the crazy mobs who were parading on that day through every street in the North." Another man in the Confederate capital city, the war clerk John Jones, found the "short inaugural message, or homily, or sermon" far more terrifying than comforting. Given Lincoln's view of God's harsh retribution, Jones had little hope that the president would treat the South with charity or mercy. Since Lincoln could quote Scripture "quite as fluently" as Jefferson Davis, "and since both Presidents resort to religious justification, it may be feared the war is about to assume a more sanguinary aspect and a more cruel nature than ever before. God help us!"

The *Hillsborough Recorder*, in North Carolina, published a mangled version of what Lincoln had said, turning it into a judgment on one side alone: "Fondly do we hope and eventually do we pray that this mighty scourge of war might speedily pass away; yet if God wills that it continue until just retribution has been visited upon the slave-holders, it must be said the judgment of the Lord is righteous." In the view of many in the South, Lincoln was merely using God as pretext for his own brutality.

* * *

The pro-Republican editors paid more attention to what Lincoln had said and how he had said it. The *Boston Transcript*, for example, found the speech powerful, moving, and utterly unique, calling it "a singular State paper, made so by the times. . . . Its omissions, even in the way of reference, are remarkable." If it failed to explore a wide range of issues— foreign affairs, the use of the nation's resources, reconstruction—the *Transcript* editor found this a cause for praise, not condemnation. "Summoned once more to the Executive chair, to be a leader in such a crisis of the world's life, no wonder the President was lifted above the level on which political leaders usually stand, and felt himself in the very presence of the awful mystery of Providence." He applauded Lincoln for casting slavery as the nation's great sin and arguing that the "day of adjudication and recompense" had come to "this vast, rich, populous republic" after its "degradation and bondage" of a "despised" people for centuries. The *Cleveland Morning Leader*, another important Republican paper, saw the address as "an imposing demonstration" of Lincoln's mind. "His views of slavery will meet the approbation of all who, as does Mr. Lincoln, believe that God is working his own purposes with this great people."

Many editors were struck by the president's unique voice. In refusing to follow "the beaten path of precedent," Lincoln had offered something "wholly original and characteristic of its distinguished author," the weekly *Delaware* (Ohio) *Gazette* argued. The *Burlington Times*, in Vermont, observed that "nobody but Lincoln ever said his say so grotesquely, or was so firmly indifferent as to how he said it." Rhode Island senator Henry B. Anthony's *Providence Journal*, which had immediately grasped the literary excellence of the Gettysburg address, found this speech, too, a remarkable example of Lincoln's "peculiar" style. "It is plain, terse, lucid, level to the commonest apprehension, and marked by some very striking and felicitous expressions," the *Journal* noted. The *Philadelphia Inquirer* rated the speech "characteristic of Mr. LINCOLN. It exhibits afresh the kindness of his heart, and the large charity which has always marked his actions toward those who are his personal enemies as well as the enemies of his country. Yet he is firm and will not deviate from the straight line of duty." The *Jeffersonian Democrat*, of Chardon, Ohio, a pro-administration paper despite its name, judged the address "remarkable for its brevity . . . but still more remarkable for its simplicity, force and clearness of style, and its nobleness of spirit. It is worthy of the man and the occasion." The *Buffalo Morning Express* agreed. "So brief, so simple, so dignified, there is an impressiveness about it which the most elaborate of orations could not" equal. Washington's *Evening Star* was to the point: "In pithy brevity, sagacity and honesty of purpose, the address is Lincolnian all over."

Wendell Phillips Garrison, son of the fiery Boston abolitionist William Lloyd Garrison, marveled over the president's growing literary powers. "Mr. Lincoln's compositions no longer stimulate criticism, but challenge admiration," he wrote from Washington on March 9 for his father's antislavery newspaper, the *Liberator*. Like others who witnessed the events of March 4, the young man prayed that Lincoln would survive his term, rather than turn the presidency over to a "drunkard" who "reels in a vertigo of conceit and intoxication, and disgraces his entrance into office by maudlin indecorum."

The British press took great interest in the address. Unlike many American journals, the *Saturday Review* of London pierced its essence: "The President regards both combatants as instruments and victims of a just retribution for a common cause." The powerful *Times* of London, long scornful of Lincoln, tepidly approved. But the *Spectator* perceived genius in the address, arguing that the "short State paper, for political weight, moral dignity, and unaffected solemnity, has had no equal in our time. . . . No statesman ever uttered words stamped at once with the seal of so deep a wisdom and so true a simplicity." The "village attorney" scorned by many sage men in 1861 seemed, the magazine maintained, "to be one of those 'foolish things of the world' which are destined to confound the wise." Charles Francis Adams Jr., the son of the U.S. ambassador to Britain, wrote to his father: "That rail-splitting lawyer is one of the wonders of the day. Once at Gettysburg and now again on a greater occasion he has shown a capacity for rising to the demands of the hour which we should not expect from orators or men of the schools. The inaugural strikes me in its grand simplicity and directness as being for all time the historical keynote of this war." In New York, lawyer George Templeton Strong found it remarkable, "unlike any American state paper of this century." Writing in his diary, he pondered how history would judge it: "I would give a good deal to know what estimate will be put on it ten or fifty years hence."

For his part, Lincoln thought it would take some time for people to appreciate his speech. He offered his own characteristically shrewd take on it after New York Republican operative and editor Thurlow Weed, a close ally of William Seward, wrote him a note effusively praising something else. Lincoln's brief and modest response the previous week to Congress's formal notification of his reelection, Weed told the president, was "not only the *neatest* but the most pregnant and effective use to which the English Language was ever put." Lincoln, perhaps racing through his correspondence, read Weed's note as a commendation of his inaugural address.

Thanking Weed, Lincoln told him that he expected the second inaugural address "to wear as well as—perhaps better than—any thing I have produced; but I believe it is not immediately popular." Americans would have to come around to his humbling interpretation of the nation's ordeal. God was *not* on their side, not entirely. The people's most earnest and selfless efforts, even their most heartfelt prayers, could neither avert nor end the carnage until God had decided it was time. "Men are not flattered by being shown that there has been a difference of purpose between the Almighty and them. To deny it, however, in this case, is to deny that there is a God governing the world," Lincoln wrote. "It is a truth which I thought needed to be told; and as whatever of humiliation there is in it, falls most directly on myself, I thought others might afford for me to tell it."

In striving to bind up the nation's wounds, Abraham Lincoln was willing to concede that he had been as wrong about this enormous catastrophe as anyone.

CHAPTER 15

A SACRED EFFORT

Saturday evening, March 4, 1865

Exhausted by it all—the rain and the mud, the mobs, the drunken vice president, the irritated VIPs, the handsome young man with the fiendish stare, the hours of pressure bracing for accidents or violence—Benjamin B. French waited until Abraham Lincoln was safely settled in the Capitol, then headed home. He dined at three p.m., then got some much-needed rest. In a few hours, he would have to rouse himself to go to the White House to help oversee the president's evening reception. In contrast to Mary Lincoln's ceremony the previous Saturday, no invitations were needed, and thousands were expected to attend, taking advantage of an opportunity to shake the hand of their president.

After Lincoln climbed into his carriage and departed, John Wilkes Booth followed the mobs on foot through the mire of Pennsylvania Avenue, heading back to his lodgings at the National Hotel, accompanying Walter Burton, the hotel's night clerk, whom Booth knew well. If the actor was agitated about Lincoln's successful inauguration and the failure of his mission, Burton did not detect it. Hundreds of others quickly filled up the city's noisy hotel bars. One of the celebrated men attending the inauguration, Benson J. Lossing, a longtime journalist and prolific historian who zealously collected primary documents of America's past, later claimed that he overheard disturbing conversations: "I remember hearing talk at Willard's, that evening, about a rash attempt, by a handsome young man, to break through a line of policemen, in the rotunda of the Capitol, who were guarding the passage of the President and his attendants through the eastern door to the platform at the portico."

There was little rest for the president. By five p.m., his ceremonial duties had resumed. Pennsylvania Republican congressman William D. Kelley, a liberal ally of Lincoln and a staunch supporter of his efforts to enlist black men in the Union Army, introduced the president to the members of Philadelphia's Perseverance Hose Company. They had splashed along in the mud earlier that day in their full uniforms, including their red shirts and leather helmets—with "Perseverance" inscribed on their helmets and their wide belts—accompanied by the Pennsylvania Cornet Band and their shiny horse-drawn fire engine. Admired by appraising women and small boys, these men were immensely proud to be select members of a historical firefighting force that dated back to 1805 and bore the motto *Perseverantia omnia vincit* (Perseverance conquers all). As a mark of respect, they awarded the president—the former rail-splitter who refused to take on airs as their social superior—their highest honor, a lifetime membership. The ceremony seemingly completed, the men were leaving when the distracted Kelley suddenly remembered that they were supposed to present the president with a silver medal bearing his own likeness. He hurried them back. Lincoln, who had posed for photographs throughout the war and fretted about the lack of silver and gold to support the nation's paper currency, looked at the medal and quipped: "I don't know but that the *material* is more scarce just now than the *picture*."

When French arrived at the White House after his nap, he had some bad news to break to the president. The civil appropriation bill had failed, having died in Congress that morning, foundering over an amendment that would have barred civilians from being tried in Lincoln's controversial military courts. With no bill, French fretted, there would be no money for public buildings and grounds, including the White House. Lincoln, focused on the war and the day's inaugural events, essentially shrugged. "We must *pick* along in some way," he told French.

A short distance from the White House that Saturday night, the district's theaters were in full operation, catering to the massive inauguration crowds. At Ford's Theatre, Elizabeth Crocker Bowers, known professionally as Mrs. D. P. Bowers, starred that night in two popular plays, a five-act sentimental drama about adultery, *The Stranger, or Misanthropy and Repentence*, and a three-act farce that followed, *The Honeymoon*. Lincoln, desperate for relief from the pressure of his presidency, had attended numerous performances at Ford's since its opening in August 1863, from Shakespeare's *Henry IV* and *Richard III* to George Sand's *Fanchon the Cricket* and such fluff as *The Marble Heart*, starring John Wilkes Booth. "Lincoln was fond of the theatre," Walt Whitman recalled. "I have myself seen him there several times. I remember thinking how funny it was that he, the leading actor in the greatest and stormiest drama known to real history's stage, should sit there and be so completely interested in those human jackstraws, moving about with their silly little gestures, foreign spirit, and flatulent text." Helen Truman, a young actress from Memphis whose career had been nurtured by Mrs. Bowers, recalled that, when seated in the audience, Lincoln seldom applauded. "His smiles were infrequent too and he would generally sit in the corner of the box away from the stage and held the curtain so that people would not stare at him," she remembered. All the same, he was one of the theatergoers, she recalled, who usually remained for the second feature, the farce or comedy that customarily followed the drama.

The first time Truman had met Lincoln had been under dire circumstances. She and her mother had come to plead for the life of her brother, sentenced to execution as a spy for running the blockade of Norfolk, Virginia. After cashing $20,000 worth of family jewels to hire lawyers, to little avail, the women had traveled to Washington, waiting for hours at the White House in hope of seeing Lincoln. When they finally got in, the president had lifted their spirits by promising to investigate the case. Ten days later, he informed them that the spy charge had fallen through, and he was able to grant a pardon. "We both fell on our knees to thank him and there were tears in his sad and weary eyes when he showed us to the door," Truman recalled. "Since that I have always adored him and my mother never ceased to bless him."

With the men of their family off at war, the two women, now destitute, needed a means to live. Trading on her budding beauty, the fourteen-year-old daughter had managed to get work as an actress at Ford's, though her Methodist mother, "exceedingly strong in her convictions," loathed the theater. "Starvation drove me to the stage," Truman recalled. There, on Christmas Eve, 1864, the teenage girl met another famous man. "It was Mr. Ford's custom to give a dinner to the members of his company after the performance of that evening and each member was permitted to bring a friend. Some one of the troop, I can't recollect who now, brought John Wilkes Booth. I was introduced to him and recalled that I had heard of him before. He appeared to be a very pleasant man but was somewhat nervous."

On inauguration night, though, the greatest show in Washington was plainly at the Executive Mansion, brightly lit with its gaslights flaring. Hours before the doors opened, a crowd formed around the White House in anticipation, and guards took up posts. By eight p.m., traffic was backed up three-quarters of a mile from the Pennsylvania Avenue portico of the house, and African American carriage drivers offered "quaint ejaculations" to guards who were bullying them about, as well as to "fellow hackmen who had the misfortune to be white and Irish," the *New York Herald* remarked. Visitors stepped down from their carriages into the mud, including "delicately dressed or undressed ladies, bareheaded and barenecked, all being promiscuously hustled and squeezed in a very dense crowd." After letting twenty or thirty people pass into the portico, the guards blocked further guests with the sides of their guns. Despite this precaution, the *Alexandria* (Virginia) *Gazette* reported, "some of the more unfortunate females, who were caught in the surging mass, actually shrieked with pain while several fainted and were carried away." One correspondent called the grand reception "more correctly, a grand jam." Another observed that it took two hours of waiting in a carriage to arrive at the portico and another two hours in line to see the president.

Inside, there were no dressing rooms and no opportunity for men to take off their overcoats with any hope of retrieving them. Male escorts accordingly put the women's mufflers over their arms and crammed their hats firmly on their heads as they were "carried through the jam of the inside passage." The carpets had been prudently covered to prevent the hordes from ruining them with the dirt they were tracking in from the muddy streets. Eager to "shake the hand that had split so many rails and written so many proclamations," the *New York Herald* recounted, they flowed in a line from the entrance hall to the Red Room and then into the roasting Blue Room, where they passed in front of Abraham Lincoln. It was the round blue room dressed in gold curtains, a depiction of a spread eagle above the central window, where Mary Lincoln had held her private reception the week before.

The college student and senator's son who had positioned himself in front of the Columbus statue earlier that day, Hamilton Gay Howard, was part of the throng. "I went alone, joined the long and rapidly-increasing procession, fell into line in the corridor of the White House and inched along toward the Blue Room, in which the great President stood, surrounded by his official family and their ladies, and he, towering like a Cedar of Lebanon above everybody who was near." Howard studied Lincoln as he came into view, standing just a few steps inside the door. "The President was in evening 'swallow-tail,' dress-suit, turn-down shirt collar, white cravat, kid gloves too large, or unduly stretched by numberless hand-shakings." Lincoln detested those white gloves, a concession to hygiene and fashion that he described to his friend Ward Hill Lamon as a violation of the statute against "cruelty to animals."

As Howard approached, Lamon asked his name and announced it to the president. "As each person was introduced, Mr. Lincoln stooped a little and cordially grasped, rather quickly, so as to get the first grip—a very essential thing in numerous hand-shakings—the right hand in his own, placed his left hand on the caller's shoulder, and gently, and amid continuous smiles and numberless 'How-de-does' shoved with his left hand each one along past him." His face covered with perspiration, Lincoln was working hard for the sake of gratifying his admirers and the curious. "I placed my hand in his great one," Howard remembered. "I looked up into those never-to-be-forgotten and magnificent eyes, and quietly said, 'God bless you, Mr. President,' to which he quickly replied: 'And you also, my young friend.'" Having shaken Lincoln's hand, Howard briefly joined the circle of dignitaries behind the president.

For a short time, the clump included Vice President Andrew Johnson, who, evidently less exhilarated than earlier, "paid considerable attention to Mrs. Lincoln." Given her distaste for the man, that may have been more trying than gratifying. Many well-known Washington figures carried on conversations in the background while the First Couple greeted the masses. Robert Lincoln was in his military uniform, as were Admiral Farragut and General Joseph Hooker, who was attended by his nieces. Navy Secretary Gideon Welles and Interior Secretary John Palmer Usher, and their wives, were in the room.

Secretary of War Edwin Stanton chatted with "one of the fairest of New York's married daughters, whose elegant and simple toilet and dress of drab silk and maroon velvet, no less than the beauty and grace of her person, made her the cynosure of neighboring eyes." Though Mrs. Stanton was with him, dressed in white satin, the usually bullying and officious Stanton was "all vivacity and smiles" in the presence of the beautiful young woman. Secretary of State William Seward's face was "still radiant with the remains of the last laugh provoked by a 'joke' of the first order." A close friend of Seward's, New York Senator Ira Harris, was in the room, as was his daughter, Clara, who with her stepbrother/fiancé, Henry Rathbone, would join the Lincolns in the presidential box at Ford's Theatre on April 14. Clara had become a favorite of the First Lady.

Elizabeth Keckley, the African American seamstress who had grown close to Mrs. Lincoln, looked in. "The jam was terrible, and the enthusiasm great," she recalled. Standing beside Lincoln, smiling at well-wishers, Mary was "dressed most charmingly," the *Evening Star* reported, "in an elegant white satin dress, the skirt tastefully draped with black lace," with "a rich black lace shawl" and a "costly pearl necklace." Elizabeth Bacon Custer expressed sympathy for what Mrs.

Lincoln and other fashionable women of 1865 had to endure in readying themselves for such ordeals. On the body, Mary's dresses were tight, and her neck and shoulders were pudgy. "There was a hard line and stiffness about the low neck of dresses then and the hourglass waist cost great struggles and vast patience if one was plump," Custer wrote. She recalled a roommate who struggled to get her waist down to size, and then endured the self-inflicted torture of sleeping encased in a bodice with an eighteen-inch waist each night, training her body to accept the restriction. "My set never allowed an increase from eighteen inches"— a brutal concession to fashion that made it hard to focus on anything else. "On some of the occasions of profound interest in the Civil War [I was] only conscious of the agonies of the suppressed, enraged, and protesting interior."

When he was through chatting, Howard moved into the East Room, where the U.S. Marine Band was pounding out patriotic songs. To leave the building, he passed through a large open window that had been transformed into an exit, with massive planks running from the low sill to the grass of the lawn, since getting people back out through the front door while others were crowding in would have been impossible. The cool of the starry darkness was a relief after the stifling heat indoors.

A woman who had spent days trying to meet Lincoln joined the line. Earlier in the day, still feeling despondent over the failure of her mission to enlist the president's help, Clara Barton had received a card from her dear cousin Anna Barton Bigelow, inviting her to dinner at Willard's Hotel. "I cheered and went," she noted in her diary. She had to walk through the crowded city, though, and by the time she arrived, the party was already eating. The group, she discovered, included George Ripley of the *New York Tribune*, a fellow Massachusetts native, former Unitarian minister, and noted transcendentalist, who was staying with his friend Charles A. Dana, the paper's former managing editor, now an assistant in the War Department. Ripley had founded the famous Utopian community Brook Farm. As a journalist, he had written glowingly about, among other topics, the speeches of Frederick Douglass. Barton stayed until after dark with this interesting group, who persuaded her to accompany them to Lincoln's reception. "Went home to dress for the levee and they called for me." She did not write about shaking the president's hand, and she could hardly have pitched her idea for locating missing soldiers during the few seconds each greeting permitted. She only noted: "President Lincoln kissed the baby—which was the most attractive feature of the levee." Which baby is not clear.

All told, some twenty thousand people "took advantage of the privilege to pour through the rooms of the Presidential mansion, to gaze at Mrs. Lincoln and to shake hands with the Chief Magistrate," the *Times* of London reported. The *New York Tribune* put the figure at fifteen thousand. French, standing near Lincoln, was more conservative, though he called it "the largest reception I ever saw." Alleviating his boredom by methodically counting, French noted that the president shook hands "steadily, at a rate of 100 every 4 minutes—with about 5,000 persons! Over, rather than under, for I counted the 100 several times, and when they came thickest he was not over 3 minutes, never over 5." Each handshake thus took about two and a half seconds.

The *New York Herald* made the obvious joke—that Lincoln's experience as a rail-splitter had prepared him well for this moment. "Certainly nothing less than the hard and sinewy arm cultivated in that occupation could be so shaken and stand it. There he stood, shaking and shaken, and still came up gallantly." The gleaming glove on his right hand gradually turned brown, then black, as thousands of hands touched it. "Mr. Lincoln looked weary, but he looked well," the paper added. Many, indeed, were struck by how tired Lincoln looked. "We were fortunate enough to gain admittance, but were pained to witness the care-worn appearance of Mr. Lincoln," wrote one correspondent. "During the whole night previous he was at the Capitol, attending upon the last hours of Congress, and the labors of the day had been immense. To crowd upon him such labors in the evening seemed almost cruel. But the people must see him, and they did."

When one visitor commiserated with Lincoln for the "infliction of courtesy," he responded good-naturedly, "I am a live man yet." "May the time be very far distant when he is not able to say so," added the

New York Herald reporter who had overhead the exchange. Noting French's presence, the *Herald* cuttingly described him as "the man who did not clean Pennsylvania avenue. The mud of Washington has, perhaps, been mentioned before." White House secretary John Hay stood in the reception line, too, no matter how much he still annoyed Mary Lincoln.

Every type of American inched in. "There was the sedate, elderly matron with faded shawl and baby in arms; the honest, sturdy, hard-handed tiller of the soil, with trousers in his boot tops; all classes and kinds, the powerful and the poor, *black and white*, yellow and brown, but orderly and respectful, all bent on one thing—to get a sight of the foremost man living on earth and *'shake his hand'*—the latter being the sine-qua-non of American good-will and respect," Howard recounted. "All the nobodies of the country were there," one journalist quipped. "Mr. Lincoln bore the infliction with manly fortitude," the *Times* of London reported, "and in numerous instances where he happened to be personally acquainted with his visitor, or to be specially introduced, inflicted so hearty a grip of welcome as to bring tears of pain rather than of gratitude into the eyes of the recipient."

Another prominent figure, who had scrupulously followed the events of the day as a correspondent for the *New York Times*, took "a notion to go" to the reception. Arriving at the White House on foot, the white-bearded, rumpled Walt Whitman found the muddy lawn packed with people—"all the grounds fill'd, and away out to the spacious sidewalks." The poet patiently waited his turn in the bracing night air, until he joined "the rush inside with the crowd" and "surged along the passage-ways," jammed with "crowds of country people, some very funny." Finally, the president came into view. "I saw Mr. Lincoln, drest all in black, with white kid gloves, and a claw-hammer coat, receiving, as in duty bound, shaking hands, looking very disconsolate, and as if he would give anything to be somewhere else." He did not record whether he shook the hand of the president he admired and loved—a curious lapse in his reporting, since the two had come to know each other by sight, and to exchange cordial bows, on the streets of Washington.

General Selden Connor's brother Virgil and his friend Cal were among the thousands. "The President must have had a lame arm the next morning if he shook hands with the whole crowd," Virgil wrote to his mother. The visitors "could not stop in the house long; go into one door and out at another." At nine thirty p.m., the Franklin Hose Company, another historic firefighting outfit from Philadelphia, was brought in to greet the president. The members of the Baltimore City Council, who had marched in the parade with the mayor, also appeared as a body, each member receiving a hearty handshake. By ten p.m., the *New York Herald* reported, the president's "glove was half torn off, and he looked perfectly exhausted." Joking about the title of a popular war song the writer added, "The cry, 'We are coming, father Abraham, five hundred thousand more,' was too much for him."

Though often bitterly critical of the president, the *Herald* sympathized with him for the "mean and unnatural" duty of shaking the hands of thousands of Americans. The writer compared Lincoln to Shakespeare's Coriolanus before the Roman people, "a man of simple nature who revolts at the artificial idea that he must be shaken by the hand by Tom, Dick and Harry, simply because he is of all the Romans the man most fit to be Consul. It is certain that Mr. Lincoln discharged this duty with a divine patience." Anyone with any integrity would seem stilted in such a setting, the writer mused. But Lincoln had not been "at all awkward on the platform in the morning, where, in front of an assemblage, representative in some degree of the people of every State, he gave utterance to the few eloquent sentences that made up his address. The tall form was in harmony with the scene, and its bold outline served only to distinguish him as the man above all others of that grand occasion." Some of the president's detractors had begun to sense the peculiar dignity of this unpolished man. One reporter noticed an expensively dressed man in the Blue Room studying Lincoln for several minutes. "Say what they will," the onlooker opined, "Old Abe is the noblest looking man in the nation."

Members of the mob, thrilled by their brush with history, indulged themselves in the nineteenth-century mania for souvenir hunting. They

EDWARD ACHORN

began slicing off swatches of the White House decor that Mary Lincoln had installed at such great expense. "A fever of vandalism seemed to seize them," said William H. Crook, one of the president's bodyguards. "A great piece of red brocade, a yard square almost, was cut from the window-hangings of the East Room, and another piece, not quite so large, from a curtain in the Green Room." Intricate flowers worked into the design of the lace curtains were sliced out, "evidently for an ornament for the top of pincushions or something of the sort." Police hunted down some of the miscreants and made arrests after the reception. Though Lincoln had presided over an immensely destructive war, he was shocked, almost hurt, when later shown this feral damage by his fellow citizens. "Why should they do it?" he asked Crook. "How can they?"

The *New York Herald* noted in its characteristically racist language that a number of African Americans had turned up at the White House, hoping to get in. "In this vestibule in the number of the visitors was a good specimen of the almighty nigger darkey, accompanied by several negro damsels," the reporter observed. "Many colored persons appeared to pay their respects to the President and lady," the *Washington Chronicle* reported, "among whom were Fred Douglass and wife." America's most famous black man was visiting that night, patiently taking his place in the line. "The negro seems quite disposed to make himself at home anywhere he pleases to go. What next?" a Vermont editor mused.

Frederick Douglass had come to make precisely that point: that black people should be "at home" anywhere in the United States. Though three African American men had, in fact, appeared at Lincoln's New Year's Day levee two months earlier, Douglass was under the impression that "no colored persons had ever ventured to present themselves" at a presidential reception. The time had come, he concluded, for black people to assert themselves as full citizens. Douglass believed, "now that freedom had become the law of the republic, and colored men were on the battle-field mingling their blood with that of white men in one common effort to save the country, that it was not too great an assumption for a colored man to offer his congratulations to the President with those of other citizens." The events of that day could only have reenforced these views, with black soldiers so prominent in the proceedings, and the president condemning slavery in his inaugural address.

To his disgust, Douglass had been unable to find any black men brave enough to accompany him to the White House that night. The disdain that whites typically showed blacks, sometimes accompanied by force, could be unpleasant, "and my colored friends had too often realized discomfiture from this cause to be willing to subject themselves to such unhappiness," Douglass noted. But his associates enthusiastically encouraged him to make the effort. It reminded Douglass of his days in New England, when black friends prodded him to buy first-class railroad tickets and seat himself among white people who were repulsed by the proximity of black people. Fellow African Americans were only too happy to have Douglass "hauled out and pounded by rough-handed brakemen," if it meant he would "make way for them" through desegregation. "It was plain, then, that someone must lead the way, and that if the colored man would have his rights, he must take them; and now, though it was plainly quite the thing for me to attend President Lincoln's reception, 'they all with one accord began to make excuse'"—a reference to the Gospel of Luke's description of the supposed followers of Jesus who found reasons not to accompany their Lord.

Douglass finally found someone of his race brave enough to join him—Mrs. Thomas J. Dorsey, the wife of a friend who had once been enslaved in Maryland but had risen as a free man to become a successful caterer in Philadelphia. With Mrs. Dorsey on his arm—rather than his own wife, the mother of their five children, Anna Murray-Douglass, who was plain, poorly educated, and often ill—Douglass was ready to mingle with the most distinguished of Mr. Lincoln's visitors at the White House. As Douglass walked in, a feeling of pride rose up in him. "I had for some time looked upon myself as a man, but now in this multitude of the élite of the land, I felt myself a man among men," he recalled. "I regret to be obliged to say, however, that this comfortable assurance was not of long duration."

When he reached the front door, "two policemen stationed there took me rudely by the arm and ordered me to stand back, for their directions were to admit no persons of my color." Douglass argued with them, insisting Lincoln would have given no such order and would, in fact, want to see him. With Douglass and his guest obstructing the entrance and refusing to step aside, police adopted a different tactic. They "assumed an air of politeness, and offered to conduct me in." But instead of bringing him to Lincoln, they took him directly to the East Room and marched him through the window and down the planks outdoors. Even after that, Douglass bravely refused to give in. "You have deceived me," he told the police. "I shall not go out of this building till I see President Lincoln." An unnamed member of Congress who knew Douglass was surprised the police would not permit this famous man to pass. "Be so kind as to say to Mr. Lincoln that Frederick Douglass is detained by officers at the door," Douglass told him. Shortly thereafter, Douglass and his companion were allowed to join the line for a handshake with the president.

The president whom Douglass had disparaged as an "excellent slave hound," no more fit to hold the presidency than the Southern apologist James Buchanan, a creature devoid of a "decided anti-slavery conviction and policy," a craven politician who was willing to sell out the black people and had allowed his pragmatism to rob his statesmanship "of all soul-moving utterances"—that very man, Douglass now knew, had doggedly undermined slavery, armed the former slaves, forced through a constitutional amendment that would abolish slavery forever, and on this day had delivered a heartrending condemnation of slavery as the grave sin that had brought this murderous war on the United States. Now he moved slowly with his fellow Americans to shake the man's hand. Finally, Douglass entered the Blue Room. "Like a mountain pine high above all others, Mr. Lincoln stood, in his grand simplicity, and homelike beauty," Douglass recalled. Lincoln recognized him in line even before Douglass reached him.

"Here comes my friend Douglass," the president said. Taking him in the firm grip reserved for important acquaintances, Lincoln said, "I am glad to see you. I saw you in the crowd today, listening to my inaugural address; how did you like it?"

Douglass was embarrassed to be taking up far more than his allotted two and a half seconds. "Mr. Lincoln, I must not detain you with my poor opinion, when there are thousands waiting to shake hands with you."

"No, no," Lincoln said, "you must stop a little, Douglass; there is no man in the country whose opinion I value more than yours. I want to know what you think of it."

Douglass replied, "Mr. Lincoln, that was a sacred effort."

"I am glad you liked it!" Lincoln said.

"I passed on," Douglass recalled, "feeling that any man, however distinguished, might well regard himself honored by such expressions, from such a man." Douglass concluded that there had been no order from Lincoln to keep out black people. The guards "were simply complying with an old custom, the outgrowth of slavery, as dogs will sometimes rub their necks, long after their collars are removed, thinking they are still there." Douglass left with the feeling that he had moved the nation one more step toward equal treatment of white and black Americans. "My colored friends were well pleased with what had seemed to them a doubtful experiment, and I believe were encouraged by its success to follow my example. I have found in my experience that the way to break down an unreasonable custom is to contradict it in practice."

The *Detroit Free Press* reported that "Fred. Douglass and lady" stuck out at the event, "the observed of all observers." The *New York Herald*, on the other hand, having failed to spot the guards' confrontation with Douglass, concluded that race was no longer an issue at such receptions: "No notice was taken of the negroes present, and no remarks were made about them." Whether he or his readers thought that was a good thing was another matter. Certainly, the *Valley Spirit*, a bitterly anti-administration journal published in Chambersburg, Pennsylvania, was displeased. "Things have greatly changed within the White House within the last four years," its editor lamented. "The star of *Niggerism* is now in the ascendant." Douglass shared the racists' perception that the world was, indeed, changing. Black Americans, he reflected after the levee, were finally winning recognition as human beings—fully entitled, as Lincoln had long argued, to the inalienable rights recognized in the nation's essential founding document, the Declaration of Independence. Skin color alone did not make anyone inferior. The "conditions of human associations are founded upon character rather than color," Douglass concluded. And since "character depends on mind and morals, there can be nothing blameworthy in people thus equal meeting each other on the plane of civil and social rights."

In the East Room, where the U.S. Marine Band played "incessantly," the *New York Herald* reported, some of the visitors refrained from heading out through the open window, choosing to linger. Women and men found themselves packed together in a "tremendous jam," while attendants fought to maintain a narrow pathway through which visitors could exit. "No chance to show or see dresses. No chance to converse with friends," the reporter noted. "The crush of the evening had been too great for comfort or enjoyment. It is said that hereafter the receptions will be more exclusive, and that tickets will be issued." But on this night, at least, American citizens by the thousands had the experience of shaking Old Abe's hand.

That evening's throng did not include the strikingly handsome man French had stopped at the Capitol earlier that day. That night, John Wilkes Booth strode down Pennsylvania Avenue in the opposite direction of the White House. At ten thirty p.m., he was in the rear room of a favorite haunt, the restaurant at the Lichau House, on Louisiana Avenue, next to the Canterbury Theatre. There he shared a drink and a private discussion with a twenty-four-year-old friend. Booth had known Michael O'Laughlen since they were boys, neighbors in Baltimore. A skilled craftsman—an engraver and a manufacturer of the ornamental plaster used in fashionable nineteenth-century homes—O'Laughlen fully shared Booth's hatred for Lincoln and his war of aggression. Though hailing from a state that was in theory still in the Union, O'Laughlen had chosen to risk his life for the cause, enlisting early and remaining in the Confederate Army until his discharge, in June 1862. After that, he had gone to work with his brother at his feed and produce business in Baltimore. In recent weeks, O'Laughlen had been spending a good deal of his time in Washington at the celebrated actor's expense, wearing flashy new clothing, including "a pair of Scotch plaid pants and vest and dark coat—tolerably large plaid, and a black slouch hat." Booth had drawn his old friend into his plot against Lincoln, and there had been many details to discuss. What the two talked about that night in the privacy of the back room is unknown, but the mysteries of this day—the failure to seize or kill the president—might well have been the topic.

At the White House, aides locked the front door at eleven p.m., leaving hundreds who had waited in line disappointed. Sometime before midnight, the band struck up "Yankee Doodle," and attendants cleared the rooms, directing people out the window. By midnight, "the lights were dead—the guests had fled." The exhausted Lincoln headed upstairs to his room, separate from Mary's, and disrobed. He was finally able to pull off his soiled and ruined right glove, which the First Lady presented to Keckley the next day as a memento of the event. But the day was not over. Officers appeared in his room to make their reports about the latest military developments while the president was "en dishabille," presumably in the nightshirt that he was prone to wear, revealing his skinny legs and big feet.

Out front, police officers and soldiers saw off the last of the visitors. "That's the end of inauguration day," said one policeman as the last carriage pulled away. "Good luck go with you."

THE STUFF TO CARRY THEM THROUGH

The events were not quite over. On Monday night, March 6, the inaugural ball was to be held in four massive second-floor rooms at the Patent Office. Two years earlier, the ornate building had been turned into a makeshift hospital, something Walt Whitman noted in his dispatch to the *New York Times*: "I have this moment been up to look at the gorgeously arrayed ball and supper-rooms, for the Inauguration Dance aforesaid, (which begins in a few hours;) and I could not help thinking of the scene [in] those rooms, where the music will sound and the dancers' feet presently tread—what a different scene they presented to my view a while since, filled with a crowded mass of the worst wounded of the war, brought in from Second Bull Run, Antietam, and Fredericksburgh." He continued with the comparison:

> To-night, beautiful women, perfumes, the violins' sweetness, the polka and the waltz; but then, the amputation, the blue face, the groan, the glassy eye of the dying, the clotted rag, the odor of the old wounds and blood, and many a mother's son amid strangers, passing away untended there, (for the crowd of the badly hurt was great, and much for nurse to do, and much for surgeon.) Think not of such grim things, gloved ladies, as you bow to your partners, and the figures of the dance this night

are loudly called, or you may drop on the floor that has known
what this one knew, but two short winters since.

Despite its preponderance of beautiful, perfumed and gloved
ladies, the ball that night proved, if anything, less edifying and more
disorderly than the reception at the White House two evenings earlier.
In the northern ballroom, blue and gold sofas on a raised platform
were set up for the president and First Lady, to the horror of the *New
York World*, which contended that "it needed but little imagination to
transform them into thrones." The paper's editor already believed that
Lincoln and his cohorts were determined to convert the Founders' free
republic into an abject tyranny of centralized power. An extravagant
dinner was prepared, but when the doors were opened to the crowd,
hungry guests in their finery made a feral rush for the tables. Men in
formal wear "with more audacity than good taste, could be seen snatch-
ing whole pates, chickens, legs of veal, halves of turkies, ornamental
pyramids, &c., from the tables and bearing them over the heads of the
shuddering crowd," including ladies who dreaded the dripping grease
would ruin their expensive gowns, the *Evening Star* reported. "The
floor of the supper room was soon sticky, pasty and oily with wasted
confections, mashed cakes and debris of foul and meat."

Professor William Withers Jr., the orchestra leader at Ford's
Theatre, was there, waving his arms and pointing his baton, directing
the main band through its performance of the "National Inauguration March," followed by quadrilles, lancers, schottisches, polkas, and
waltzes. Unsurprisingly, Lincoln proved himself not particularly adept
at the graces of a formal ball. Yet Elizabeth Bacon Custer felt great
sympathy toward him for gamely trying, as she danced in the set next
to the president. "I was so absorbed watching dear Mr. Lincoln, this
tall, gaunt man walking through the dance so patiently, I was nearly
lifted around by my arm when I forgot an a la mande left. The patience
and sadness of his expressive face has not been exaggerated in the best
portraits; the war had almost broken his heart," she wrote. "Girl that

I was, I could not fail to see that any fashionable life to which he had to submit was a trial, that he was so tolerant for it was heaven to Mrs. Lincoln." In the dances, Mary "swung, as was the custom, the seven breadths of her brocaded dress from side to side as she went through a la mande left or curtsied to her partner in the old-time quadrilles." President Lincoln, on the other hand, "seemed not to be one of us, [in this] gay thoughtless crowd, but he moved among the gay throng, as intent on doing the stupid, tiresome a la mande left and chasse to your partners as if he were reading a proclamation."

Among the matters weighing on the president's mind was a new round of patronage appointments, which he always regarded as vital to securing political power. Former Republican senator John P. Hale, out of the job he had held off and on since 1847, was aggressively seeking a lucrative government post that would take his family, including his Booth-obsessed daughter Lucy, far from Washington. On Thursday, three days after the ball, Lincoln awarded Hale the highly prized position of ambassador to Spain. When Assistant Navy Secretary Gustavus Fox complained that Hale had repeatedly criticized the administration —and Fox in particular—Lincoln replied, "You have more of that feeling of personal resentment than I. . . . Perhaps I may have too little of it, but I never thought it paid. A man has not time to spend half his life in quarrels. If any man ceases to attack me, I never remember the past against me." Despite efforts to break up their relationship, however, Booth and Lucy remained "the most devoted lovers," according to Booth's sister Asia. Over the next month, they would concoct a plan: after spending a year with her father, Lucy would "return from Spain for [Booth], either with her father or without him."

On the day after the inauguration, surely knowing that a separation might be imminent, Booth had added some words to the back of an envelope already almost covered with verses scrawled by Lucy and her visiting cousin John Parker Hale Wentworth: *Now in this moment.*

Booth crossed out the line. He chose another noun.

Now in this hour that we part,
I will ask to be forgotten <u>never.</u>
But in thy pure and guileless heart,
Consider me thy friend, dear, Ever.

He signed it "J. Wilkes Booth."

Booth was still planning with his co-conspirators to kidnap Lincoln and hold him for ransom, but with thousands of prisoners being traded, and the South's military position increasingly precarious, the plot was becoming pointless.

Walt Whitman, meanwhile, returned to Brooklyn, where he could embrace his brother George, back home after five months of suffering, sickness, and hunger in a Confederate prison. The poet also had to oversee the publication of his new book of Civil War poems, *Drum-Taps*. Whitman planned to publish it himself, signing a contract with Peter Eckler, a printer on Fulton Street, for five hundred copies for $254. Desperate to produce it as cheaply as possible, Whitman altered his carefully arranged order of the poems, saving paper by cramming them onto fewer pages.

On April 3, Richmond fell to Union forces. The next night, Booth traveled on an overnight steamship from New York City to Newport, Rhode Island. He arrived on the morning of April 5, with an unnamed woman many historians have taken to be Lucy Hale. Checking in at the Aquidneck House, he registered boldly as "J.W. Booth and lady"—not Mrs. Booth, as would have been required by a seemingly respectable hotel—yet he got away with it. Such a stay would have been a reckless act by an unmarried senator's daughter, who had to preserve her reputation to live and marry in respectable society. But Booth and the unnamed "lady" certainly seemed to have some sort of relationship. After breakfast, they set off for a long walk in the seaside town. When they returned at two p.m., Booth requested that dinner be sent up to the room "for the lady; the excuse being indisposition." Perhaps they had squabbled, since Booth was devastated that the Confederate capital, a city he had loved for many years, had been defiled by Lincoln's soldiers.

Before the dinner could be delivered, the couple abruptly departed on the three p.m. train for Boston, a city where Lucy had family and friends.

When Booth arrived in Boston, he set off on his own. Friend and fellow actor McKee Rankin found him "in a most unsettled frame of mind." While the citadel of abolitionism and Republicanism wildly celebrated the fall of Richmond, Booth engaged in target practice in a basement shooting gallery near his hotel. He visited his friend Orlando Tompkins at his drugstore, giving him a bloodstone ring and asking him to wear it in his memory. "I may never see you again," he said. He visited his pro-Lincoln brother Edwin, who was appearing at the Boston Theatre. The subject of Richmond's fall inevitably arose. "You and I could never agree upon that question," John said. "Goodbye, Ned." They were his last words to his brother.

Frederick Douglass was in the same city that night, speaking to a jubilant audience celebrating at Faneuil Hall. "I, for the first time in my life, have the assurance, not only of a country redeemed, a country regenerated, but of my race free and having a future in this land," Douglass told the crowd.

Booth returned to Washington by steamer on April 9, and that night learned that Robert E. Lee had surrendered the forces of the Army of Northern Virginia to Ulysses S. Grant at Appomattox. Grant followed the lead of Lincoln's second inaugural speech in acting with charity, not malice, permitting the soldiers to take their guns and horses home so that they could start life anew. The Army of the Potomac showed deep respect for its defeated foes. Returned to his home in Rochester, New York, Douglass joined in another celebration over the surrender. Firefighters rang the city hall bell from eleven p.m. until two a.m.

On the evening of April 11, Booth joined the crowds thronging the White House, in a Washington lit up in celebration. Lincoln spoke from a window, a halo of light silhouetting his figure. He discussed reconstruction in rather tedious detail, dropping each page to the ground after he finished reading it. Touching on the explosive issue of civil rights for former slaves, he revealed he favored states' conferring voting rights "on the very intelligent and on those who serve our cause as soldiers." "That means nigger citizenship," Booth seethed to his friend David Herold, according to Herold's defense counsel, Frederick Stone. "Now, by God! I'll put him through." When they caught up with Lewis Powell, another member of the conspiracy, Booth vowed, "That is the last speech he will ever make."

On April 14, Booth checked his mail at Ford's Theatre, and opened a four-page letter. Reading to himself, he laughed out loud and shook his head. "The damned woman," he was heard to remark. At Ford's, he learned that President and Mrs. Lincoln intended to attend the show there that night, something that the theater's managers proudly advertised in a broadside.

The flag-raising ceremony at Fort Sumter in Charleston Harbor that War Secretary Edwin Stanton had arranged took place that day, ex-governor John Clifford among the many dignitaries in attendance. It was on this lovely sunny afternoon, with a light breeze blowing from the east, that preacher Henry Ward Beecher—no believer in charity for all and malice toward none after such evil had been unleashed—denounced "the ambitious, educated, plotting leaders of the South," and promised that God would punish them severely for shedding an "ocean of blood."

At five p.m., the Lincolns took a carriage ride to the navy yard. Lincoln startled Mary with his unusual cheerfulness, she recalled six months later. "We must both be more cheerful in the future—between the war and the loss of our darling Willie—we have both been very miserable," he told her. They clambered aboard the USS *Montauk* anchored there, "going all over her, accompanied by us all," wrote navy surgeon George B. Todd, in a letter to his brother. "Both seemed very happy, and so expressed themselves,—glad that this war was over, or so near its end, and then drove back to the White House."

In their festive mood, the Lincolns had made plans to attend a "celebrated eccentric comedy" (as Ford's broadside put it) that night, *Our American Cousin*, by British playwright Tom Taylor, the story of a crude but shrewd and honest American who gets the better of a snobby and dim-witted English nobleman. While Lincoln had invited the Grants— the victorious president joined by the victorious general would create quite a public stir—they declined the invitation. The night before, Grant had accompanied Mrs. Lincoln on a ride through the city to marvel at the brilliantly illuminated buildings and fireworks in celebration of Lee's surrender. The mercurial First Lady was irritated by the wild cheers for the general rather than her husband, behavior that Grant found unsettling. He was happy when his wife, Julia, who "objected strenuously to accompanying Mrs. Lincoln," insisted that they decline the invitation and set off immediately for Burlington, New Jersey, on the Delaware River near Philadelphia, where the couple, with their children, hoped to enjoy a brief respite from the war. Two young friends of the Lincoln family agreed to attend instead: Clara Harris, daughter of New York senator Ira Harris, and her stepbrother and fiancé, Colonel Henry Rathbone. They had stood near the First Couple during the mobbed reception at the White House on the evening of the inauguration.

The play was already underway when the party arrived. Some seventeen hundred people, joyful over the virtual end of the war, rose in a standing ovation when they saw Lincoln enter the presidential box, perched to the right above the stage. Professor Withers's orchestra struck up "Hail to the Chief," and when the applause faded, the play resumed. After ten p.m., Booth, concealing a small single-shot derringer and a large bowie knife, mounted the steps of Ford's Theatre to the dress circle. Unfortunately, Lincoln's guard that night, Washington police officer John Parker, was not known for his attention to detail and devotion to duty. He had been reprimanded previously for falling asleep on a streetcar during his beat, using intemperate language, extorting prostitutes, and being drunk on duty, among other offenses that had cost him neither his job nor a posting at the White House, a mark of the lax standards of both police work and presidential security during that era. On that night at Ford's, expecting no trouble, he had left his seat outside the presidential box, according to several witnesses. Indeed, earlier in the evening, while the Lincolns enjoyed the play, Parker stepped out for a quick drink at the bar next door with the president's coachman, Francis Burke, and his messenger, Charles Forbes.

By the time Booth arrived that night, the messenger was back in the theater, biding his time near the presidential box should his services be required. There were two doors: one leading from the general audience to a narrow vestibule, and another opening to the box itself. According to eyewitness Helen Du Barry, Booth claimed he had a communication for the president, showed Forbes an official envelope, and pulled from his pocket and presented to him "a card with the name of a Senator written on it." The calling card of an esteemed U.S. senator might have persuaded Lincoln's messenger that nothing was amiss with the visitor. "The watch stepped aside & the assassin entered," Du Barry recounted in a letter to her mother two days later. It is thus possible that Booth's love affair with John Hale's daughter gained him admittance not only to the second inauguration, but also to the presidential box at Ford's Theatre. One theatergoer taking in the play from a seat not far from the box was the navy surgeon who had greeted the president a few hours earlier. Dr. Todd heard a man say, "There's Booth," and turned his head to see the actor. "He was still walking very slow and was near the box door when he stopped took a card from his pocket, wrote something on it, and gave it to the usher who took it to the box. In a minute the door was opened and he walked in," the surgeon wrote to his brother the next day, while the memory was fresh.

The play was nearing one of the moments when the crowd's laughter was loudest. In act 3, scene 2, a pushy English mother who has tried to pair her daughter off with the boorish American, Asa Trenchard, in the mistaken belief that he possesses a rich inheritance, stiffly responds to his rudeness after the truth emerges that he is not wealthy after all: "I am aware, Mr. Trenchard, you are not used to the manners of good society, and that, alone will excuse the impertinence of which you have been guilty." Like Groucho Marx, Trenchard delights the audience by puncturing her pomposity with the kind of bluntness that elites found deplorable: "Don't know the manners of good society, eh? Well, I guess

I know enough to turn you inside out, old gal—you sockdologizing old man-trap."

As the audience roared, Booth aimed his small pistol at the back of the president's head, pulled the trigger, and sent a ball into Abraham Lincoln's brain, plunging him into unconsciousness. When Rathbone leapt up to stop him, Booth slashed his arm with the bowie knife. The famous actor, noted for his acrobatic performances, leapt to the stage, awkwardly this time, catching a spur on the bunting decorating the box. Many saw him shake his fist and heard him shout *Sic semper tyrannis*— "Thus always to tyrants," the motto of his beloved Virginia, home of George Washington, Thomas Jefferson, and James Madison. He left the stage before the audience could even comprehend what had happened.

While Mary screamed and wept, a twenty-three-year-old army surgeon named Charles A. Leale made it into the box. Leale, who oversaw the wounded commissioned officers' ward at the Army's general hospital at Armory Square, ascertained the president had been shot in the head and mortally wounded. Two other doctors joined Leale. They all concluded Lincoln could not survive a trip to the White House. Some on the scene were concerned that a president should not die in a theater, a place that many religious Americans still considered unrespectable. With the help of several soldiers, men lifted Lincoln up, forced their way through the crowd, and carried him across the street to a boardinghouse owned by a German immigrant tailor named William Petersen. Lincoln was laid on a bed in the first floor's back room, at an angle because of his height. A month earlier, Ford's callboy William Ferguson, delivering parts for actors to memorize, had seen Booth stretched out "lazily" on that very bed, "a pipe in his mouth, his handsome hair disheveled," during a visit to fellow actors Charles Warwick and John Mathews, who had rented the room.

As Booth struck at the theater, one of his co-conspirators, Lewis Powell, gained access to William Seward's house and brutally stabbed the secretary of state, who was recovering from a bad carriage accident and lay helpless in bed. Fearing an organized attempt to decapitate the government, War Secretary Stanton raced to the Petersen house and, as was his wont, immediately took charge. At one point during the night, Dr. Leale recalled, the First Lady "sprang up suddenly with a piercing cry and fell fainting to the floor." Stanton entered the back room and issued a stern order: "Take that woman out and do not let her in again." Mary Lincoln never saw her husband alive again. Benjamin Brown French, who had ordered the Capitol closed in the emergency, rushed to the house to lend any assistance he could. "I took Mrs. Lincoln by the hand, and she made some exclamation indicating the deepest agony of mind. I also shook hands with Robert, who was crying audibly," Brown wrote the next day in his diary. Before Lincoln passed away, Stanton had already launched an investigation. Louis J. Weichmann would finally spill his guts to the authorities, saving his life by telling everything he knew. John Surratt would flee the country. Mary Surratt would be hanged for running the boardinghouse where Booth and his associates gathered.

Shortly after Lincoln died that morning, John P. Hale met privately with the next president, Andrew Johnson, at his room in Kirkwood House. "It was of a strictly confidential character," Hale told the press, insisting he had "no right to communicate what passed between them." For the record, the ambassador declared his strong confidence in Johnson's leadership. The two may well have discussed keeping the Hale name out of the probe of the assassination. Strangely, Lucy—who surely had extensive knowledge of Booth's activities leading up to the tragedy—would be left out of the investigation entirely. So too would Charles Forbes, who had evidently let Booth pass into the presidential box on the strength of Hale's calling card.

Salmon P. Chase arrived at Johnson's hotel. The chief justice, who still dreamed of becoming president, administered the oath of office to another man for the second time in six weeks. Hale was among the elite group of eleven men in Johnson's room watching this moment in American history. The former tailor from Tennessee—drunk before the gathered dignitaries on March 4, prompting prayers from even the administration's enemies that Lincoln would survive his term—was subdued this day. "All were deeply impressed by the solemnity of the occasion," said a wire account sent to the nation's newspapers.

Johnson offered a few humble words this time. "I feel incompetent to perform duties so important and responsible as those which have been so unexpectedly thrown upon me," the new president said, adding that he did not yet know what policies he would pursue. He addressed Hale and the others in the room that morning. "I shall ask and rely upon you and others in carrying the government through its present perils. I feel in making this request that it will be heartily responded to by you and all other patriots and lovers of the rights and interests of a free people."

Booth's act had replaced the shrewd and careful Lincoln with an impulsive man far less sympathetic to the plight of black Americans and far less attuned to the difficult work of balancing factions and easing along change. The result would be political overreaching by congressional Republicans, a fierce reaction by Southern whites, and brutal oppression of African Americans for the next century—a bitter tragedy for the United States after all it had sacrificed. Of all the tragic what-ifs of American history, the loss of Lincoln's political touch in dealing with the terrible challenges of reconstruction must rank at the top.

Walt Whitman was at his mother's house in Brooklyn that morning when he heard the shouts in the streets and learned of Lincoln's death from telegraphed accounts published in the newspapers. "Mother prepared breakfast—and other meals afterward—as usual; but not a mouthful was eaten all day by either of us," he recalled. "We each drank half a cup of coffee; that was all. Little was said. We got every newspaper morning and evening, and the frequent extras of that period, and pass'd them silently to each other."

That afternoon, he left the house, walked to the Fulton Street ferry, and crossed to Manhattan, curious to see how New York was reacting. "All Broadway is black with mourning—the facades of the houses are festooned with black," he wrote in his notebook. "Towards noon the sky darkened & it began to rain. Drip, drip & heavy moist black weather—the stores are all closed—the rain sent the women from the street & black-clothed men only remain." He gathered his thoughts about Lincoln. "He leaves, in my opinion, the greatest, best, most characteristic, artistic, moral personality," Whitman wrote. "He was assassinated—but the Union is not assassinated. Death does its work, obliterates a hundred, a thousand—President, general, captain, private—but the Nation is immortal."

Whitman began working on poems in commemoration of Lincoln —including the most popular of his career, "O Captain! My Captain!"— halting the publication of *Drum-Taps* to include them. But his spookier, more profound elegy was the 206-line poem "When Lilacs Last in the Door-Yard Bloom'd." In it, he returned to his fascination with the "lustrous" star he had seen at the inauguration, and keenly remembered the lovely and fragrant lilacs that were in bloom when the president he treasured was killed:

> *O ever-returning spring! Trinity sure to me you bring;*
> *Lilac blooming perennial, and drooping star in the west,*
> *And thought of him I love.*

Lucy Hale, staggered to learn that her beautiful, exuberant lover had killed Lincoln, wrote in anguish to Edwin Booth, John's brother. "I have had a heart-broken letter from the poor little girl to whom he had promised so much happiness," he revealed to his sister Asia Booth Clarke. Asia later wrote to another correspondent that Lucy had "written heart-broken letters to Edwin about it."

In the coming days, some newspapers even leaked details of the engagement. The Washington correspondent for the *New York Tribune* reported that an "unhappy lady—the daughter of a New England Senator—is plunged in the profoundest grief; but with womanly fidelity, is slow to believe him guilty of this appalling crime, and asks, with touching pathos, for evidence of his innocence." John's brother Junius Brutus Booth, the *Dayton* (Ohio) *Daily Empire* reported, "stated in the presence of several gentlemen that he had only a day or two previous received a letter from his brother, John Wilkes, and that Wilkes stated his engagement with Miss Hale, and that there was opposition to their marriage, but that the marriage would take place, notwithstanding the opposition, and that, too, before Mr. Hale left for Spain."

The *Springfield* (Massachusetts) *Republican* found the story hard to believe, since "Booth wasn't the kind of a man that any young lady of character would have noticed, much less married." A day later, however, the paper conceded: "It cannot be denied, we are afraid, that John Wilkes Booth, the assassin, was engaged to be married to a daughter of Senator Hale. He has been very much of a beau among the ladies of the National Hotel at Washington the past winter." But disavowals soon followed, newspapers insisting that there was nothing to the story. For the most part, Ambassador Hale and his allies managed to hush up the matter with remarkable effectiveness. Editors of the time were willing to respect the privacy of a young woman of Lucy Hale's social class, rather than ruin her life. As journalist Benjamin Perley Poore noted, her name "was honorably kept a secret." Correspondence was apparently destroyed. The family archives at Concord, New Hampshire, are devoid of letters by Lucy during this period. Nine years later, Lucy married a widowed corporation lawyer, William E. Chandler, who had ardently admired her in her youth. He became a senator from New Hampshire—and she an ornament of Washington society until her death in 1915.

Booth broke another woman's heart, a lover who had addressed him as "My Darling Baby," even as he proceeded with his engagement to Lucy Hale. Ella Turner, the petite blond prostitute he had enjoyed at the Class 1 house at 62 Ohio Avenue, tried to kill herself after the news of Lincoln's assassination broke. At eleven a.m. on April 15, housemates entered her room. At first they thought she was still asleep but could not rouse her. "Several physicians were called in, when it was discovered she had taken chloroform," the Washington *Evening Star* reported that night, happy to link the president's murderer to a whore. When the doctors revived her, she immediately asked for a photograph of Booth that she "had concealed under the pillow of her bed." Miserable, she informed the physicians that "she did not thank them for saving her life." When authorities later questioned Turner about her connection with Booth, she fed them palpable lies—such as, "I have never heard him speak unfavorable of the President" and "I heard him speak of the President as being a good man just as other people did."

In Rochester, New York, that same day, Frederick Douglass wandered into city hall for a memorial gathering, and sat at the back, in a daze. Called on to speak, he protested, "This is not an occasion for speech making, but for silence." But pressed, he spoke a few words from the heart. "I feel it as a personal as well as national calamity; on account of the race to which I belong and the deep interest which that good man ever took in its elevation."

Booth expected to be embraced as a courageous hero, and some were indeed thrilled. "Hurrah! Old Abe Lincoln has been assassinated!" Emma LeConte, of devastated Columbia, South Carolina, wrote in her diary on April 21. "It may be abstractedly wrong to be so jubilant, but I just can't help it. After all the heaviness and gloom of yesterday this blow to our enemies comes like a gleam of light." She was delighted that Lincoln had been shot in the sleazy setting of a theater, and that his assassin had proclaimed *Sic semper tyrannis*. "Virginia is avenged," she wrote. "Could there have been a fitter death for such a man?" She added bitterly that "Andy Johnson will succeed him—the rail-splitter will be succeeded by the drunken ass. Such are the successors of Washington and Jefferson—such are to rule the South."

Even some Republicans in the North were happy to see Lincoln gone. Indiana congressman George Washington Julian, who had briefly supported Chase's bid for the 1864 Republican nomination, met on the afternoon of Lincoln's death with a group of fellow radicals in Washington, including Ohio senator Benjamin Wade, Michigan senator Zachariah Chandler, Pennsylvania congressman John Covode, U.S. District Court judge David K. Carter, and *New York Tribune* reporter Samuel Wilkinson. "Their hostility towards Lincoln's policy of conciliation and contempt for his weakness were undisguised; and the universal feeling among radical men here is that his death is a godsend," Julian wrote in his journal that night. Lincoln's policy of charity toward the defeated Southern leaders would neither protect black people in the South nor secure Northern control, radicals feared. Julian's entry continued: "The dastardly attack upon Lincoln and Seward, the great leaders in the policy of mercy, puts to flight utterly every vestige of humanitarian weakness, and makes it seem that justice shall be done and the righteous ends of the war made sure. The government could not have survived the policy on which it had entered."

In short, hard times were coming for the ex-Confederates and their society. Some in the South grasped that point. "I know this foul murder will bring down worse miseries on us," Mary Chesnut, having fled from Union forces to Chester, South Carolina, wrote in her diary on April 22. She quoted a friend's observation that the Yankees, for all their crimes against God and country, were at least loyal to Lincoln. "If they did choose a baboon to reign over them, they were true to him, they stuck to him through weal and through woe. Oh! they were sharp Yankees and saw in his ugly hide the stuff to carry them through, and he saved them—if he could not save himself." One person in Mary's hearing lamented: "That mad man that killed him! Now he will be Saint Abe for all time, saint and martyr."

Booth, the object of an intense manhunt, was in agony from a broken leg, the result of his jump to the stage or some mishap later in his flight. At four a.m. after the shooting, he made his way to the Southern Maryland house of Samuel Mudd, the doctor who had been seen in Washington, looking for Booth, on the morning of March 3. For treating the assassin's leg and sending him on his way, Dr. Mudd was later found guilty of conspiring to kill the president, and sent to the fever-plagued hellhole of Fort Jefferson, in the Dry Tortugas Islands, off the Florida keys. He was later pardoned and released. Mudd's ministrations could not stop the misery of Booth, forced to travel on his shattered limb. A hounded animal, Booth hid shivering in the damp and cold and got food where he could, dismayed to learn that the newspapers regarded him a coward and knave instead of a national liberator. Determined to be heard by history, he scrawled his thoughts into a pocket diary as he fled. "I struck boldly and not as the papers say," he wrote. "I can never repent it, though we hated to kill: Our country owed all her troubles to him, and God simply made me the instrument of his punishment. The country is not what it *was*. This forced union is not what I *have* loved. I care not what *becomes* of me. I have no desire to out-live my country."

After twelve days at bay, Booth was finally cornered in a tobacco barn in Virginia. Union forces set it on fire, and a sergeant named Boston Corbett took aim through cracks in the boards, shooting Booth through the neck. The handsome actor was hauled in agonizing pain to a grassy area twenty-five feet away. "Tell my mother I die for my country," he gasped. His captors found in his possession the photographs of five women, one of them Lucy Hale. Unable to raise his hands, Booth asked to see them. "Useless, useless," he mumbled, gazing at them. Again, he said, "I die for my country. I did what I thought was best." He perished there and then on the lawn.

In 1891, when a reporter from the *New York World* looked over War Department records of the assassination and came across the photos of Booth's women, he was informed he could not obtain a copy of one of them. It was "the picture of the daughter of one distinguished senator from a New England state and the wife of another now living in the same section," the reporter discreetly hinted, describing Lucy Hale precisely.

In the weeks that followed the assassination, Mary Lincoln, with the help of Elizabeth Keckley, sent keepsakes of the late president to those who were most important to him. Douglass was amazed to receive Lincoln's "favorite walking staff." The black leader assured Mrs. Lincoln he would keep "this inestimable memento of his Excellency" as "an object of sacred interest," not only because of the president's regard for him but also as an indication of Lincoln's humane regard for "the welfare of my whole race." The remainder of Mary Lincoln's life was a series of horrors. She lost her eighteen-year-old son, Tad, to an illness in 1871, the third of her four boys to die before her. She spoke out bitterly about the country's failure to provide for her. Her surviving son, Robert, placed her in an insane asylum for a time. A troubled woman to the last, Mary Lincoln died of a stroke, at sixty-three, in 1882.

In a speech at New York's Cooper Union two months after Lincoln's assassination, Douglass argued that Booth's act was the product of the diseased view of humanity fostered by slavery—"the concentrated *virus* the moral poison, accumulated by more than two centuries of human slavery, pouring itself out upon the nation as a vial of wrath in one dreadful and shocking crime, the first of its kind in the annals of the nation. . . . Hereafter when men think of southern honor, they will think of the assassination of Abraham Lincoln." Still, Douglass found it astonishing that anyone would turn his wrath on Lincoln, given the "gentle, the amiable, character of the man—the man, with malice toward none, but charity towards—all."

Upon Lincoln's death, much of the nation embraced those words from the second inauguration as the essence of their lost president. As Lincoln's funeral train made its way across the country, banners proclaimed them—sometimes incorrectly, as in Columbus, Ohio, where a sign declared, "With malice to no one / with charity to all." Throughout the summer—and then for decades to come—the phrase would be printed in newspapers across the country, as words that embodied the great and good man. They helped transform the Confederacy's determined enemy into the very thing Mary Chesnut's friend had feared: a secular saint and a martyr.

Douglass found himself forever bound with Lincoln, a man he had once despised as a craven opportunist. Among African Americans, Lincoln assumed the stature of the race's sacred liberator, his fears of black assimilation and his slow and deliberate movements toward emancipation long forgotten. When Douglass died, in 1895, South Carolina Republican George W. Murray, then the only African American member of the U.S. House of Representatives, said of the great black orator, "We looked up to him almost as we do to the memory of Abraham Lincoln."

* * *

On April 14, 1887, Walt Whitman gave his last speech. A reporter described the ancient poet: "Long, flowing white beard; hair like spun silver hanging down in wild profusion under a wide sombrero; a strong patriarchal face, with soft, benevolent eyes; a tall imposing frame, over six feet high, and still muscular and almost straight, despite the weight of years and the ravages of disease." His topic that night was Abraham Lincoln. Despite significant publicity and the appearance of literary friends, the turnout at New York's Madison Square Theatre was so small that a friend had to kick in a significant amount to make sure the elderly, impoverished poet could go home with $200 from the event. Whitman passed on five years later. The widely detested *Leaves of Grass* came to be regarded as a towering American classic, and his Civil War writings as treasured glimpses of the time.

Whitman's great, hairy Scottish American friend, Alexander Gardner, also left behind priceless insights into his day, through his brilliantly evocative photographs. After the war, Gardner took a series of remarkably powerful images of the doomed Lincoln conspirators, each bound in irons, and later recorded faces of Native Americans. He said of his work: "It is designed to speak for itself. As mementos of the fearful struggle through which the country has just passed, it is confidently hoped that it will possess an enduring interest." Beyond his scenes of the war dead, which still have the power to shock and move, he left the world the priceless gift of Abraham Lincoln's face. Gardner took more pictures of him—thirty-eight all told—than any other photographer. Unable to sustain himself in his profession, Gardner put his art behind him and founded an insurance company in Washington, D.C., where he died at the age of sixty-one in 1882.

Salmon P. Chase never won the presidency, though he made one last desperate attempt in 1872, despite failing health. He helped to found the Liberal Republican Party, which teamed up that year with Democrats in a bid to topple President Ulysses Grant. In the end, the party nominated newspaper editor Horace Greeley instead, who went down to defeat and died three weeks after the election. As chief justice, Chase presided over the 1868 impeachment trial of Andrew Johnson, who escaped removal by the Senate by one vote. Seven Republicans bravely defied their party to vote against conviction; Chase's son-in-law William Sprague was not one of them. Chase died of a stroke, at sixty-five, in 1873.

His daughter Kate's unhappy marriage to Sprague, who increasingly indulged himself in drinking and abusive behavior, ended in divorce in 1882 after she was accused of having an affair with flashy New York senator Roscoe Conkling. Resuming her maiden name, Kate Chase over time dissipated the remainder of her once extraordinary fortune and spent her last days raising chickens and vegetables to survive, selling her meager harvest door to door. She died of Bright's disease at fifty-eight. A small gathering attended her permanent burial at Cincinnati's Spring Grove Cemetery, as she was laid to rest beside her illustrious father. "No Queen has ever reigned under the Stars and Stripes," the *Cincinnati Enquirer* observed, "but this remarkable woman came closer to being Queen than any American woman has." However far she had fallen in life, Kate still seemed to outshine dumpy Mary Lincoln. "She was in many respects the most remarkable woman that has ever been seen in Washington society," the *Boston Globe* contended. "In those days Mrs. Sprague's snub would kill socially. Her smile opened society's doors to those who received it. But all her powers could not make her father president."

Benjamin B. French retained his job as commissioner of public buildings into the Johnson administration, showing intense loyalty to the new president. As the radical Republicans became increasingly disgusted with Johnson for his leniency to the South, French drove them into a frenzy by composing a poem comparing Andrew Johnson to Andrew Jackson, regarded as an infinitely greater president. Congressman Robert C. Schenck of Ohio, sneeringly calling French the "Poet Laureate of the Administration," led Republicans to retaliate on March 4,

1867—two years to the day after Lincoln's second inauguration—by using an appropriations bill to abolish his well-paying job. French managed to scrape by through an appointment to a minor clerk's position in the Treasury Department. The following year, he had the honor of dedicating a statue to Abraham Lincoln in front of the District of Columbia's city hall. French spoke admiringly of the "peculiar" use of language by his former boss: "terse, pointed, plain; never wandering among the mazes of rhetoric after adornment" but "going as straight to the mark at which he aimed as an arrow from the bow of Tell." One speech stayed with French and had the power to make his eyes well up: "That single sentence in his last inaugural coming up undefiled from the pure well of his noble heart—'With malice toward none; with charity for all; with firmness in the right, as God gives us [to] see the right, let us strive on to finish the work we are in'—spoke the character of the man, and will live among the sayings of great and good men as long as human lips can speak or types can print; and as we read it now, we can scarcely repress a tear as we reflect how soon after it was said the voice that said it was silenced forever, and the *work that he was in* was finished." French died of heart disease two years later, on August 12, 1870.

The monuments French had seen installed at the Capitol succumbed to the ravages of time and political fashion. Horatio Greenough's much-maligned statue of a half-nude George Washington was moved from the Capitol grounds to a less prominent spot outside the Patent Office, then indoors to the Smithsonian Institution castle. In 1962, it was moved to what became the National Museum of American History, where it sits on the second floor, reduced to the status of a colossal piece in a curiosity cabinet. Greenough's statue *The Rescue* had it worse. Both it and Luigi Persico's *Discovery of America*—long criticized by Native American groups—were removed during a 1958 renovation of the Capitol and quietly placed into storage. In 1976, while workers were using a crane to move *The Rescue* to a new Smithsonian storage area in Maryland, they dropped it, shattering it into pieces. The sad remnants of the statuary group that Americans of the nineteenth century called "Daniel Boone Protects His Family" rest in storage to this day, unlamented, beside the deteriorating *Discovery*.

In 1867, French made a present of the table he had fashioned for Lincoln's second inauguration—and had hoped the president might take home with him to Springfield—to the Massachusetts Historical Society. Both Ronald Reagan and Barack Obama used the sacred object in their inaugurations. According to the *Washingtonian* magazine, one of Reagan's junior staffers wasn't very impressed. "He thought it looked dingy, and spray-painted it white," giving the preservationists at the Massachusetts Historical Society "a heart attack." Restored, it was put on display at the U.S. Capitol Visitor Center.

On March 11, one week after the inauguration and the day after her beloved brother Stephen died, Clara Barton got the help she so desperately wanted from the president. "To the friends of missing persons: Miss Clara Barton has kindly offered to search for the missing prisoners of war. Please address her at Annapolis, Maryland giving name, regiment, and company of any missing prisoner," said the letter of recommendation. It was signed, "A. Lincoln." She spent the next four years striving to find out what had become of soldiers gone missing in the terrible war. By 1869, her office had received sixty-three thousand letters and determined what had become of twenty-two thousand men. After the fighting was over, she delivered hundreds of lectures about her experiences, becoming friendly with Frederick Douglass. Active in the civil rights and woman suffrage movements, she founded the American Red Cross. Barton died at ninety of pneumonia, on April 12, 1912. In 1997, when the Washington building she had occupied, at 437 Seventh Street, one block from Alexander Gardner's photography studio, was facing demolition, a search of the attic uncovered a treasure trove of letters, Civil War artifacts, and even the original Missing Soldiers Office sign from 1865. The National Park Service managed to save the structure and, in 2015, opened the Clara Barton Missing Soldiers Office Museum there.

*   *   *

Selden Connor eventually lost his leg to amputation, surviving the operation. Though he endured pain the rest of his life, he married Henrietta W. Bailey of Washington, fathered three children, became active in veterans' affairs, and as an acclaimed citizen of Maine, delivered a celebrated address after the death of Lincoln's first vice president, Hannibal Hamlin. The state also chose Connor to deliver the oration at the dedication of its monument on the Gettysburg battlefield. In 1875, Connor was elected governor of Maine, serving three one-year terms and advancing such liberal causes as civil service reform and free public education for the state's children. At their 1878 state convention, Maine Republicans briefly considered the sixty-eight-year-old Hamlin for governor, until Lincoln's onetime running mate appeared before the delegates with "both hands in his pockets" and insisted that the public's strenuous "duties should devolve upon younger men." Connor was unanimously renominated, hailed for "the intelligence, the integrity, the fidelity and the ability with which he has discharged" the office.

In a message on Memorial Day, 1915, the aged Civil War general, still said to be "weak" and "hovering between life and death" because of his terrible war wound, spoke optimistically: "I rejoice, as do all survivors of that great struggle, that there is today no North and no South, in the sense of division, but more than ever we stand a solid and united country." Connor finally surrendered on July 9, 1917, dying at the age of seventy-eight. His daughter Mabel, given life only because he had barely survived, became a leader in the fight for the women's vote, while working with the American Red Cross and the Maine State Society for the Protection of Animals. Selden's exuberant younger brother Virgil, who had seen the "big bugs" at Lincoln's second inauguration, attended Harvard College, then made his living in lumber, real estate, and agriculture, serving on important local boards and winning election as a state senator in Maine. "A public-spirited man, he has given freely of his time and energy to the public service," a contemporary wrote admiringly.

*   *   *

After his friend Ulysses S. Grant was elected president twice, William Tecumseh Sherman repeatedly and emphatically denied any interest in the job, supposedly declaring: "I will not accept if nominated and will not serve if elected." He died in 1891, at the age of seventy-one. Sherman's legacy was the hard truth that, as he told the attendees of a soldiers' reunion in August 1880, war "is all hell." There was no way to sugarcoat its horrors; in his view, wars were to be avoided at almost any cost and, once begun, ended as quickly as possible. In his autobiography *It Doesn't Take a Hero*, U.S. general Norman Schwarzkopf noted something he did at the start of the Gulf War, in 1991: "I copied out a quote from *The Memoirs of General William T. Sherman* and taped it to my desk: 'War is the remedy our enemies have chosen. And I say let us give them all they want.'"

Generations of Southerners, however, vowed never to forget Sherman's cruelty and destruction. In Cheraw, South Carolina, Harriet Powe Godfrey would not allow the general's name to be spoken in her house, nor permit any American flag ever to be flown on her property. "She would not even let the mailman deliver her mail because he wore a blue uniform and worked for the Government!" her granddaughter Adeline Godfrey Pringle Merrill recalled. Decades after the war, Mrs. Godfrey still had her son stop by the post office every day to pick up her mail. Emma Holmes, another South Carolina woman, could not envision a future for her proud and brutalized people in a reunited country. "To go back into the Union!!!" she wrote in her diary on April 22, 1865, the day news arrived of Lincoln's assassination. "No words can describe all the horrors contained in those few words. Our souls recoiled shuddering at the bare idea. What can ever bridge over that fearful abyss of blood, suffering, affliction, desolation and unsummed anguish stretching through these past four years. The blood of slain heroes cries out against such an end—as if end it could be. Peace on such terms, is war for the rising generation."

Yet the fearful abyss was bridged. On May 30, 1922, while jazz-loving young men in straw skimmer hats looked on, a feeble and bent seventy-eight-year-old with a white beard, his arms locked with those of dapper military officers, painfully ascended the marble stairs of the

Lincoln Memorial on the day of its dedication. He wore rimless round glasses, an old-fashioned frock coat, and a Victorian top hat, looking like what he was: a strange visitor from another world that had all but vanished. "Few persons recognized in the decrepit old man who was assisted up the steps of the memorial the son of Abraham Lincoln, Robert Todd Lincoln," the *Washington Herald* reported. Lincoln effected a smile but looked sad and tired, as if all too familiar with the excesses of human nature, including the deification of his very human father.

Installed in the massive mock-Greek temple was a nineteen-foot-high statue of Abraham Lincoln—powerful, solid, enthroned—in stern contemplation staring out at the unknown masses to come. It was the work of Benjamin Brown French's own nephew, Daniel Chester French, whose nascent talent Benjamin had recognized decades earlier, in 1869. "*Dan is a sculptor.* I mean it," he wrote in his diary. A mighty symbol of the nation's ability to grow and change, to become a more perfect expression of its founding ideals of liberty without shattering to pieces, the Lincoln Memorial became a setting for countless events and addresses. On Easter Sunday in 1939, famed contralto Marian Anderson struck a blow against racial division by giving a free concert from the memorial, with Lincoln's statue looming behind her, to an audience of seventy-five thousand. The Daughters of the American Revolution had banned her from Washington's Constitution Hall, which the group co-owned, because she was African American. "Genius draws no color line," Interior Secretary Harold Ickes asserted when introducing her. And there, on August 28, 1963, Baptist minister and civil rights leader Martin Luther King Jr. delivered his "I Have a Dream" speech, helping to reshape America again, through eloquence of a power matched only by Thomas Jefferson, Frederick Douglass, and Abraham Lincoln before him.

Inside the majestic white building, engraved on walls to the left and the right, behind pillars that set them off as mini-temples of their own, were two short speeches of Lincoln, the Gettysburg Address and the second inaugural address. Derided by many in their time as grotesque expressions of a rude country lawyer's peculiar sensibility, they had been lifted forever to the realm of American scripture.

ABRAHAM LINCOLN'S SECOND INAUGURAL ADDRESS

Fellow countrymen:

At this second appearing to take the oath of the presidential office, there is less occasion for an extended address than there was at the first. Then a statement, somewhat in detail, of a course to be pursued, seemed fitting and proper. Now, at the expiration of four years, during which public declarations have been constantly called forth on every point and phase of the great contest which still absorbs the attention, and engrosses the energies of the nation, little that is new could be presented. The progress of our arms, upon which all else chiefly depends, is as well known to the public as to myself; and it is, I trust, reasonably satisfactory and encouraging to all. With high hope for the future, no prediction in regard to it is ventured.

On the occasion corresponding to this four years ago, all thoughts were anxiously directed to an impending civil-war. All dreaded it—all sought to avert it. While the inaugural address was being delivered from this place, devoted altogether to *saving* the Union without war, insurgent agents were in the city seeking to *destroy* it without war— seeking to dissolve the Union, and divide effects, by negotiation. Both parties deprecated war; but one of them would *make* war rather than let the nation survive; and the other would *accept* war rather than let it perish. And the war came.

One eighth of the whole population were colored slaves, not distributed generally over the Union, but localized in the Southern part of it. These slaves constituted a peculiar and powerful interest. All knew that this interest was, somehow, the cause of the war. To strengthen, perpetuate, and extend this interest was the object for which the insurgents would rend the Union, even by war; while the government claimed no right to do more than to restrict the territorial enlargement of it. Neither party expected for the war, the magnitude, or the duration, which it has already attained. Neither anticipated that the *cause* of the conflict might cease with, or even before, the conflict itself should cease. Each looked for an easier triumph, and a result less fundamental and astounding. Both read the same Bible, and pray to the same God; and each invokes His aid against the other. It may seem strange that any men should dare to ask a just God's assistance in wringing their bread from the sweat of other men's faces; but let us judge not that we be not judged. The prayers of both could not be answered; that of neither has been answered fully. The Almighty has His own purposes. "Woe unto the world because of offences! for it must needs be that offences come; but woe to that man by whom the offence cometh!" If we shall suppose that American Slavery is one of those offences which, in the providence of God, must needs come, but which, having continued through His appointed time, He now wills to remove, and that He gives to both North and South, this terrible war, as the woe due to those by whom the offence came, shall we discern therein any departure from those divine attributes which the believers in a Living God always ascribe to Him? Fondly do we hope—fervently do we pray—that this mighty scourge of war may speedily pass away. Yet, if God wills that it continue, until all the wealth piled by the bond-man's two hundred and fifty years of unrequited toil shall be sunk, and until every drop of blood drawn with the lash, shall be paid by another drawn with the sword, as was said three thousand years ago, so still it must be said "the judgments of the Lord, are true and righteous altogether."

With malice toward none; with charity for all; with firmness in the right, as God gives us to see the right, let us strive on to finish the work we are in; to bind up the nation's wounds; to care for him who shall have borne the battle, and for his widow, and his orphan—to do all which may achieve and cherish a just, and a lasting peace, among ourselves, and with all nations.

ACKNOWLEDGMENTS

A while back, my friend Phil Swann, with whom I wrote *How to Land a Job in Journalism* (so long ago that there *were* jobs in journalism then), suggested a book idea to me. He had always been struck by John Wilkes Booth's presence at Lincoln's second inauguration with the obvious intention of killing the president. That germ of an idea led me to this book, which follows several famous people interacting with Lincoln at the inauguration and their perceptions of the anguishing war that forever changed America. Thank you, Phil.

John Arnold has been a dear friend since the sixth grade at Forbes School in Westborough, Massachusetts, and a tech guru who, in endlessly providing me free IT support, helped me recover my long-lost files on floppy disks that I used in writing two baseball books, *Fifty-Nine in '84* and *The Summer of Beer and Whiskey*. He has been so close to me for so long that I flat out forgot to acknowledge him in either of those books. John, my profound gratitude for all you have done to make these books possible.

Former Rhode Island Supreme Court chief justice Frank J. Williams, the founder of the Lincoln Forum and author of *Judging Lincoln*, offered kindness and encouragement. He read the manuscript and suggested many improvements. Historian Maury Klein, whose classic *Days of Deliverance* was a key inspiration, was kind enough to read the manuscript—attesting that it held his attention even as home renovations were making a racket around him—and strengthened it with some thoughtful suggestions. Playwright Ken Dooley was hugely enthusiastic about the book. J. William Middendorf, former secretary of the navy and U.S. ambassador to the European Union, encouraged this pursuit and shared his memories of the hatred of Lincoln that persisted in pockets of Maryland, where he grew up seven decades after the war. James Tackach, author of *Lincoln's Moral Vision: The Second Inaugural Address*, was intrigued by my approach and offered me ideas. Llewellyn King, the great newspaperman and executive producer and host of public television's *White House Chronicle*, was a big fan of the project and welcomed me on his show to discuss Lincoln with Brown University professor Michael Vorenberg, author of *Final Freedom*. Jim Weidman kindly assisted me in my travels in Maryland, with the bonus of taking me to a Baltimore Orioles game. Marine colonel and military historian Theodore L. Gatchel shared his thoughts and unfailing enthusiasm. With the generosity and intellectual curiosity that are his hallmarks, the great Gordon S. Wood listened to me prattle on about the book during our lunches and shared his remarkable insights about the country that shaped Lincoln.

A lifetime of reading into Lincoln leaves me with profound debts to the many scholars who have shaped my understanding of him. Douglas L. Wilson's reassessment of the historical material intrepidly gathered by Lincoln's law partner, William Herndon, opened the eyes of a generation of readers, and his Lincoln Prize–winning books *Lincoln's Sword* and *Honor's Voice* were particularly helpful. I am grateful for the superb works of Harold Holzer, too numerous to mention. However far I have fallen short of their example, Bruce Catton, Shelby Foote, and James M. McPherson taught me through their classic narratives how great writing and telling detail might illuminate the war that made us who we are.

Terry Alford, author of the deeply researched *Fortune's Fool: The Life of John Wilkes Booth*, shared some of his insights about Booth at the inauguration. Richard S. Lowry, author of the engaging *The Photographer of the President*, provided some helpful insights about Alexander Gardner. Todd Harrington, who takes photographs using 1865 techniques, helped me better understand the technology of the collodion wet-plate process that Gardner used at the second inauguration to take his historic photos of the event. Historian and writer Ted Widmer, former director of the John Carter Brown Library at Brown University and contributor to the *New York Times*' tremendous digital history of the Civil War, was encouraging and supportive. The staff at the Library of Congress, Ford's Theatre, and the John Hay Library at Brown University were also unfailingly helpful. Jill Redding, vice president of the Junius B. Booth Society, kindly took me through the Booth family home, Tudor Hall, in Bel Air, Maryland.

I thank Lisa Adams and David Miller of the Garamond Agency for their tireless dedication to this book, as to my last two. Special thanks to Karen Potter, a big fan of my baseball books who used her skills as a budding historian to help track down information. I am grateful to my many colleagues at the *Providence Journal* for their support, including publisher Peter Meyer, former publishers Howard Sutton, Bernie Szachara, and Janet Hasson, and former executive vice president Mark Ryan.

I feel especially fortunate that the book was in the hands of such a brilliant editor as George Gibson at Grove Atlantic. He made it infinitely stronger with his numerous and deft suggestions. Amy Hughes's intrepid copyediting saved me from countless errors and infelicities.

Special thanks, of course, go to my wife, Valerie. She eagerly listened to me read the entire manuscript out loud to make sure it sounded all right. She has patiently endured my extended and lonely forays into the nineteenth century and has come to know my books' peculiar characters perhaps more familiarly than she expected. But, through it all, she has never flagged in her faith that these stories are worth my telling.

Herndon recalled Lincoln saying of Nancy Hanks Lincoln: "God bless my mother; all that I am or ever hope to be I owe to her." My own mother, Jean Marie (Berlo) Achorn, died decades ago, when I was twenty-three, but my amazement over her generosity, sense of fun, and capacity for love continues to grow. She well knew, all those years ago, how much I admired Lincoln and would, I think, have been touched to hold this volume. To her, this book is dedicated.

BIBLIOGRAPHY

ABBREVIATIONS USED IN THE NOTES

BBF: French, Benjamin Brown. *Witness to the Young Republic: A Yankee's Journal, 1828–1870*, ed. Donald B. Cole and John Joseph (Lebanon, New Hampshire: University Press of New England, 1989).

CW: Lincoln, Abraham. *The Collected Works of Abraham Lincoln*, 8 vols., ed. Roy P. Basler (New Brunswick, New Jersey: Rutgers University Press, 1953–55).

GWD: Welles, Gideon. *Diary of Gideon Wells, Secretary of the Navy under Lincoln and Johnson*, 2 vols. (Boston: Houghton Mifflin, 1911).

SCC: Selden Connor Correspondence. Lincoln Collection, John Hay Library, Brown University.

NEWSPAPERS AND PERIODICALS

The Age, Philadelphia

Alexandria (Virginia) *Gazette*

Appleton (Wisconsin) *Motor*

Argus and Patriot, Montpelier, Vermont

The Baltimore Sun

The Bedford (Pennsylvania) *Inquirer*

The Boston Globe

Boston Intelligencer

The Brooklyn Daily Eagle

The Buffalo Courier

The Buffalo Evening News

The Buffalo Morning Express

The Burlington (Vermont) *Times*

The Burlington (Vermont) *Weekly Sentinel*

The Caledonian, Saint Johnsbury, Vermont

Chicago Inter-Ocean
The Chicago Times
The Chicago Tribune
The Christian Recorder, Philadelphia
The Cincinnati Commercial
Cincinnati Daily Gazette
The Cincinnati Enquirer
Clearfield (Pennsylvania) *Republican*
Cleveland Morning Leader
The Cleveland Plain Dealer
The Critic, London
Daily Davenport (Iowa) *Democrat*
The Daily Dispatch, Richmond, Virginia
The Daily Exchange, Baltimore
The Daily Graphic, New York
The Daily Milwaukee News
Daily Ohio Statesman, Columbus
The Daily Pittsburgh Gazette
Daily Richmond (Virginia) *Examiner*
The Daily Whig & Courier, Bangor, Maine
Dayton (Ohio) *Daily Empire*
Dayton (Ohio) *Daily Journal*
The Delaware Gazette, Delaware, Ohio
The Delawarean, Dover, Delaware
The Detroit Free Press
Douglass Monthly
The Dubuque (Iowa) *Herald*
The Evening Star, Washington, D.C.
The Evening Telegraph, Philadelphia
The Fairfield Courier, Winnsboro, South Carolina
The Grand Haven (Michigan) *News*
Harper's Weekly
The Hillsborough (North Carolina) *Recorder*
The Holmes County Farmer, Millersburg, Ohio
Illinois State Register, Springfield
The Indianapolis News
The Indianapolis Star

The Jeffersonian Democrat, Chardon, Ohio

Kansas City Star

La Crosse (Wisconsin) *Democrat*

The Liberator, Boston

Littell's Living Age, Boston

Los Angeles Herald

Los Angeles Times

The Louisville Daily Journal

The Memphis Daily Appeal

The Minneapolis Tribune

The Nashville Times and True Union

The National Gazette, Philadelphia

The National Republican, Washington, D.C.

Newcastle Courant, Newcastle upon Tyne, England

The New York Express

The New York Herald

New York Leader

The New York Times

The New York Tribune

The New York World

The North Branch Democrat, Tunkhannock, Pennsylvania

The Ottawa (Illinois) *Free Trader*

Petersburg (Virginia) *Daily Express*

The Philadelphia Inquirer

The Philadelphia Sunday Mercury

The Pittsburgh Commercial

The Practical Christian, Hopedale, Massachusetts

The Providence (Rhode Island) *Journal*

The Rochester (New York) *Democrat and American*

The Rutland (Vermont) *Weekly Herald*

The San Francisco Chronicle

Selma (Alabama) *Morning Dispatch*

The Spectator, London

Spirit of the Times, Batavia, New York

Springfield (Massachusetts) *Republican*

The Standard, London

The Star of the North, Bloomsburg, Pennsylvania

Syracuse (New York) *Daily Courier and Union*
The Times, of London
Utica (New York) *Telegraph*
The Valley Spirit, Chambersburg, Pennsylvania
Washington (D.C.) *Chronicle*
The Washington Herald
The Washington Post
The Weekly Advertiser, Montgomery, Alabama
Weekly State Journal, Raleigh, North Carolina
The Wheeling (West Virginia) *Intelligencer*
Wilmington (North Carolina) *Journal*
Wisconsin State Journal

COLLECTIONS

Clara Barton Papers. Diaries and Journals: Jan. 1862–Dec. 1865. Library of Congress.

Richard Cary Letters. Massachusetts Historical Society, Boston.

Zachariah Chandler Papers, 1854–1899. Library of Congress.

Asia Booth Clarke Letters. Maryland Historical Society, Baltimore.

Clifford Family Papers. Massachusetts Historical Society, Boston.

Selden Connor Correspondence, Lincoln Collection. John Hay Library, Brown University.

Dana Family Papers. Massachusetts Historical Society, Boston.

David Davis Papers. Chicago History Museum.

James R. Doolittle Papers. State Historical Society of Wisconsin.

Hamilton Fish Papers. Library of Congress.

Benjamin B. French Family Papers. Library of Congress.

Gilder Lehrman Collection. New York.

Warren S. Gurney Papers. John Hay Library, Brown University.

John Parker Hale Papers, 1820–1914. New Hampshire Historical Society, Concord.

Herndon-Weik Collection of Lincolniana, circa 1824–1933. Library of Congress.

Abraham Lincoln Papers. Library of Congress.

James G. Randall Papers. Library of Congress.

Thomas H. Seymour Papers. Connecticut Historical Society, Hartford.

Katherine Chase Sprague Papers, 1850–1900. John Hay Library, Brown University.

Tilton Papers. Buffalo Public Library.

Carter G. Woodson Papers. Library of Congress.

MAGAZINE ARTICLES

Adger, John B., "Northern and Southern Views of the Province of the Church," *Southern Presbyterian Review*, March 1866.

Bachman, John, "Types of Mankind," *The Charleston Medical Journal and Review*, September 1854.

Brooks, Noah, "The Boy in the White House," *St. Nicholas: An Illustrated Magazine for Young Folks*, November 1882.

———. "Personal Reminiscences of Lincoln," *Scribner's Monthly*, February and March 1878.

Chittenden, L. E., "The Faith of President Lincoln," *Harper's New Monthly Magazine*, February 1891.

Clark, Achilles V., "A Letter of Account," ed. Dan E. Pomeroy, *Civil War Times Illustrated*, June 1985.

Cobb, Howell, Maj. General, Letter to Hon. J. A. Seddon, Secretary of War, Macon, Georgia, January 8, 1865, "Documents," *The American Historical Review*, October 1895.

Conway, Moncure D., "Walt Whitman," *Fortnightly Review* 6, October 15, 1866.

Crook, William H. (His Body-Guard), "Lincoln as I Knew Him," *Harper's Magazine*, June 1907.

Du Barry, Helen A., "Eyewitness Account of Lincoln's Assassination," *Journal of the Illinois State Historical Society* 39, no. 3 (1946).

Ferguson, William J., "I Saw Lincoln Shot!," *American Magazine*, August 1920.

Fryd, Vivien Green, "Two Sculptures for the Capitol: Horatio Greenough's 'Rescue' and Luigi Persico's 'Discovery of America,'" *American Art Journal*, Spring 1987.

Genoways, Ted., "The Disorder of *Drum-Taps*," *Walt Whitman Quarterly Review*, Fall 2006/Winter 2007.

Gleason, D. H. L., "The Conspiracy Against Lincoln," *Magazine of History with Notes and Queries*, February 1911.

"The Curious Paternity of Abraham Lincoln," *Great Smoky Mountains Colloquy*, Spring 2008.

Griswold, Rufus, "Leaves of Grass. By Walt Whitman. 1855," *The Criterion*, November 10, 1855.

Hatch, Frederick, "Lincoln's Missing Guard," *Lincoln Herald* 107 (Fall 2005).

Hawthorne, Nathaniel, "Chiefly about War Matters, by a Peaceable Man," *Atlantic Monthly*, July 1862.

Henderson, General John B., "Emancipation and Impeachment," *Century Illustrated Monthly Magazine*, December 1912.

Herndon, William H., "An Analysis of the Character of Abraham Lincoln" [lecture delivered in Springfield, Illinois, on December 12, 1865], *Abraham Lincoln Quarterly*, September 1941.

Higginson, Thomas Wentworth, "Literature as an Art," *Atlantic Monthly*, December 1867.

Horton, Dexter, "Diary of an Officer in Sherman's Army Marching Through the Carolinas," *Journal of Southern History*, May 1943.

Houmes, Blaine, "Robert Todd Lincoln, John Wilkes Booth, & Lucy Lambert Hale," *Manuscripts*, Winter 2007.

Joynt, Carol Ross, "The Untold Story of the Lincoln Table, the Reagan Inaugural, and the Spray Paint," *Washingtonian*, December 5, 2012.

Julian, George W., "George Julian's Journal—The Assassination of Lincoln," *Indiana Magazine of History* 11, no. 4 (December 1915).

MacCulloch, Campbell, "This Man Saw Lincoln Shot," *Good Housekeeping*, February 1927.

McCandless, Peter, "The Political Evolution of John Bachman: From New York Yankee to South Carolina Secessionist," *South Carolina Historical Magazine*, January 2007.

McCulloch, Hugh, "Memories of Some Contemporaries," *Scribner's Magazine*, September 1888.

Morcom, Richard, "They All Loved Lucy," *American Heritage*, October 1970.

Murray, Martin G., "'Pete the Great': A Biography of Peter Doyle," *Walt Whitman Quarterly Review* 12, Summer 1994.

O'Sullivan, John L., "The Great Nation of Futurity," *United States Democratic Review*, November 1839.

Our Special Correspondent in America, "Washington during the War," *Macmillan's Magazine*, May 1862.

Reed, J. A. Rev., "Religious Sentiments of Abraham Lincoln," *Scribner's Monthly*, July 1873.

Schurz, Carl, "Reminiscences of a Long Life: The Campaign of 1860," *McClure Magazine*, February 1907.

Schwartz, J. W., "Kahler's Advertising," *Printer's Ink: A Journal for Advertisers*, New York, December 13, 1899.

Shettel, James W., "J. Wilkes Booth at School," *New York Dramatic Mirror*, February 26, 1916.

Smith, Goldwin, "President Lincoln," *Macmillan's Magazine*, February 1865.

Stowe, Harriet Beecher, "A Reply," *Atlantic Monthly*, January 1863.

Turner, Arlin, "Elizabeth Peabody Visits Lincoln, February, 1865," *New England Quarterly*, March 1975.

Whitney, Henry C., "Abraham Lincoln: A Study from Life," *The Arena*, April 1898.

Wilson, Col. J. Grant, "Lieutenant General Grant," *Hours at Home*, June 1866.

BOOKS

Adams, Charles Francis. *Charles Francis Adams, 1835–1915: An Autobiography*, ed. Massachusetts Historical Society (Boston: Houghton Mifflin, 1916).

Adams, Lois Bryan. *Letter from Washington, 1863–1865* (Detroit: Wayne State University, 1999).

Alford, Terry. *Fortune's Fool: The Life of John Wilkes Booth* (New York: Oxford University Press, 2015).

American Series of Popular Biographies, Maine Edition (Boston: New England Historical Society, 1903).

Ames, Mary Clemmer. *Ten Years in Washington: Life and Scenes in the National Capital, as a Woman Sees Them* (Hartford: A. D. Worthington, 1874).

Angle, Paul M., ed. *A Portrait of Abraham Lincoln in Letters by His Oldest Son* (Chicago: Chicago Historical Society, 1968).

Arnold, Isaac N. *The History of Abraham Lincoln and the Overthrow of Slavery* (Chicago: Clarke & Co, 1866).

———. *The Life of Abraham Lincoln*, 2 vols. (Chicago: Jansen, McClurg, 1885).

Baker, Jean H. *Mary Todd Lincoln: A Biography* (New York: W. W. Norton, 1987).

Barrus, Clara. *Whitman and Burroughs: Comrades* (Boston: Houghton Mifflin, 1931).

Bayne, Julia Taft. *Tad Lincoln's Father* (Lincoln: University of Nebraska Press, 2001).

Belden, Thomas Graham, and Marva Robins. *So Fell the Angels* (Boston: Little, Brown, 1956).

Bigelow, John. *Retrospections of an Active Life*, 5 vols. (New York: Baker and Taylor, 1909–13).

Boine, Albert. *A Social History of Modern Art: Art in the Age of Counterrevolution, 1815–1848* (Chicago: University of Chicago Press, 2004).

Booth, John Wilkes. *Right or Wrong, God Judge Me: The Writings of John Wilkes Booth*, eds. John H. Rhodehamel and Louise Taper (Urbana: University of Illinois Press, 2000).

Brooks, Noah. *Lincoln Observed: Civil War Dispatches of Noah Brooks*. ed. Michael Burlingame (Baltimore: Johns Hopkins University Press, 1998).

———. *Mr. Lincoln's Washington: Selections from the Writings of Noah Brooks, Civil War Correspondent*, ed. P. J. Staudenraus (South Brunswick, New Jersey: Thomas Yoseloff, 1967).

———. *Washington, D.C., in Lincoln's Time*, ed. Herbert Mitgang (Chicago: Quadrangle Books, 1971).

Brown, Norman D., ed. *Journey to Pleasant Hill: The Civil War Letters of Captain Elijah P. Petty, Walker's Texas Division, CSA* (San Antonio: University of Texas, 1982).

Bucke, Richard Maurice. *Walt Whitman*, ed. Edward Dowden (Glasgow, Scotland: Wilson & McCormick, 1884).

Burge, Dolly Lunt. *The Diary of Dolly Lunt Burge, 1848–1979*, ed. Christine Jacobson Carter (Athens: University of Georgia Press, 1997).

Burlingame, Michael. *Abraham Lincoln: A Life, Vol. 2* (Baltimore: Johns Hopkins University Press, 2013).

Burton, Elijah Pierce. *Diary of E. P. Burton, Surgeon, 7th Reg. Illinois, 3rd Brig., 2nd Div. 16 A.C.* (Des Moines, Iowa: Historical Records Survey, 1939).

Burwell, Letitia M. *A Girl's Life in Virginia before the War* (New York: Frederick A. Stokes, 1895).

Campbell, Jacqueline Glass. *When Sherman Marched North from the Sea: Resistance on the Confederate Home Front* (Chapel Hill: University of North Carolina Press, 2003).

Carpenter, Francis Bicknell. *Six Months at the White House with Abraham Lincoln: The Story of a Picture* (New York: Hurd, Houghton, 1867).

Castel, Albert. *The Presidency of Andrew Johnson* (Lawrence: Regents Press of Kansas, 1979).

Catton, Bruce. *Grant Takes Command* (Boston: Little, Brown, 1968).

Chambrun, Charles Adolphe de Pineton. *Impressions of Lincoln and the Civil War: A Foreigner's Account; Translated from the French*. Trans., Gen. Aldebert de Chambrun (New York: Random House, 1952).

Chase, Salmon P. *The Salmon P. Chase Papers, Vol. 1, Journals 1829–1872*, ed. John Niven (Kent, Ohio: Kent State University Press, 1993).

———. *The Salmon P. Chase Papers, Vol. 5, Correspondence, April 1863–1864*, ed. John Niven (Kent, Ohio: Kent State University Press, 1997).

Chernow, Ron. *Grant* (New York: Penguin Press, 2017).

Chesnut, Mary. *Mary Chesnut's Civil War*, ed. C. Vann Woodward (New Haven: Yale University Press, 1981).

The Chicago Copperhead Convention: The Treasonable and Revolutionary Utterances of the Men Who Composed It (Washington, D.C.: Congressional Union Committee, 1864).

Child, Lydia Maria. *Letters of Lydia Maria Child, with a Biographical Introduction* (Boston: Houghton Mifflin, 1883).

Clarke, Asia Booth. *John Wilkes Booth: A Sister's Memoir*, ed. Terry Alford (Jackson: University Press of Mississippi, 1996).

Committee from South Carolina State Division, U.D.C. *South Carolina Women in the Confederacy, Vol. 2* (Columbia, South Carolina: State, 1903).

Conrad, Thomas Nelson (Capt., C.S.A). *The Rebel Scout: A Thrilling History of Scouting Life in the Southern Army* (Washington, D.C.: National, 1904).

Conyngham, David P. *Sherman's March Through the South* (New York: Sheldon, 1865).

Croffut, William A., *Now I Recollect—Souvenirs of the Sanctum: Lincoln as I Saw Him* (Washington, D.C.: Colonial Press, 1943).

Crook, W. H. *Memories of the White House: The Home Life of Our Presidents from Lincoln to Roosevelt*, ed. Henry Rood (Boston: Little, Brown, 1911).

Curtis, William Eleroy. *The True Abraham Lincoln* (Philadelphia: J. B. Lippincott, 1903).

Custer, Elizabeth Bacon. *The Civil War Memories of Elizabeth Bacon Custer*, ed. Arlene Reynolds (Austin: University of Texas Press, 1994).

Dabney, William H. *Sketch of the Dabneys of Virginia, with Some of Their Family Records* (Chicago: S. D. Childs, 1888).

Daly, Joseph Francis. *The Life of Augustin Daly* (New York: Macmillan, 1917).

Davis, Burke. *Sherman's March: The First Full-Length Narrative of General William T. Sherman's Devastating March Through Georgia and the Carolinas* (New York: Vintage, 1988).

Davis, Jefferson. *The Papers of Jefferson Davis*, eds. Lynda Lasswell Christ et al., 14 vols. (Baton Rouge: Louisiana State University Press, 1971–2015).

———. *The Rise and Fall of the Confederate Government*, 2 vols. (New York: D. Appleton, 1912).

Donald, David Herbert. *Lincoln* (New York: Simon & Schuster, 1996).

Douglass, Frederick. *The Frederick Douglass Papers*, 6 vols., ed. John W. Blassingame (New Haven, Connecticut: Yale University Press, 1991).

———. *Frederick Douglass: Selected Speeches and Writings*, ed. Philip S. Foner (Chicago: Lawrence Hill, 1999).

———. *The Life and Times of Frederick Douglass, Written by Himself* (Boston: De Wolfe & Fisk, 1892).

———. *The Life and Writings*, 5 vols., ed. Philip S. Foner (New York: International, 1950).

———. *My Bondage and My Freedom* (New York: Miller, Orton & Mulligan, 1855).

———. *Narrative of the Life of Frederick Douglass, An American Slave, Written by Himself* (Dublin: Webb and Chapman, 1845).

Douglass, Helen. *In Memoriam: Frederick Douglass* (Philadelphia: John C. Yorston, 1897).

Dowdey, Clifford, and Louis H. Manarin, eds. *The Wartime Papers of R. E. Lee* (Boston: Little, Brown, 1961).

Downing, Alexander G. *Downing's Civil War Diary: August 15, 1861–July 31, 1865*, ed. Olynthus B. Clark (Des Moines, Iowa: Homstead Printing, 1916).

Eaton, Harriet. *This Birth Place of Souls: The Civil War Nursing Diary of Harriet Eaton*, ed. Jane E. Schultz (New York: Oxford University Press, 2012).

Eaton, John, and Ethel Osgood Mason. *Grant, Lincoln, and the Freedmen: Reminiscences of the Civil War* (New York: Longmans, Green, 1907).

Edwards, William C., and Edward Steers Jr., eds. *The Lincoln Assassination: The Evidence* (Urbana: University of Illinois Press, 2009).

Emerson, Ralph Waldo. *The Heart of Emerson's Journals*, ed. Bliss Perry (Boston: Houghton Mifflin, 1926).

English, Thos. Dunn, ed. *The Old Guard, Vol. 8* (New York: English, 1870).

Epler, Percy Harold. *The Life of Clara Barton* (New York: Macmillan, 1915).

Fehrenbacher, Don, and Virginia Fehrenbacher, eds. *Recollected Words of Abraham Lincoln* (Redwood City, California: Stanford University Press, 1996).

Ferguson, W. J. *I Saw Booth Shoot Lincoln* (Boston: Houghton Mifflin, 1930).

Field, Maunsell B. *Memories of Many Men and of Some Women: Being Personal Recollections of Emperors, Kings, Queens, Princes, Presidents, Statesmen, Authors, and Artists, at Home and Abroad, during the Last Thirty Years* (New York: Harper & Brothers, 1874).

Fleming, Walter L. *Documentary History of Reconstruction: Political, Military, Social, Religious, Educational & Industrial, 1865 to the Present Time, Vol. 1* (Cleveland: Arthur H. Clark, 1906).

Ford, Worthington Chauncey, ed. *A Cycle of Adams Letters*, 2 vols. (Boston: Houghton Mifflin, 1920).

Forney, John W. *Anecdotes of Public Men*, 2 vols. (New York: Harper & Brothers, 1873 and 1881).

Fox, Dorus M. *History of Political Parties, National Reminiscences, and the Tippecanoe Movement* (Des Moines, Iowa: Col. Dorus M. Fox, 1895).

French, Benjamin Brown. *Witness to the Young Republic: A Yankee's Journal, 1828–1870*, ed. Donald B. Cole and John Joseph (Lebanon, New Hampshire: University Press of New England, 1989).

Furgurson, Ernest B. *Freedom Rising: Washington in the Civil War* (New York: Alfred A. Knopf, 2004).

Gardner, Alexander. *Gardner's Photographic Sketch Book of the War* (Washington, D.C.: Philip and Solomons, 1866).

General Assembly of the State of Kentucky. *Biographical Sketch of the Hon. Lazarus W. Powell (of Henderson, Kentucky), Governor of the State of Kentucky from 1851 to 1855 and a Senator in Congress from 1859 to 1865* (Frankfort, Kentucky: S.I.M Major, Printer, 1868).

Glatthaar, Joseph T. *The March to the Sea and Beyond: Sherman's Troops in the Savannah and Carolinas Campaign* (Baton Rouge: Louisiana State University Press, 1997).

Gordon, John B. *Reminiscences of the Civil War* (New York: Charles Scribner's Sons, 1903).

Gragg, Rod, *The Illustrated Confederate Reader* (New York: Harper & Row, 1989).

Grant, Julia Dent. *The Personal Memoirs of Julia Dent Grant*, ed. John Y. Simon (Carbondale: Southern Illinois University Press, 2016).

Grant, U. S. *Personal Memoirs of U. S. Grant* (New York: Charles L. Webster, 1894).

———. *The Papers of Ulysses S. Grant, Vol. 14*, ed. John Y. Simon (Carbondale: Southern Illinois University Press, 1985).

Greenough, Horatio. *The Travels, Observations, and Experience of a Yankee Stonecutter* (1852, Gainesville, Florida: Scholars' Facsimiles & Reprints, 1958).

Grinnell, Josiah Bushnell. *Men and Events of Forty Years: Autobiographical Reminiscences of an Active Career from 1850 to 1890* (Boston: D. Lothrop, 1891).

Hamlin, Charles Eugene. *The Life and Times of Hannibal Hamlin* (Boston: Riverside Press, 1899).

Hart, Albert Bushnell. *Salmon Portland Chase* (Boston: Houghton Mifflin, 1899).

Hart, Albert Bushnell, and Elizabeth Stevens, eds. *The Romance of the Civil War* (New York: Macmillan, 1917).

Hay, John. *Addresses of John Hay* (New York: Century, 1906).

———. *At Lincoln's Side: John Hay's Civil War Correspondence and Selected Writings*, ed. Michael Burlingame (Carbondale: Southern Illinois University Press, 2006).

———. *Inside Lincoln's White House: The Complete Civil War Diary of John Hay*, eds. Michael Burlingame and John R. T. Ettlinger (Carbondale: Southern Illinois University Press, 1999).

———. *Lincoln and the Civil War in the Diaries and Letters of John Hay*, ed. Tyler Dennett (Boston: Da Capo Press, 1988).

———. *Lincoln's Journalist: John Hay's Anonymous Writings for the Press, 1860–1864*, ed. Michael Burlingame (Carbondale: Southern Illinois University Press, 1998).

Hazen, William Babcock. *A Narrative of Military Service* (Boston: Ticknor, 1885).

Henry, Matthew, and Thomas Scott. *A Commentary upon the Holy Bible, from Henry and Scott. Isaiah to Malachi*, 6 vols. (London: Religious Tract Society, 1834).

Herndon, William H., and Jesse William Weik. *Herndon's Lincoln: The True Story of a Great Life*, 3 vols. (Chicago: Belford-Clarke, 1890).

Herndon, William H. *The Hidden Lincoln: From the Letters and Papers of William H. Herndon*, ed. Emanuel Hertz (New York: Blue Ribbon Books, 1940).

Holmes, Emma. *The Diary of Miss Emma Holmes, 1861–1866*, ed. John F. Marszalek (Baton Rouge: Louisiana State University Press, 1979).

Holzer, Harold. *Lincoln and the Power of the Press: The War for Public Opinion* (New York: Simon & Schuster, 2014).

Holzer, Harold, ed. *President Lincoln Assassinated!! The Firsthand Story of the Murder, Manhunt, Trial, and Mourning* (New York: Library of America, 2014).

Howard, Frank Key. *Fourteen Months in American Bastiles* (Baltimore: Kelly, Hedian, and Piet, 1863).

Howard, Hamilton Gay, *Civil-War Echoes: Character Sketches and State Secrets* (Washington, D.C.: Howard, 1907).

Howe, Julia Ward. *Reminiscences, 1819–1899* (Boston: Houghton Mifflin, 1900).

Hunt, Harry Draper. *Hannibal Hamlin of Maine, Lincoln's First Vice-President* (Syracuse, New York: Syracuse University Press, 1969).

Hurst, Samuel H. *Journal-History of the Seventy-Third Ohio Volunteer Infantry* (Chillicothe Ohio: S.H. Hurst, 1866).

Jefferson, Thomas. *Notes on the State of Virginia, with an Appendix*, 9th American ed. (Boston: H. Sprague, 1802).

Johnson, Andrew. *The Papers of Andrew Johnson, Vols. 6 and 7*. Eds. Leroy P. Graf and Ralph W. Haskins (Knoxville: University of Tennessee Press, 1983, 1986).

Jones, J. B. *A Rebel War Clerk's Diary at the Confederate States Capital*, 2 vols. (Philadelphia: J. B. Lippincott, 1866).

Jones, Jenkin Lloyd. *An Artilleryman's Diary* (Maidson: Wisconsin History Commission: Democrat Printing, 1914).

Keckley, Elizabeth. *Behind the Scenes; or, Thirty Years a Slave, and Four Years in the White House* (New York: G. W. Carleton, 1868).

Kieffer, Harry M. *The Recollections of a Drummer-Boy* (Boston: James R. Osgood, 1883).

Lamon, Ward H. *The Life of Abraham Lincoln; From His Birth to His Inauguration as President* (Boston: James R. Osgood, 1872).

Lamon, Ward Hill, and Dorothy Lamon Teillard, eds. *Recollections of Abraham Lincoln, 1847–1865* (Washington, D.C.: Published by the editors, 1911).

Leale, Charles A., M.D. *Lincoln's Last Hours* (New York: Estate of Charles A. Leale, 1909).

LeConte, Emma Florence. *A Journal, Kept by Emma Florence LeConte, from Dec. 31, 1864, to Aug. 6, 1865* (Durham: University of North Carolina, 1998).

Lee, Elizabeth Blair. *Wartime Washington: The Civil War Letters of Elizabeth Blair Lee*, ed. Virginia Jeans Laas (Urbana: University of Illinois Press, 1991).

Leonard, John W., ed. *Men of America: A Biographical Dictionary of Contemporaries, Vol. 1* (New York: L. R. Hamersley, 1907).

Lincoln, Abraham. *The Collected Works of Abraham Lincoln*, 8 vols., ed. Roy P. Basler (New Brunswick, New Jersey: Rutgers University Press, 1953).

Lindsay, Debra. *Maria Martin's World: Art and Science, Faith and Family in Audubon's America* (Tuscaloosa, Alabama: The University of Alabama Press, 2018).

Longstreet, James. *From Manassas to Appomattox: Memoirs of the Civil War in America* (Philadelphia: J. B. Lippincott, 1896).

Lowry, Thomas P. *Love and Lust: Private and Amorous Letters of the Civil War* (BookSurge, 2009).

———. *The Story the Soldiers Wouldn't Tell: Sex in the Civil War* (Mechanicsburg, Pennsylvania: Stackpole Books, 2012).

Masur, Louis P., ed. *The Real War Will Never Get in the Books: Selections from Writers during the Civil War* (New York: Oxford University Press, 1995).

McBride, Robert W. *Lincoln's Body Guard, the Union Light Guard of Ohio: With Some Personal Recollections of Abraham Lincoln* (Indianapolis, Indiana: Edward J. Hecker, 1911).

McCall, Samuel W. *Thaddeus Stevens* (Boston: Houghton Mifflin, 1899).

McClure, A. K. *Abraham Lincoln and Men of War-Times: Some Personal Recollections of War and Politics during the Lincoln Administration* (Philadelphia: Times, 1892).

McClure, Col. Alexander K. *"Abe" Lincoln's Yarns and Stories* (Philadelphia: Educational, 1901).

Merrill, Adeline Godfrey. *Sherman in Cheraw and the Aftermath* (Privately printed, 2009).

Military Order of the Loyal Legion of the United States, Wisconsin Commandery, *War Papers* (Milwaukee: Burdick, Armitage & Allen, 1903).

Miller, Ernest C. *Booth in the Pennsylvania Oil Region* (Meadville, Pennsylvania: Crawford County Historical Society, 1987).

Moore, Frank, ed. *The Rebellion Record: A Diary of American Events*, 11 vols. (New York: D. Van Nostrand, 1868).

Morel, Lucas E. *Lincoln's Sacred Effort: Defining Religion's Role in America's Self-Government* (Lanham, Maryland: Lexington Books, 2000).

Morris, Clara. *Life on the Stage: My Personal Experiences and Recollections* (New York: McClure, 1901).

Nelson, Larry E. *Sherman's March Through the Upper Pee Dee Region of South Carolina* (Florence, South Carolina: Pee Dee Heritage Center, 2001).

New Hampshire General Court, Committee on Hale Statue. *The Statue of John P. Hale Erected in Front of the Capitol and Presented to the State of New Hampshire by William E. Chandler* (Concord, New Hampshire: Republican Press Association, 1892).

Nicolay, John George. *An Oral History of Abraham Lincoln: John G. Nicolay's Interviews and Essays*, ed. Michael Burlingame (Carbondale: Southern Illinois University Press, 2006).

———. *With Lincoln in the White House: Letters, Memoranda, and Other Writings of John G. Nicolay, 1860–1865*, ed. Michael Burlington (Carbondale: Southern Illinois University Press, 2000).

Nicolay, John George, and John Hay, *Abraham Lincoln: A History*, 10 vols. (New York: Century, 1890).

Palmer, B. M. *National Responsibility before God. A Discourse, Delivered on the Day of Fasting, Humiliation and Prayer Appointed by the President of the Confederate State of America, June 13, 1861* (New Orleans: Price-Current Steam Book and Job Printing, 1861).

Pepper, Capt. George W., *Personal Recollections of Sherman's Campaigns in Georgia and the Carolinas* (Zanesville, Ohio: Hugh Dunne, 1866).

Pittman, Ben. *The Assassination of President Lincoln and the Trial of the Conspirators: David E. Herold, Mary E. Surratt, Lewis Payne, George A. Atzerodt, Edward Spangler, Samuel A. Mudd, Samuel Arnold, Michael O'Laughlin* (New York: Moore, Wilstach & Boldwin, 1865).

Poore, Benjamin Perley. *Perley's Reminiscences of Sixty Years in the National Metropolis*, 2 vols. (Philadelphia: Hubbard Brothers, 1886).

Porter, General Horace. *Campaigning with Grant* (New York: Century, 1897).

Pratt, Harry E. "David Davis, 1815–1886," PhD diss. (University of Illinois, 1930).

Proceedings of the American Anti-Slavery Society, and Its Third Decade, Held in the City of Philadelphia, Dec. 3d and 4th, 1863 (New York: American Anti-Slavery Society, 1864).

Proceedings of the Massachusetts Historical Society, 1866–1867 (Boston: Wiggin and Lunt, 1867).

Pryor, Elizabeth Brown. *Six Encounters with Lincoln: A President Confronts Democracy and Its Demons* (New York: Viking, 2017).

Rankin, Henry B. *Personal Recollections of Abraham Lincoln* (New York: Putnam, 1916).

Raymond, Henry J. *Life, Public Services and State Papers of Abraham Lincoln* (New York: Darby and Miller Publishers, 1865).

Retter, Corey S. *1861–1865 Union Executions* (Raleigh, North Carolina: Lulu Press, 2016).

Rhodes, James Ford, ed. *History of the United States from the Compromise of 1850 to the Final Restoration of Home Rule at the South in 1877, Vol. 5: 1865–1866* (New York: Macmillan, 1906).

Rice, Allen Thorndike. *Reminiscences of Abraham Lincoln by Distinguished Men of His Time* (New York: Harper, 1909).

Russell, William Howard. *My Diary, North and South* (Boston: T.O.H.P. Burnham, 1863).

Samples, Gordon. *Lust for Fame: The Stage Career of John Wilkes Booth* (Jefferson, North Carolina: McFarland, 1982).

Schwarzkopf, Norman. *It Doesn't Take a Hero: The Autobiography of General Norman Schwarzkopf* (New York: Random House, 2010).

Seaman, L. *What Miscegenation Is! And What We Are to Expect Now That Mr. Lincoln Is Re-elected* (New York: Waller & Willets, 1864).

Sears, Stephen W. *For Country Cause and Leader: The Civil War Journals of Charles B. Haydon* (Boston: Houghton Mifflin, 1993).

Shenk, Joshua Wolf. *Lincoln's Melancholy: How Depression Challenged a President and Fueled His Greatness* (Boston: Houghton Mifflin, 2006).

Sherman, John. *John Sherman's Recollections of Forty Years in the House, Senate and Cabinet*, 2 vols. (Chicago: Werner, 1895).

Sherman, William T. *Memoirs of General William T. Sherman*, 2 vols. (New York: D. Appleton, 1875).

———. *Sherman's Civil War: Selected Correspondence of William T. Sherman, 1860–1865*, eds. Brooks D. Simpson and Jean V. Berlin (Chapel Hill: University of North Carolina Press, 1999).

Slave Narratives: A Folk History of Slavery in the United States from Interviews with Former Slaves, Vol. 14: South Carolina Narratives, pt. 3. (Washington, D.C.: Federal Writers Project for the Library of Congress, 1941).

Stanton, R. L. *The Church and the Rebellion: A Consideration of the Rebellion Against the Government of the United States; and the Agency of the Church, North and South, in Relation Thereto* (New York: Derby & Miller, 1864).

Stevens, Walter B. *A Reporter's Lincoln*, ed. Michael Burlingame (Lincoln: University of Nebraska Press, 1998).

Stoddard, William Osborn. *Inside the White House in War Times: Memoirs and Reports of Lincoln's Secretary*, ed. Michael Burlingame (Lincoln: University of Nebraska Press, 2000).

Stout, Harry S., *Upon the Altar of the Nation: A Moral History of the Civil War* (New York: Penguin Books, 2007).

Stowe, Harriet Beecher. *Men of Our Times; or Leading Patriots of the Day* (Hartford: Hartford, 1868).

Strong, George Templeton. *Diary, Vol. 3: The Civil War, 1860–1865*, eds. Allan Nevins and Milton Halsey Thomas (New York: Macmillan, 1952).

Taylor, Tom. *Our American Cousin: A Drama, in 3 Acts* (New York: Samuel French, 1869).

Thayer, William Roscoe. *John Hay: In Two Volumes* (Boston: Houghton Mifflin, 1915).

Thomas, Emory M. *Bold Dragoon: The Life of J. E. B. Stuart* (Norman: University of Oklahoma Press, 1988).

Thompson, S. Millett. *Thirteenth Regiment of New Hampshire Volunteer Infantry in the War of the Rebellion, 1861–1865: A Diary Covering Three Years and a Day* (Boston: Houghton Mifflin, 1888).

Townsend, George Alfred. *Kate of Catoctin, or The Chain-Breakers: A National Romance* (New York: D. Appleton, 1886).

Traubel, Horace. *With Walt Whitman in Camden*, 5 vols. (New York: Mitchell Kennerley, 1914).

Trowbridge, John Townsend. *My Own Story: With Recollections of Noted Persons* (Boston: Houghton Mifflin, 1903).

Turner, Justin G., and Linda Levitt Turner. *Mary Todd Lincoln: Her Life and Letters* (New York: Fromm International, 1987).

U.L.A. *"Going Home to Vote": Authentic Speeches of S. P. Chase, Secretary to the Treasury, during His Visit to Ohio, with His Speeches at Indianapolis, and at the Mass Meeting in Baltimore, October, 1863* (Washington, D.C.: W. H. Moore, 1863).

U.S. Congress, House. *Impeachment Investigation, Testimony Taken before the Judiciary Committee of the House of Representatives in the Investigation of Charges Against Andrew Johnson* (39th Congress, 2nd sess., and 40th Congress, 1st sess., 1867).

U.S. War Department. *The War of the Rebellion: A Compilation of the Official Records of the Union and Confederate Armies* (Washington, D.C.: Government Printing Office, 1891–1895).

Wagenknect, Edward, *Nathaniel Hawthorne: Man and Writer* (New York: Oxford University Press, 1961).

War Papers Read before the Commandery of the State of Maine, Military Order of the Loyal Legion of the United States, Vols. 1–4 (Portland, Maine: Thurston Print and Lefavor-Tower, 1898–1915).

Warren, Louis A. *Lincoln's Youth: Indiana Years, Seven to Twenty-one, 1816–1830* (New York: Appleton, Century, Crofts, 1959).

Washington, John E., and Kate Masur. *They Knew Lincoln* (New York: Oxford University Press, 2018).

Weichmann, Louis J. *A True History of the Assassination of Abraham Lincoln and of the Conspiracy of 1865*, ed. Floyd E. Risvold (New York: Vintage Books, 1977).

Weik, Jesse William. *The Real Lincoln: A Portrait* (Boston: Houghton Mifflin, 1922).

Welles, Gideon. *Diary of Gideon Welles, Secretary of the Navy under Lincoln and Johnson*, 2 vols. (Boston: Houghton Mifflin, 1911).

White, Horace. *The Life of Lyman Trumbull* (Boston: Houghton Mifflin, 1913).

Whitman, Walt. *Complete Prose Works* (Philadelphia: David McKay, 1892).

———. *The Correspondence*, 6 vols., ed. Edwin Haviland Miller (New York: New York University Press, 1961–1977).

———. *Drum-Taps: The Complete 1865 Edition*, ed. Lawrence Kramer (New York: New York Review of Books, 2015).

———. *Leaves of Grass* (New York: W. E. Chapin, 1867).

———. *Notebooks and Unpublished Prose Manuscripts*, 6 vols., ed. Edward F. Grier (New York: New York University Press, 1984).

———. *November Boughs* (Philadelphia: David McKay, 1888).

Whitney, Henry C. *Life on the Circuit with Lincoln* (Boston: Estes and Lauriat, 1892).

Wilkie, Franc B. *Pen and Power* (Boston: Ticknor, 1888).

Wilson, Douglas L. *Lincoln's Sword: The Presidency and the Power of Words* (Vintage Books, New York, 2006).

Wilson, Douglas L., and Rodney O. Davis, eds. *Herndon's Informants: Letters, Interviews, and Statements about Abraham Lincoln* (Champaign: University of Illinois Press, 1997).

Winthrop, Robert C. Jr. *A Memoir of Robert C. Winthrop* (Boston: Little, Brown, 1897).

Witt, John Fabian. *Lincoln's Code: The Laws of War in American History* (New York: Free Press, 2012).

Wooster, Louise Catherine. *The Autobiography of a Magdalen* (Birmingham, Alabama: Birmingham, 1911).

ONLINE SOURCES

American Battlefield Trust, "Photography and the Civil War." Accessed September 8, 2018. (www.battlefields.org/learn/articles/photography-and-civil-war).

The Architect of the Capitol, "Philip Reid and the Statue of Freedom." Accessed September 8, 2018. (www.aoc.gov/philip-reid-and-statue-freedom).

Clara Barton Missing Soldiers Office Museum, "Our Story." Accessed October 5, 2018. (http://www.clarabartonmuseum.org/ourstory/).

"Emigh, Benjamin F.," *David Schooley's Independent Artillery* (blog). Accessed September 1, 2018. (https://millardallan.wordpress.com/officers/sergeants/benjamin-emigh/).

Ford's Theatre, "What Lincoln Wore." Accessed October 5, 2018. (www.fords.org/lincolns-assassination/lincolns-clothes/).

James Cummins Bookseller, "The Surgeon of the 'Montauk' Gives an Eye-Witness Account." Accessed April 14, 2019. (https://www.jamescumminsbookseller.com/pages/books/100185/lincoln-assassination-george-b-todd-m-d/autograph-letter-signed-george-to-his-brother-giving-his-eye-witness-account-of-the-assassination).

United States Senate Historical Office, "George T. Brown, Sergeant At Arms, 1861–1869." Accessed September 30, 2018. (www.senate.gov/artandhistory/history/common/generic/SAA_George_Brown.htm).

Vermont Historical Society, "William Scott Letters." Accessed September 30, 2018. (www.vermonthistory.org/research/research-resources-online/civil-war-transcriptions/william-the-sleeping-sentinel-scott-letters).

The Walt Whitman Archive, eds. Ed Folsom and Kenneth M. Price. Accessed September 8, 2018. (http://www.whitmanarchive.org).

"The Washington Canal: Cesspool in the Midst of the Nation's Capital," *Civil War Washington, D.C.* (blog), April 1, 2012. Accessed September 2, 2018. (www.civilwarwashingtondc1861-1865.blogspot.com/2012/04/washington-canal-cesspool-in-midst-of.html).

Will Hughes, "Horatio Greenough's Near Naked Washington," *Boundary Stones*, WETA's Local History Blog, May 22, 2013. Accessed on October 5, 1918. (https://blogs.weta.org/boundarystones/2013/05/22/horatio-greenough's-near-naked-washington).

NOTES

PROLOGUE: THE NATION'S WOUNDS

xi *Nearly ten months after*: SCC, 1864–65.

xi *Connor was a strikingly*: Biographical details from John W. Leonard, ed., *Men of America: A Biographical Dictionary of Contemporaries, Vol. 1* (New York: L. R. Hamersley, 1907), 509.

xii *"military force would not only be useless"*: *The New York Times*, November 20, 1860.

xii *"it was the havoc of the war"*: Ward Hill Lamon and Dorothy Lamon Teillard, eds., *Recollections of Abraham Lincoln, 1847–1865* (Washington, D.C.: Published by the editors, 1911), 103.

xiii *"The dead, the dead, the dead"*: Walt Whitman, *Complete Prose Works* (Philadelphia: David McKay, 1892), 79–80.

xiii *"death was on every hand"*: W.H. Crook, *Memories of the White House: The Home Life of Our Presidents from Lincoln to Roosevelt*, ed. Henry Rood (Boston: Little, Brown, 1911), 21.

xiii *jailing of journalists*: Harold Holzer describes Lincoln's battles with the press extensively in *Lincoln and the Power of the Press: The War for Public Opinion* (New York: Simon & Schuster, 2014).

xiv *"a bitter and unrelenting hatred"*: Elijah P. Petty to Margaret Elizabeth Pinner Petty, September 11, 1862; Norman D. Brown, ed., *Journey to Pleasant Hill: The Civil War Letters of Captain Elijah P. Petty, Walker's Texas Division, CSA* (San Antonio: University of Texas, 1982), 79–80.

xiv *"You god damned bloody"*: Thomas P. Lowry, *Love and Lust: Private and Amorous Letters of the Civil War* (BookSurge, 2009), 111.

xv *"The flag which he had then"*: Frank Key Howard, *Fourteen Months in American Bastiles* (Baltimore: Kelly, Hedian, and Piet, 1863), 9.

xv *"a foul-tongued and ribald"*: *The Standard*, London, October 8, 1864.

xv *"No wonder the President"*: *Dubuque (IA) Herald*, quoted in *The Delaware Gazette*, Delaware, Ohio, June 19, 1863.

xv *"There is death at the heart"*: Sabin Hough to Thomas H. Seymour, May 15, 1864, Thomas H. Seymour Papers.

xv *"Patriotism is played out"*: *La Crosse (Wisconsin) Democrat*, quoted in *The Daily Milwaukee News*, July 19, 1863.

xv *"Dishonest Abe"*: Elizabeth Cady Stanton quotes cited in Michael Burlingame, *Abraham Lincoln: A Life*, *Vol. 2* (Baltimore: Johns Hopkins University Press, 2013), 685.

xv *"This morning, as for"*: August 23, 1864, memorandum, Abraham Lincoln Papers, Series 3, General Correspondence.

xvi *"a vulgar tyrant"*: Richmond *Daily Dispatch*, November 9, 1864, quoted in *The New York Herald*, November 12, 1864.

xvi *"in the hands of those"*: *Daily Richmond Examiner*, November 11, 1864, quoted in *The Indianapolis Star*, November 19, 1864.

xvii *"a new and irrepressible fire"*: *The Times*, of London, March 20, 1865.

xvii *"teach the insolent enemy"*: *The Chicago Tribune*, February 15, 1865.

xviii *"combinations too powerful"*: CW, 4:332.

xviii *"The motive that impelled"*: "The Boys of 1861," *War Papers Read before the Commandery of the State of Maine, Military Order of the Loyal Legion of the United States*, *Vols. 1–4* (Portland, Maine: Thurston Print and Lefavor-Tower, 1898–1915), 1:323–43.

xviii *"something like a sledgehammer"*: "In the Wilderness," *War Papers Read before the Commandery of the State of Maine*, 4:200–229.

xix *"Boatloads of unfortunate"*: Noah Brooks, *Mr. Lincoln's Washington: Selections from the Writings of Noah Brooks, Civil War Correspondent*, ed. P. J. Staudenraus (South Brunswick, New Jersey: Thomas Yoseloff, 1967), 320.

xix *"Look yonder at those"*: Isaac N. Arnold, *The Life of Abraham Lincoln* (Chicago: Jansen, McClurg, 1885), 2:375.

xix *"The day before his death"*: *The Daily Whig & Courier*, Bangor, Maine, June 24, 1864.

xix *Benjamin Emigh of Pittston*: "Emigh, Benjamin F.," *David Schooley's Independent Artillery* (blog). Accessed September 1, 2018. (https://millardallan.wordpress. com/officers/sergeants/benjamin-emigh/).

xx *"Noble-looking man"*: Harriet Eaton, *This Birth Place of Souls: The Civil War Nursing Diary of Harriet Eaton*, ed. Jane E. Schultz (New York: Oxford University Press, 2012), 153.

xx *"I tried to get him"*: SCC, letter from Virgil Connor to his mother, February 19, 1865.

xx *"One year ago today"*: SCC, letter from Selden Connor to his mother, May 6, 1865.

xx *"a view of the elite"*: SCC, letter from Virgil Connor to his mother, February 19, 1865.

xx *marveled at the spectacular*: SCC, letter from Virgil Connor to his sister, February 27, 1865.

xxi *"she kept her tongue"*: Ibid.

xxi *Chambrun had paid a visit*: Account of the day's activities, February 27, 1865, Charles Adolphe de Pineton Chambrun, *Impressions of Lincoln and the Civil War: A Foreigner's Account; Translated from the French*. Trans., Gen. Aldebert de Chambrun (New York: Random House, 1952), 20–29.

xxii *"To say that he is ugly"*: "Washington during the War," *Macmillan's Magazine*, May 1862, 23.

xxiii *"Such a shapeless mass"*: May 4, 2864 letter by Richard Henry Dana Jr., Dana Family Papers.

xxiv *"a fool—the laughing stock"*: David Herbert Donald, *Lincoln* (New York: Simon & Schuster, 1996), 324.

xxiv *"vulgar doll"*: Louis P. Masur, ed., *The Real War Will Never Get in the Books: Selections from Writers during the Civil War* (New York: Oxford University Press, 1995), 47.

xxiv *"a sallow, fleshy, uninteresting"*: Burlingame, *Abraham Lincoln: A Life*, 272.

xxiv *"had her bosom on exhibition"*: James W. Nesmith to his wife, Washington, February 5, 1862, photocopy, James G. Randall Papers.

xxvi *"rare virtues of heart"*: *Washington Chronicle*, November 13, 1863, quoted in *The Chicago Tribune*, November 17, 1863.

xxvi *"tall and slender"*: Carl Schurz, "Reminiscences of a Long Life: The Campaign of 1860," *McClure Magazine*, February 1907, 410.

xxvii *"the Hell Cat"*: John Hay, *Lincoln and the Civil War in the Diaries and Letters of John Hay*, ed. Tyler Dennett (Boston: Da Capo Press, 1988), 41.

xxvii *"Her Satanic Majesty"*: John G. Nicolay, *With Lincoln in the White House: Letters, Memoranda, and Other Writings of John G. Nicolay, 1860–1865*, ed. Michael Burlington (Carbondale: Southern Illinois University Press, 2000), 125.

xxvii *"statuesque Kate cry"*: Thomas Graham Belden and Marva Robins, *So Fell the Angels* (Boston: Little, Brown, 1956), 94.

xxvii *"a small insignificant youth"*: John Hay, *Inside Lincoln's White House: The Complete Civil War Diary of John Hay*, eds. Michael Burlingame and John R. T. Ettlinger (Carbondale: Southern Illinois University Press, 1999), 12

xxvii *"Personally, Mr. Sprague"*: *The Brooklyn Daily Eagle*, October 14, 1863.

xxviii *"'take the cuss off'"*: Noah Brooks, *Lincoln Observed: Civil War Dispatches of Noah Brooks*. ed. Michael Burlingame (Baltimore: Johns Hopkins University Press, 1998), 90–91.

xxviii *"Kate looked tired out"*: Hay, *Inside Lincoln's White House*, 111.

xxviii *"The Chief Justice"*: *The Evening Star*, February 27, 1865.

xxviii *"Magnificent salons"*: *The New York Express*, quoted in *The Cincinnati Enquirer*, March 4, 1865.

xxix *"shoddy upstarts"*: *Wisconsin State Journal* (Madison), correspondence from January 29, 1865, quoted in *Appleton* (Wisconsin) *Motor*, February 9, 1865.

xxix *"Point lace, diamonds, &c."*: Ibid.

xxix *"We are not only fighting"*: U.S. War Department, *The War of the Rebellion: A Compilation of the Official Records of the Union and Confederate Armies* (Washington, D.C.: Government Printing Office, 1891–1895), ser. 1, vol. 44, 799.

xxx *"One would imagine"*: *Richmond Whig*, February 24, 1865, quoted in *The Rutland* (Vermont) *Weekly Herald*, March 2, 1865.

xxx *"bowing at the footstool"*: *Richmond Whig*, February 25, 1865, quoted in *The New York Times*, February 28, 1865.

CHAPTER 1: BLOODY GASHES ON THE FACE OF HEAVEN

1 *"the liquefied condition"*: *The New York Herald*, March 4, 1865.

1 *"the weather was dry"*: *The Evening Star*, March 4, 1865.

2 *Cal and Virgil decided*: SCC, letter from Virgil Connor to his mother, March 6, 1865.

2 *known thugs and pickpockets*: *The Evening Star*, March 4, 1865.

2 *Like many in Washington*: GWD, 2:250.

2 *"The city full of people"*: Ibid., 251.

2 *"something was going on"*: *The Evening Star*, March 4, 1865.

3 *"Are you hit, Colonel?"*: "In the Wilderness," *War Papers Read before the Commandery of the State of Maine*, 4:221.

3 *"I sent back the reply"*: Ibid., 223

4 *"may be more justly called"*: Nathaniel Hawthorne, "Chiefly about War Matters, by a Peaceable Man," *Atlantic Monthly*, July 1862.

4 *"Of all the detestable"*: George Templeton Strong, *Diary, Vol. 3: The Civil War, 1860–1865*, ed. Allan Nevins and Milton Halsey Thomas (New York: Macmillan, 1952), 164.

4 *"Its buildings, like its population"*: Lois Bryan Adams, *Letter from Washington, 1863–1865* (Detroit: Wayne State University, 1999), 35.

4 *"a cesspool into which"*: Franc B. Wilkie, *Pen and Power* (Boston: Ticknor, 1888), 181.

5 *"politicians & prostitutes"*: Stephen W. Sears, *For Country Cause and Leader: The Civil War Journals of Charles B. Haydon* (Boston: Houghton Mifflin, 1993), 138.

5 *"It is the grand receptacle"*: "The Washington Canal: Cesspool in the Midst of the Nation's Capital," *Civil War Washington, D.C.* (blog), April 1, 2012. Accessed September 2, 2018. (www.civilwarwashingtondc1861-1865.blogspot. com/2012/04/washington-canal-cesspool-in-midst-of.html).

5 *"Lincoln's dog"*: Thos. Dunn English, ed., *The Old Guard, Vol. 8* (New York: English, 1870), 474.

6 *"My guests were always"*: John W. Forney, *Anecdotes of Public Men*, 2 vols. (New York: Harper & Brothers, 1873 and 1881), 1:75.

6 *"beau-ideal of a"*: Andrew Johnson, *The Papers of Andrew Johnson* (Knoxville: University of Tennessee Press, 1983, 1986), 7:288.

6 *"a coarse, vulgar creature"*: GWD, 2:557.

7 *"Mr. President, Andrew Johnson is a rank demagogue"*: Charles Eugene Hamlin, *The Life and Times of Hannibal Hamlin* (Boston: Riverside Press, 1899), 472.

7 *"pseudo Democratic party"*: Johnson, *The Papers*, 7:237.

7 *"I found fault"*: Ibid., 298.

7 *"Treason must be"*: Walter L. Fleming, *Documentary History of Reconstruction: Political, Military, Social, Religious, Educational & Industrial, 1865 to the Present Time, Vol. 1* (Cleveland: Arthur H. Clark, 1906), 116.

8 *"No man in Tennessee"*: *Nashville Press*, February 9, 1864, quoted in *Wilmington* (North Carolina) *Journal*, March 3, 1864.

8 *"the very lick spittle"*: Johnson, *The Papers*, 7:123.

8 *"untiring energy"*: *The Nashville Times and True Union*, February 25, 1865.

8 *privately referred to as "niggers"*: Ron Chernow, *Grant* (New York: Penguin Press, 2017), 550.

9 *"The personal partizans"*: Johnson, *The Papers*, 7:439.

9 *"it is unsafe"*: Ibid., 7:427.

9 *"This Johnson is a queer man"*: Walter B. Stevens, *A Reporter's Lincoln*, ed. Michael Burlingame (Lincoln: University of Nebraska Press, 1998), 156.

9 *"You and I were old Democrats"*: U.S. Congress, House, *Impeachment Investigation* (39th Congress, 2nd sess., and 40th Congress, 1st sess., 1867), 781.

9 *"the same plain citizen"*: Johnson, *The Papers*, 7:494.

10 *"There are at present"*: *The Evening Star*, October 27, 1863.

10 *Fort Sumter; the Ironclad*: Thomas P. Lowry, *The Story the Soldiers Wouldn't Tell: Sex in the Civil War* (Mechanicsburg, Pennsylvania: Stackpole Books, 2012), 63.

10 *"and the feet of the people"*: *The Washington Post*, July 8, 1888.

11 *Three found themselves arrested*: *The Evening Star*, March 16, 1863.

12 *"There may be circumstances"*: *The National Republican*, Washington, D.C., March 4, 1865.

12 *"the fog of the avenue"*: *The Evening Star*, March 4, 1865.

12 *"please pump the water"*: CW, 8:319.

12 *"The streets resound"*: *The New York Herald*, March 4, 1865.

13 *"Numbers of bands"*: Louis J. Weichmann, *A True History of the Assassination of Abraham Lincoln and of the Conspiracy of 1865*, ed. Floyd E. Risvold (New York: Vintage Books, 1977), 87.

13 *"tall, erect, slender"*: Ibid., 14.

13 *"an impetuous southerner"*: Thomas Nelson Conrad (Capt., C.S.A), *The Rebel Scout: A Thrilling History of Scouting Life in the Southern Army* (Washington, D.C.: National, 1904), 153.

14 *"We had a regular established line"*: *The Evening Star*, December 7, 1870.

14 *"just as orderly, decent, and respectable"*: Weichmann, *A True History*, 29.

14 *"Her steel gray eye"*: Ibid., 20.

15 *"We have reason to"*: Ibid., 87.

15 *"Physically and intellectually"*: D. H. L. Gleason, "The Conspiracy Against Lincoln," *Magazine of History with Notes and Queries*, 59–65.

15 *"I was chaffing him"*: William C. Edwards and Edward Steers Jr., eds., *The Lincoln Assassination: The Evidence* (Urbana: University of Illinois Press, 2009), 594.

15 *"His face wore a look"*: Gleason, "The Conspiracy," 59.

16 *strolled down Sixth Street*: Weichmann, *A True History*, 88.

17 *"I rather considered it"*: Ibid., 103.

17 *"Do you want"*: *The Cleveland Plain Dealer*, November 5, 1865.

18 *"This country was formed"*: John Wilkes Booth, *Right or Wrong, God Judge Me: The Writings of John Wilkes Booth*, eds. John H. Rhodehamel and Louise Taper (Urbana: University of Illinois Press, 2000), 124–27.

18 *"Whenever I hear"*: CW, 8:361.

19 *"How I have loved"*: Booth, *Right or Wrong*, 126.

20 *"He appeared somewhat excited"*: Ben Pittman, *The Assassination of President Lincoln and the Trial of the Conspirators: David E. Herold, Mary E. Surratt, Lewis Payne, George A. Atzerodt, Edward Spangler, Samuel A. Mudd, Samuel Arnold, Michael O'Laughlin* (New York: Moore, Wilstach & Boldwin, 1865), 177.

CHAPTER 2: ONE AND A HALF TIMES BIGGER

21 *"What, to the American slave"*: Frederick Douglass, *Frederick Douglass: Selected Speeches and Writings*, ed. Philip S. Foner (Chicago: Lawrence Hill, 1999), 196–97.

22 *"I hate it"*: CW, 2:255.

23 *"refused to be inoculated"*: Frederick Douglass, *The Life and Times of Frederick Douglass, Written by Himself* (Boston: De Wolfe & Fisk, 1892), 366.

23 *"welcomed me to"*: Ibid., 439.

23 *"tall, of good presence"*: William Howard Russell, *My Diary, North and South* (Boston: T.O.H.P. Burnham, 1863), 42.

23 *"Chase is about one and a half"*: Albert Bushnell Hart, *Salmon Portland Chase* (Boston: Houghton Mifflin, 1899), 435.

24 *"If in 1864"*: Salmon P. Chase, *The Salmon P. Chase Papers, Vol. 5, Correspondence, April 1863–1864*, ed. John Niven (Kent, Ohio: Kent State University Press, 1997), 146.

24 *"proposed plan for collecting"*: Salmon P. Chase, *The Salmon P. Chase Papers, Vol. 1, Journals 1829–1872,* ed. John Niven (Kent, Ohio: Kent State University Press, 1993), 459.

24 *"Let the dead"*: Francis Bicknell Carpenter, *Six Months at the White House with Abraham Lincoln: The Story of a Picture* (New York: Hurd, Houghton, 1867), 38.

24 *"Even after the rebellion"*: U.L.A. *"Going Home to Vote": Authentic Speeches of S. P. Chase, Secretary to the Treasury, during His Visit to Ohio, with His Speeches at Indianapolis, and at the Mass Meeting in Baltimore, October, 1863* (Washington, D.C.: W. H. Moore, 1863), 27–29.

25 *"Abraham Lincoln is no"*: *Douglass Monthly,* August 1862.

26 *"If there be those"*: CW, 5:389.

26 *"pre-eminently the white man's"*: Douglass, *The Life and Times,* 372.

26 *"When there was any shadow of a hope"*: Frederick Douglass to Theodore Tilton, October 15, 1864, Tilton Papers.

26 *"planted agony"*: *The New York Tribune,* January 14, 1864.

28 *"Mr. Chase honestly felt"*: Maunsell B. Field, *Memories of Many Men and of Some Women* (New York: Harper & Brothers, 1874), 280.

28 *"reserved, unappreciative as to jokes"*: Brooks, *Lincoln Observed,* 47.

28 *"with Axminster carpets"*: Ibid., 125.

28 *"Chase is a good man"*: Hay, *Inside Lincoln's White House,* 77.

28 *"I see Chase"*: Belden, *So Fell the Angels,* 29.

29 *"If you are going to put"*: Alexander K. McClure, *"Abe" Lincoln's Yarns and Stories* (Philadelphia: Educational, 1901), 400.

29 *"the higher priced notes"*: John George Nicolay and John Hay, *Abraham Lincoln: A History* (New York: Century, 1890), 9:395.

29 *"Mr. Chase is large"*: Brooks, *Lincoln Observed,* 47.

29 *"An ambition for"*: Ibid., 69.

30 *"was at work night and day"*: Hay, *Inside Lincoln's White House,* 120.

30 *"the want of energy"*: GWD, 1:520–21.

30 *"eating a man's bread"*: David Davis to Julius Rockwell, Washington, January 24, 1864, David Davis Papers.

30 *"I have determined"*: Nicolay and Hay, *Abraham Lincoln,* 8:316.

30 *Lincoln even joked*: Carpenter, *Six Months at the White House,* 129–30.

30 *"much amused at Chase's mad hunt"*: Hay, *Inside Lincoln's White House,* 103.

31 *"nothing could induce me"*: Bruce Catton, *Grant Takes Command* (Boston: Little, Brown, 1968), 111–12.

31 *"My son, I can't tell"*: Chernow, *Grant,* 329.

31 *"Treasury report is very able"*: John Bigelow, *Retrospections of an Active Life,* 5 vols. (New York: Baker and Taylor, 1909–13), 2:110.

32 *"union of influences"*: *The New York Times,* February 23, 1864.

32 *"The treasury rats"*: Nicolay, *With Lincoln in the White House*, 127.

32 *"it would be more dangerous"*: GWD, 1:529.

32 *"I do not believe in"*: *The New York Times*, March 5, 1864.

33 *"ask that no further consideration"*: *The Chicago Tribune*, March 11, 1864.

33 *"the salmon is a queer fish"*: *The New York Herald*, March 12, 1864.

33 *"Whether you shall remain"*: CW, 7:213.

33 *"Of all I have said"*: Ibid., 419.

34 *"Mr. President, this is worse"*: L. E. Chittenden, "The Faith of President Lincoln," *Harper's New Monthly Magazine*, February 1891, 389.

34 *"Are you sure"*: Josiah Bushnell Grinnell, *Men and Events of Forty Years: Autobiographical Reminiscences of an Active Career from 1850 to 1890* (Boston: D. Lothrop, 1891), 173.

34 *"put the blacks and whites"*: Montgomery Blair letter to Abraham Lincoln, December 6, 1864, Abraham Lincoln Papers.

35 *"the complete, absolute, unqualified"*: Frederick Douglass, *The Frederick Douglass Papers*, ed. John W. Blassingame (New Haven, Connecticut: Yale University Press, 1991), 4:527, 530–31.

35 *"Do evil by choice"*: Douglass, *Selected Speeches and Writings*, 568.

36 *"would only be sustaining himself"*: Brooks, *Lincoln Observed*, 154.

36 *"Mr. Chase is a very able"*: James Ford Rhodes, ed. *History of the United States from the Compromise of 1850 to the Final Restoration of Home Rule at the South in 1877, Vol. 5: 1865–1866* (New York: Macmillan, 1906), 46.

36 *"Probably no other man"*: Nicolay, *With Lincoln in the White House*, 166.

36 *"I should despise myself"*: Isaac N. Arnold, *The History of Abraham Lincoln and the Overthrow of Slavery* (Chicago: Clarke & Co, 1866), 575.

36 *"upon the subject of"*: William Sprague to Kate Chase Sprague, December 27, 1864, Katherine Chase Sprague Papers.

36 *"Those politicians who counted"*: *The New York Herald*, December 27, 1864.

37 *"There is no man"*: GWD, 2:246.

37 *"I fear our good President"*: Nicolay and Hay, *Abraham Lincoln*, 9:389.

37 *"I most respectfully"*: Ibid., 397.

37 *"Shall the loyal blacks"*: *The Liberator*, Boston, March 10, 1865.

37 *"My country 'tis of thee"*: Adams, *Letter from Washington*, 239.

CHAPTER 3: A MESSAGE FROM GRANT

39 *"illuminating the heavens"*: *The Evening Star*, March 4, 1865.

39 *"If people see the Capitol"*: John Eaton and Ethel Osgood Mason, *Grant, Lincoln, and the Freedmen: Reminiscences of the Civil War* (New York: Longmans, Green, 1907), 89.

39 *"Tonight I have been"*: Whitman, *Complete Prose Works*, 63.

40 *"were bolting in every direction"*: *The Evening Star*, March 4, 1865.

40 *"They behave disgracefully"*: Ernest B. Furgurson, *Freedom Rising: Washington in the Civil War* (New York: Alfred A. Knopf, 2004), 355.

40 *"the august assemblies"*: Adams, *Letter from Washington*, 240.

40 *"not disgraced by personal quarrels"*: *The New York Times*, March 6, 1865.

40 *"not calculated to elevate"*: John H. Clifford to Sarah Clifford, March 4, 1865, Clifford Family Papers.

41 *Noah Brooks, thirty-four*: Brooks, *Lincoln Observed*, 1–12.

41 *"He's a dangerous man"*: Noah Brooks, "Personal Reminiscences of Lincoln," *Scribner's Monthly*, February 1878, 562.

41 *"We crawled under"*: Ibid.

42 *"he immediately sent word"*: Noah Brooks, *Washington, D.C., in Lincoln's Time*, ed. Herbert Mitgang (Chicago: Quadrangle Books, 1971), 15.

42 *"There was over his whole face"*: Brooks, "Personal," 563.

42 *"his face was often full"*: Ibid.

42 *"The great rotunda"*: Brooks, *Mr. Lincoln's Washington*, 415.

42 *"The Capitol is literally jammed"*: *The Baltimore Sun*, March 5, 1865.

42 *"The galleries of the House"*: Brooks, *Mr. Lincoln's Washington*, 415.

43 *"most beautiful to behold"*: Ibid., 417.

43 *"but as a similar excuse"*: Elizabeth Blair Lee, *Wartime Washington: The Civil War Letters of Elizabeth Blair Lee*, ed. Virginia Jeans Laas (Urbana: University of Illinois Press, 1991), 479.

43 *"gay and festive in silk"*: Brooks, *Mr. Lincoln's Washington*, 417.

43 *"exhibited the extraordinary spectacle"*: Ibid., 416.

44 *"Grave senators"*: Ibid.

44 *"bills, which were reckoned"*: Ibid., 417.

44 *"to high as well as low"*: *The Buffalo Courier*, March 6, 1865.

44 *"did a thriving business"*: Brooks, *Mr. Lincoln's Washington*, 418.

45 *"Who's that?"*: Weichmann, *A True History*, 88.

45 *"Having served four years"*: CW, 8:326.

46 *"As usual, the time passed"*: GWD, 2:251.

46 *"Gilding, frescoes, arabesques"*: Mary Clemmer Ames, *Ten Years in Washington: Life and Scenes in the National Capital, as a Woman Sees Them* (Hartford: A. D. Worthington, 1874), 95.

47 *"the incredible gorgeousness"*: Walt Whitman, *The Correspondence*, ed. Edwin Haviland Miller (New York: New York University Press, 1961–1977), 1:74–75.

47 *"who were born free"*: Jefferson Davis, *The Papers of Jefferson Davis*, eds. Lynda Lasswell Christ et al. (Baton Rouge: Louisiana State University Press, 1971–2015), 6:6.

47 *In yet another irony*: The Architect of the Capitol, "Philip Reid and the Statue of Freedom." Accessed September 8, 2018. (www.aoc.gov/philip-reid-and-statue-freedom).

48 *"standing in the mud"*: *The New York Times*, October 4, 1863.

48 *"making her twenty times brighter"*: Whitman, *The Correspondence*, 1:80–85.

48 *"huge and delicate"*: *The New York Times*, October 4, 1863.

49 *"We know what hole"*: John Sherman, *John Sherman's Recollections of Forty Years in the House, Senate and Cabinet* (Chicago: Werner, 1895), 1:348.

49 *"Sherman went in at Atlanta"*: *The New York Tribune*, March 4, 1865.

49 *"There are some people"*: Brooks, *Lincoln Observed*, 152–53.

50 *"and is full of aspirations"*: GWD, 2:251

50 *"receiving the congratulations"*: *The Philadelphia Inquirer*, March 4, 1865.

50 *"I don't think that he would steal"*: Samuel W. McCall, *Thaddeus Stevens* (Boston: Houghton Mifflin, 1899), 311.

50 *"Every one appeared to be happy"*: Lamon, *Recollections*, 249–53.

51 *William H. Cunnington*: *The Philadelphia Inquirer*, March 4, 1865.

51 *"We have had several good"*: Warren S. Gurney to his mother, March 1, 1865, Warren S. Gurney Papers.

51 *"It is very true"*: Gurney to Uncle Lekla, March 10, 1865, Warren S. Gurney Papers.

51 *"The box was elegantly"*: Gurney to his mother, March 1, 1865, Warren S. Gurney Papers.

52 *"the war had gone on"*: James Longstreet, *From Manassas to Appomattox: Memoirs of the Civil War in America* (Philadelphia: J. B. Lippincott, 1896), 586.

53 *"Oh! How enchanting!"*: Julia Dent Grant, *The Personal Memoirs of Julia Dent Grant*, ed. John Y. Simon (Carbondale: Southern Illinois University Press, 2016), 141.

53 *"expressed especial approval"*: Longstreet, *From Manassas*, 586.

54 *"I can't spare this man"*: A. K. McClure, *Abraham Lincoln and Men of War-Times: Some Personal Recollections of War and Politics during the Lincoln Administration* (Philadelphia: Times, 1892), 180.

54 *"It was not war, but murder"*: Harry S. Stout, *Upon the Altar of the Nation: A Moral History of the Civil War* (New York: Penguin Books, 2007), xi.

55 *"I had always supposed"*: U. S. Grant, *Personal Memoirs of U. S. Grant* (New York: Charles L. Webster, 1894), 590–92.

55 *"having read it, handed it"*: Lamon, *Recollections*, 250.

55 *"a coarse, abusive and arbitrary"*: Brooks, *Lincoln Observed*, 98.

55 *"towering rage"*: Lamon, *Recollections*, 250.

56 *"Stanton, you are right"* : Ibid., 251.

56 *"The President directs me"*: CW, 8:330–31.

56 *"unduly anxious"*: Horace Porter, *Campaigning with Grant* (New York: Century, 1897), 390.

56 *"I can assure you"*: Ulysses S. Grant, *The Papers of Ulysses S. Grant*, ed. John Y. Simon (Carbondale: Southern Illinois University Press, 1985), 14:100.

57 *"I have no authority"*: Ibid., 14:98–99.

57 *"expressed himself more unreservedly"*: GWD, 2:251.

CHAPTER 4: THE REAL PRECIOUS AND ROYAL ONES

58 *"everything dim, leaden, and soaking"*: *The New York Times*, March 12, 1865.

58 *"serene, proud, cheerful"*: William Douglas O'Connor, "The Good Gray Poet," The Walt Whitman Archive, eds. Ed Folsom and Kenneth M. Price. Accessed Sept. 8, 2018. (http://www.whitmanarchive.org).

58 *"so large and well"*: Whitman, *The Correspondence*, 89.

59 *"I sound my barbaric"*: *Leaves of Grass* (1855), 55, The Walt Whitman Archive.

59 *"Walt Whitman is as unacquainted"*: *The Critic* (London), April 1, 1856.

59 *"mass of stupid filth"*: Rufus Griswold, "Leaves of Grass. By Walt Whitman. 1855," *The Criterion*, November 10, 1855.

59 *"It is no discredit"*: Thomas Wentworth Higginson, "Literature as an Art," *Atlantic Monthly*, December 1867, 753.

59 *"heterogeneous mass"*: *Boston Intelligencer*, May 3, 1856.

60 *"Nothing can more clearly"*: Richard Maurice Bucke, *Walt Whitman*, ed. Edward Dowden (Glasgow, Scotland: Wilson & McCormick, 1884), 198.

60 *"reading aloud a dozen"*: Henry B. Rankin, *Personal Recollections of Abraham Lincoln* (New York: Putnam, 1916), 124–27.

60 *"How is it possible"*: Ralph Waldo Emerson to Salmon P. Chase, January, 10, 1863, note, The Walt Whitman Archive.

60 *"He went strong"*: Horace Traubel, *With Walt Whitman in Camden* (New York: Mitchell Kennerley, 1914), 3:234.

61 *"Gardner was a real"*: Ibid., 346.

61 *The plate was coated*: American Battlefield Trust, "Photography and the Civil War," Accessed September 8, 2018 (www.battlefields.org/learn/articles/photography-and-civil-war).

62 *"The living that throng Broadway"*: *The New York Times*, October 20, 1862.

63 *"The members were nervous"*: *The New York Times*, March 12, 1865.

63 *"little mannikins"*: Walt Whitman, *Notebooks and Unpublished Prose Manuscripts*, ed. Edward F. Grier (New York: New York University Press, 1984), 2:567.

63 *"even here amid"*: Whitman, *The Correspondence*, 1:99.

63 *"different from any"*: Ibid., 249–50.

64 *"Mrs. Grayson gives"*: Ibid., 278.

64 *"the healthiest sweetest part"*: Whitman, *The Correspondence*, 2:39.

64 *"I wander'd through the"*: Whitman, *Complete Prose Works*, 63.

64 *"It beat like a deluge"*: *The New York Times*, March 12, 1865.

64 *"a tornado had overwhelmed the building"*: Brooks, *Mr. Lincoln's Washington*, 418.

64 *"as if Lee's batteries"*: *The National Republican*, March 4, 1865.

65 *"Rained—almost a hurricane"*: diary entry for March 4, 1865, Clara Barton Papers.

65 *"He was as a father"*: S. Millett Thompson, *Thirteenth Regiment of New Hampshire Volunteer Infantry in the War of the Rebellion, 1861–1865: A Diary Covering Three Years and a Day* (Boston: Houghton Mifflin, 1888), 620.

65 *"to return to the front"*: diary entry for March 4, 1865, Clara Barton Papers.

65 *"In my feeble estimation"*: Albert Bushnell Hart and Elizabeth Stevens, eds., *The Romance of the Civil War* (New York: Macmillan, 1917), 418.

66 *"care worn face"*: Elizabeth Brown Pryor, *Six Encounters with Lincoln: A President Confronts Democracy and Its Demons* (New York: Viking, 2017), 222.

66 *"Miss Barton calls"*: Ibid.

66 *"one of the most useful"*: Ibid.

67 Conway's *"success"*: CW, 8:326

67 *"I . . . do not feel it"*: Pryor, *Six Encounters*, 222.

67 *"I was always between"*: Traubel, *With Walt Whitman in Camden*, 3:581.

68 *"Out doors, at the foot"*: *The New York Times*, December 11, 1864.

68 *"I cannot tell you"*: Percy Harold Epler, *The Life of Clara Barton* (New York: Macmillan, 1915), 66–71.

69 *"Permit me to say"*: Ralph Waldo Emerson to Salmon P. Chase, January 10, 1863, The Walt Whitman Archive.

69 *"he considered Leaves of Grass"*: Ibid.

70 *"There are twice as many"*: *The New York Times*, December 11, 1864.

70 *"Who is there in Brooklyn"*: *The Brooklyn Daily Eagle*, December 3, 1863.

70 *"is considered by many"*: *The Daily Dispatch*, Richmond, Virginia, March 30, 1864.

70 *"Walt Whitman is now"*: *The Memphis Daily Appeal*, June 17, 1863.

70 *"I can't recall"*: Traubel, *With Walt Whitman in Camden*, 4:63.

71 *"That be Walt Whitman"*: Moncure D. Conway, "Walt Whitman," *Fortnightly Review* 6, October 15, 1866, 538–48.

71 *"Many of the soldiers"*: Whitman, *The Correspondence*, 1:89.

71 *"Walt just passed"*: Clara Barrus, *Whitman and Burroughs: Comrades* (Boston: Houghton Mifflin, 1931), 6.

71 *"I went sometimes at night"*: *The New York Times*, February 26, 1863.

71 *"O, ma'am"*: Adams, *Letter from Washington*, 152.

72 *"The brightest memory"*: Ibid., 21.

72 *"there is something in personal"*: *The New York Times*, December 11, 1864.

72 *Oscar F. Wilber*: Ibid.

72 *"I have the consciousness"*: Whitman, *The Correspondence*, 1:115–16.

72 *"It is curious"*: Walt Whitman, *November Boughs* (Philadelphia: David McKay, 1888), 113.

73 *"I see such awful"*: Whitman, *The Correspondence*, 1:224.

73 *"We receive them here"*: Ibid., 1:231.

73 *"the real precious and royal"*: Ibid., 1:129.

73 *"My opinion is to"*: Whitman, *Notebooks*, 2:573.

73 *"Mother, one's heart"*: Whitman, *The Correspondence*, 1:114.

73 *"This country can't be broken"*: Ibid., 1:92.

74 *"fresh and affectionate"*: Whitman, *Notebooks*, 2:487.

74 *"My womb is clean"*: Susan Garnet Smith to Walt Whitman, July 11, 1860, The Walt Whitman Archive.

74 *"once more in the hotbed"*: Ibid., Alonzo S. Bush to Walt Whitman, December 22, 1863.

75 *"Walt had his blanket"*: Bucke, *Walt Whitman*, 23.

75 *The conductor's name was Peter*: Martin G. Murray, "'Pete the Great': A Biography of Peter Doyle." *Walt Whitman Quarterly Review* 12, Summer 1994.

75 *"We were familiar at once"*: Bucke, *Walt Whitman*, 23.

75 *"bare and desolate back room"*: John Townsend Trowbridge, *My Own Story: With Recollections of Noted Persons* (Boston: Houghton Mifflin, 1903), 377.

75 *"We have got so"*: Whitman, *Complete Prose Works*, 43.

76 *"I love the President"*: Whitman, *Notebooks*, 2:539.

76 *"that underneath his outside"*: Whitman, *The Correspondence*, 1:80–85.

76 *"I have finally made up"*: Ibid., 1:124.

76 *"to electioneer and vote"*: Hay, *Inside Lincoln's White House*, 102.

77 *"Now, dear Walt"*: William D. O'Connor to Walt Whitman, December 30, 1864, The Walt Whitman Archive.

77 *"the seething hell"*: Whitman, *Complete Prose Works*, 80.

77 *"Come up from the fields"*: Walt Whitman, *Drum-Taps: The Complete 1865 Edition*, ed. Lawrence Kramer (New York: New York Review of Books, 2015), 47–49.

CHAPTER 5: MEDITATION ON THE DIVINE WILL

79 *"He was very abstemious"*: John Hay, *At Lincoln's Side: John Hay's Civil War Correspondence and Selected Writings*, ed. Michael Burlingame (Carbondale: Southern Illinois University Press, 2006), 110.

79 *"because it made him cross"*: Douglas L. Wilson and Rodney O. Davis, eds., *Herndon's Informants: Letters, Interviews, and Statements about Abraham Lincoln* (Champaign: University of Illinois Press, 1997), 631–32.

79 *in a new suit*: Ford's Theatre, "What Lincoln Wore." Accessed October 5, 2018. (www.fords.org/lincolns-assassination/lincolns-clothes/).

80 *"Let this man"*: J. W. Schwartz, "Kahler's Advertising," *Printer's Ink: A Journal for Advertisers*, New York, December 13, 1899.

80 *"a Virginian of distinguished"*: John E. Washington and Kate Masur, *They Knew Lincoln* (New York: Oxford University Press, 2018), 108.

80 *William Johnson*: Ibid., 127–28.

80 *"his demeanor and disposition"*: Hay, *At Lincoln's Side*, 139.

81 *"a deranged mind"*: Joshua Wolf Shenk, *Lincoln's Melancholy: How Depression Challenged a President and Fueled His Greatness* (Boston: Houghton Mifflin, 2006), 12.

81 *"I am now the most miserable"*: CW, 1:229.

81 *"His melancholy dripped"*: *The New York Times*, December 31, 1865.

81 *"All that I am"*: quoted in William Henry Herndon to Jesse William Weik, January 19, 1886, Herndon-Weik Collection.

81 *"It was a wild region"*: CW, 3:511.

82 *"the sad, if not pitiful"*: Jesse William Weik, *The Real Lincoln: A Portrait* (Boston: Houghton Mifflin, 1922), 293.

82 *"When my father settled"*: CW, 1:386.

82 *"In this sad world"*: Ibid., 6:16.

82 *"Lincoln's melancholy never"*: William H. Herndon and Jesse William Weik, *Herndon's Lincoln: The True Story of a Great Life* (Chicago: Belford-Clarke, 1890), 3:588.

82 *"I used to be a slave"*: quoted in *Los Angeles Herald*, September 8, 1895.

83 *"Say to him"*: CW, 2:96–97.

83 *Abraham's paternity was in question*: "The Curious Paternity of Abraham Lincoln," *Great Smoky Mountains Colloquy*, Spring 2008.

83 *"I have been too familiar"*: CW, 1:9.

83 *"His ambition was a little engine"*: *Herndon's Lincoln*, 2:375.

84 *"the most reticent"*: *Herndon's Informants*, 348.

84 *"growing feeble"*: BBF, 417.

85 *"Just when everybody"*: *Herndon's Informants*, 255.

85 *"shocked in the change"*: Arnold, *The Life*, 2:453–54.

85 *"the hearty, blithesome, genial"*: Brooks, *Lincoln Observed*, 211.

85 *a religious home*: Louis A. Warren, *Lincoln's Youth: Indiana Years, Seven to Twenty-one, 1816–1830* (New York: Appleton, Century, Crofts, 1959), 112–24.

86 *"Lincoln maintained that God"*: quoted in Ward H. Lamon, *The Life of Abraham Lincoln; From His Birth to His Inauguration as President* (Boston: James R. Osgood, 1872), 495.

86 *"Indeed I tremble"*: Thomas Jefferson, *Notes on the State of Virginia, with an Appendix*, 9th American ed. (Boston: H. Sprague, 1802), 224.

86 *"Those who deny freedom"*: CW, 3:376.

86 *"cold, calculating, unimpassioned reason"*: CW, 1:115.

87 *"When I do good"*: *Herndon's Lincoln*, 3:439.

87 *"Mr. Lincoln had not"*: quoted in Lamon, *The Life of Abraham Lincoln*, 492.

87 *book on infidelity*: Ibid., 493–94.

87 *"believed in predestination, foreordination"*: William H. Herndon, *The Hidden Lincoln: From the Letters and Papers of William H. Herndon*, ed. Emanuel Hertz (New York: Blue Ribbon Books, 1940), 167.

87 *"the Doctrine of Necessity"*: CW, 1:382.

88 *"Things were to be"*: Herndon, *The Hidden Lincoln*, 180.

88 *"smiled at my philosophy"*: Ibid., 408.

89 *"jealousy, envy, and avarice"*: CW, 1:114.

89 *"neither better, nor worse"*: Ibid., 2:230.

89 *"A house divided"*: Ibid., 2:461.

90 *"It is the eternal struggle"*: Ibid., 3:315.

90 *"I have a notion"*: Julia Taft Bayne, *Tad Lincoln's Father* (Lincoln: University of Nebraska Press, 2001), 76.

90 *"Every educated person"*: Ibid.

90 *"He reached forth"*: Elizabeth Keckley, *Behind the Scenes; or, Thirty Years a Slave, and Four Years in the White House* (New York: G. W. Carleton, 1868), 119.

91 *"In regard to this Great Book"*: CW, 7:542.

91 *"President Lincoln was deeply"*: William Osborn Stoddard, *Inside the White House in War Times: Memoirs and Reports of Lincoln's Secretary*, ed. Michael Burlingame (Lincoln: University of Nebraska Press, 2000), 176.

91 *"That he had an abiding"*: Ibid., 216.

91 *"our highest wisdom"*: CW, 6:39.

91 *"I have often wished"*: Ibid., 6:535–36.

92 *"There's a divinity"*: Herndon, *The Hidden Lincoln*, 142.

92 *"with the care of a great Nation"*: Justin G. Turner and Linda Levitt Turner, *Mary Todd Lincoln: Her Life and Letters* (New York: Fromm International, 1987), 567–68.

92 *"he kept up the habit"*: J. A. Reed, "Religious Sentiments of Abraham Lincoln," *Scribner's Monthly*, July 1873, 52.

92 *"Lincoln was a praying man"*: William Eleroy Curtis, *The True Abraham Lincoln* (Philadelphia: J. B. Lippincott, 1903), 385–86.

92 *"There is a good deal"*: Bayne, *Tad Lincoln's Father*, 76.

92 *"the most lovable boy"*: Ibid., 3.

92 *"This town is"*: Jean H. Baker, *Mary Todd Lincoln: A Biography* (New York: W. W. Norton, 1987), 218.

93 *"children literally ran over"*: Herndon, *The Hidden Lincoln*, 289.

93 *"and all the while"*: Allen Thorndike Rice, *Reminiscences of Abraham Lincoln by Distinguished Men of His Time* (New York: Harper, 1909), 346.

93 *"in Lincoln's hat"*: quoted in William Herndon to Jesse William Weik, February 18, 1887, Herndon-Weik Collection.

93 *"We were sitting in the office"*: Stevens, *A Reporter's Lincoln*, 193.

93 *"Get out of the way"*: Noah Brooks, "The Boy in the White House," *St. Nicholas: An Illustrated Magazine for Young Folks*, November 1882, 58.

93 *"It is my pleasure"*: *Herndon's Lincoln*, 3:512.

93 *After Willie died*: Donald, *Lincoln*, 336–37.

94 *"Reverently let us"*: Davis, *The Papers*, 7:51.

94 *"public humiliation"*: CW, 4:482.

94 *"the awful calamity"*: CW, 6:156.

96 *"into the most secret recesses"*: John Hay, *Addresses of John Hay* (New York: Century, 1906), 239.

96 *"The will of God prevails"*: CW, 5:403–04.

96 *"In telling this tale"*: Ibid., 6:535–36.

97 *"The purposes of the Almighty"*: Ibid., 7:535.

CHAPTER 6: PUBLIC SENTIMENT IS EVERYTHING

98 *"an act unparalleled"*: Carpenter, *Six Months at the White House*, 10–11.

99 *"look at and admire"*: Adams, *Letter from Washington*, 180.

99 The *"whole picture"*: William Roscoe Thayer, *John Hay: In Two Volumes* (Boston: Houghton Mifflin, 1915), 1:268.

99 *"the happy family"*: Henry J. Raymond, *Life, Public Services and State Papers of Abraham Lincoln* (New York: Darby and Miller Publishers, 1865), 763.

100 *"Well, wife"*: Carpenter, *Six Months at the White House*, 113.

100 *"the saddest man"*: *The Washington Herald*, July 17, 1921.

100 *"holding in his hand"*: Carpenter, *Six Months at the White House*, 234.

100 *"Abe read all the books"*: *Herndon's Informants*, 107.

101 *"Among my earliest recollections"*: Carpenter, *Six Months at the White House*, 312–13.

101 *"Don't shoot too high"*: *Herndon's Lincoln*, 2:325.

102 *"see the thing or idea"*: Herndon, *The Hidden Lincoln*, 132.

102 *"I catch the idea"*: Ibid., 95.

102 *"aroused . . . as he"*: CW, 4:67.

103 *"If you would win a man"*: Ibid., 1:273.

103 *"Our government rests"*: Ibid., 2:385.

103 *"In this and like communities"*: Ibid., 3:27.

104 *"Nothing would have more amazed him"*: Nicolay and Hay, *Abraham Lincoln*, 10:351.

104 *"I am loth to close"*: CW, 4:271

104 *"It presents to the whole family"*: Ibid., 4:426.

105 *"conceived in liberty"*: Ibid., 7:23.

105 *"sugar-coated"*: Carpenter, *Six Months at the White House*, 127.

106 *"Was there ever such a curious"*: Henry C. Whitney, *Life on the Circuit with Lincoln* (Boston: Estes and Lauriat, 1892), 126.

106 *"You cannot refine"*: Ralph Waldo Emerson, *The Heart of Emerson's Journals*, ed. Bliss Perry (Boston: Houghton Mifflin, 1926), 300. Also see Douglas L. Wilson, *Lincoln's Sword: The Presidency and the Power of Words* (Vintage Books, New York, 2006), 197. Wilson's classic analysis of Lincoln's writing was invaluable to me.

106 *"involved, coarse, colloquial"*: Burlingame, *Abraham Lincoln: A Life*, 63.

106 *"We pass over the silly remarks"*: *Clearfield* (Pennsylvania) *Republican*, December 2, 1864.

106 *"The Gettysburg ceremony was rendered"*: *The Times*, of London, December 4, 1863.

106 *"there are passages"*: Harriet Beecher Stowe, *Men of Our Times; or Leading Patriots of the Day* (Hartford: Hartford, 1868), 60.

107 *"some hideously bad rhetoric"*: Hay, *At Lincoln's Side*, 54.

107 *"Uncle Sam's web-feet"*: CW, 6:409.

107 *"as if the government"*: Burlingame, *Abraham Lincoln: A Life*, 563.

107 *"there are sentences"*: Strong, *Diary*, 355.

000 *"Fellow-citizens, we cannot"*: CW, 5:537.

107 *"The President is not generally"*: *The New York Tribune*, quoted in *The Daily Pittsburgh Gazette*, May 2, 1864.

107 *"something more than a boor"*: Goldwin Smith, "President Lincoln," *Macmillan's Magazine*, February 1865.

107 *"It is interesting and curious"*: Brooks, *Lincoln Observed*, 155.

108 *"You have a very trying"*: Arlin Turner, "Elizabeth Peabody Visits Lincoln, February, 1865," *New England Quarterly*, March 1975, 124.

108 *"But for the great practical"*: *The New York Times*, March 4, 1865.

109 *"not a new man"*: *The Pittsburgh Commercial*, March 4, 1865.

109 *"Mr. Lincoln commences"*: *The Cincinnati Enquirer*, March 6, 1865.

109 *"He is a most remarkable man"*: *The New York Herald*, March 4, 1865.

110 *"a public letter must"*: CW, 8:2.

110 *"anything requiring thought"*: Brooks, *Lincoln Observed*, 151.

111 *"He was a very deliberate"*: Paul M. Angle, ed., *A Portrait of Abraham Lincoln in Letters by His Oldest Son* (Chicago: Chicago Historical Society, 1968), 15.

111 *the printed version back*: Abraham Lincoln Papers, Image 10 of Series 3, General Correspondence.

CHAPTER 7: INDEFINABLE FASCINATION

112 *"booted, spurred, gauntlets"*: *The Daily Graphic*, New York, November 6, 1873.

113 *Dramatic Oil Company*: Booth, *Right or Wrong*, 97.

113 *"I would rather have my"*: Ernest C. Miller, *Booth in the Pennsylvania Oil Region* (Meadville, Pennsylvania: Crawford County Historical Society, 1987), 72.

113 *"I hardly know"*: Edwards, *The Lincoln Assassination*, 1156.

114 *"going to do something"*: Terry Alford, *Fortune's Fool: The Life of John Wilkes Booth* (New York: Oxford University Press, 2015), 249.

114 *"Booth was crazy for fame"*: *The Daily Graphic*, New York, November 6, 1873.

114 *"Apollo's own grace"*: *The New York World*, quoted in *The Louisville Daily Journal*, October 20, 1868.

114 *"one of the simplest"*: Alford, *Fortune's Fool*, 153.

114 *"a most winning, captivating"*: Edwards, *The Lincoln Assassination*, 848.

114 *"a marvelously clever and amusing"*: W. J. Ferguson, *I Saw Booth Shoot Lincoln* (Boston: Houghton Mifflin, 1930), 15.

114 *"little trotters"*: Asia Booth Clarke, *John Wilkes Booth: A Sister's Memoir*, ed. Terry Alford (Jackson: University Press of Mississippi, 1996), 18.

114 *"He lies on the floor"*: Ibid., 11.

114 *Joseph Hazelton*: Campbell MacCulloch, "This Man Saw Lincoln Shot," *Good Housekeeping*, February 1927.

115 *John Deery's billiards saloon*: Gordon Samples, *Lust for Fame: The Stage Career of John Wilkes Booth* (Jefferson, North Carolina: McFarland, 1982), 169.

115 *"the only non-utilitarian"*: Henry C. Whitney, "Abraham Lincoln: A Study

115 *"He frequently remarked"*: James W. Shettel, "J. Wilkes Booth at School," *New York Dramatic Mirror*, February 26, 1916.

115 *"Seldom has the stage"*: quoted in Booth, *Right or Wrong*, 6.

116 *"five-act tragedy"*: Joseph Francis Daly, *The Life of Augustin Daly* (New York: Macmillan, 1917), 19.

116 *"by far the greatest histrion"*: Whitman, *The Correspondence*, 3:376.

116 *"The words fire, energy"*: Whitman, *Complete Prose Works*, 428.

117 *"John has more of the"*: Clara Morris, *Life on the Stage: My Personal Experiences and Recollections* (New York: McClure, 1901), 103.

117 *"It is about as much"*: *New York Leader*, May 3, 1862.

117 *"lay rather in his romantic"*: Nicolay and Hay, *Abraham Lincoln*, 10:289.

117 *"Did not like him"*: Richard Cary to his wife, March 14, 1862, Richard Cary Letters.

117 *"In truth, he would not study"*: Shettel, "J. Wilkes Booth at School."

118 *"He was a brave"*: Clarke, *John Wilkes Booth*, 81.

118 *"Roman firmness"*: *The Brooklyn Daily Eagle*, November 3, 1859.

118 *"My brains are worth"*: Clarke, *John Wilkes Booth*, 82.

119 *"He was so young"*: Morris, *Life on the Stage*, 97.

119 *"many of his best qualities"*: *The National Republican*, November 9, 1863.

119 *"fine, expressive face"*: *The Evening Star*, November 3, 1863.

119 *"Rather tame than otherwise"*: Hay, *Inside Lincoln's White House*, 110.

119 *"round him like doves"*: Morris, *Life on the Stage*, 99.

120 *"a young man of remarkable"*: Julia Ward Howe, *Reminiscences, 1819–1899* (Boston: Houghton Mifflin, 1900), 242.

120 *piles of passionate letters*: Morris, *Life on the Stage*, 100.

120 *"strikingly handsome"*: Louise Catherine Wooster, *The Autobiography of a Magdalen* (Birmingham, Alabama: Birmingham, 1911), 3.

120 *"I was young, rather pretty"*: Ibid., 50–53.

120 *Henrietta Irving*: *The Daily Exchange*, Baltimore, May 10, 1861.

121 *"My Darling Baby"*: Edwards, *The Lincoln Assassination*, 156.

121 *"He was a welcome guest"*: Clarke, *John Wilkes Booth*, 85.

121 *"well-looking elderly"*: John Hay, *Lincoln's Journalist: John Hay's Anonymous Writings for the Press, 1860–1864*, ed. Michael Burlingame (Carbondale: Southern Illinois University Press, 1998), 115.

121 *"To all human seeming"*: New Hampshire General Court, Committee on Hale Statue, *The Statue of John P. Hale Erected in Front of the Capitol and Presented to the State of New Hampshire by William E. Chandler* (Concord, New Hampshire: Republican Press Association, 1892), 154.

122 *Hale's "moral heroism"*: Ibid., 138.

122 *"[T]here is a mysterious"*: Traubel, *With Walt Whitman in Camden*, 5:454–55.

122 *"real live Democratic Party"*: Walt Whitman to John P. Hale, August 14, 1852, Whitman, *The Correspondence*, 1:39.

123 *"I invite him"*: *The Statue of John P. Hale*, 52.

123 *set upon by a drunk*: *The Chicago Tribune*, August 30, 1861.

123 *"ceaseless and merciless attacks"*: Hay, *Lincoln's Journalist*, 184.

123 *"This loud-mouthed paragon"*: GWD, 1:489.

124 *"Although it was a"*: John P. Hale letter to wife, Lucy, October 9, 1863, John Parker Hale Papers.

124 *"I do not believe"*: Ibid., December 8, 1863.

124 *"An unusually large number"*: *The Burlington* (Vermont) *Weekly Sentinel*, February 21, 1862.

125 *When not attending parties*: Richard Morcom, "They All Loved Lucy," *American Heritage*, October 1970.

125 *"Among the ladies present"*: *The Evening Star*, January 27, 1864.

125 *"a slightly jealous disposition"*: Oliver Wendell Holmes Jr. to Lucy Hale, April 24, 1858, John Parker Hale Papers.

125 *"How many young gentlemen"*: Ibid., April 30, 1858.

126 *"the kind tone"*: Ibid., William Kemp to Lucy Hale, December 2, 1860.

126 *"charming privilege"*: Ibid., E. P. Turner to Lucy Hale, December 14, 1862.

126 *"I am passionately fond"*: Ibid., Captain Clayton MacMichael to Lucy Hale, November 23, 1864.

126 *"there were anyone else"*: Ibid., John Hay to Lucy Hale, August 9, 1869.

127 *An 1878 newspaper article*: *Chicago Inter-Ocean*, June 18, 1878.

127 *fragrant bouquets*: Blaine Houmes, "Robert Todd Lincoln, John Wilkes Booth, & Lucy Lambert Hale," *Manuscripts*, Winter 2007.

127 *On Valentine's Day, 1862*: "A Stranger" to Lucy Hale, John Parker Hale Papers.

128 *"every now and then using"*: Clarke, *John Wilkes Booth*, 86.

128 *"was very intimate"*: *Springfield* (Massachusetts) *Republican*, quoted in *The Brooklyn Daily Eagle*, May 5, 1865.

128 *"Last evening, the ladies"*: Lucy Hale to her mother, January 1, 1864, John Parker Hale Papers.

128 *"resulted in a secret"*: Clarke, *John Wilkes Booth*, 85.

128 *"there were two young women"*: *The San Francisco Chronicle*, July 30, 1882.

129 *That spring, while visiting*: Edwards, *The Lincoln Assassination*, 345–346.

129 *"that he was in love"*: Ibid., 182.

129 *"The secret you have"*: Booth, *Right or Wrong*, 136.

129 *requested from John Nicolay*: John P. Hale to John G. Nicolay, Thursday, March 2, 1865, Abraham Lincoln Papers, Series 2, General Correspondence, 1858–64.

129 *"He . . . meditated seizing"*: *The Daily Graphic*, New York, November 6, 1873.

129 *"It was the day"*: Ibid.

CHAPTER 8: THE BLIGHTING PESTILENCE

130 *"although far removed"*: Letitia M. Burwell, *A Girl's Life in Virginia before the War* (New York: Frederick A. Stokes, 1895), 154.

130 *Dabney, who had graduated first*: William H. Dabney, *Sketch of the Dabneys of Virginia, with Some of Their Family Records* (Chicago: S. D. Childs, 1888), 110–11.

130 *"the Adonis of the staff"*: Emory M. Thomas, *Bold Dragoon: The Life of J. E. B. Stuart* (Norman: University of Oklahoma Press, 1988), 91.

131 *"They may succeed"*: Stout, *Upon the Altar of the Nation*, 431.

131 *"like a dream or a nightmare"*: Emma Holmes, *The Diary of Miss Emma Holmes, 1861–1866*, ed. John F. Marszalek (Baton Rouge: Louisiana State University Press, 1979), 398–412.

132 *"Thousands of people"*: William T. Sherman, *Sherman's Civil War: Selected Correspondence of William T. Sherman, 1860–1865*, eds. Brooks D. Simpson and Jean V. Berlin (Chapel Hill: University of North Carolina Press, 1999), 853.

132 *"Our march over the country"*: Dexter Horton, "Diary of an Officer in Sherman's Army Marching Through the Carolinas," *Journal of Southern History*, May 1943, 248.

132 *"This ended the passing"*: Dolly Lunt Burge, *The Diary of Dolly Lunt Burge, 1848–1979*, ed. Christine Jacobson Carter (Athens, University of Georgia Press, 1997), 163.

132 *"If the people raise a howl"*: Sherman, *Sherman's Civil War*, 697.

133 *"the bravest and best"*: Joseph T. Glatthaar, *The March to the Sea and Beyond: Sherman's Troops in the Savannah and Carolinas Campaign* (Baton Rouge: Louisiana State University Press, 1997), 15.

133 *"car windows were smashed"*: Committee from South Carolina State Division, U.D.C. *South Carolina Women in the Confederacy* (Columbia, South Carolina: State, 1903), 2:182.

133 *"right and left"*: Rod Gragg, *The Illustrated Confederate Reader* (New York: Harper & Row, 1989), 189–90.

133 *"If I saw any rebels"*: Jacqueline Glass Campbell, *When Sherman Marched North from the Sea: Resistance on the Confederate Home Front* (Chapel Hill: University of North Carolina Press, 2003), 64.

133 *"a synonym for all"*: Emma Florence LeConte, *A Journal, Kept by Emma Florence LeConte, from Dec. 31, 1864, to Aug. 6, 1865* (Durham: University of North Carolina, 1998), 46–47.

133 *"I wonder if the vengeance"*: Ibid., 42.

133 *"The fiends acted"*: *The Fairfield Courier*, Winnsboro, South Carolina, March 23, 1865.

134 *"It is not an unwillingness"*: U.S. War Department, *The War of the Rebellion*, ser. 1, vol. 44, 906.

134 *"The state of despondency"*: Ibid., ser. 1, Vol.47, pt. 2, 1270.

134 *"With General Lee"*: Campbell, *When Sherman Marched*, 73.

134 *"I fired volley after volley"*: Holmes, *The Diary*, 402.

135 *"If all the men who had taken"*: Ibid., 407.

135 *"a manufacturing center"*: Alexander G. Downing, *Downing's Civil War Diary: August 15, 1861–July 31, 1865*, ed. Olynthus B. Clark (Des Moines, Iowa: Homstead Printing, 1916), 258.

136 *"His dress is as unassuming"*: Glatthaar, *The March*, 16.

136 *"you se him"*: Ibid.

136 *"He stood by me"*: J. Grant Wilson, "Lieutenant General Grant," *Hours at Home*, June 1866, 179.

136 *"Oh! no, master"*: William T. Sherman, *Memoirs of General William T. Sherman* (New York: D. Appleton, 1875), 2:290.

137 *"money, silver, gold"*: Henry D. Jenkins, in *Slave Narratives: A Folk History of Slavery in the United States from Interviews with Former Slaves, Vol. 14: South Carolina Narratives, pt. 3.* (Washington, D.C.: Federal Writers Project for the Library of Congress, 1941).

137 *"I want the foragers"*: U.S. War Department, *The War of the Rebellion*, ser. 1, vol. 47, pt. 2, 537.

137 *"South Carolina has commenced"*: Campbell, *When Sherman Marched*, 35.

137 *"an old negro woman"*: Ibid., 66

137 *"the robbing of some negroes"*: U.S. War Department, *The War of the Rebellion*, ser. 1, vol. 47, pt. 2, 33.

137 *"nothing but these damn"*: Campbell, *When Sherman Marched*, 46.

138 *"We could not resist"*: Samuel H. Hurst, *Journal-History of the Seventy-Third Ohio Volunteer Infantry* (Chillicothe: S.H. Hurst, 1866), 156.

138 *"I like niggers"*: Sherman, *Sherman's Civil War*, 727.

138 *"All ages, sizes"*: David P. Conyngham, *Sherman's March Through the South* (New York: Sheldon, 1865), 344.

138 *"We must go"*: Glatthaar, *The March*, 61.

139 *"so wet that we all"*: Sherman, *Memoirs*, 2:291.

139 *"his implacable hatred"*: Burke Davis, *Sherman's March: The First Full-Length Narrative of General William T. Sherman's Devastating March Through Georgia and the Carolinas* (New York: Vintage, 1988), 203.

139 *"amiable and respected citizen"*: William Babcock Hazen, *A Narrative of Military Service* (Boston: Ticknor, 1885), 357–58.

140 *"FIRST GUN FIRED"*: Davis, *Sherman's March*, 203.

141 *"Old honest Abe"*: Glatthaar, *The March*, 51.

141 *"This is the day"*: Jenkin Lloyd Jones, *An Artilleryman's Diary* (Maidson: Wisconsin History Commission: Democrat Printing, 1914), 309.

141 *"The explosion shattered"*: Adeline Godfrey Merrill, *Sherman in Cheraw and the Aftermath* (Privately printed, 2009), 29.

141 *One woman recalled*: Larry E. Nelson, *Sherman's March Through the Upper Pee Dee Region of South Carolina* (Florence, South Carolina: Pee Dee Heritage Center, 2001), 49.

141 *"Those five days"*: Merrill, *Sherman in Cheraw*, 35.

141 *"Nothing left but ashes"*: Ibid., 25.

142 *Many years later, she told*: Ibid., 33.

142 *"the barbarities inflicted"*: Jefferson Davis, *The Rise and Fall of the Confederate Government*, 2 vols. (New York: D. Appleton, 1912), 2:710–17.

142 *Dr. Bachman was an*: Peter McCandless, "The Political Evolution of John Bachman: From New York Yankee to South Carolina Secessionist," *South Carolina Historical Magazine*, January 2007.

143 *"That the negro will remain"*: John Bachman, "Types of Mankind," *The Charleston Medical Journal and Review*, September 1854, 657.

143 *"enable us to protect & bless"*: Debra Lindsay, *Maria Martin's World: Art and Science, Faith and Family in Audubon's America* (Tuscaloosa, Alabama: The University of Alabama Press, 2018), 201–202.

144 *"A lady of delicacy and refinement"*: Davis, *The Rise and Fall*, 2:710.

144 *"cut open the trunks"*: Ibid., 2:712.

145 *"Vast clouds of"*: Elijah Pierce Burton, *Diary of E. P. Burton, Surgeon, 7th Reg. Illinois, 3rd Brig., 2nd Div. 16 A.C.* (Des Moines, Iowa: Historical Records Survey, 1939), 67.

145 *"a crow could not"*: Military Order of the Loyal Legion of the United States, Wisconsin Commandery, *War Papers* (Milwaukee: Burdick, Armitage & Allen, 1903), 3:384.

146 *"Dead horses all along"*: Nelson, *Sherman's March*, 37.

146 *"The thousands of homes"*: George W. Pepper, *Personal Recollections of Sherman's Campaigns in Georgia and the Carolinas* (Zanesville, Ohio: Hugh Dunne, 1866), 330.

146 *"What would you do"*: CW, 5:346.

147 *"To save the country"*: John Fabian Witt, *Lincoln's Code: The Laws of War in American History* (New York: Free Press, 2012), 4.

147 *"Enroute from the pens"*: *The Wheeling* (West Virginia) *Intelligencer*, March 4, 1865.

147 *"allowed, as have thousands"*: *Spirit of the Times*, Batavia, New York, March 4, 1865.

148 *"dirty, filled with vermin,"*: U.S. War Department, *The War of the Rebellion*, ser. 1, vol. 46, pt. 2, 1151.

148 "cold-blooded policy": *The New York Times*, December 27, 1864.

149 *"We cannot spare one"*: Booth, *Right or Wrong*, 12.

149 *Booth had met with Confederate*: Ibid., 119.

CHAPTER 9: THERE WAS MURDER IN THE AIR

150 *"The dawn came slowly"*: Adams, *Letter from Washington*, 242.

150 *"The wind howled viciously"*: *The New York Herald*, March 6, 1865

150 *"Such a wet, dirty"*: *The Delawarean*, Dover, Delaware, March 11, 1865.

151 *"mud, (and such mud!)"*: *The New York Times*, March 12, 1865.

151 *"but it was found"*: *The Evening Star*, March 4, 1865.

151 *"a vile yellow fluid"*: *The New York Herald*, March 6, 1865.

151 *"the triumph of their race"*: *The Times*, of London, March 20, 1865.

152 *"Now, what do I see"*: *Newcastle Courant*, Newcastle upon Tyne, England, March 10, 1865.

153 *"It is a long time since we"*: *The Bedford* (Pennsylvania) *Inquirer*, March 10, 1865.

153 *"and the ribbons waved"*: *The New York Herald*, March 6, 1865.

153 *"mammoth or miniature"*: *The Evening Star*, March 4, 1865.

153 *"his dear little face"*: Lee, *Wartime Washington*, 479–80.

155 *"The mingled noises"*: *The Bedford* (Pennsylvania) *Inquirer*, March 10, 1865.

156 *"crowd almost innumerable"*: SCC, Virgil Connor to his mother, March 6, 1865.

156 *"It was a play of Hamlet"*: *The New York Herald*, March 5, 1865.

157 *"deluged the country"*: *The Chicago Copperhead Convention: The Treasonable and Revolutionary Utterances of the Men Who Composed It* (Washington, D.C.: Congressional Union Committee, 1864), 7.

157 *"the infamous orders of"*: Ibid., 11.

157 *"The people will soon rise"*: *The Buffalo Morning Express*, October 10, 1864.

157 *"The man who votes"*: *La Crosse* (Wisconsin) *Democrat*, August 23, 1864.

157 *"fully one-third"*: *The Times*, of London, March 20, 1865.

157 *"vulgar, uncouth animal"*: Holmes, *The Diary*, 382.

158 *"to cause the lives"*: *Selma* (Alabama) *Morning Dispatch*, December 1, 1864.

158 *"There was no enthusiasm"*: Lydia Maria Child, *Letters of Lydia Maria Child, with a Biographical Introduction* (Boston: Houghton Mifflin, 1883), 183.

158 *"the heaviest calamity"*: *Illinois State Register*, Springfield, November 10, 1864.

158 *"All for the"*: *The Grand Haven* (Michigan) *News*, September 21, 1864, and *Argus and Patriot*, Montpelier, Vermont, March 30, 1865.

159 *"Fight for the"*: *The Philadelphia Sunday Mercury*, quoted in the *Weekly State Journal*, Raleigh, North Carolina, March 11, 1863.

159 *"The thick tufts"*: L. Seaman, *What Miscegenation Is! And What We Are to Expect Now That Mr. Lincoln Is Re-elected* (New York: Waller & Willets, 1864), 4–8.

160 *"I felt then that there was murder"*: Rice, *Reminiscences*, 320.

160 *"milky bulging dome"*: *The New York Times*, March 12, 1865.

160 *"he was gruff and moody"*: *The Philadelphia Inquirer*, April 18, 1865.

161 *"Well, even if true"*: Carpenter, *Six Months at the White House*, 62–63.

161 *"his mail was infested"*: Nicolay and Hay, *Abraham Lincoln*, 10:284–88.

161 *"In that place"*: Forney, *Anecdotes*, 2:425.

161 *One tourist from Dubuque*: GWD, 1:528.

162 *Lincoln wandered out*: William A. Croffut, *Now I Recollect—Souvenirs of the Sanctum: Lincoln as I Saw Him* (Washington, D.C.: Colonial Press, 1943), 6.

162 *"To-night, as you have"*: Lamon, *Recollections*, 274–75.

162 *"He believed that if anybody"*: Crook, *Memories*, 20–21.

162 *"furnish no ground"*: Bigelow, *Retrospections*, 1:505.

163 *"he and Mrs. Lincoln couldn't"*: Carpenter, *Six Months at the White House*, 67.

163 *"Often did I see"*: Harry M. Kieffer, *The Recollections of a Drummer-Boy* (Boston: James R. Osgood, 1883), 56.

163 *"I see the President"*: *The New York Times*, August 16, 1863.

164 *"The reb cavalry"*: Walt Whitman to John P. Hale, August 14, 1852, 1:111–14.

164 *"To my unsophisticated judgment"*: Brooks, *Lincoln Observed*, 57.

164 *"jogging along"*: Lamon, *Recollections*, 267.

165 *"The shot had been fired"*: *The New York Times*, April 6, 1887.

CHAPTER 10: A FUTURE WITH HOPE IN IT

166 *"The ladies giggled"*: *The New York Herald*, March 6, 1865.

167 *"heard the sound of"*: Harriet Beecher Stowe, "A Reply," *Atlantic Monthly*, January 1863.

168 *"I have no purpose"*: CW, 4:250.

168 *"The Yankee soldiers"*: Washington, *They Knew Lincoln*, 117.

169 *"the noble framers"*: Booth, *Right or Wrong*, 147.

169 *"If God's design"*: Adams, *Letter from Washington*, 38.

170 The *"whispered" rumor*: Frederick Douglass, *Narrative of the Life of Frederick Douglass, An American Slave, Written By Himself* (Dublin: Webb and Chapman, 1845), 2.

170 *"seem to think themselves"*: Mary Chesnut, *Mary Chesnut's Civil War*, ed. C. Vann Woodward (New Haven: Yale Universal Press, 1981), li.

170 *"the patriarchs of old"*: Ibid., 29.

170 *"The man must be a"*: Jefferson, *Notes*, 223.

170 *"supposed one human being"*: Douglass, *Narrative*, 37.

171 *"first decidedly antislavery"*: Frederick Douglass, *My Bondage and My Freedom* (New York: Miller, Orton & Mulligan, 1855), 146.

171 *"Every opportunity I got"*: Douglass, *Narrative*, 39.

171 *"The thought of only being"*: Douglass, *My Bondage*, 273.

171 *"I felt assured that if"*: Douglass, *Narrative*, 107.

171 *"the magnetism and melody"*: *The Christian Recorder*, Philadelphia, January 18, 1862.

172 *"stood there like an"*: Douglass, Helen, *In Memoriam: Frederick Douglass* (Philadelphia: John C. Yorston, 1897), 44.

172 *"He stands erect"*: Douglass, Frederick, *The Life and Writings*, ed. Philip S. Foner (New York: International, 1950), 1:130.

172 *"We wish that everyone"*: *The New York Tribune*, June 10, 1845.

172 *"Frederick is a strong man"*: *The Practical Christian*, Hopedale, Massachusetts, May 31, 1845.

172 *Communion wine*: Douglass, *Selected Speeches and Writings*, 3.

173 *"While we are here"*: *The Liberator*, Boston, May 26, 1848.

174 *"Fred Douglass for his"*: CW, 3:10.

174 *"I have reason to recollect"*: Ibid., 3:55–56.

174 *"a blot upon"*: Ibid., 8:83.

174 *"I do not question"*: Ibid., 3:10.

175 *"I am not nor ever"*: Ibid., 3:145–46.

175 *"What I would most desire"*: Ibid., 2:521.

176 *"You and we are different races"*: Ibid., 5:371–75.

176 *"an itinerant Colonization lecturer"*: Douglass, *Selected Speeches and Writings*, 511.

177 *"Ohio will be overrun"*: Donald, *Lincoln*, 417.

178 *"It is my last card"*: quoted in Robert C. Winthrop Jr., *A Memoir of Robert C. Winthrop* (Boston: Little, Brown, 1897), 229.

178 *"a measure by which"*: *The Weekly Advertiser*, Montgomery, Alabama, January 21, 1863.

178 *"serious offense"*: Douglass, *The Life and Times*, 423.

179 *"There is no time for delay"*: *Douglass Monthly*, March 1863.

179 *"the stairway was crowded"*: *Proceedings of the American Anti-Slavery Society, and Its Third Decade, Held in the City of Philadelphia, Dec. 3d and 4th, 1863* (New York: American Anti-Slavery Society, 1864), 116–18.

180 *"had larger motives"*: Douglass, *The Life and Times*, 423.

180 *"We had to make some concessions"*: Dorus M. Fox, *History of Political Parties, National Reminiscences, and the Tippecanoe Movement* (Des Moines, Iowa: Col. Dorus M. Fox, 1895), 229.

180 *"Shall colored men enlist"*: *Douglass Monthly*, March 1863.

180 *"noble little"*: Masur, *The Real War*, 154.

181 *"Men fell all around"*: Lewis Henry Douglass to Helen Amelia Loguen, July 20, 1863, Carter G. Woodson Papers.

181 *"No quarter!"*: *The New York Times*, May 6, 1864.

181 *"The slaughter was awful"*: Achilles V. Clark, "A Letter of Account," *Civil War Times Illustrated*, June 1985, 24–25.

181 *"Some officers undertook"*: Adams, *Letter from Washington*, 149.

182 *"The problem is solved"*: Frank Moore, ed., *The Rebellion Record: A Diary of American Events* (New York: D. Van Nostrand, 1868), 11:580.

182 *"The dimmed light"*: Douglass, *The Frederick Douglass Papers*, 4:542.

182 *"a band of scouts"*: Douglass, *The Life and Times*, 435.

182 *"He saw the danger"*: Ibid.

182 *"He thought that now was"*: Frederick Douglass to Theodore Tilton, October 15, 1864, Tilton Papers.

182 *"What he said on this day"*: Douglass, *The Life and Times*, 435.

183 *After visiting Lincoln, Douglass*: Frederick Douglass to Theodore Tilton, October 15, 1864, Tilton Papers.

183 *"Lincoln seemed tardy, cold"*: Douglass, *Selected Speeches and Writings*, 621.

183 *Soldiers' Home*: Douglass, *The Life and Times*, 437.

183 *"I am not doing much"*: Frederick Douglass to Theodore Tilton, October 15, 1864, Tilton Papers.

184 *"Slavery is not abolished"*: Douglass, *The Frederick Douglass Papers*, 4:578.

185 *"the day may not be"*: Adams, *Letter from Washington*, 234.

185 *"with silent tongue"*: CW, 6:410.

185 *"sloughed off"*: Hay, *Inside Lincoln's White House*, 217.

185 *"I would myself prefer"*: CW, 8:403.

185 *Confederate House*: *The New York Herald*, March 4, 1865.

185 *"spare nothing"*: Sherman, *Memoirs*, 2:185.

185 *"The day you make"*: Howell Cobb, "Documents," *The American Historical Review*, October 1895, 97.

186 *"their business, not mine"*: CW, 8:361.

186 *"What we now want"*: Douglass, *Selected Speeches and Writings*, 562.

CHAPTER 11: ANDY AIN'T A DRUNKARD

187 *"talismanic pass"*: *The Evening Star*, March 4, 1865; *The Chicago Tribune*, March 6, 1865.

187 *"oratorical captain"*: *The New York Herald*, March 6, 1865.

187 *"such a crowd"*: John H. Clifford to Sarah Clifford, March 4, 1865, Clifford Family Papers.

187 *"If Old Abe don't arrive"*: *The New York Herald*, March 6, 1865.

188 *"flocks of women streamed"*: Brooks, *Mr. Lincoln's Washington*, 419.

188 *"The mud in the city of Washington"*: Brooks, *Washington, D.C., in Lincoln's Time*, 210.

188 *"grand national display"*: *The New York Herald*, March 6, 1865.

189 *"I pushed with some"*: Chambrun, *Impressions*, 35.

189 *"There was great want"*: GWD, 2:251.

189 *"heartless ruffians"*: General Assembly of the State of Kentucky, *Biographical Sketch of the Hon. Lazarus W. Powell (of Henderson, Kentucky), Governor of the State of Kentucky from 1851 to 1855 and a Senator in Congress from 1859 to 1865* (Frankfort, Kentucky: S.I.M Major, Printer, 1868), 80.

189 *"The rush and scramble"*: *The Chicago Tribune*, March 6, 1865.

190 *"Their elegant costumes"*: *The New York Herald*, March 6, 1865.

190 *"the gorgeous hues"*: *The Caledonian*, Saint Johnsbury, Vermont, March 10, 1865.

190 *"greatly discomfited to find"*: Brooks, *Washington, D.C., in Lincoln's Time*, 210.

190 *Another reporter observed*: *The New York Herald*, March 6, 1865.

190 *"The gay people in the galleries"*: Brooks, *Washington, D.C., in Lincoln's Time*, 210.

191 *"handsome, rosy, and gorgeous"*: Ibid.

191 *"Of course it was"*: CW, 6:78–79.

191 *"a place no self-respecting"*: Charles Francis Adams, *Charles Francis Adams, 1835–1915: An Autobiography*, ed. Massachusetts Historical Society (Boston: Houghton Mifflin, 1916), 161.

191 *"brilliant in gold lace"*: Brooks, *Washington, D.C., in Lincoln's Time*, 211.

192 *"looking very young"*: Ibid.

192 *"every inch like a judge"*: *The Times*, of London, March 20, 1865.

192 *"engaged in a lively battle"*: *Herndon's Informants*, 731–32.

193 *"but for the extraordinary"*: Harry E. Pratt, "David Davis, 1815–1886," PhD diss. (University of Illinois, 1930), 82.

193 *"If Judge Davis, with his tact"*: *Herndon's Lincoln*, 3:503.

193 *"Lincoln was a peculiar"*: *Herndon's Informants*, 346.

193 *"We go hence"*: *The National Republican*, March 7, 1865.

194 *"gorgeous array of foreign ministers"*: Brooks, *Washington, D.C., in Lincoln's Time*, 211.

194 *"massive crinoline"*: *The New York Herald*, March 6, 1865.

194 *"Mr. Edward De Stoeckl"*: Ibid.

194 *"nullity"*: John George Nicolay, *An Oral History of Abraham Lincoln: John G. Nicolay's Interviews and Essays*, ed. Michael Burlingame (Carbondale: Southern Illinois University Press, 2006), 68.

195 *"[Lincoln's] treatment of me"*: Ibid.

195 *"slow and unsatisfactory"*: Harry Draper Hunt, *Hannibal Hamlin of Maine, Lincoln's First Vice-President* (Syracuse, New York: Syracuse University Press, 1969), 155.

195 *"was craftily and rigidly"*: Brooks, *Washington, D.C., in Lincoln's Time*, 151.

195 *John Nicolay assured*: Hamlin, *The Life and Times*, 471.

195 *Lincoln "leaned forward"*: McClure, *Abraham Lincoln*, 439.

195 *"I was with the President"*: Johnson, *The Papers*, 6:730.

195 *"perfect accord of feeling"*: Ibid., 6:731.

196 *"ask favor of the Administration"*: Hunt, *Hannibal Hamlin*, 194.

196 *expressing his "high regard"*: Johnson, *The Papers*, 7:498.

196 *"In one of the darkest"*: Ibid., 7:498–99.

196 *"I have the honor"*: Ibid., 7:497.

197 *"I need all the strength"*: Albert Castel, *The Presidency of Andrew Johnson* (Lawrence: Regents Press of Kansas, 1979), 9.

197 *"The warmth of the"*: Brooks, *Washington, D.C., in Lincoln's Time*, 237.

197 *"I'm a-goin' for"*: Castel, *The Presidency*, 10–11.

197 *Johnson pointed accusingly*: The New York Herald, March 6, 1865.

198 *"a rambling and strange"*: GWD, 2:252.

198 *"The vice president's friend Forney"*: The Indianapolis Star, March 10, 1865.

198 *"No one thinks"*: The Times, of London, March 20, 1865.

198 *"Is he crazy, or what"*: The New York Herald, March 6, 1865.

199 *"The crowd began to buzz"*: Ibid.

199 *"acquired the wretched"*: Chambrun, *Impressions*, 36.

199 *"I was never so mortified"*: Zachariah Chandler to his wife, March 6, 1865, Zachariah Chandler Papers.

199 *"the new Vice president"*: John H. Clifford to Sarah Clifford, March 4, 1865, Clifford Family Papers.

199 *"The sound of a harsh, shrill voice"*: The New York Herald, March 6, 1865.

200 *"slobbered the Holy Book"*: The Evening Telegraph (Philadelphia), December 1, 1866.

201 *"But the subject is really"*: The Cincinnati Commercial, quoted in The Detroit Free Press, March 11, 1865.

201 *"in great haste"*: Weichmann, *A True History*, 91.

202 *"Don't let Johnson speak"*: John B. Henderson, "Emancipation and Impeachment," *Century Illustrated Monthly Magazine*, December 1912, 198.

202 *"I have known Andy"*: Hugh McCulloch, "Memories of Some Contemporaries," *Scribner's Magazine*, September 1888, 292.

CHAPTER 12: AN EXCELLENT CHANCE TO KILL THE PRESIDENT

203 *Five years earlier*: BBF, 326.

203 *"a very brilliant affair"*: Ibid., 465.

203 *"all the aid"*: Ibid., 466.

204 *"The hopes of the crowd"*: Wisconsin State Journal, reported in *Appleton* (Wisconsin) *Motor*, March 16, 1865.

204 *"poor devil"*: BBF, 24.

205 *"She is evidently a smart"*: Ibid., 375.

205 *"Republican Queen"*: Benjamin B. French to Henry F. French, October 13, 1861, Benjamin B. French Family Papers.

205 *First Lady wildly overspent*: BBF, 382.

206　*"a few brief"*: BBF, 435–37.

206　*visited Gardner's studio*: Ibid., 441.

207　*"It is unique"*: Proceedings of the Massachusetts Historical Society, 1866–1867 (Boston: Wiggin and Lunt, 1867), 353–55.

207　*But they got caught*: Cleveland Morning Leader, March 9, 1865.

208　*"Every one was left"*: The Times, of London, March 20, 1865.

208　*"when he began to wrangle"*: Benjamin B. French to Francis O. French, April 24, 1865, Benjamin B. French Family Papers.

209　*"A tragedy was planned"*: Lamon, *Recollections*, 271.

209　*John Plants*: Weichmann, *A True History*, 90.

209　*Charles J. Cleary*: Ibid., 90–91.

209　*William J. Belshan*: Ibid., 93.

209　*"phenomenal audacity"*: Lamon, *Recollections*, 273.

210　*"The appearance of the tall form"*: The Bedford (Pennsylvania) *Inquirer*, March 10, 1865.

210　*"thunder of shouts"*: Chambrun, *Impressions*, 38–39.

211　*"sea of heads"*: Brooks, *Lincoln Observed*, 167.

211　*"with a monitory finger"*: The New York Herald, March 6, 1865.

211　*French had been there*: BBF, 129–31.

211　*"Did anybody ever see"*: Edward Wagenknect, *Nathaniel Hawthorne: Man and Writer* (New York: Oxford University Press, 1961), 135.

211　*"a nasty, lousy dungeon"*: Whitman, *The Correspondence*, 1:77–78.

212　*Charles Sperry*: Corey S. Retter, *1861–1865 Union Executions* (Raleigh, North Carolina: Lulu Press, 2016), 185–86.

212　*"The Sleeping Sentinel"*: The Rutland (Vermont) *Weekly Herald*, March 5, 1863.

212　*William Scott of Groton*: Vermont Historical Society, "William Scott Letters." Accessed September 30, 2018. (www.vermonthistory.org/research/research-resources-online/civil-war-transcriptions/william-the-sleeping-sentinel-scott-letters).

213　*"Thousands of colored folk"*: Chambrun, *Impressions*, 39.

213　*"I think there were"*: Nicolay, *With Lincoln in the White House*, 175.

214　*"Ladies, senators, negroes"*: The New York Herald, March 6, 1865.

214　*"Whilst Mr. L was speaking"*: Lee, *Wartime Washington*, 479.

215　*"to convey the idea"*: Albert Boine, *A Social History of Modern Art: Art in the Age of Counterrevolution, 1815–1848* (Chicago: University of Chicago Press, 2004), 527.

215　*"I avoid a black man"*: Horatio Greenough, *The Travels, Observations, and Experience of a Yankee Stonecutter* (1852, Gainesville, Florida: Scholars' Facsimiles & Reprints, 1958), 74–75.

216 *"to establish on earth"*: John L. O'Sullivan, "The Great Nation of Futurity," *United States Democratic Review*, November 1839, 426–30.

216 *"Shall we expect some"*: CW, 1:109.

217 *"Our heavenly neighbor"*: *The New York Times*, March 12, 1865.

218 *"The United States themselves"*: *Leaves of Grass* (1855), introduction, The Walt Whitman Archive.

218 *"bitter contempt"*: Douglass, *The Life and Times*, 442–43.

219 *"What an excellent chance"*: Pittman, *The Assassination*, 45.

219 *"what good it would do"*: Edwards, *The Lincoln Assassination*, 345.

CHAPTER 13: WITH MALICE TOWARD NONE

220 *"shambling, loose, irregular"*: Russell, *My Diary*, 37.

220 *"A marble placed"*: William H. Herndon, "An Analysis of the Character of Abraham Lincoln," *Abraham Lincoln Quarterly*, September 1941, 358.

220 *"smiled to himself"*: *The New York Herald*, March 6, 1865.

220 *George T. Brown*: United States Senate Historical Office, "George T. Brown, Sergeant At Arms, 1861–1869." Accessed September 30, 2018. (www.senate.gov/artandhistory/history/common/generic/SAA_George_Brown.htm).

221 *"as cunning as a fox"*: Horace White, *The Life of Lyman Trumbull* (Boston: Houghton Mifflin, 1913), 428.

221 *"historic Brown"*: Brooks, *Washington, D.C., in Lincoln's Time*, 238–41.

222 *"The sun shone out"*: John H. Clifford to Sarah Clifford, March 4, 1865, Clifford Family Papers.

222 *"clouds were rolled"*: *The National Republican*, March 4, 1865.

222 *"Did you notice that"*: Brooks, "Personal," March 1878, 678.

222 *"like whirling demons"*: *The New York Times*, March 12, 1865.

222 *published lithographs*: *Harper's Weekly*, March 18, 1865, 168–69.

223 *"Doug must have"*: *The Cincinnati Commercial*, March 11, 1861.

224 *"His voice was singularly"*: Robert W. McBride, *Lincoln's Body Guard, the Union Light Guard of Ohio: With Some Personal Recollections of Abraham Lincoln* (Indianapolis, Indiana: Edward J. Hecker, 1911), 29–30.

224 *"Fellow countrymen"*: CW, 8:332–33.

225 *The pledge disgusted Frederick*: Douglass, *Selected Speeches and Writings*, 433–36.

225 *"We are not enemies"*: CW, 4:271.

227 *"The whole proceeding"*: Douglass, *The Life and Times*, 441.

228 *"Your purpose, then"*: CW, 3:543. Also see Lucas E. Morel, *Lincoln's Sacred Effort: Defining Religion's Role in America's Self-Government* (Lanham, Maryland: Lexington Books, 2000), 173. I found Morel's keen insights into Lincoln and religion helpful, especially pages 163–210.

228 *"I think I have no"*: Ibid., 2:255.

229 *"You consider yourselves"*: Ibid., 3:535–36.

230 *"except the Lord"*: *The National Gazette*, Philadelphia, March 7, 1825.

231 *"the whole guilt of"*: *The Liberator*, Boston, April 28, 1865.

231 *"We cherish the institution"*: R.L. Stanton, *The Church and the Rebellion: A Consideration of the Rebellion Against the Government of the United States; and the Agency of the Church, North and South, in Relation Thereto* (New York: Derby & Miller, 1864), 458.

231 *"The American nation"*: B. M. Palmer, *National Responsibility before God* (New Orleans: Price-Current Steam Book and Job Printing, 1861), 13.

232 *"a cruel, unjust, and wicked"*: John B. Adger, "Northern and Southern Views of the Province of the Church," *Southern Presbyterian Review*, March 1866, 398.

233 *"vast iron machine"*: William Herndon to Jesse William Weik, February 25, 1887, Herndon-Weik Collection.

235 *"Fellow-citizens, we"*: CW, 5:537.

236 *"printed letters of gold"*: Brooks, *Lincoln Observed*, 168.

237 *"If I were in your place"*: Don Fehrenbacher and Virginia Fehrenbacher, eds., *Recollected Words of Abraham Lincoln* (Redwood City, California: Stanford University Press, 1996), 182.

237 *"the tall, pathetic, melancholy figure"*: Brooks, *Washington, D.C., in Lincoln's Time*, 215.

CHAPTER 14: A TRUTH THAT NEEDED TO BE TOLD

238 *"I saw Mr. Lincoln"*: Chambrun, *Impressions*, 39–40.

238 *"a clear, solemn voice"*: *The Philadelphia Inquirer*, March 6, 1865.

239 *"When God comes"*: Matthew Henry and Thomas Scott, *A Commentary upon the Holy Bible, from Henry and Scott. Isaiah to Malachi* (London: Religious Tract Society, 1834), 4:16.

239 *"I hope the sacred"*: Salmon P. Chase to Mary Todd Lincoln, March 4, 1865, Abraham Lincoln Papers.

239 *"God Save the President"*: *The Philadelphia Inquirer*, March 6, 1865.

241 *"I was very near Mr. Lincoln"*: Elizabeth Bacon Custer, *The Civil War Memories of Elizabeth Bacon Custer*, ed. Arlene Reynolds (Austin: University of Texas Press, 1994), 131.

241 *"secured a coign"*: Hamilton Gay Howard, *Civil-War Echoes: Character Sketches and State Secrets* (Washington, D.C.: Howard, 1907), 74.

241 *"rivals the greatest"*: James R. Doolittle Jr. to his brother, March 4, 1865, James R. Doolittle Papers.

242 *"Heard Abe deliver"*: SCC, Virgil Connor to his mother, March 6, 1865.

242 *"He rubbed his red face"*: *The New York Herald*, March 6, 1865.

243 *"struck me"*: Douglass, *The Life and Times*, 442.

243 *"unless coupled"*: Clifford Dowdey and Louis H. Manarin, eds., *The Wartime Papers of R. E. Lee* (Boston: Little, Brown, 1961), 911.

244 *"The revelation was startling"*: John B. Gordon, *Reminiscences of the Civil War* (New York: Charles Scribner's Sons, 1903), 387–90.

244 *"There is almost a panic"*: J. B. Jones, *A Rebel War Clerk's Diary at the Confederate States Capital* (Philadelphia: J. B. Lippincott, 1866), 2:439–40.

244 *"a nice talk"*: John H. Clifford to Sarah Clifford, March 4, 1865, Clifford Family Papers.

245 *"looked very much worn"*: *The New York Times*, March 12, 1865.

245 *"With all the bands"*: Adams, *Letter from Washington*, 243.

246 *"Laboring through"*: *The Times*, of London, March 20, 1865.

246 *"and our power press"*: *The Evening Star*, March 4, 1865.

247 *"It speaks—through"*: quoted in *Littell's Living Age*, March 25, 1865.

247 *"a little speech of"*: *The New York Herald*, March 5, 1865.

247 less "politic" and "humane": *The New York Tribune*, March 5, 1865.

248 *"calmness" and "modesty"*: *The New York Times*, March 6, 1865.

248 *"It is with a blush"*: *The New York World*, March 6, 1865.

248 *"as chilly and dreary"*: *Daily Ohio Statesman*, Columbus, March 6, 1865.

249 *"We had looked for something"*: *The Chicago Times*, March 6, 1865.

249 *"an exceedingly brief"*: *The Chicago Tribune*, March 6, 1865.

249 *"abolition ceremony"*: *The Grand Haven* (Michigan) *News*, March 6, 1865.

250 *"[The] administration that has"*: *The Holmes County Farmer*, Millersburg, Ohio, March 8, 1865.

250 *"In lieu of any such attempt"*: quoted in *The North Branch Democrat*, Tunkhannock, Pennsylvania, March 8, 1865.

250 *"that was Old Abe's"*: *The Cincinnati Enquirer*, March 8, 1865.

250 *"labors and stumbles"*: quoted in *Syracuse* (New York) *Daily Courier and Union*, March 18, 1865.

251 *"an obscure village lawyer"*: Ibid.

251 *"Who has made Abraham"*: *The Ottawa* (Illinois) *Free Trader*, March 11, 1865.

251 *"at once the most absurd"*: *The Cincinnati Enquirer*, March 7, 1865.

251 *"Inaugural with the Bark Off"*: *The Star of the North*, Bloomsburg, Pennsylvania, March 15, 1865.

252 *"a queer sort"*: Petersburg (Virginia) *Daily Express*, March 7, 1865.

252 *"manifesto" of "Abraham the First"*: *Daily Richmond* (Virginia) *Examiner*, March 8, 1865.

252 *"short inaugural message, or homily"*: Jones, *A Rebel War Clerk's Diary*, 2:443.

252 mangled version: *The Hillsborough* (North Carolina) *Recorder*, March 15, 1865.

253 *"a singular State paper"*: quoted in *Littell's Living Age*, March 25, 1865.

253 *"an imposing demonstration"*: *Cleveland Morning Leader*, March 6, 1865.

253 *"the beaten path of precedent"*: *The Delaware Gazette*, Delaware, Ohio, March 10, 1865.

253 *"nobody but Lincoln"*: *The Burlington* (Vermont) *Times*, March 11, 1865.

253 *"It is plain, terse"*: *The Providence* (Rhode Island) *Journal*, March 6, 1865.

253 *"characteristic of Mr. LINCOLN"*: *The Philadelphia Inquirer*, March 6, 1865.

254 *"remarkable for its"*: *The Jeffersonian Democrat*, Chardon, Ohio, March 10, 1865.

254 *"So brief, so simple"*: *The Buffalo Morning Express*, March 6, 1865.

254 *"In pithy brevity"*: *The Evening Star*, March 4, 1865.

254 *"Mr. Lincoln's compositions"*: *The Liberator*, Boston, March 17, 1865.

254 *"The President regards"*: quoted in *Littell's Living Age*, March 25, 1865.

254 *The powerful* Times: *The Times*, of London, March 20, 1865.

254 *"short State paper"*: *The Spectator*, London, March 18, 1865.

254 *"That rail-splitting lawyer"*: Worthington Chauncey Ford, ed., *A Cycle of Adams Letters*, (Boston: Houghton Mifflin, 1920), 2:257–58.

255 *"unlike any American"*: Strong, *Diary*, 561.

255 *"not only the neatest"*: CW, 8:356.

255 *"to wear as well"*: Ibid.

CHAPTER 15: A SACRED EFFORT

256 *dined at three p.m.*: BBF, 466.

256 *Walter Burton*: Alford, *Fortune's Fool*, 227.

256 *"I remember hearing"*: *The Chicago Tribune*, February 19, 1884.

257 *ceremonial duties had resumed*: *The Philadelphia Inquirer*, March 6, 1865

257 *"I don't know but that"*: Ibid.

257 *"We must pick along"*: BFF, 466.

258 *At Ford's Theatre*: *The Evening Star*, March 4, 1865.

258 *"Lincoln was fond"*: *The Minneapolis* (Minnesota) *Tribune*, April 21, 1879.

258 *"His smiles were infrequent"*: *Kansas City Star*, February 8, 1925.

259 *"exceedingly strong"*: *Los Angeles Times*, February 21, 1916.

259 *"quaint ejaculations"*: *The New York Herald*, March 6, 1865.

259 *"some of the more unfortunate"*: *Alexandria* (Virginia) *Gazette*, March 7, 1865.

259 *"more correctly, a grand jam"*: *Appleton* (Wisconsin) *Motor*, March 16, 1865.

260 *"I went alone"*: Howard, *Civil-War Echoes*, 74–77.

260 *"cruelty to animals"*: Lamon, *Recollections*, 97.

261 *"paid considerable attention"*: *The Philadelphia Inquirer*, March 6, 1865.

261 *"one of the fairest of"*: *The New York Herald*, March 6, 1865.

261 *"still radiant with the remains"*: Ibid.

261 *"The jam was terrible"*: Keckley, *Behind the Scenes*, 158.

261 *"dressed most charmingly"*: *The Evening Star*, March 6, 1865.

262 *"There was a hard line"*: Custer, *The Civil War Memories*, 134.

262 *"I cheered and went"*: Diary entry for March 4, 1865, Clara Barton Papers.

263 *"took advantage of"*: *The Times*, of London, March 20, 1865.

263 *figure at fifteen thousand*: *The New York Tribune*, March 6, 1865.

263 *"the largest reception"*: BBF, 466.

263 *"We were fortunate enough"*: *Appleton* (Wisconsin) *Motor*, March 16, 1865.

264 *"All the nobodies"*: *Cleveland Morning Leader*, March 9, 1865.

264 *"a notion to go"*: *The New York Times*, March 12, 1865.

265 *"The President must have"*: SCC, Virgil Connor to his mother, March 6, 1865.

265 *"glove was half torn off"*: *The New York Herald*, March 5, 1865.

265 *"Say what they will"*: March 16, 1865.

266 *"A fever of vandalism"*: William H. Crook, "Lincoln as I Knew Him," *Harper's Magazine*, June 1907, 42.

266 *"Many colored persons"*: quoted in *Cleveland Morning Leader*, March 9, 1865.

266 *"The negro seems"*: *The Burlington* (Vermont) *Weekly Sentinel*, March 10, 1865.

266 *"no colored persons had ever"*: Douglass, *The Life and Times*, 443–45.

269 *"Fred. Douglass and lady"*: *The Detroit Free Press*, March 10, 1865.

269 *"Things have greatly changed"*: *The Valley Spirit*, Chambersburg, Pennsylvania, March 15, 1865.

269 *U.S. Marine Band played "incessantly"*: *The New York Herald*, March 6, 1865.

269 *at the Lichau House*: Edwards, *The Lincoln Assassination*, 620.

270 *"a pair of Scotch plaid pants"*: Ibid., 619.

271 *"the lights were dead"*: *The New York Herald*, March 6, 1865.

271 *"en dishabille"*: Ibid.

271 *"That's the end"*: Ibid.

EPILOGUE: THE STUFF TO CARRY THEM THROUGH

273 *"I have this moment"*: *The New York Times*, March 12, 1865.

274 *"it needed but little"*: quoted in *Daily Davenport* (Iowa) *Democrat*, March 16, 1865.

274 *"with more audacity"*: *The Evening Star*, March 7, 1865.

274 *"I was so absorbed"*: Custer, *The Civil War Memories*, 132–33.

275 *"You have more of that"*: Hay, *Inside Lincoln's White House*, 245.

275 *"the most devoted lovers"*: Asia Boothe Clarke to Jean Anderson, May 22, 1865, Asia Booth Clarke Letters.

275 *Booth had added some words*: Alford, *Fortune's Fool*, 288.

276 *Peter Eckler*: Ted Genoways, "The Disorder of *Drum-Taps*," *Walt Whitman Quarterly Review*, Fall 2006/Winter 2007, 98–116.

276 *"J.W. Booth and lady"*: Edwards, *The Lincoln Assassination*, 1163.

277 *"in a most unsettled"*: Alford, *Fortune's Fool*, 252.

277 *Orlando Tompkins*: Ibid.

277 *"I, for the first time"*: *The Liberator*, Boston, April 7, 1865.

277 *Lincoln spoke from a window*: CW, 8:399–405.

278 *"That means nigger citizenship"*: George Alfred Townsend, *Kate of Catoctin, or The Chain-Breakers: A National Romance* (New York: D. Appleton, 1886), 490.

278 *"That's the last speech"*: *Impeachment Investigation*, 674.

278 *"The damned woman"*: Alford, *Fortune's Fool*, 260.

278 *"the ambitious, educated"*: *The Liberator*, Boston. April 28, 1865.

278 *"We must both be"*: Mary Todd Lincoln to Francis B. Carpenter, November 15, 1865, Turner, *Mary Todd Lincoln*, 284–85.

278 *"going all over her"*: George B. Todd to his brother, April 15, 1865, James Cummins Bookseller, "The Surgeon of the 'Montauk' Gives an Eye-Witness Account." Accessed April 14, 2019. (https://www.jamescumminsbookseller.com/pages/books/100185/lincoln-assassination-george-b-todd-m-d/autograph-letter-signed-george-to-his-brother-giving-his-eye-witness-account-of-the-assassination).

279 *The night before*: Hamilton Fish diary, November 12, 1869, Hamilton Fish Papers.

279 *"objected strenuously to accompanying"*: Ibid.

279 *Lincoln's guard that night*: Frederick Hatch, "Lincoln's Missing Guard," *Lincoln Herald* 107 (Fall 2005), 106–17.

280 *"a card with the name"*: Helen A. Du Barry, "Eyewitness Account of Lincoln's Assassination," *Journal of the Illinois State Historical Society* 39, no. 3 (1946), 368.

280 *"He was still walking"*: George B. Todd to his brother, April 15, 1865, "The Surgeon of the 'Montauk.'"

280 *"I am aware"*: Tom Taylor, *Our American Cousin: A Drama, in 3 Acts* (New York: Samuel French, 1869), 37.

281 *Charles A. Leale*: Charles A. Leale, M.D., *Lincoln's Last Hours* (New York: Estate of Charles A. Leale, 1909), 2–11.

281 *callboy William Ferguson*: William J. Ferguson, "I Saw Lincoln Shot!," *American Magazine*, August 1920, 86.

282 *"I took Mrs. Lincoln by the hand"*: BBF, 470.

282 *"It was of a strictly"*: Alford, *Fortune's Fool*, 415.

283 *"All were deeply impressed"*: *The New York Times*, April 17, 1865.

283 *"I feel incompetent"*: Ibid.

283 *"Mother prepared breakfast"*: Whitman, *Complete Prose Works*, 26.

284 *"He leaves"*: Ibid., 68.

284 *"O ever-returning spring!"*: Whitman, Walt, *Leaves of Grass* (New York: W. E. Chapin, 1867), "Sequel to Drum-Taps," 3.

284 *"I have had a heart-broken"*: Clarke, *John Wilkes Booth*, 92.

284 *"written heart-broken letters"*: Asia Boothe Clarke to Jean Anderson, May 22, 1865, Asia Booth Clarke Letters.

284 *"unhappy lady"*: quoted in *The Cincinnati Enquirer*, April 26, 1865.

284 *"stated in the presence"*: Dayton (Ohio) *Daily Empire*, April 21, 1865.

285 *"Booth wasn't the kind"*: *Springfield* (Massachusetts) *Republican*, April 21, 1865.

285 *"It cannot be denied"*: Ibid., April 22, 1865.

285 *"was honorably kept"*: Benjamin Perley Poore, *Perley's Reminiscences of Sixty Years in the National Metropolis* (Philadelphia: Hubbard Brothers, 1886), 2:184.

285 *"Several physicians"*: *The Evening Star*, April 15, 1865.

286 *authorities later questioned*: Edwards, *The Lincoln Assassination*, 1194.

286 *"This is not an occasion"*: *The Rochester* (New York) *Democrat and American*, April 17, 1865.

286 *"Hurrah! Old Abe"*: LeConte, *A Journal*, 65.

286 *"Their hostility"*: George W. Julian, "George Julian's Journal—The Assassination of Lincoln," *Indiana Magazine of History* 11, no. 4 (December 1915), 335.

287 *"I know this foul murder"*: *Mary Chesnut's Civil War*, 791.

287 *"If they did choose a baboon"*: Harold Holzer, ed., *President Lincoln Assassinated!! The Firsthand Story of the Murder, Manhunt, Trial, and Mourning* (New York: Library of America, 2014), 244.

288 *"I struck boldly"*: House, *Impeachment Investigation*, 286.

288 *"Tell my mother"*: Ibid., 328.

288 *"Useless, useless"*: Ibid., 483.

288 *"the picture of the daughter"*: *The New York World*, April 26, 1891.

288 *"favorite walking staff"*: Frederick Douglass to Mary Lincoln, August 17, 1865, Gilder Lehrman Collection.

289 *"the concentrated virus"*: Holzer, *Lincoln Assassinated!!*, 316–20.

289 *"With malice to no one"*: *The Cincinnati Enquirer*, May 1, 1865.

289 *"We looked up"*: *The Evening Star*, February 21, 1895.

290 *"Long, flowing white"*: *The Buffalo Evening News*, March 28, 1892.

290 *"It is designed to speak"*: Alexander Gardner, *Gardner's Photographic Sketch Book of the War* (Washington, D.C.: Philip and Solomons, 1866), introduction.

291 *"No Queen has ever"*: *The Cincinnati Enquirer*, August 6, 1899.

291 *"She was in many respects"*: *The Boston Globe*, July 31, 1899.

291 *"Poet Laureate"*: *The Chicago Tribune*, February 27, 1867.

292 *"terse, pointed, plain"*: *The National Republican*, April 16, 1868.

292 *much-maligned statue*: Will Hughes, "Horatio Greenough's Near Naked Washington," *Boundary Stones*, WETA's Local History Blog, May 22, 2013. Accessed on October 5, 1918. (https://blogs.weta.org/boundarystones/2013/05/22/horatio-greenough's-near-naked-washington).

292 *Both it and*: Vivien Green Fryd, "Two Sculptures for the Capitol: Horatio Greenough's 'Rescue' and Luigi Persico's 'Discovery of America,'" *American Art Journal*, Spring 1987, 93–100.

293 *"He thought it looked dingy"*: Carol Ross Joynt, "The Untold Story of the Lincoln Table, the Reagan Inaugural, and the Spray Paint," *Washingtonian*, December 5, 2012.

293 *"To the friends of missing persons"*: CW, 8: Appendix I

293 *437 Seventh Street*: Clara Barton Missing Soldiers Office Museum, "Our Story." Accessed October 5, 2018. (http://www.clarabartonmuseum.org/ourstory/).

294 *"both hands in his pockets"*: *The Boston Globe*, July 31, 1878.

294 *message on Memorial Day*: *The Boston Globe*, May 30, 1915.

294 *daughter Mabel*: *The Indianapolis News*, November 10, 1917.

294 *"A public-spirited man"*: *American Series of Popular Biographies, Maine Edition* (Boston: New England Historical, 1903), 119.

295 *"I will not accept"*: *The Boston Globe*, June 5, 1884, renders this less poetically: "I will not accept if the convention nominates me. If the people elect me I will not serve . . ."

295 *"is all hell"*: *The New York Times*, August 19, 1880.

295 *"I copied out"*: Norman Schwarzkopf, *It Doesn't Take a Hero: The Autobiography of General Norman Schwarzkopf* (New York: Random House, 2010), 498.

295 *"She would not even"*: Merrill, *Sherman in Cheraw*, 57.

295 *"To go back into"*: Holmes, *The Diary*, 436.

296 *"Few persons recognized"*: *The Washington Herald*, May 31, 1922.

296 *"Dan is a sculptor"*: BBF, 596.

296 *"Genius draws no color line"*: *The Cincinnati Enquirer*, April 10, 1939.

INDEX